W9-BUC-310

LITERATURE SALES ORDER FORM

NAME: _____

COMPANY: _____

ADDRESS: _____

CITY: _____ STATE: _____ ZIP: _____

COUNTRY: _____

PHONE NO.: (_____) _____

ORDER NO.	TITLE	QTY.		PRICE		TOTAL
☐☐☐☐☐☐	_____	_____	×	_____	=	_____
☐☐☐☐☐☐	_____	_____	×	_____	=	_____
☐☐☐☐☐☐	_____	_____	×	_____	=	_____
☐☐☐☐☐☐	_____	_____	×	_____	=	_____
☐☐☐☐☐☐	_____	_____	×	_____	=	_____
☐☐☐☐☐☐	_____	_____	×	_____	=	_____
☐☐☐☐☐☐	_____	_____	×	_____	=	_____
☐☐☐☐☐☐	_____	_____	×	_____	=	_____
☐☐☐☐☐☐	_____	_____	×	_____	=	_____
☐☐☐☐☐☐	_____	_____	×	_____	=	_____

Subtotal _____

Must Add Your
Local Sales Tax _____

Must add appropriate postage to subtotal
(10% U.S. and Canada, 20% all other) ⟶ Postage _____

Total _____

Pay by Visa, MasterCard, American Express, Check, Money Order, or company purchase order payable to Intel Literature Sales. Allow 2-4 weeks for delivery.

☐ Visa   ☐ MasterCard   ☐ American Express   Expiration Date _____

Account No. _____

Signature: _____

Mail To: Intel Literature Sales
P.O. Box 58130
Santa Clara, CA
95052-8130

International Customers outside the U.S. and Canada should contact their local Intel Sales Office or Distributor listed in the back of most Intel literature.

Call Toll Free: (800) 548-4725 for phone orders

Prices good until 12/31/87.

Source HB

CUSTOMER SUPPORT

CUSTOMER SUPPORT

Customer Support is Intel's complete support service that provides Intel customers with hardware support, software support, customer training, and consulting services. For more information contact your local sales offices.

After a customer purchases any system hardware or software product, service and support become major factors in determining whether that product will continue to meet a customer's expectations. Such support requires an international support organization and a breadth of programs to meet a variety of customer needs. As you might expect, Intel's customer support is quite extensive. It includes factory repair services and worldwide field service offices providing hardware repair services, software support services, customer training classes, and consulting services.

HARDWARE SUPPORT SERVICES

Intel is committed to providing an international service support package through a wide variety of service offerings available from Intel Hardware Support.

SOFTWARE SUPPORT SERVICES

Intel's software support consists of two levels of contracts. Standard support includes TIPS (Technical Information Phone Service), updates and subscription service (product-specific troubleshooting guides and COMMENTS Magazine). Basic support includes updates and the subscription service. Contracts are sold in environments which represent product groupings (i.e., iRMX environment).

CONSULTING SERVICES

Intel provides field systems engineering services for any phase of your development or support effort. You can use our systems engineers in a variety of ways ranging from assistance in using a new product, developing an application, personalizing training, and customizing or tailoring an Intel product to providing technical and management consulting. Systems Engineers are well versed in technical areas such as microcommunications, real-time applications, embedded microcontrollers, and network services. You know your application needs; we know our products. Working together we can help you get a successful product to market in the least possible time.

CUSTOMER TRAINING

Intel offers a wide range of instructional programs covering various aspects of system design and implementation. In just three to ten days a limited number of individuals learn more in a single workshop than in weeks of self-study. For optimum convenience, workshops are scheduled regularly at Training Centers worldwide or we can take our workshops to you for on-site instruction. Covering a wide variety of topics, Intel's major course categories include: architecture and assembly language, programming and operating systems, bitbus and LAN applications.

80286 AND 80287 PROGRAMMER'S REFERENCE MANUAL

1987

Intel Corporation makes no warranty for the use of its products and assumes no responsibility for any errors which may appear in this document nor does it make a commitment to update the information contained herein.

Intel retains the right to make changes to these specifications at any time, without notice.

Contact your local sales office to obtain the latest specifications before placing your order.

The following are trademarks of Intel Corporation and may only be used to identify Intel Products:

Above, BITBUS, COMMputer, CREDIT, Data Pipeline, FASTPATH, Genius, i, î, ICE, iCEL, iCS, iDBP, iDIS, I²ICE, iLBX, i_m, iMDDX, iMMX, Inboard, Insite, Intel, intel, intelBOS, Intel Certified, Intelevision, inteligent Identifier, inteligent Programming, Intellec, Intellink, iOSP, iPDS, iPSC, iRMK, iRMX, iSBC, iSBX, iSDM, iSXM, KEPROM, Library Manager, MAPNET, MCS, Megachassis, MICROMAINFRAME, MULTIBUS, MULTICHANNEL, MULTIMODULE, MultiSERVER, ONCE, OpenNET, OTP, PC BUBBLE, Plug-A-Bubble, PROMPT, Promware, QUEST, QueX, Quick-Pulse Programming, Ripplemode, RMX/80, RUPI, Seamless, SLD, SugarCube, SupportNET, UPI, and VLSiCEL, and the combination of ICE, iCS, iRMX, iSBC, iSBX, iSXM, MCS, or UPI and a numerical suffix, 4-SITE.

MDS is an ordering code only and is not used as a product name or trademark. MDS® is a registered trademark of Mohawk Data Sciences Corporation.

*MULTIBUS is a patented Intel bus.

Additional copies of this manual or other Intel literature may be obtained from:

Intel Corporation
Literature Distribution
Mail Stop SC6-59
3065 Bowers Avenue
Santa Clara, CA 95051

CG-5/26/87

PREFACE

This manual describes the 80286, the most powerful 16-bit microprocessor in the 8086 family, and the 80287 Numeric Processor Extension (NPX).

ORGANIZATION OF THIS MANUAL

This manual is, essentially, two books in one. The first book describes the 80286, the second the 80287 NPX.

80286

The 80286 contains a table of contents, eleven chapters, four appendices, and an index. For more information on the 80286 book's organization, see its first chapter, Chapter 1, "Introduction to the 80286." Section 1.4 in that chapter explains the organization in detail.

80287 NPX

The 80287 NPX contains a preface, table of contents, four chapters, three appendices, and a glossary. For more information on the 80287 NPX book's organization, see its preface.

TABLE OF CONTENTS

Page

Figures

Tables

CUSTOMER SUPPORT

CUSTOMER SUPPORT

Customer Support is Intel's complete support service that provides Intel customers with hardware support, software support, customer training, and consulting services. For more information contact your local sales offices.

After a customer purchases any system hardware or software product, service and support become major factors in determining whether that product will continue to meet a customer's expectations. Such support requires an international support organization and a breadth of programs to meet a variety of customer needs. As you might expect, Intel's customer support is quite extensive. It includes factory repair services and worldwide field service offices providing hardware repair services, software support services, customer training classes, and consulting services.

HARDWARE SUPPORT SERVICES

Intel is committed to providing an international service support package through a wide variety of service offerings available from Intel Hardware Support.

SOFTWARE SUPPORT SERVICES

Intel's software support consists of two levels of contracts. Standard support includes TIPS (Technical Information Phone Service), updates and subscription service (product-specific troubleshooting guides and COMMENTS Magazine). Basic support includes updates and the subscription service. Contracts are sold in environments which represent product groupings (i.e., iRMX environment).

CONSULTING SERVICES

Intel provides field systems engineering services for any phase of your development or support effort. You can use our systems engineers in a variety of ways ranging from assistance in using a new product, developing an application, personalizing training, and customizing or tailoring an Intel product to providing technical and management consulting. Systems Engineers are well versed in technical areas such as microcommunications, real-time applications, embedded microcontrollers, and network services. You know your application needs; we know our products. Working together we can help you get a successful product to market in the least possible time.

CUSTOMER TRAINING

Intel offers a wide range of instructional programs covering various aspects of system design and implementation. In just three to ten days a limited number of individuals learn more in a single workshop than in weeks of self-study. For optimum convenience, workshops are scheduled regularly at Training Centers worldwide or we can take our workshops to you for on-site instruction. Covering a wide variety of topics, Intel's major course categories include: architecture and assembly language, programming and operating systems, bitbus and LAN applications.

Introduction to the 80286 1

CHAPTER 1
INTRODUCTION TO THE 80286

The 80286 is the most powerful 16-bit processor in the 8086 series of microprocessors, which includes the 8086, the 8088, the 80186, the 80188, and the 80286. It is designed for applications that require very high performance. It is also an excellent choice for sophisticated "high end" applications that will benefit from its advanced architectural features: memory management, protection mechanisms, task management, and virtual memory support. The 80286 provides, on a single VLSI chip, computational and architectural characteristics normally associated with much larger minicomputers.

Sections 1.1, 1.2, and 1.3 of this chapter provide an overview of the 80286 architecture. Because the 80286 represents an extension of the 8086 architecture, some of this overview material may be new and unfamiliar to previous users of the 8086 and similar microprocessors. But the 80286 is also an evolutionary development, with the new architecture superimposed upon the industry standard 8086 in such a way as to affect only the design and programming of operating systems and other such system software. Section 1.4 of this chapter provides a guide to the organization of this manual, suggesting which chapters are relevant to the needs of particular readers.

1.1 GENERAL ATTRIBUTES

The 80286 base architecture has many features in common with the architecture of other members of the 8086 family, such as byte addressable memory, I/O interfacing hardware, interrupt vectoring, and support for both multiprocessing and processor extensions. The entire family has a common set of addressing modes and basic instructions. The 80286 base architecture also includes a number of extensions which add to the versatility of the computer.

The 80286 processor can function in two modes of operation (see section 1.2 of this chapter, Modes of Operation). In one of these modes only the base architecture is available to programmers, whereas in the other mode a number of very powerful advanced features have been added, including support for virtual memory, multitasking, and a sophisticated protection mechanism. These advanced features are described in section 1.3 of this chapter.

The 80286 base architecture was designed to support programming in high-level languages, such as Pascal, C or PL/M. The register set and instructions are well suited to compiler-generated code. The addressing modes (see section 2.6.3 in Chapter 2) allow efficient addressing of complex data structures, such as static and dynamic arrays, records, and arrays within records, which are commonly supported by high-level languages. The data types supported by the architecture include, along with bytes and words, high level language constructs such as strings, BCD, and floating point.

The memory architecture of the 80286 was designed to support modular programming techniques. Memory is divided into segments, which may be of arbitrary size, that can be used to contain procedures and data structures. Segmentation has several advantages over more conventional linear memory architectures. It supports structured software, since segments can contain meaningful program units and data, and more compact code, since references within a segment can be shorter (and locality of reference usually insures that the next few references will be within the same segment). Segmentation also lends itself to efficient implementation of sophisticated memory management, virtual memory, and memory protection.

In addition, new instructions have been added to the base architecture to give hardware support for procedure invocations, parameter passing, and array bounds checking.

1.2 MODES OF OPERATION

The 80286 can be operated in either of two different modes: Real Address Mode or Protected Virtual Address Mode (also referred to as Protected Mode). In either mode of operation, the 80286 represents an upwardly compatible addition to the 8086 family of processors.

In Real Address Mode, the 80286 operates essentially as a very high-performance 8086. Programs written for the 8086 or the 80186 can be executed in this mode without any modification (the few exceptions are described in Appendix C, "Compatibility Considerations"). Such upward compatibility extends even to the object code level; for example, an 8086 program stored in read-only memory will execute successfully in 80286 Real Address Mode. An 80286 operating in Real Address Mode provides a number of instructions not found on the 8086. These additional instructions, also present with the 80186, allow for efficient subroutine linkage, parameter validation, index calculations, and block I/O transfers.

The advanced architectural features and full capabilities of the 80286 are realized in its native Protected Mode. Among these features are sophisticated mechanisms to support data protection, system integrity, task concurrency, and memory management, including virtual storage. Nevertheless, even in Protected Mode, the 80286 remains upwardly compatible with most 8086 and 80186 application programs. Most 8086 applications programs can be re-compiled or re-assembled and executed on the 80286 in Protected Mode.

1.3 ADVANCED FEATURES

The architectural features described in section 1.1 of this chaper are common to both operating modes of the processor. In addition to these common features, Protected Mode provides a number of advanced features, including a greatly extended physical and logical address space, new instructions, and support for additional hardware-recognized data structures. The Protected Mode 80286 includes a sophisticated memory management and multilevel protection mechanism. Full hardware support is included for multitasking and task switching operations.

1.3.1 Memory Management

The memory architecture of the Protected Mode 80286 represents a significant advance over that of the 8086. The physical address space has been increased from1 megabyte to 16 megabytes (2^{24} bytes), while the virtual address space (i.e., the address space visible to a program) has been increased from 1 megabyte to 1 gigabyte (2^{30} bytes). Moreover, separate virtual address spaces are provided for each task in a multi-tasking system (see the next section, 1.3.2, "Task Management").

The 80286 supports on-chip memory management instead of relying on an external memory management unit. The one-chip solution is preferable because no software is required to manage an external memory management unit, performance is much better, and hardware designs are significantly simpler.

Mechanisms have been included in the 80286 architecture to allow the efficient implementation of virtual memory systems. (In virtual memory systems, the user regards the combination of main and external storage as a single large memory. The user can write large programs without worrying about the physical memory limitations of the system. To accomplish this, the operating system places some of the user programs and data in external storage and brings them into main memory only as they are needed.) All instructions that can cause a segment-not-present fault are fully restartable. Thus, a not-present segment can be loaded from external storage, and the task can be restarted at the point where the fault occurred.

The 80286, like all members of the 8086 series, supports a segmented memory architecture. The 80286 also fully integrates memory segmentation into a comprehensive protection scheme. This protection scheme includes hardware-enforced length and type checking to protect segments from inadvertent misuse.

1.3.2 Task Management

The 80286 is designed to support multi-tasking systems. The architecture provides direct support for the concept of a task. For example, task state segments (see section 8.2 in Chapter 8) are hardware-recognized and hardware-manipulated structures that contain information on the current state of all tasks in the system.

Very efficient context-switching (task-switching) can be invoked with a single instruction. Separate logical address spaces are provided for each task in the system. Finally, mechanisms exist to support intertask communication, synchronization, memory sharing, and task scheduling. Task Management is described in Chapter 8.

1.3.3 Protection Mechanisms

The 80286 allows the system designer to define a comprehensive protection policy to be applied, uniformly and continuously, to all ongoing operations of the system. Such a policy may be desirable to ensure system reliability, privacy of data, rapid error recovery, and separation of multiple users.

The 80286 protection mechanisms are based on the notion of a "hierarchy of trust." Four privilege levels are distinguished, ranging from Level 0 (most trusted) to Level 3 (least trusted). Level 0 is usually reserved for the operating system kernel. The four levels may be visualized as concentric rings, with the most privileged level in the center (see figure 1-1).

This four-level scheme offers system reliability, flexibility, and design options not possible with the typical two-level (supervisor/user) separation provided by other processors. A four-level division is capable of separating kernel, executive, system services, and application software, each with different privileges.

At any one time, a task executes at one of the four levels. Moreover, all data segments and code segments are also assigned to privilege levels. A task executing at one level cannot access data at a more privileged level, nor can it call a procedure at a less privileged level (i.e., trust a less privileged procedure to do work for it). Thus, both access to data and transfer of control are restricted in appropriate ways.

A complete separation can exist between the logical address spaces local to different tasks, providing users with automatic protection against accidental or malicious interference by other users. The hardware also provides immediate detection of a number of fault and error conditions, a feature that can be useful in the development and maintenance of software.

Finally, these protection mechanisms require relatively little system overhead because they are integrated into the memory management and protection hardware of the processor itself.

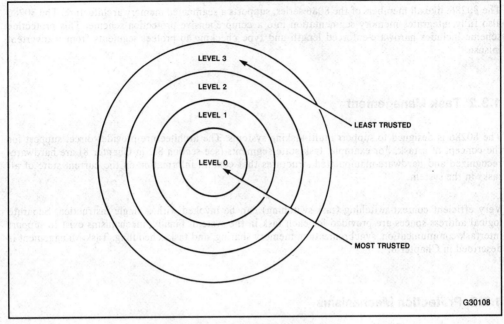

Figure 1-1. Four Privilege Levels

1.3.4 Support for Operating Systems

Most operating systems involve some degree of concurrency, with multiple tasks vying for system resources. The task management mechanisms described above provide the 80286 with inherent support for such multi-tasking systems. Moreover, the advanced memory management features of the 80286 allow the implementation of sophisticated virtual memory systems.

Operating system implementors have found that a multi-level approach to system services provides better security and more reliable systems. For example, a very secure kernel might implement critical functions such as task scheduling and resource allocation, while less fundamental functions (such as I/O) are built around the kernel. This layered approach also makes program development and enhancement simpler and facilitates error detection and debugging. The 80286 supports the layered approach through its four-level privilege scheme.

1.4 ORGANIZATION OF THIS BOOK

To facilitate the use of this book both as an introduction to the 80286 architecture and as a reference guide, the remaining chapters are divided into three major parts.

Part I, comprising chapters 2 through 4, should be read by all those who wish to acquire a basic familiarity with the 80286 architecture. These chapters provide detailed information on memory segmentation, registers, addressing modes and the general (application level) 80286 instruction set. In conjunction with the *80286 Assembly Language Reference Manual*, these chapters provide sufficient information for an assembly language programmer to design and write application programs.

The chapters in Part I are:

Chapter 2, "Architectural Features." This chapter discusses those features of the 80286 architecture that are significant for application programmers. The information presented can also function as an introduction to the machine for system programmers. Memory organization and segmentation, processor registers, addressing modes, and instruction formats are all discussed.

Chapter 3, "Basic Instruction Set." This chapter presents the core instructions of the 8086 family.

Chapter 4, "Extended Instruction Set." This chapter presents the extended instructions shared by the 80186 and 80286 processors.

Part II of the book consists of a single chapter:

Chapter 5, "Real Address Mode." This chapter presents the system programmer's view of the 80286 when the processor is operated in Real Address Mode.

Part III of the book comprises chapters 6 through 11. Aimed primarily at system programmers, these chapters discuss the more advanced architectural features of the 80286, which are available when the processor is in Protected Mode. Details on memory management, protection mechanisms, and task switching are provided.

The chapters in Part III are:

Chapter 6, "Virtual Memory." This chapter describes the 80286 address translation mechanisms that support virtual memory. Segment descriptors, global and local descriptor tables, and descriptor caches are discussed.

Chapter 7, "Protection." This chapter describes the protection features of the 80286. Privilege levels, segment attributes, access restrictions, and call gates are discussed.

Chapter 8, "Tasks and State Transitions." This chapter describes the 80286 mechanisms that support concurrent tasks. Context-switching, task state segments, task gates, and interrupt tasks are discussed.

Chapter 9, "Interrupts, Traps and Faults." This chapter describes interrupt and trap handling. Special attention is paid to the exception traps, or faults, which may occur in Protected Mode. Interrupt gates, trap gates, and the interrupt descriptor table are discussed.

Chapter 10, "System Control and Initialization." This chapter describes the actual instructions used to implement the memory management, protection, and task support features of the 80286. System registers, privileged instructions, and the initial machine state are discussed.

Chapter 11, "Advanced Topics." This chapter completes Part III with a description of several advanced topics, including special segment attributes and pointer validation.

1.5 RELATED PUBLICATIONS

The following manuals also contain information of interest to programmers of 80287 systems:

- *Introduction to the 80286*, order number 210308
- *ASM286 Assembly Language Reference Manual*, order number 121924
- *80286 Operating System Writer's Guide*, order number 121960

- *80286 Hardware Reference Manual*, order number 210760
- *Microprocessor and Peripheral Handbook*, order number 230843
- *PL/M-286 User's Guide*, order number 121945
- *80287 Support Library Reference Manual*, order number 122129
- *8086 Software Toolbox Manual*, order number 122203 (includes information about 80287 Emulator Software)

80286 Base Architecture

2

CHAPTER 2
80286 BASE ARCHITECTURE

This chapter describes the 80286 application programming environment as seen by assembly language programmers. It is intended to introduce the programmer to those features of the 80286 architecture that directly affect the design and implementation of 80286 application programs.

2.1 MEMORY ORGANIZATION AND SEGMENTATION

The main memory of an 80286 system makes up its physical address space. This address space is organized as a sequence of 8-bit quantities, called bytes. Each byte is assigned a unique address ranging from 0 up to a maximum of 2^{20} (1 megabyte) in Real Address Mode, and up to 2^{24} (16 megabytes) in Protected Mode.

A virtual address space is the organization of memory as viewed by a program. Virtual address space is also organized in units of bytes. (Other addressable units such as words, strings, and BCD digits are described below in section 2.2, "Data Types.") In Real Address Mode, as with the 8086 itself, programs view physical memory directly, inasmuch as they manipulate pure physical addresses. Thus, the virtual address space is identical to the physical address space (1 megabyte).

In Protected Mode, however, programs have no direct access to physical addresses. Instead, memory is viewed as a much larger virtual address space of 2^{30} bytes (1 gigabyte). This 1 gigabyte virtual address is mapped onto the Protected Mode's 16-megabyte physical address space by the address translation mechanisms described in Chapter 6.

The programmer views the virtual address space on the 80286 as a collection of up to sixteen thousand linear subspaces, each with a specified size or length. Each of these linear address spaces is called a segment. A segment is a logical unit of contiguous memory. Segment sizes may range from one byte up to 64K (65,536) bytes.

80286 memory segmentation supports the logical structure of programs and data in memory. Programs are not written as single linear sequences of instructions and data, but rather as modules of code and data. For example, program code may include a main routine and several separate procedures. Data may also be organized into various data structures, some private and some shared with other programs in the system. Run-time stacks constitute yet another data requirement. Each of these several modules of code and data, moreover, may be very different in size or vary dynamically with program execution.

Segmentation supports this logical structure (see figure 2-1). Each meaningful module of a program may be separately contained in individual segments. The degree of modularization, of course, depends on the requirements of a particular application. Use of segmentation benefits almost all applications. Programs execute faster and require less space. Segmentation also simplifies the design of structured software.

2.2 DATA TYPES

Bytes and words are the fundamental units in which the 80286 manipulates data, i.e., the fundamental data types.

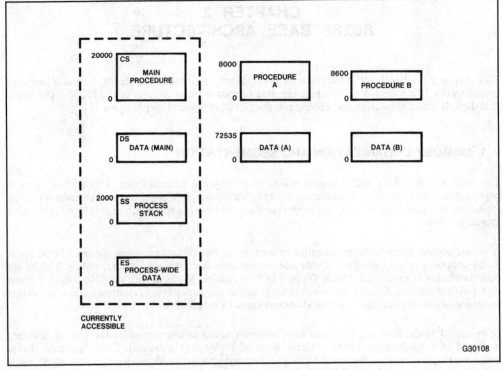

Figure 2-1. Segmented Virtual Memory

A byte is 8 contiguous bits starting on an addressable byte boundary. The bits are numbered 0 through 7, starting from the right. Bit 7 is the most significant bit:

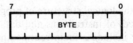

A word is defined as two contiguous bytes starting on an arbitrary byte boundary; a word thus contains 16 bits. The bits are numbered 0 through 15, starting from the right. Bit 15 is the most significant bit. The byte containing bit 0 of the word is called the low byte; the byte containing bit 15 is called the high byte.

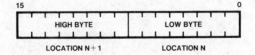

Each byte within a word has its own particular address, and the smaller of the two addresses is used as the address of the word. The byte at this lower address contains the eight least significant bits of the word, while the byte at the higher address contains the eight most significant bits. The arrangement of bytes within words is illustrated in figure 2-2.

Note that a word need not be aligned at an even-numbered byte address. This allows maximum flexibility in data structures (e.g., records containing mixed byte and word entries) and efficiency in memory utilization. Although actual transfers of data between the processor and memory take place at physically aligned word boundaries, the 80286 converts requests for unaligned words into the appropriate sequences of requests acceptable to the memory interface. Such odd aligned word transfers, however, may impact performance by requiring two memory cycles to transfer the word rather than one. Data structures (e.g., stacks) should therefore be designed in such a way that word operands are aligned on word boundaries whenever possible for maximum system performance. Due to instruction prefetching and queueing within the CPU, there is no requirement for instructions to be aligned on word boundaries and no performance loss if they are not.

Although bytes and words are the fundamental data types of operands, the processor also supports additional interpretations on these bytes or words. Depending on the instruction referencing the operand, the following additional data types can be recognized:

Integer:

A signed binary numeric value contained in an 8-bit byte or a 16-bit word. All operations assume a 2's complement representation. (Signed 32- and 64-bit integers are supported using the 80287 Numeric Data Processor.)

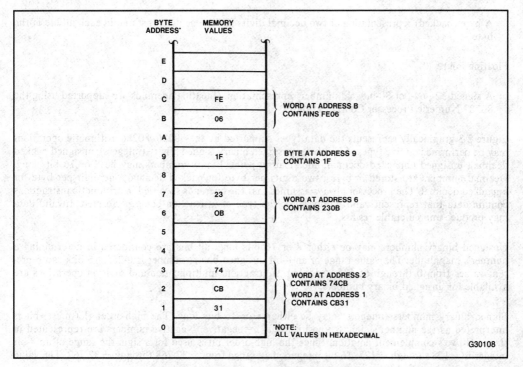

Figure 2-2. Bytes and Words in Memory

Ordinal:

An unsigned binary numeric value contained in an 8-bit byte or 16-bit word.

Pointer:

A 32-bit address quantity composed of a segment selector component and an offset component. Each component is a 16-bit word.

String:

A contiguous sequence of bytes or words. A string may contain from 1 byte to 64K bytes.

ASCII:

A byte representation of alphanumeric and control characters using the ASCII standard of character representation.

BCD:

A byte (unpacked) representation of the decimal digits (0-9).

Packed BCD:

A byte (packed) representation of two decimal digits (0-9). One digit is stored in each nibble of the byte.

Floating Point:

A signed 32-, 64-, or 80-bit real number representation. (Floating operands are supported using the 80287 Numeric Processor Configuration.)

Figure 2-3 graphically represents the data types supported by the 80286. 80286 arithmetic operations may be performed on five types of numbers: unsigned binary, signed binary (integers), unsigned packed decimal, unsigned unpacked decimal, and floating point. Binary numbers may be 8 or 16 bits long. Decimal numbers are stored in bytes; two digits per byte for packed decimal, one digit per byte for unpacked decimal. The processor always assumes that the operands specified in arithmetic instructions contain data that represent valid numbers for the type of instruction being performed. Invalid data may produce unpredictable results.

Unsigned binary numbers may be either 8 or 16 bits long; all bits are considered in determining a number's magnitude. The value range of an 8-bit unsigned binary number is 0-255; 16 bits can represent values from 0 through 65,535. Addition, subtraction, multiplication and division operations are available for unsigned binary numbers.

Signed binary numbers (integers) may be either 8 or 16 bits long. The high-order (leftmost) bit is interpreted as the number's sign: 0=positive and 1=negative. Negative numbers are represented in standard two's complement notation. Since the high-order bit is used for a sign, the range of an 8-bit integer is −128 through +127; 16-bit integers may range from −32,768 through +32,767. The value zero has a positive sign.

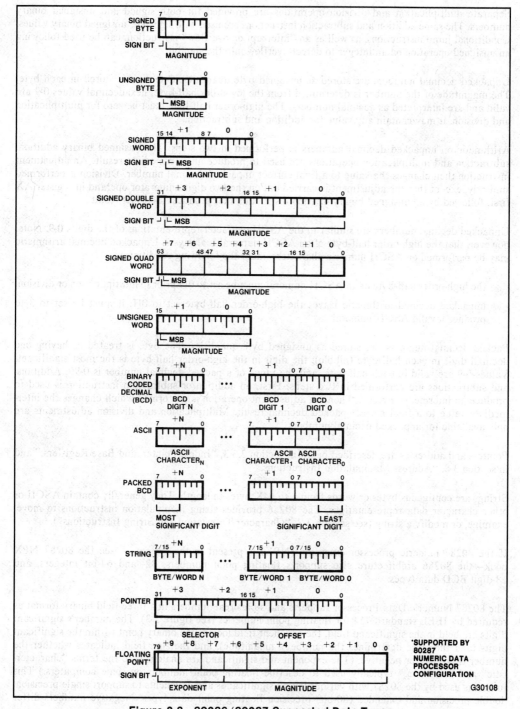

Figure 2-3. 80286/80287 Supported Data Types

Separate multiplication and division operations are provided for both signed and unsigned binary numbers. The same addition and subtraction instructions are used with signed or unsigned binary values. Conditional jump instructions, as well as an "interrupt on overflow" instruction, can be used following an unsigned operation on an integer to detect overflow into the sign bit.

Unpacked decimal numbers are stored as unsigned byte quantities. One digit is stored in each byte. The magnitude of the number is determined from the low-order half-byte; hexadecimal values 0-9 are valid and are interpreted as decimal numbers. The high-order half-byte must be zero for multiplication and division; it may contain any value for addition and subtraction.

Arithmetic on unpacked decimal numbers is performed in two steps. The unsigned binary addition, subtraction and multiplication operations are used to produce an intermediate result. An adjustment instruction then changes the value to a final correct unpacked decimal number. Division is performed similarly, except that the adjustment is carried out on the two digit numerator operand in register AX first, followed by an unsigned binary division instruction that produces a correct result.

Unpacked decimal numbers are similar to the ASCII character representations of the digits 0-9. Note, however, that the high-order half-byte of an ASCII numeral is always 3. Unpacked decimal arithmetic may be performed on ASCII numeric characters under the following conditions:

- the high-order half-byte of an ASCII numeral must be set to 0H prior to multiplication or division.

- unpacked decimal arithmetic leaves the high-order half-byte set to 0H; it must be set to 3 to produce a valid ASCII numeral.

Packed decimal numbers are stored as unsigned byte quantities. The byte is treated as having one decimal digit in each half-byte (nibble); the digit in the high-order half-byte is the most significant. Values 0-9 are valid in each half-byte, and the range of a packed decimal number is 0-99. Additions and subtractions are performed in two steps. First, an addition or subtraction instruction is used to produce an intermediate result. Then, an adjustment operation is performed which changes the intermediate value to a final correct packed decimal result. Multiplication and division adjustments are only available for unpacked decimal numbers.

Pointers and addresses are described below in section 2.3.3, "Index, Pointer, and Base Registers," and in section 3.8, "Address Manipulation Instructions."

Strings are contiguous bytes or words from 1 to 64K bytes in length. They generally contain ASCII or other character data representations. The 80286 provides string manipulation instructions to move, examine, or modify a string (see section 3.7, "Character Translation and String Instructions").

If the 80287 numeric processor extension (NPX) is present in the system — see the 80287 NPX book—the 80286 architecture also supports floating point numbers, 32- and 64-bit integers, and 18-digit BCD data types.

The 80287 Numeric Data Processor supports and stores real numbers in a three-field binary format as required by IEEE standard 754 for floating point numerics (see figure 2-3). The number's significant digits are held in the significand field, the exponent field locates the binary point within the significant digits (and therefore determines the number's magnitude), and the sign field indicates whether the number is positive or negative. (The exponent and significand are analogous to the terms "characteristic" and "mantissa," typically used to describe floating point numbers on some computers.) This format is used by the 80287 with various length significands and exponents to support single precision, double precision and extended (80-bit) precision floating point data types. Negative numbers differ from positive numbers only in their sign bits.

2.3 REGISTERS

The 80286 contains a total of fourteen registers that are of interest to the application programmer. (Five additional registers used by system programmers are covered in section 10.1.) As shown in figure 2-4, these registers may be grouped into four basic categories:

- General registers. These eight 16-bit general-purpose registers are used primarily to contain operands for arithmetic and logical operations.
- Segment registers. These four special-purpose registers determine, at any given time, which segments of memory are currently addressable.
- Status and Control registers. These three special-purpose registers are used to record and alter certain aspects of the 80286 processor state.

2.3.1 General Registers

The general registers of the 80286 are the 16-bit registers AX, BX, CX, DX, SP, BP, SI, and DI. These registers are used interchangeably to contain the operands of logical and arithmetic operations.

Some instructions and addressing modes (see section 2.4), however, dedicate certain general registers to specific uses. BX and BP are often used to contain the base address of data structures in memory (for example, the starting address of an array); for this reason, they are often referred to as the *base registers*. Similarly, SI and DI are often used to contain an index value that will be incremented to step through a data structure; these two registers are called the *index registers*. Finally, SP and BP are used for stack manipulation. Both SP and BP normally contain offsets into the current stack. SP generally contains the offset of the top of the stack and BP contains the offset or base address of the current

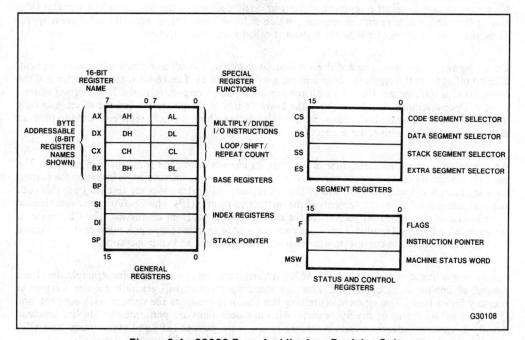

Figure 2-4. 80286 Base Architecture Register Set

stack frame. The use of these general-purpose registers for operand addressing is discussed in section 2.3.3, "Index, Pointer, and Base Registers." Register usage for individual instructions is discussed in chapters 3 and 4.

As shown in figure 2-4, eight byte registers overlap four of the 16-bit general registers. These registers are named AH, BH, CH, and DH (high bytes); and AL, BL, CL, and DL (low bytes); they overlap AX, BX, CX, and DX. These registers can be used either in their entirety or as individual 8-bit registers. This dual interpretation simplifies the handling of both 8- and 16-bit data elements.

2.3.2 Memory Segmentation and Segment Registers

Complete programs generally consist of many different code modules (or segments), and different types of data segments. However, at any given time during program execution, only a small subset of a program's segments are actually in use. Generally, this subset will include code, data, and possibly a stack. The 80286 architecture takes advantage of this by providing mechanisms to support direct access to the working set of a program's execution environment and access to additional segments on demand.

At any given instant, four segments of memory are immediately accessible to an executing 80286 program. The segment registers DS, ES, SS, and CS are used to identify these four current segments. Each of these registers specifies a particular kind of segment, as characterized by the associated mnemonics ("code," "stack," "data," or "extra") shown in figure 2-4.

An executing program is provided with concurrent access to the four individual segments of memory—a code segment, a stack segment, and two data segments—by means of the four segment registers. Each may be said to select a segment, since it uniquely determines the one particular segment from among the numerous segments in memory, which is to be immediately accessible at highest speed. Thus, the 16-bit contents of a segment register is called a segment selector.

Once a segment is selected, a base address is associated with it. To address an element within a segment, a 16-bit offset from the segment's base address must be supplied. The 16-bit segment selector and the 16-bit offset taken together form the high and low order halves, respectively, of a 32-bit virtual address pointer. Once a segment is selected, only the lower 16-bits of the pointer, called the offset, generally need to be specified by an instruction. Simple rules define which segment register is used to form an address when only a 16-bit offset is specified.

An executing program requires, first of all, that its instructions reside somewhere in memory. The segment of memory containing the currently executing sequence of instructions is known as the current code segment; it is specified by means of the CS register. All instructions are fetched from this code segment, using as an offset the contents of the instruction pointer (IP). The CS:IP register combination therefore forms the full 32-bit pointer for the next sequential program instruction. The CS register is manipulated indirectly. Transitions from one code segment to another (e.g., a procedure call) are effected implicitly as the result of control-transfer instructions, interrupts, and trap operations.

Stacks play a fundamental role in the 80286 architecture; subroutine calls, for example, involve a number of implicit stack operations. Thus, an executing program will generally require a region of memory for its stack. The segment containing this region is known as the current stack segment, and it is specified by means of the SS register. All stack operations are performed within this segment, usually in terms of address offsets contained in the stack pointer (SP) and stack frame base (BP) registers. Unlike CS, the SS register can be loaded explicitly for dynamic stack definition.

Beyond their code and stack requirements, most programs must also fetch and store data in memory. The DS and ES registers allow the specification of two data segments, each addressable by the currently executing program. Accessibility to two separate data areas supports differentiation and access requirements like local procedure data and global process data. An operand within a data segment is addressed by specifying its offset either directly in an instruction or indirectly via index and/or base registers (described in the next subsection).

Depending on the data structure (e.g., the way data is parceled into one or more segments), a program may require access to multiple data segments. To access additional segments, the DS and ES registers can be loaded under program control during the course of a program's execution. This simply requires loading the appropriate data pointer prior to accessing the data.

The interpretation of segment selector values depends on the operating mode of the processor. In Real Address Mode, a segment selector is a physical address (figure 2-5). In Protected Mode, a segment selector selects a segment of the user's virtual address space (figure 2-6). An intervening level of logical-to-physical address translation converts the logical address to a physical memory address. Chapter 6, "Memory Management," provides a detailed discussion of Protected Mode addressing. In general, considerations of selector formats and the details of memory mapping need not concern the application programmer.

2.3.3 Index, Pointer, and Base Registers

Five of the general-purpose registers are available for offset address calculations. These five registers, shown in figure 2-4, are SP, BP, BX, SI, and DI. SP is called a *pointer register*; BP and BX are called *base registers*; SI and DI are called *index registers*.

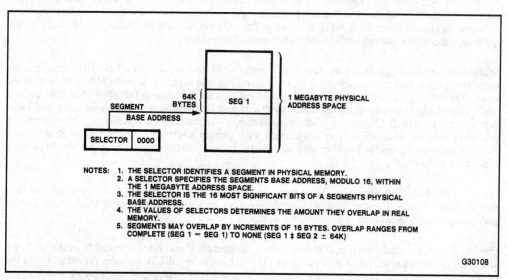

NOTES:
1. THE SELECTOR IDENTIFIES A SEGMENT IN PHYSICAL MEMORY.
2. A SELECTOR SPECIFIES THE SEGMENTS BASE ADDRESS, MODULO 16, WITHIN THE 1 MEGABYTE ADDRESS SPACE.
3. THE SELECTOR IS THE 16 MOST SIGNIFICANT BITS OF A SEGMENTS PHYSICAL BASE ADDRESS.
4. THE VALUES OF SELECTORS DETERMINES THE AMOUNT THEY OVERLAP IN REAL MEMORY.
5. SEGMENTS MAY OVERLAP BY INCREMENTS OF 16 BYTES. OVERLAP RANGES FROM COMPLETE (SEG 1 = SEG 1) TO NONE (SEG 1 ≠ SEG 2 ± 64K)

G30108

Figure 2-5. Real Address Mode Segment Selector Interpretation

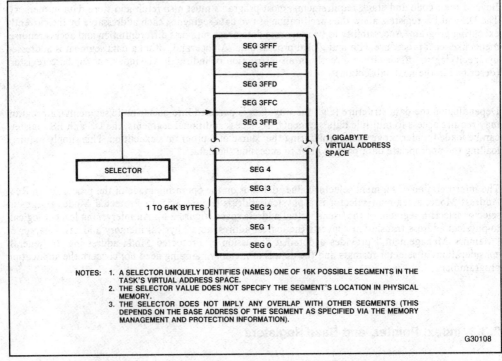

NOTES:
1. A SELECTOR UNIQUELY IDENTIFIES (NAMES) ONE OF 16K POSSIBLE SEGMENTS IN THE TASK'S VIRTUAL ADDRESS SPACE.
2. THE SELECTOR VALUE DOES NOT SPECIFY THE SEGMENT'S LOCATION IN PHYSICAL MEMORY.
3. THE SELECTOR DOES NOT IMPLY ANY OVERLAP WITH OTHER SEGMENTS (THIS DEPENDS ON THE BASE ADDRESS OF THE SEGMENT AS SPECIFIED VIA THE MEMORY MANAGEMENT AND PROTECTION INFORMATION).

G30108

Figure 2-6. Protected Mode Segment Selector Interpretation

As described in the previous section, segment registers define the set of four segments currently addressable by a program. A pointer, base, or index register may contain an offset value relative to the start of one of these segments; it thereby points to a particular operand's location within that segment. To allow for efficient computations of effective address offsets, all base and index registers may participate interchangeably as operands in most arithmetical operations.

Stack operations are facilitated by the stack pointer (SP) and stack frame base (BP) registers. By specifying offsets into the current stack segment, each of these registers provides access to data on the stack. The SP register is the customary top-of-stack pointer, addressing the uppermost datum on a push-down stack. It is referenced implicitly by PUSH and POP operations, subroutine calls, and interrupt operations. The BP register provides yet another offset into the stack segment. The existence of this stack relative base register, in conjunction with certain addressing modes described in section 2.6.3, is particularly useful for accessing data structures, variables and dynamically allocated work space within the stack.

Stacks in the 80286 are implemented in memory and are located by the stack segment register (SS) and the stack pointer register (SP). A system may have an unlimited number of stacks, and a stack may be up to 64K bytes long, the maximum length of a segment.

One stack is directly addressable at a time; this is the current stack, often referred to simply as "the" stack. SP contains the current top of the stack (TOS). In other words, SP contains the offset to the top of the push down stack from the stack segment's base address. Note, however, that the stack's base address (contained in SS) is not the "bottom" of the stack (figure 2-7).

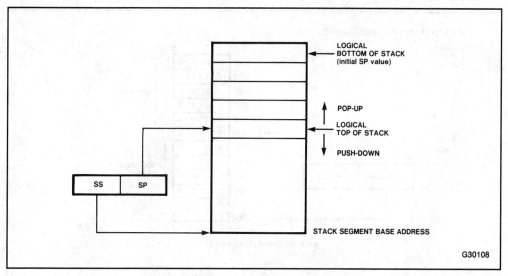

G30108

Figure 2-7. 80286 Stack

80286 stack entries are 16 bits wide. Instructions operate on the stack by adding and removing stack items one word at a time. An item is pushed onto the stack (see figure 2-8) by *decrementing* SP by 2 and writing the item at the new TOS. An item is popped off the stack by copying it from TOS and then *incrementing* SP by 2. In other words, the stack grows *down* in memory toward its base address. Stack operations never move items on the stack; nor do they erase them. The top of the stack changes only as a result of updating the stack pointer.

The stack frame base pointer (BP) is often used to access elements on the stack relative to a *fixed* point on the stack rather than relative to the *current* TOS. It typically identifies the base address of the current stack frame established for the current procedure (figure 2-9). If an index register is used relative to BP (e.g., base + index addressing mode using BP as the base), the offset will be calculated automatically in the current stack segment.

Accessing data structures in data segments is facilitated by the BX register, which has the same function in addressing operands within data segments that BP does for stack segments. They are called base registers because they may contain an offset to the base of a data structure. The similar usage of these two registers is especially important when discussing addressing modes (see section 2.4, "Addressing Modes").

Operations on data are also facilitated by the SI and DI registers. By specifying an offset relative to the start of the currently addressable data segment, an index register can be used to address an operand in the segment. If an index register is used in conjunction with the BX base register (i.e., base + index addressing) to form an offset address, the data is also assumed to reside in the current data segment. As a rule, data referenced through an index register or BX is presumed to reside in the current data segment. That is, if an instruction invokes addressing for one of its operands using either BX, DI, SI, or BX with SI or DI, the contents of the register(s) (BX, DI, or SI) implicitly specify an offset in the current data segment. As previously mentioned, data referenced via SP, BP or BP with SI or DI implicitly specify an operand in the current stack segment (refer to table 2-1).

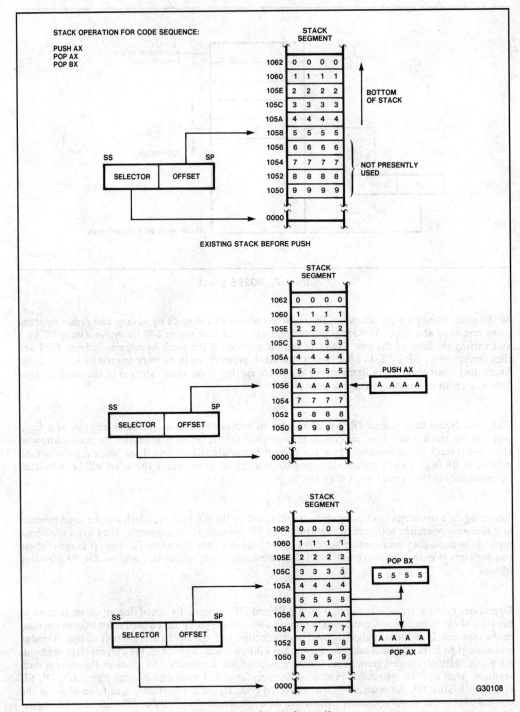

Figure 2-8. Stack Operation

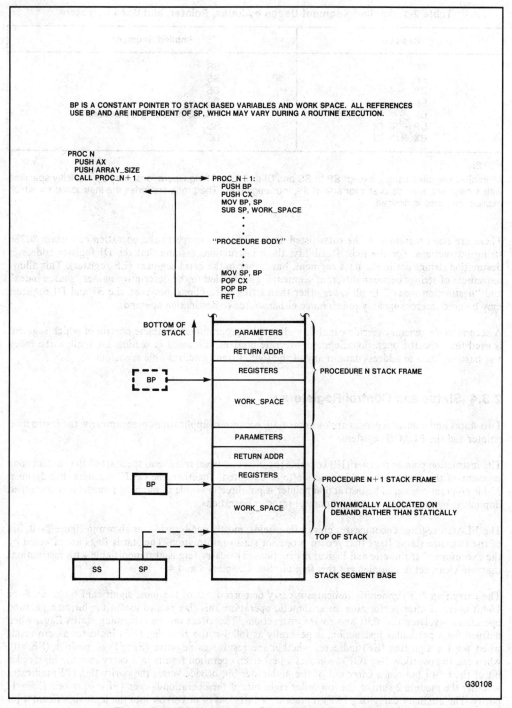

BP IS A CONSTANT POINTER TO STACK BASED VARIABLES AND WORK SPACE. ALL REFERENCES
USE BP AND ARE INDEPENDENT OF SP, WHICH MAY VARY DURING A ROUTINE EXECUTION.

```
PROC N
    PUSH AX
    PUSH ARRAY_SIZE
    CALL PROC_N+1  ─────────────▶  PROC_N+1:
                                      PUSH BP
                                      PUSH CX
                                      MOV BP, SP
                                      SUB SP, WORK_SPACE
                                         •
                                         •
                                         •
                                   "PROCEDURE BODY"
                                         •
                                         •
                                         •
                                      MOV SP, BP
                                      POP CX
                                      POP BP
                                      RET
```

BOTTOM OF
STACK

PARAMETERS	
RETURN ADDR	
REGISTERS	PROCEDURE N STACK FRAME
WORK_SPACE	
PARAMETERS	
RETURN ADDR	
REGISTERS	PROCEDURE N+1 STACK FRAME
WORK_SPACE	DYNAMICALLY ALLOCATED ON DEMAND RATHER THAN STATICALLY

BP

BP

TOP OF STACK

SS   SP

STACK SEGMENT BASE

G30108

Figure 2-9. BP Usage as a Stack Frame Base Pointer

Table 2-1. Implied Segment Usage by Index, Pointer, and Base Registers

Register	Implied Segment
SP	SS
BP	SS
BX	DS
SI	DS
DI	DS, ES for String Operations
BP + SI, DI	SS
BX + SI, DI	DS

NOTE:
All implied Segment usage, except SP to SS and DI to ES for String Operations, may be explicitly specified with a segment override prefix for any of the four segments. The prefix precedes the instruction for which explicit reference is desired.

There are two exceptions to the rules listed above. The first concerns the operation of certain 80286 string instructions. For the most flexibility, these instructions assume that the DI register addresses destination strings not in the data segment, but rather in the extra segment (ES register). This allows movement of strings between different segments. This has led to the descriptive names "source index" and "destination index." In all cases other than string instructions, however, the SI and DI registers may be used interchangeably to reference either source or destination operands.

A second more general override capability allows the programmer complete control of which segment is used for a specific operation. Segment-override prefixes, discussed in section 2.4.3, allow the index and base registers to address data in any of the four currently addressable segments.

2.3.4 Status and Control Registers

Two status and control registers are of immediate concern to applications programmers: the instruction pointer and the FLAGS registers.

The instruction pointer register (IP) contains the offset address, relative to the start of the current code segment, of the next sequential instruction to be executed. Together, the CS:IP registers thus define a 32-bit program-counter. The instruction pointer is not directly visible to the programmer; it is controlled implicitly, by interrupts, traps, and control-transfer operations.

The FLAGS register encompasses eleven flag fields, mostly one-bit wide, as shown in figure 2-10. Six of the flags are status flags that record processor status information. The status flags are affected by the execution of arithmetic and logical instructions. The carry flag is also modifiable with instructions that will clear, set or complement this flag bit. See Chapters 3 and 4.

The carry flag (CF) generally indicates a carry or borrow out of the most significant bit of an 8- or 16-bit operand after performing an arithmetic operation; this flag is also useful for bit manipulation operations involving the shift and rotate instructions. The effect on the remaining status flags, when defined for a particular instruction, is generally as follows: the zero flag (ZF) indicates a zero result when set; the sign flag (SF) indicates whether the result was negative (SF=1) or positive (SF=0); when set, the overflow flag (OF) indicates whether an operation results in a carry into the high order bit of the result but not a carry out of the high-order bit, or vice versa; the parity flag (PF) indicates whether the modulo 2 sum of the low-order eight bits of the operation is even (PF=0) or odd (PF=1) parity. The auxiliary carry flag (AF) represents a carry out of or borrow into the least significant 4-bit digit when performing binary coded decimal (BCD) arithmetic.

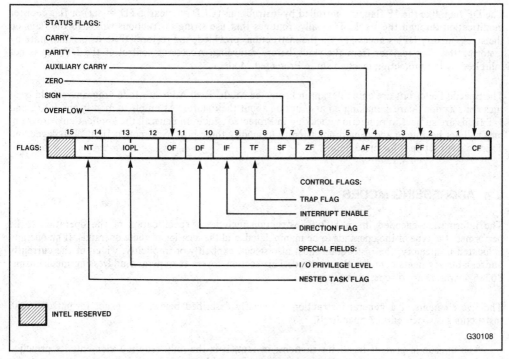

Figure 2-10. Flags Register

The FLAGS register also contains three control flags that are used, under program control, to direct certain processor operations. The interrupt-enable flag (IF), if set, enables external interrupts; otherwise, interrupts are disabled. The trap flag (TF), if set, puts the processor into a single-step mode for debugging purposes where the target program is automatically interrupted to a user supplied debug routine after the execution of each target program instruction. The direction flag (DF) controls the forward or backward direction of string operations: 0 = forward or auto increment the address register(s) (SI, DI or SI and DI), 1 = backward or auto-decrement the address register(s) (SI, DI or SI and DI).

In general, the interrupt enable flag may be set or reset with special instructions (STI = set, CLI = clear) or by placing the flags on the stack, modifying the stack, and returning the flag image from the stack to the flag register. If operating in Protected Mode, the ability to alter the IF bit is subject to protection checks to prevent non-privileged programs from effecting the interrupt state of the CPU. This applies to both instruction and stack options for modifying the IF bit.

The TF flag may only be modified by copying the flag register to the stack, setting the TF bit in the stack image, and returning the modified stack image to the flag register. The trap interrupt occurs on completion of the next instruction. Entry to the single step routine saves the flag register on the stack with the TF bit set, and resets the TF bit in the register. After completion of the single step routine, the TF bit is automatically set on return to the program being single stepped to interrupt the program again after completion of the next instruction. Use of TF is not inhibited by the protection mechanism in Protected Mode.

The DF flag, like the IF flag, is controlled by instructions (CLD = clear, STD = set) or flag register modification through the stack. Typically, routines that use string instructions will save the flags on the stack, modify DF as necessary via the instructions provided, and restore DF to its original state by restoring the Flag register from the stack before returning. Access or control of the DF flag is not inhibited by the protection mechanism in Protected Mode.

The Special Fields bits are only relevant in Protected Mode. Real Address Mode programs should treat these bits as don't-care's, making no assumption about their status. Attempts to modify the IOPL and NT fields are subject to protection checking in Protected Mode. In general, the application's programmer will not be able to and should not attempt to modify these bits. (See section 10.3, "Privileged and Trusted Instructions" for more details.)

2.4 ADDRESSING MODES

The information encoded in an 80286 instruction includes a specification of the operation to be performed, the type of the operands to be manipulated, and the location of these operands. If an operand is located in memory, the instruction must also select, explicitly or implicitly, which of the currently addressable segments contains the operand. This section covers the operand addressing mechanisms; 80286 operators are discussed in Chapter 3.

The five elements of a general instruction are briefly described below. The exact format of 80286 instructions is specified in Appendix B.

- The opcode is present in all instructions; in fact, it is the only required element. Its principal function is the specification of the operation performed by the instruction.

- A register specifier.

- The addressing mode specifier, when present, is used to specify the addressing mode of an operand for referencing data or performing indirect calls or jumps.

- The displacement, when present, is used to compute the effective address of an operand in memory.

- The immediate operand, when present, directly specifies one operand of the instruction.

Of the four elements, only one, the opcode, is always present. The other elements may or may not be present, depending on the particular operation involved and on the location and type of the operands.

2.4.1 Operands

Generally speaking, an instruction is an operation performed on zero, one, or two operands, which are the data manipulated by the instruction. An operand can be located either in a register (AX, BX, CX, DX, SI, DI, SP, or BP in the case of 16-bit operands; AH, AL, BH, BL, CH, CL, DH, or DL in the case of 8-bit operands; the FLAG register for flag operations in the instruction itself (as an immediate operand)), or in memory or an I/O port. Immediate operands and operands in registers can be accessed more rapidly than operands in memory since memory operands must be fetched from memory while immediate and register operands are available in the processor.

An 80286 instruction can reference zero, one, or two operands. The three forms are as follows:

- Zero-operand instructions, such as RET, NOP, and HLT. Consult Appendix B.

- One-operand instructions, such as INC or DEC. The location of the single operand can be specified *implicitly*, as in AAM (where the register AX contains the operand), or *explicitly*, as in INC (where the operand can be in any register or memory location). Explicitly specified operands are accessed via one of the addressing modes described in section 2.4.2.

- Two operand instructions such as MOV, ADD, XOR, etc., generally overwrite one of the two participating operands with the result. A distinction can thus be made between the source operand (the one left unaffected by the operation) and the destination operand (the one overwritten by the result). Like one-operand instructions, two-operand instructions can specify the location of operands either explicitly or implicitly. If an instruction contains two explicitly specified operands, only one of them—either the source or the destination—can be in a register or memory location. The other operand must be in a register or be an immediate source operand. Special cases of two-operand instructions are the string instructions and stack manipulation. Both operands of some string instructions are in memory and are explicitly specified. Push and pop stack operations allow transfer between memory operands and the memory based stack.

Thus, the two-operand instructions of the 80286 permit operations of the following sort:

- Register-to-register
- Register-to-memory
- Memory-to-register
- Immediate-to-register
- Immediate-to-memory
- Memory-to-memory

Instructions can specify the location of their operands by means of eight addressing modes, which are described in sections 2.4.2 and 2.4.3.

2.4.2 Register and Immediate Modes

Two addressing modes are used to reference operands contained in registers and instructions:

- Register Operand Mode. The operand is located in one of the 16-bit registers (AX, BX, CX, DX, SI, DI, SP, or BP) or in one of the 8-bit general registers (AH, BH, CH, DH, AL, BL, CL, or DL).

  Special instructions are also included for referencing the CS, DS, ES, SS, and Flag registers as operands also.

- Immediate Operand Mode. The operand is part of the instruction itself (the immediate operand element).

2.4.3 Memory Addressing Modes

Six modes are used to access operands in memory. Memory operands are accessed by means of a pointer consisting of a segment selector (see section 2.3.2) and an offset, which specifies the operand's displacement in bytes from the beginning of the segment in which it resides. Both the segment selector component and the offset component are 16-bit values. (See section 2.1 for a discussion of segmentation.) Only some instructions use a full 32-bit address.

Most memory references do not require the instruction to specify a full 32-bit pointer address. Operands that are located within one of the currently addressable segments, as determined by the four segment registers (see section 2.3.2, "Segment Registers"), can be referenced very efficiently simply by means of the 16-bit offset. This form of address is called by short address. The choice of segment (CS, DS, ES, or SS) is either implicit within the instruction itself or explicitly specified by means of a segment override prefix (see below).

See figure 2-11 for a diagram of the addressing process.

2.4.3.1 SEGMENT SELECTION

All instructions that address operands in memory must specify the segment and the offset. For speed and compact instruction encoding, segment selectors are usually stored in the high speed segment registers. An instruction need specify only the desired segment register and an offset in order to address a memory operand.

Most instructions need not explicitly specify which segment register is used. The correct segment register is automatically chosen according to the rules of table 2-1 and table 2-2. These rules follow the way programs are written (see figure 2-12) as independent modules that require areas for code and data, a stack, and access to external data areas.

There is a close connection between the type of memory reference and the segment in which that operand resides (see the next section for a discussion of how memory addressing mode calculations are performed). As a rule, a memory reference implies the current data segment (i.e., the implicit segment selector is in DS) unless the BP register is involved in the address specification, in which case the current stack segment is implied (i.e, SS contains the selector).

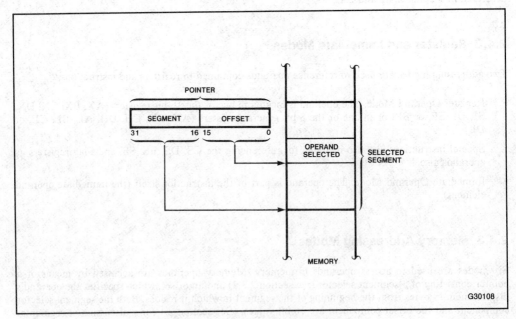

Figure 2-11. Two-Component Address

Table 2-2. Segment Register Selection Rules

Memory Reference Needed	Segment Register Used	Implicit Segment Selection Rule
Instructions	Code (CS)	Automatic with instruction prefetch.
Stack	Stack (SS)	All stack pushes and pops. Any memory reference which uses BP as a base register.
Local Data	Data (DS)	All data references except when relative to stack or string destination.
External (Global) Data	Extra (ES)	Alternate data segment and destination of string operation.

The 80286 instruction set defines special instruction prefix elements (see Appendix B). One of these is SEG, the segment-override prefix. Segment-override prefixes allow an explicit segment selection. Only in two special cases—namely, the use of DI to reference destination strings in the ES segment, and the use of SP to reference stack locations in the SS segment—is there an implied segment selection which cannot be overridden. The format of segment override prefixes is shown in Appendix B.

2.4.3.2 OFFSET COMPUTATION

The offset within the desired segment is calculated in accordance with the desired addressing mode. The offset is calculated by taking the sum of up to three components:

- the displacement element in the instruction
- the base (contents of BX or BP—a base register)
- the index (contents of SI or DI—an index register)

Each of the three components of an offset may be either a positive or negative value. Offsets are calculated modulo 2^{16}.

The six memory addressing modes are generated using various combinations of these three components. The six modes are used for accessing different types of data stored in memory:

addressing mode	offset calculation
direct address	displacement alone
register indirect	base or index alone
based	base + displacement
indexed	index + displacement
based indexed	base + index
based indexed with displacement	base + index + disp

In all six modes, the operand is located at the specified offset within the selected segment. All displacements, except direct address mode, are optionally 8- or 16-bit values. 8-bit displacements are automatically sign-extended to 16 bits. The six addressing modes are described and demonstrated in the following section on memory addressing modes.

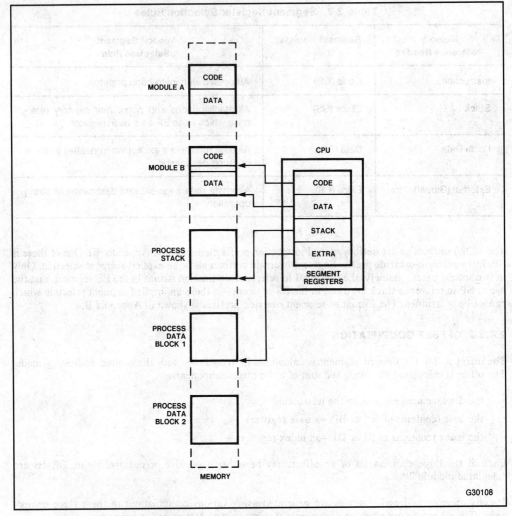

Figure 2-12. Use of Memory Segmentation

2.4.3.3 MEMORY MODE

Two modes are used for simple scalar operands located in memory:

- Direct Address Mode. The offset of the operand is contained in the instruction as the displacement element. The offset is a 16-bit quantity.

- Register Indirect Mode. The offset of the operand is in one of the registers SI, DI, or BX. (BP is excluded; if BP is used as a stack frame base, it requires an index or displacement component to reference either parameters passed on the stack or temporary variables allocated on the stack. The instruction level bit encoding for the BP only address mode is used to specify Direct Address mode. See Chapter 12 for more details.)

The following four modes are used for accessing complex data structures in memory (see figure 2-13):

- Based Mode. The operand is located within the selected segment at an offset computed as the sum of the displacement and the contents of a base register (BX or BP). Based mode is often used to access the same field in different copies of a structure (often called a record). The base register points to the base of the structure (hence the term "base" register), and the displacement selects a particular field. Corresponding fields within a collection of structures can be accessed simply by changing the base register. (See figure 2-13, example 1.)

- Indexed Mode. The operand is located within the selected segment at an offset computed as the sum of the displacement and the contents of an index register (SI or DI). Indexed mode is often used to access elements in a static array (e.g., an array whose starting location is fixed at translation time). The displacement locates the beginning of the array, and the value of the index register selects one element. Since all array elements are the same length, simple arithmetic on the index register will select any element. (See figure 2-13, example 2.)

- Based Indexed Mode. The operand is located within the selected segment at an offset computed as the sum of the base register's contents and an index register's contents. Based Indexed mode is often used to access elements of a dynamic array (i.e., an array whose base address can change during execution). The base register points to the base of the array, and the value of the index register is used to select one element. (See figure 2-13, example 3.)

- Based Indexed Mode with Displacement. The operand is located with the selected segment at an offset computed as the sum of a base register's contents, an index register's contents, and the displacement. This mode is often used to access elements of an array within a structure. For example, the structure could be an activation record (i.e., a region of the stack containing the register contents, parameters, and variables associated with one instance of a procedure); and one variable could be an array. The base register points to the start of the activation record, the displacement expresses the distance from the start of the record to the beginning of the array variable, and the index register selects a particular element of the array. (See figure 2-13, example 4.)

Table 2-3 gives a summary of all memory operand addressing options.

2.5 INPUT/OUTPUT

The 80286 allows input/output to be performed in either of two ways: by means of a separate I/O address space (using specific I/O instructions) or by means of memory-mapped I/O (using general-purpose operand manipulation instructions).

Table 2-3. Memory Operand Addressing Modes

Addressing Mode	Offset Calculation
Direct	16-bit Displacement in the instruction
Register Indirect	BX, SI, DI
Based	(BX or BP) + Displacement*
Indexed	(SI or DI) + Displacement*
Based Indexed	(BX or BP) + (SI or DI)
Based Indexed + Displacement	(BX or BP) + (SI or DI) + Displacement*

* The displacement can be a 0, 8 or 16-bit value.

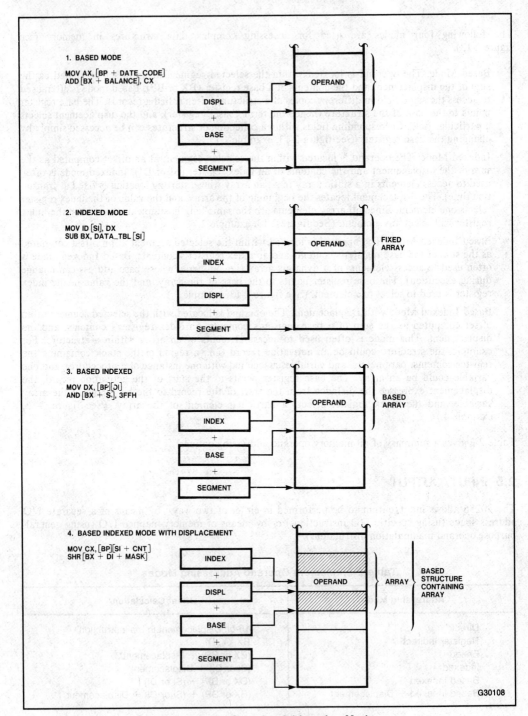

Figure 2-13. Complex Addressing Modes

2.5.1 I/O Address Space

The 80286 provides a separate I/O address space, distinct from physical memory, to address the input/output ports that are used for external devices. The I/O address space consists of 2^{16} (64K) individually addressable 8-bit ports. Any two consecutive 8-bit ports can be treated as a 16-bit port. Thus, the I/O address space can accommodate up to 64K 8-bit ports or up to 32K 16-bit ports. I/O port addresses 00F8H to 00FFH are reserved by Intel.

The 80286 can transfer either 8 or 16 bits at a time to a device located in the I/O space. Like words in memory, 16-bit ports should be aligned at even-numbered addresses so that the 16 bits will be transferred in a single access. An 8-bit port may be located at either an even or odd address. The internal registers in a given peripheral controller device should be assigned addresses as shown below.

Port Register	Port Addresses	Example
16-bit	even word addresses	OUT FE,AX
8-bit; device on lower half of 16-bit data bus	even byte addresses	IN AL,FE
8-bit; device on upper half of 16-bit data bus	odd byte addresses	OUT FF,AL

The I/O instructions IN and OUT (described in section 3.11.3) are provided to move data between I/O ports and the AX (16-bit I/O) or AL (8-bit I/O) general registers. The block I/O instructions INS and OUTS (described in section 4.1) move blocks of data between I/O ports and memory space (as shown below). In Protected Mode, an operating system may prevent a program from executing these I/O instructions. Otherwise, the function of the I/O instructions and the structure of the I/O space are identical for both modes of operation.

```
INS    es:byte ptr [di], DX
OUTS  DX, byte ptr [si]
```

IN and OUT instructions address I/O with either a direct address to one of up to 256 port addresses, or indirectly via the DX register to one of up to 64K port addresses. Block I/O uses the DX register to specify the I/O address and either SI or DI to designate the source or destination memory address. For each transfer, SI or DI are either incremented or decremented as specified by the direction bit in the flag word while DX is constant to select the I/O device.

2.5.2 Memory-Mapped I/O

I/O devices also may be placed in the 80286 memory address space. So long as the devices respond like memory components, they are indistinguishable to the processor.

Memory-mapped I/O provides additional programming flexibility. Any instruction that references memory may be used to access an I/O port located in the memory space. For example, the MOV instruction can transfer data between any register and a port; and the AND, OR, and TEST instructions may be used to manipulate bits in the internal registers of a device (see figure 2-14). Memory-mapped I/O performed via the full instruction set maintains the full complement of addressing modes for selecting the desired I/O device.

Memory-mapped I/O, like any other memory reference, is subject to access protection and control when executing in protected mode.

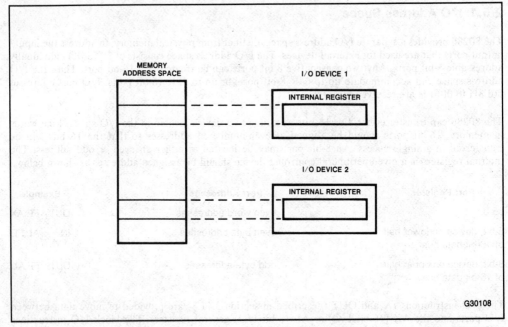

Figure 2-14. Memory-Mapped I/O

2.6 INTERRUPTS AND EXCEPTIONS

The 80286 architecture supports several mechanisms for interrupting program execution. Internal interrupts are synchronous events that are the responses of the CPU to certain events detected during the execution of an instruction. External interrupts are asynchronous events typically triggered by external devices needing attention. The 80286 supports both maskable (controlled by the IF flag) and non-maskable interrupts. They cause the processor to temporarily suspend its present program execution in order to service the requesting device. The major distinction between these two kinds of interrupts is their origin: an internal interrupt is always reproducible by re-executing with the program and data that caused the interrupt, whereas an external interrupt is generally independent of the currently executing task.

Interrupts 0-31 are reserved by Intel.

Application programmers will normally not be concerned with servicing external interrupts. More information on external interrupts for system programmers may be found in Chapter 5, section 5.2, "Interrupt Handling for Real Address Mode," and in Chapter 9, "Interrupts, Traps and Faults for Protected Virtual Address Mode."

In Real Address Mode, the application programmer is affected by two kinds of internal interrupts. (Internal interrupts are the result of executing an instruction which causes the interrupt.) One type of interrupt is called an exception because the interrupt only occurs if a particular fault condition exists. The other type of interrupt generates the interrupt every time the instruction is executed.

The exceptions are: *divide error, INTO detected overflow, bounds check, segment overrun, invalid operation code*, and *processor extension error* (see table 2-4). A divide error exception results when the instructions DIV or IDIV are executed with a zero denominator; otherwise, the quotient will be too large for the destination operand (see section 3.3.4 for a discussion of DIV and IDIV). An overflow exception results when the INTO instruction is executed and the OF flag is set (after an arithmetic operation that set the overflow (OF) flag). (See section 3.6.3, "Software Generated Interrupts," for a discussion of INTO.) A bounds check exception results when the BOUND instruction is executed and the array index it checks falls outside the bounds of the array. (See section 4.2 for a discussion of the BOUND instruction.) The segment overrun exception occurs when a word memory reference is attempted which extends beyond the end of a segment. An invalid operation code exception occurs if an attempt is made to execute an undefined instruction operation code. A processor extension error is generated when a processor extension detects an illegal operation. Refer to Chapter 5 for a more complete description of these exception conditions.

The instruction INT generates an internal interrupt whenever it is executed. The effects of this interrupt (and the effects of all interrupts) is determined by the interrupt handler routines provided by the application program or as part of the system software (provided by system programmers). See Chapter 5 for more on this topic. The INT instruction itself is discussed in section 3.6.3.

In Protected Mode, many more fault conditions are detected and result in internal interrupts. Protected Mode interrupts and faults are discussed in Chapter 9.

2.7 HIERARCHY OF INSTRUCTION SETS

For descriptive purposes, the 80286 instruction set is partitioned into three distinct subsets: the Basic Instruction Set, the Extended Instruction Set, and the System Control Instruction Set. The "hierarchy" of instruction sets defined by this partitioning helps to clarify the relationships between the various processors in the 8086 family (see figure 2-15).

The Basic Instruction Set, presented in Chapter 3, comprises the common subset of instructions found on all processors of the 8086 family. Included are instructions for logical and arithmetic operations, data movement, input/output, string manipulation, and transfer of control.

The Extended Instruction Set, presented in Chapter 4, consists of those instructions found only on the 80186, 80188, and 80286 processors. Included are instructions for block structured procedure entry and exit, parameter validation, and block I/O transfers.

The System Control Instruction Set, presented in Chapter 10, consists of those instructions unique to the 80286. These instructions control the memory management and protection mechanisms of the 80286.

Table 2-4. 80286 Interrupt Vector Assignments (Real Address Mode)

Function	Interrupt Number	Related Instructions	Return Address Before Instruction Causing Exception?
Divide error exception	0	DIV, IDIV	Yes
Single step interrupt	1	All	
NMI interrupt	2	All	
Breakpoint interrupt	3	INT	
INTO detected overflow exception	4	INTO	No
BOUND range exceeded exception	5	BOUND	Yes
Invalid opcode exception	6	Any undefined opcode	Yes
Processor extension not available exception	7	ESC or WAIT	Yes
Interrupt table limit too small exception	8	INT vector is not within table limit	Yes
Processor extension segment overrun interrupt	9	ESC with memory operand extending beyond offset FFFF(H)	No
Reserved	10-12		
Segment overrun exception	13	Word memory reference with offset = FFFF(H) or an attempt to execute past the end of a segment	Yes
Reserved	14, 15		
Processor extension error interrupt	16	ESC or WAIT	
Reserved	17–31		
User defined	32–255		

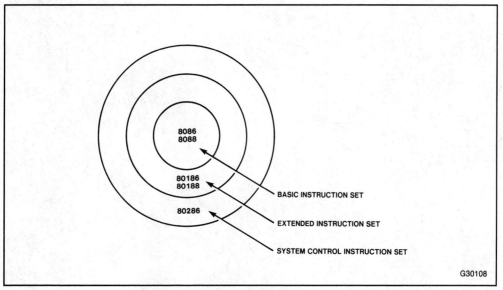

G30108

Figure 2-15. Hierarchy of Instructions

Figure 2-13. Hierarchy of Instructions

Basic Instruction Set

CHAPTER 3
BASIC INSTRUCTION SET

The base architecture of the 80286 is identical to the complete instruction set of the 8086, 8088, 80188, and 80186 processors. The 80286 instruction set includes new forms of some instructions. These new forms reduce program size and improve the performance and ease of implementation of source code.

This chapter describes the instructions which programmers can use to write application software for the 80286. The following chapters describe the operation of more complicated I/O and system control instructions.

All instructions described in this chapter are available for both Real Address Mode and Protected Virtual Address Mode operation. The instruction descriptions note any differences that exist between the operation of an instruction in these two modes.

This chapter also describes the operation of each application program-relative instruction and includes an example of using the instruction. The Instruction Dictionary in Appendix B contains formal descriptions of all instructions. Any opcode pattern that is not described in the Instruction Dictionary is undefined and results in an opcode violation trap (interrupt 6).

3.1 DATA MOVEMENT INSTRUCTIONS

These instructions provide convenient methods for moving bytes or words of data between memory and the registers of the base architecture.

3.1.1 General-Purpose Data Movement Instructions

MOV (Move) transfers a byte or a word from the source operand to the destination operand. The MOV instruction is useful for transferring data to a register from memory, to memory from a register, between registers, immediate-to-register, or immediate-to-memory. Memory-to-memory or segment register-to-segment register moves are not allowed.

Example: MOV DS,AX. Replaces the contents of register DS with the contents of register AX.

XCHG (Exchange) swaps the contents of two operands. This instruction takes the place of three MOV instructions. It does not require a temporary memory location to save the contents of one operand while you load the other.

The XCHG instruction can swap two byte operands or two word operands, but not a byte for a word or a word for a byte. The operands for the XCHG instruction may be two register operands, or a register operand with a memory operand. When used with a memory operand, XCHG automatically activates the LOCK signal.

Example: XCHG BX,WORDOPRND. Swaps the contents of register BX with the contents of the memory word identified by the label WORDOPRND after asserting bus lock.

3.1.2 Stack Manipulation Instructions

PUSH (Push) decrements the stack pointer (SP) by two and then transfers a word from the source operand to the top of stack indicated by SP. See figure 3-1. PUSH is often used to place parameters on the stack before calling a procedure; it is also the basic means of storing temporary variables on the stack. The PUSH instruction operates on memory operands, immediate operands (new with the 80286), and register operands (including segment registers).

Example: PUSH WORDOPRND. Transfers a 16-bit value from the memory word identified by the label WORDOPRND to the memory location which represents the current top of stack (byte transfers are not allowed).

PUSHA (Push All Registers) saves the contents of the eight general registers on the stack. See figure 3-2. This instruction simplifies procedure calls by reducing the number of instructions required to retain the contents of the general registers for use in a procedure. PUSHA is complemented by POPA (see below).

The processor pushes the general registers on the stack in the following order: AX, CX, DX, BX, the initial value of SP before AX was pushed, BP, SI, and DI.

Example: PUSHA. Pushes onto the stack the contents of the eight general registers.

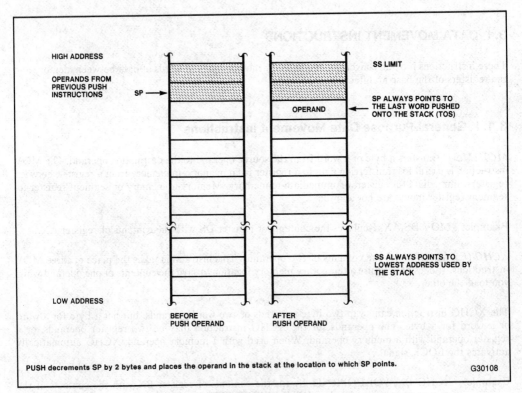

PUSH decrements SP by 2 bytes and places the operand in the stack at the location to which SP points.

G30108

Figure 3-1. PUSH

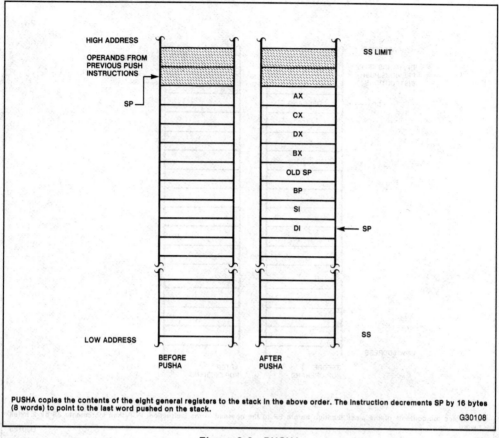

PUSHA copies the contents of the eight general registers to the stack in the above order. The instruction decrements SP by 16 bytes (8 words) to point to the last word pushed on the stack.

G30108

Figure 3-2. PUSHA

POP (Pop) transfers the word at the current top of stack (indicated by SP) to the destination operand, and then increments SP by two to point to the new top of stack. See figure 3-3. POP moves information from the stack to either a register or memory. The only restriction on POP is that it cannot place a value in register CS.

Example: POP BX. Replaces the contents of register BX with the contents of the memory location at the top of stack.

POPA (Pop All Registers) restores the registers saved on the stack by PUSHA, except that it ignores the value of SP. See figure 3-4.

Example: POPA. Pops from the stack the saved contents of the general registers, and restores the registers (except SP) to their original state.

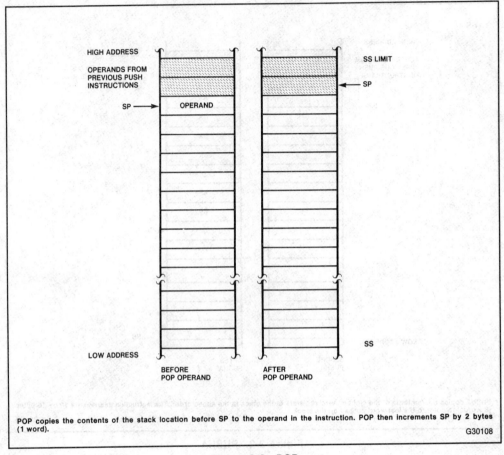

POP copies the contents of the stack location before SP to the operand in the instruction. POP then increments SP by 2 bytes (1 word).

G30108

Figure 3-3. POP

3.2 FLAG OPERATION WITH THE BASIC INSTRUCTION SET

3.2.1 Status Flags

The status flags of the FLAGS register reflect conditions that result from a previous instruction or instructions. The arithmetic instructions use OF, SF, ZF, AF, PF, and CF.

The SCAS (Scan String), CMPS (Compare String), and LOOP instructions use ZF to signal that their operations are complete. The base architecture includes instructions to set, clear, and complement CF before execution of an arithmetic instruction. See figure 3-5 and tables 3-1 and 3-2.

3.2.2 Control Flags

The control flags of the FLAGS register determine processor operations for string instructions, maskable interrupts, and debugging.

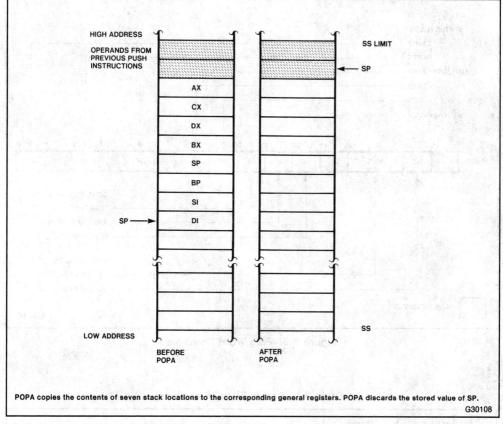

POPA copies the contents of seven stack locations to the corresponding general registers. POPA discards the stored value of SP.

G30108

Figure 3-4. POPA

Setting *DF (direction flag)* causes string instructions to auto-decrement; that is, to process strings from high addresses to low addresses, or from "right-to-left." Clearing DF causes string instructions to auto-increment, or to process strings from "left-to-right."

Setting *IF (interrupt flag)* allows the CPU to recognize external (maskable) interrupt requests. Clearing IF disables these interrupts. IF has no effect on either internally generated interrupts, nonmaskable external interrupts, or processor extension segment overrun interrupts.

Setting *TF (trap flag)* puts the processor into single-step mode for debugging. In this mode, the CPU automatically generates an internal interrupt after each instruction, allowing a program to be inspected as it executes each instruction, instruction by instruction.

3.3 ARITHMETIC INSTRUCTIONS

The arithmetic instructions of the 8086-family processors simplify the manipulation of numerical data. Multiplication and division instructions ease the handling of signed and unsigned binary integers as well as unpacked decimal integers.

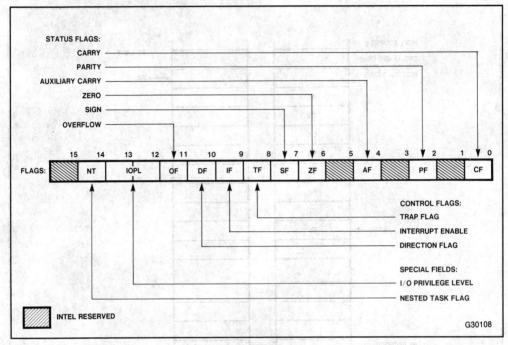

Figure 3-5. Flag Word Contents

Table 3-1. Status Flags' Functions

Bit Position	Name	Function
0	CF	Carry Flag—Set on high-order bit carry or borrow; cleared otherwise.
2	PF	Parity Flag—Set if low-order eight bits of result contain an even number of 1 bits; cleared otherwise.
4	AF	Set on carry from or borrow to the low order four bits of AL; cleared otherwise.
6	ZF	Zero Flag—Set if result is zero; cleared otherwise.
7	SF	Sign Flag—Set equal to high-order bit of result (0 if positive, 1 if negative).
11	OF	Overflow Flag—Set if result is too-large a positive number or too-small a negative number (excluding sign-bit) to fit in destination operand; cleared otherwise.

Table 3-2. Control Flags' Functions

Bit Position	Name	Function
8	TF	Trap (Single Step) Flag—Once set, a single step interrupt occurs after the next instruction executes. TF is cleared by the single step interrupt.
9	IF	Interrupt-enable Flag—When set, maskable interrupts will cause the CPU to transfer control to an interrupt vector-specified location.
10	DF	Direction Flag—Causes string instructions to auto decrement the appropriate index registers when set. Clearing DF causes auto increment.

An arithmetic operation may consist of two register operands, a general register source operand with a memory destination operand, a memory source operand with a register destination operand, or an immediate field with either a register or memory destination operand, but not two memory operands. Arithmetic instructions can operate on either byte or word operands.

3.3.1 Addition Instructions

ADD (Add Integers) replaces the destination operand with the sum of the source and destination operands. ADD affects OF, SF, AF, PF, CF, and ZF.

Example: ADD BL, BYTEOPRND. Adds the contents of the memory byte labeled BYTEOPRND to the contents of BL, and replaces BL with the resulting sum.

ADC (Add Integers with Carry) sums the operands, adds one if CF is set, and replaces the destination operand with the result. ADC can be used to add numbers longer than 16 bits. ADC affects OF, SF, AF, PF, CF, and ZF.

Example: ADC BX, CX. Replaces the contents of the destination operand BX with the sum of BX, CS, and 1 (if CF is set). If CF is cleared, ADC performs the same operation as the ADD instruction.

INC (Increment) adds one to the destination operand. The processor treats the operand as an unsigned binary number. INC updates AF, OF, PF, SF, and ZF, but it does not affect CF. Use ADD with an immediate value of 1 if an increment that updates carry (CF) is needed.

Example: INC BL. Adds 1 to the contents of BL.

3.3.2 Subtraction Instructions

SUB (Subtract Integers) subtracts the source operand from the destination operand and replaces the destination operand with the result. If a borrow is required, carry flag is set. The operands may be signed or unsigned bytes or words. SUB affects OF, SF, ZF, AF, PF, and CF.

Example: SUB WORDOPRND, AX. Replaces the contents of the destination operand WORDOPRND with the result obtained by subtracting the contents of AX from the contents of the memory word labeled WORDOPRND.

SBB (Subtract Integers with Borrow) subtracts the source operand from the destination operand, subtracts 1 if CF is set, and returns the result to the destination operand. The operands may be signed or unsigned bytes or words. SBB may be used to subtract numbers longer than 16 bits. This instruction affects OF, SF, ZF, AF, PF, and CF. The carry flag is set if a borrow is required.

Example: SBB BL, 32. Subtracts 32 from the contents of BL and then decrements the result of this subtraction by one if CF is set. If CF is cleared, SBB performs the same operation as SUB.

DEC (Decrement) subtracts 1 from the destination operand. DEC updates AF, OF, PF, SF, and ZF, but it does not affect CF. Use SUB with an immediate value of 1 to perform a decrement that affects carry.

Example: DEC BX. Subtracts 1 from the contents of BX and places the result back in BX.

3.3.3 Multiplication Instructions

MUL (Unsigned Integer Multiply) performs an unsigned multiplication of the source operand and the accumulator. If the source is a byte, the processor multiplies it by the contents of AL and returns the double-length result to AH and AL.

If the source operand is a word, the processor multiplies it by the contents of AX and returns the double-length result to DX and AX. MUL sets CF and OF to indicate that the upper half of the result is nonzero; otherwise, they are cleared. This instruction leaves SF, ZF, AF, and PF undefined.

Example: MUL BX. Replaces the contents of DX and AX with the product of BX and AX. The low-order 16 bits of the result replace the contents of AX; the high-order word goes to DX. The processor sets CF and OF if the unsigned result is greater than 16 bits.

IMUL (Signed Integer Multiply) performs a signed multiplication operation. IMUL uses AX and DX in the same way as the MUL instruction, except when used in the immediate form.

The immediate form of IMUL allows the specification of a destination register other than the combination of DX and AX. In this case, the result cannot exceed 16 bits without causing an overflow. If the immediate operand is a byte, the processor automatically extends it to 16 bits before performing the multiplication.

The immediate form of IMUL may also be used with unsigned operands because the low 16 bits of a signed or unsigned multiplication of two 16-bit values will always be the same.

IMUL clears CF and OF to indicate that the upper half of the result is the sign of the lower half. This instruction leaves SF, ZF, AF, and PF undefined.

Example: IMUL BL. Replaces the contents of AX with the product of BL and AL. The processor sets CF and OF if the result is more than 8 bits long.

Example: IMUL BX, SI, 5. Replaces the contents of BX with the product of the contents of SI and an immediate value of 5. The processor sets CF and OF if the signed result is longer than 16 bits.

3.3.4 Division Instructions

DIV (Unsigned Integer Divide) performs an unsigned division of the accumulator by the source operand. If the source operand is a byte, it is divided into the double-length dividend assumed to be in registers AL and AH (AH = most significant byte; AL = least significant byte). The single-length quotient is returned in AL, and the single-length remainder is returned in AH.

If the source operand is a word, it is divided into the double-length dividend in registers AX and DX. The single-length quotient is returned in AX, and the single-length remainder is returned in DX. Non-integral quotients are truncated to integers toward 0. The remainder is always less than the quotient.

For unsigned byte division, the largest quotient is 255. For unsigned word division, the largest quotient is 65,535. DIV leaves OF, SF, ZF, AF, PF, and CF undefined. Interrupt (INT 0) occurs if the divisor is zero or if the quotient is too large for AL or AX.

Example: DIV BX. Replaces the contents of AX with the unsigned quotient of the doubleword value contained in DX and AX, divided by BX. The unsigned modulo replaces the contents of DX.

Example: DIV BL. Replaces the contents of AL with the unsigned quotient of the word value in AX, divided by BL. The unsigned modulo replaces the contents of AH.

IDIV (Signed Integer Divide) performs a signed division of the accumulator by the source operand. IDIV uses the same registers as the DIV instruction.

For signed byte division, the maximum positive quotient is +127 and the minimum negative quotient is −128. For signed word division, the maximum positive quotient is +32,767 and the minimum negative quotient is −32,768. Non-integral results are truncated towards 0. The remainder will always have the same sign as the dividend and will be less than the divisor in magnitude. IDIV leaves OF, SF, ZF, AF, PF, and CF undefined. A division by zero causes an interrupt (INT 0) to occur if the divisor is 0 or if the quotient is too large for AL or AX.

Example: IDIV WORDOPRND. Replaces the contents of AX with the signed quotient of the double-word value contained in DX and AX, divided by the value contained in the memory word labeled WORDOPRND. The signed modulo replaces the contents of DX.

3.4 LOGICAL INSTRUCTIONS

The group of logical instructions includes the Boolean operation instructions, rotate and shift instructions, type conversion instructions, and the no-operation (NOP)instruction.

3.4.1 Boolean Operation Instructions

Except for the NOT and NEG instructions, the Boolean operation instructions can use two register operands, a general purpose register operand with a memory operand, an immediate operand with a general purpose register operand, or a memory operand. The NOT and NEG instructions are unary operations that use a single operand in a register or memory.

AND (And) performs the logical "and" of the operands (byte or word) and returns the result to the destination operand. AND clears OF and DF, leaves AF undefined, and updates SF, ZF, and PF.

Example: AND WORDOPRND, BX. Replaces the contents of WORDOPRND with the logical "and" of the contents of the memory word labeled WORDOPRND and the contents of BX.

NOT (Not) inverts the bits in the specified operand to form a one's complement of the operand. NOT has no effect on the flags.

Example: NOT BYTEOPRND. Replaces the original contents of BYTEOPRND with the one's complement of the contents of the memory word labeled BYTEOPRND.

OR (Or) performs the logical "inclusive or" of the two operands and returns the result to the destination operand. OR clears OF and DF, leaves AF undefined, and updates SF, ZF, and PF.

Example: OR AL,5. Replaces the original contents of AL with the logical "inclusive or" of the contents of AL and the immediate value 5.

XOR (Exclusive OR) performs the logical "exclusive or" of the two operands and returns the result to the destination operand. XOR clears OF and DF, leaves AF undefined, and updates SF, ZF, and PF.

Example: XOR DX, WORDOPRND. Replaces the original contents of DX with the logical "exclusive or" or the contents of DX and the contents of the memory word labeled WORDOPRND.

NEG (Negate) forms a two's complement of a signed byte or word operand. The effect of NEG is to reverse the sign of the operand from positive to negative or from negative to positive. NEG updates OF, SF, ZF, AF, PF, and CF.

Example: NEG AX. Replaces the original contents of AX with the two's complement of the contents of AX.

3.4.2 Shift and Rotate Instructions

The shift and rotate instructions reposition the bits within the specified operand. The shift instructions provide a convenient way to accomplish division or multiplication by binary power. The rotate instructions are useful for bit testing.

3.4.2.1 SHIFT INSTRUCTIONS

The bits in bytes and words may be shifted arithmetically or logically. Depending on the value of a specified count, up to 31 shifts may be performed.

A shift instruction can specify the count in one of three ways. One form of shift instruction implicitly specifies the count as a single shift. The second form specifies the count as an immediate value. The third form specifies the count as the value contained in CL. This last form allows the shift count to be a variable that the program supplies during execution. Only the low order 5 bits of CL are used.

Shift instructions affect the flags as follows. AF is always undefined following a shift operation. PF, SF, and ZF are updated normally as in the logical instructions.

CF always contains the value of the last bit shifted out of the destination operand. In a single-bit shift, OF is set if the value of the high-order (sign) bit was changed by the operation. Otherwise, OF is cleared. Following a multibit shift, however, the content of OF is always undefined.

SAL (Shift Arithmetic Left) shifts the destination byte or word operand left by one or by the number of bits specified in the count operand (an immediate value or the value contained in CL). The processor shifts zeros in from the right side of the operand as bits exit from the left side. See figure 3-6.

Example: SAL BL,2. Shifts the contents of BL left by 2 bits and replaces the two low-order bits with zeros.

Example: SAL BL,1. Shifts the contents of BL left by 1 bit and replaces the low-order bit with a zero. Because the processor does not have to decode the immediate count operand to obtain the shift count, this form of the instruction takes 2 clock cycles rather than the 6 clock cycles (5 cycles + 1 cycle for each bit shifted) required by the previous example.

SHL (Shift Logical Left) is physically the same instruction as SAL (see SAL above).

SHR (Shift Logical Right) shifts the destination byte or word operand right by one or by the number of bits specified in the count operand (an immediate value or the value contained in CL). The processor shifts zeros in from the left side of the operand as bits exit from the right side. See figure 3-7.

Example: SHR BYTEOPRND, CL. Shifts the contents of the memory byte labeled BYTEOPRND right by the number of bits specified in CL, and pads the left side of BYTEOPRND with an equal number of zeros.

SAR (Shift Arithmetic Right) shifts the destination byte or word operand to the right by one or by the number of bits specified in the count operand (an immediate value or the value contained in CL). The processor preserves the sign of the operand by shifting in zeros on the left side if the value is positive or by shifting by ones if the value is negative. See figure 3-8.

Example: SAR WORDPRND,1. Shifts the contents of the memory byte labeled WORDPRND right by one, and replaces the high-order sign bit with a value equal to the original sign of WORDPRND.

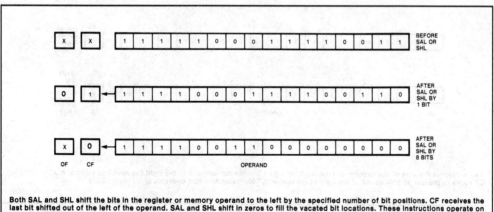

Both SAL and SHL shift the bits in the register or memory operand to the left by the specified number of bit positions. CF receives the last bit shifted out of the left of the operand. SAL and SHL shift in zeros to fill the vacated bit locations. These instructions operate on byte operands as well as word operands.

G30108

Figure 3-6. SAL and SHL

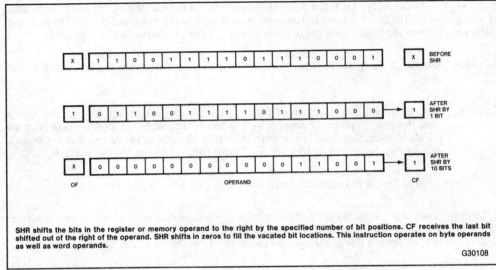

SHR shifts the bits in the register or memory operand to the right by the specified number of bit positions. CF receives the last bit shifted out of the right of the operand. SHR shifts in zeros to fill the vacated bit locations. This instruction operates on byte operands as well as word operands.

G30108

Figure 3-7. SHR

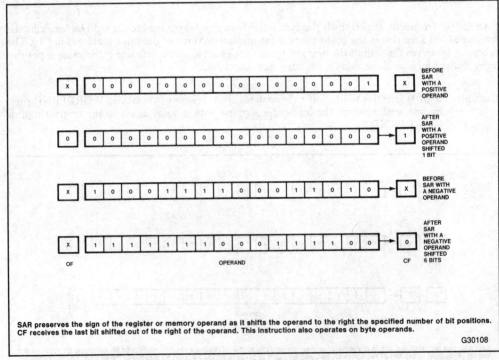

SAR preserves the sign of the register or memory operand as it shifts the operand to the right the specified number of bit positions. CF receives the last bit shifted out of the right of the operand. This instruction also operates on byte operands.

G30108

Figure 3-8. SAR

3.4.2.2 ROTATE INSTRUCTIONS

Rotate instructions allow bits in bytes and words to be rotated. Bits rotated out of an operand are not lost as in a shift, but are "circled" back into the other "end" of the operand.

Rotates affect only the carry and overflow flags. CF may act as an extension of the operand in two of the rotate instructions, allowing a bit to be isolated and then tested by a conditional jump instruction (JC or JNC). CF always contains the value of the last bit rotated out, even if the instruction does not use this bit as an extension of the rotated operand.

In single-bit rotates, OF is set if the operation changes the high-order (sign) bit of the destination operand. If the sign bit retains its original value, OF is cleared. On multibit rotates, the value of OF is always undefined.

ROL (Rotate Left) rotates the byte or word destination operand left by one or by the number of bits specified in the count operand (an immediate value or the value contained in CL). For each rotation specified, the high-order bit that exists from the left of the operand returns at the right to become the new low-order bit of the operand. See figure 3-9.

Example: ROL AL, 8. Rotates the contents of AL left by 8 bits. This rotate instruction returns AL to its original state but isolates the low-order bit in CF for testing by a JC or JNC instruction.

ROR (Rotate Right) rotates the byte or word destination operand right by one or by the number of bits specified in the count operand (an immediate value or the value contained in CL). For each rotation specified, the low-order bit that exits from the right of the operand returns at the left to become the new high-order bit of the operand. See figure 3-10.

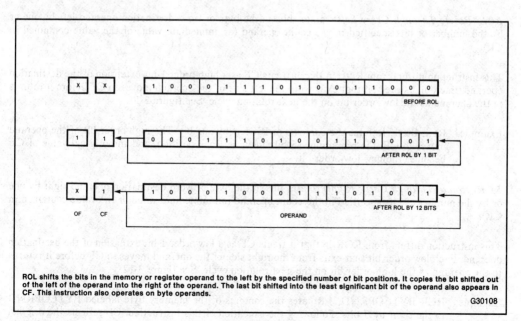

ROL shifts the bits in the memory or register operand to the left by the specified number of bit positions. It copies the bit shifted out of the left of the operand into the right of the operand. The last bit shifted into the least significant bit of the operand also appears in CF. This instruction also operates on byte operands.

G30108

Figure 3-9. ROL

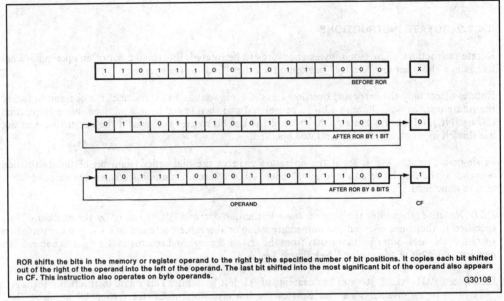

ROR shifts the bits in the memory or register operand to the right by the specified number of bit positions. It copies each bit shifted out of the right of the operand into the left of the operand. The last bit shifted into the most significant bit of the operand also appears in CF. This instruction also operates on byte operands.

G30108

Figure 3-10. ROR

Example: ROR WORDOPRND, CL. Rotates the contents of the memory word labeled WORDOPRND by the number of bits specified by the value contained in CL. CF reflects the value of the last bit rotated from the right to the left side of the operand.

RCL (Rotate Through Carry Left) rotates bits in the byte or word destination operand left by one or by the number of bits specified in the count operand (an immediate value or the value contained in CL).

This instruction differs from ROL in that it treats CF as a high-order 1-bit extension of the destination operand. Each high-order bit that exits from the left side of the operand moves to CF before it returns to the operand as the low-order bit on the next rotation cycle. See figure 3-11.

Example: RCL BX,1. Rotates the contents of BX left by one bit. The high-order bit of the operand moves to CF, the remaining 15 bits move left one position, and the original value of CF becomes the new low-order bit.

RCR (Rotate Through Carry Right) rotates bits in the byte or word destination operand right by one or by the number of bits specified in the count operand (an immediate value or the value contained in CL).

This instruction differs from ROR in that it treats CF as a low-order 1-bit extension of the destination operand. Each low-order bit that exits from the right side of the operand moves to CF before it returns to the operand as the high-order bit on the next rotation cycle. See figure 3-12.

Example: RCR BYTEOPRND,3. Rotates the contents of the memory byte labeled BYTEOPRND to the right by 3 bits. Following the execution of this instruction, CF reflects the original value of bit number 5 of BYTEOPRND, and the original value of CF becomes bit 2.

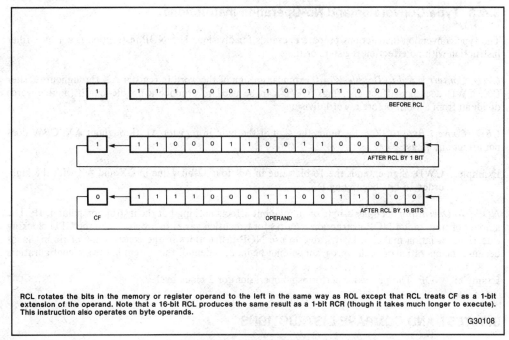

RCL rotates the bits in the memory or register operand to the left in the same way as ROL except that RCL treats CF as a 1-bit extension of the operand. Note that a 16-bit RCL produces the same result as a 1-bit RCR (though it takes much longer to execute). This instruction also operates on byte operands.

G30108

Figure 3-11. RCL

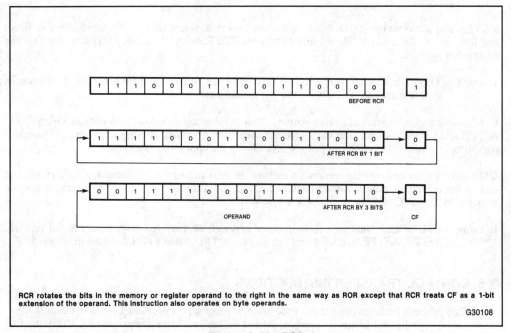

RCR rotates the bits in the memory or register operand to the right in the same way as ROR except that RCR treats CF as a 1-bit extension of the operand. This instruction also operates on byte operands.

G30108

Figure 3-12. RCR

3.4.3 Type Conversion and No-Operation Instructions

The type conversion instructions prepare operands for division. The NOP instruction is a 1-byte filler instruction with no effect on registers or flags.

CWD (Convert Word to Double-Word) extends the sign of the word in register AX throughout register DX. CWD does not affect any flags. CWD can be used to produce a double-length (double-word) dividend from a word before a word division.

CBW (Convert Byte to Word) extends the sign of the byte in register AL throughout AX. CBW does not affect any flags.

Example: CWD. Sign-extends the 16-bit value in AX to a 32-bit value in DX and AX with the high-order 16-bits occupying DX.

NOP (No Operation) occupies a byte of storage but affects nothing but the instruction pointer, IP. The amount of time that a NOP instruction requires for execution varies in proportion to the CPU clocking rate. This variation makes it inadvisable to use NOP instructions in the construction of timing loops because the operation of such a program will not be independent of the system hardware configuration.

Example: NOP. The processor performs no operation for 2 clock cycles.

3.5 TEST AND COMPARE INSTRUCTIONS

The test and compare instructions are similar in that they do not alter their operands. Instead, these instructions perform operations that only set the appropriate flags to indicate the relationship between the two operands.

TEST (Test) performs the logical "and" of the two operands, clears OF and DF, leaves AF undefined, and updates SF, ZF, and PF. The difference between TEST and AND is that TEST does not alter the destination operand.

Example: TEST BL,32. Performs a logical "and" and sets SF, ZF, and PF according to the results of this operation. The contents of BL remain unchanged.

CMP (Compare) subtracts the source operand from the destination operand. It updates OF, SF, ZF, AF, PF, and CF but does not alter the source and destination operands. A subsequent signed or unsigned conditional transfer instruction can test the result using the appropriate flag result.

CMP can compare two register operands, a register operand and a memory operand, a register operand and an immediate operand, or an immediate operand and a memory operand. The operands may be words or bytes, but CMP cannot compare a byte with a word.

Example: CMP BX,32. Subtracts the immediate operand, 32, from the contents of BX and sets OF, SF, ZF, AF, PF, and CF to reflect the result. The contents of BX remain unchanged.

3.6 CONTROL TRANSFER INSTRUCTIONS

The 80286 provides both conditional and unconditional program transfer instructions to direct the flow of execution. Conditional program transfers depend on the results of operations that affect the flag register. Unconditional program transfers are always executed.

3.6.1 Unconditional Transfer Instructions

JMP, CALL, RET, INT and IRET instructions transfer control from one code segment location to another. These locations can be within the same code segment or in different code segments.

3.6.1.1 JUMP INSTRUCTION

JMP (Jump) unconditionally transfers control to the target location. JMP is a one-way transfer of execution; it does not save a return address on the stack.

The JMP instruction always performs the same basic function of transferring control from the current location to a new location. Its implementation varies depending on the following factors:

- Is the address specified directly within the instruction or indirectly through a register or memory?
- Is the target location inside or outside the current code segment selected in CS?

A direct JMP instruction includes the destination address as part of the instruction. An indirect JMP instruction obtains the destination address indirectly through a register or a pointer variable.

Control transfers through a gate or to a task state segment are available only in Protected Mode operation of the 80286. The formats of the instructions that transfer control through a call gate, a task gate, or to a task state segment are the same. The label included in the instruction selects one of these three paths to a new code segment.

Direct JMP within the current code segment. A direct JMP that transfers control to a target location within the current code segment uses a relative displacement value contained in the instruction. This can be either a 16-bit value or an 8-bit value sign extended to 16 bits. The processor forms an effective address by adding this relative displacement to the address contained in IP. IP refers to the next instruction when the additions are performed.

Example: JMP NEAR_NEWCODE. Transfers control to the target location labeled NEAR_NEWCODE, which is within the code segment currently selected in CS.

Indirect JMP within the current code segment. Indirect JMP instructions that transfer control to a location within the current code segment specify an absolute address in one of several ways. First, the program can JMP to a location specified by a 16-bit register (any of AX, DX, CX, BX, BP, SI, or DI). The processor moves this 16-bit value into IP and resumes execution.

Example: JMP SI. Transfers control to the target address formed by adding the 16-bit value contained in SI to the base address contained in CS.

The processor can also obtain the destination address within a current segment from a memory word operand specified in the instruction.

Example: JMP PTR_X. Transfers control to the target address formed by adding the 16-bit value contained in the memory word labeled PTR X to the base address contained in CS.

A register can modify the address of the memory word pointer to select a destination address.

Example: JMP CASE_TABLE [BX]. CASE_TABLE is the first word in an array of word pointers. The value of BX determines which pointer the program selects from the array. The JMP instruction then transfers control to the location specified by the selected pointer.

Direct JMP outside of the current code segment. Direct JMP instructions that specify a target location outside the current code segment contain a full 32-bit pointer. This pointer consists of a selector for the new code segment and an offset within the new segment.

Example: JMP FAR_NEWCODE_FOO. Places the selector contained in the instruction into CS and the offset into IP. The program resumes execution at this location in the new code segment.

Indirect JMP outside of the current code segment. Indirect JMP instructions that specify a target location outside the current code segment use a double-word variable to specify the pointer.

Example: JMP NEWCODE. NEWCODE the first word of two consecutive words in memory which represent the new pointer. NEWCODE contains the new offset for IP and the word following NEWCODE contains the selector for CS. The program resumes execution at this location in the new code segment. (Protected mode programs treat this differently. See Chapters 6 and 7).

Direct JMP outside of the current code segment to a call gate. If the selector included with the instruction refers to a call gate, then the processor ignores the offset in the instruction and takes the pointer of the routine being entered from the call gate.

JMP outside of current code segment may only go to the same level.

Example: JMP CALL_GATE_FOO. The selector in the instruction refers to the call gate CALL_GATE_FOO, and the call gate actually provides the new contents of CS and IP to specify the address of the next instructions.

Indirect JMP outside the current code segment to a call gate. If the selector specified by the instruction refers to a call gate, the processor ignores the offset in the double-word and takes the address of the routine being entered from the call gate. The JMP instruction uses the same format to indirectly specify a task gate or a task state segment.

Example: JMP CASE_TABLE [BX]. The instruction refers to the double-word in the array of pointers called CASE_TABLE. The specific double-word chosen depends on the value in BX when the instruction executes. The selector portion of this double-word selects a call gate, and the processor takes the address of the routine being entered from the call gate.

3.6.1.2 CALL INSTRUCTION

CALL (Call Procedure) activates an out-of-line procedure, saving on the stack the address of the instruction following the CALL for later use by a RET (Return) instruction. An intrasegment CALL places the current value of IP on the stack. An intersegment CALL places both the value of IP and CS on the stack. The RET instruction in the called procedure uses this address to transfer control back to the calling program.

A long CALL instruction that invokes a task-switch stores the outgoing task's task state segment selector in the incoming task state segment's link field and sets the nested task flag in the new task. In this case, the IRET instruction takes the place of the RET instruction to return control to the nested task.

Examples:

CALL NEAR_NEWCODE
· CALL SI
CALL PTR_X
CALL CASE_TABLE [BP]
CALL FAR_NEWCODE_FOO
CALL NEWCODE
CALL CALL_GATE_FOO
CALL CASE_TABLE [BX]

See the previous treatment of JMP for a discussion of the operations of these instructions.

3.6.1.3 RETURN AND RETURN FROM INTERRUPT INSTRUCTION

RET (Return From Procedure) terminates the execution of a procedure and transfers control through a back-link on the stack to the program that originally invoked the procedure.

An intrasegment RET restores the value of IP that was saved on the stack by the previous intrasegment CALL instruction. An intersegment RET restores the values of both CS and IP which were saved on the stack by the previous intersegment CALL instruction.

RET instructions may optionally specify a constant to the stack pointer. This constant specifies the new top of stack to effectively remove any arguments that the calling program pushed on the stack before the execution of the CALL instruction.

Example: RET. If the previous CALL instruction did not transfer control to a new code segment, RET restores the value of IP pushed by the CALL instruction. If the previous CALL instruction transferred control to a new segment, RET restores the values of both IP and CS which were pushed on the stack by the CALL instruction.

Example: RET n. This form of the RET instruction performs identically to the above example except that it adds n (which must be an even value) to the value of SP to eliminate n bytes of parameter information previously pushed by the calling program.

IRET (Return From Interrupt or Nested Task) returns control to an interrupted routine or, optionally, reverses the action of a CALL or INT instruction that caused a task switch. See Chapter 8 for further information on task switching.

Example: IRET. Returns from an interrupt with or without a task switch based on the value of the NT bit.

3.6.2 Conditional Transfer Instructions

The conditional transfer instructions are jumps that may or may not transfer control, depending on the state of the CPU flags when the instruction executes. Instruction encoding is most efficient when the target for the conditional jumps is in the current code segment and within −128 to +127 bytes of the first byte of the next instruction. Alternatively, the opposite sense of the conditional jump can skip around an unconditional jump to the destination.

3.6.2.1 CONDITIONAL JUMP INSTRUCTIONS

Table 3-3 shows the conditional transfer mnemonics and their interpretations. The conditional jumps that are listed as pairs are actually the same instruction. The assembler provides the alternate mnemonics for greater clarity within a program listing.

3.6.2.2 LOOP INSTRUCTIONS

The loop instructions are conditional jumps that use a value placed in CX to specify the number of repetitions of a software loop. All loop instructions automatically decrement CX and terminate the loop when CX=0. Four of the five loop instructions specify a condition of ZF that terminates the loop before CX decrements to zero.

LOOP (Loop While CX Not Zero) is a conditional transfer that auto-decrements the CX register before testing CX for the branch condition. If CX is non-zero, the program branches to the target label specified in the instruction. The LOOP instruction causes the repetition of a code section until the operation of the LOOP instruction decrements CX to a value of zero. If LOOP finds CX=0, control transfers to the instruction immediately following the LOOP instruction. If the value of CX is initially zero, then the LOOP executes 65,536 times.

Example: LOOP START_LOOP. Each time the program encounters this instruction, it decrements CX and then tests it. If the value of CX is non-zero, then the program branches to the instruction labeled START_LOOP. If the value in CX is zero, then the program continues with the instruction that follows the LOOP instruction.

Table 3-3. Interpretation of Conditional Transfers

Unsigned Conditional Transfers		
Mnemonic	**Condition Tested**	**"Jump If. . ."**
JA/JNBE	(CF or ZF) = 0	above/not below nor equal
JAE/JNB	CF = 0	above or equal/not below
JB/JNAE	CF = 1	below/not above nor equal
JBE/JNA	(CF or ZF) = 1	below or equal/not above
JC	CF = 1	carry
JE/JZ	ZF = 1	equal/zero
JNC	CF = 0	not carry
JNE/JNZ	ZF = 0	not equal/not zero
JNP/JPO	PF = 0	not parity/parity odd
JP/JPE	PF = 1	parity/parity even

Signed Conditional Transfers		
Mnemonic	**Condition Tested**	**"Jump If. . ."**
JG/JNLE	((SF xor OF) or ZF) = 0	greater/not less nor equal
JGE/JNL	(SF xor OF) = 0	greater or equal/not less
JL/JNGE	(SF xor OF) = 0	less/not greater nor equal
JLE/JNG	((SF xor OF) or ZF) = 1	less or equal/not greater
JNO	OF = 0	not overflow
JNS	SF = 0	not sign (positive, including 0)
JO	OF = 1	overflow
JS	SF = 1	sign (negative)

LOOPE (Loop While Equal) and *LOOPZ (Loop While Zero)* are physically the same instruction. These instructions auto-decrement the CX register before testing CX and ZF for the branch conditions. If CX is non-zero and ZF=1, the program branches to the target label specified in the instruction. If LOOPE or LOOPZ finds that CX=0 or ZF=0, control transfers to the instruction immediately succeeding the LOOPE or LOOPZ instruction.

Example: LOOPE START_LOOP (or LOOPZ START_LOOP). Each time the program encounters this instruction, it decrements CX and tests CX and ZF. If the value in CX is non-zero and the value of ZF is 1, the program branches to the instruction labeled START_LOOP. If CX=0 or ZF=0, the program continues with the instruction that follows the LOOPE (or LOOPZ) instruction.

LOOPNE (Loop While Not Equal) and *LOOPNZ (Loop While Not Zero)* are physically the same instruction. These instructions auto-decrement the CX register before testing CX and ZF for the branch conditions. If CX is non-zero and ZF=0, the program branches to the target label specified in the instruction. If LOOPNE or LOOPNZ finds that CX=0 or ZF=1, control transfers to the instruction immediately succeeding the LOOPNE or LOOPNZ instruction.

Example: LOOPNE START_LOOP (or LOOPNZ START_LOOP). Each time the program encounters this instruction, it decrements CX and tests CX and ZF. If the value of CX is non-zero and the value of ZF is 0, the program branches to the instruction labeled START_LOOP. If CX=0 or ZF=1, the program continues with the instruction that follows the LOOPNE (or LOOPNZ) instruction.

3.6.2.3 EXECUTING A LOOP OR REPEAT ZERO TIMES

JCXZ (Jump if CX Zero) branches to the label specified in the instruction if it finds a value of zero in CX. Sometimes, it is desirable to design a loop that executes zero times if the count variable in CX is initialized to zero. Because the LOOP instructions (and repeat prefixes) decrement CX before they test it, a loop will execute 65,536 times if the program enters the loop with a zero value in CX. A programmer may conveniently overcome this problem with JCXZ, which enables the program to branch around the code within the loop if CX is zero when JCXZ executes.

Example: JCXZ TARGETLABEL. Causes the program to branch to the instruction labeled TARGETLABEL if CX=0 when the instruction executes.

3.6.3 Software-Generated Interrupts

The INT n and INTO instructions allow the programmer to specify a transfer to an interrupt service routine from within a program. Interrupts 0-31 are reserved by Intel.

3.6.3.1 SOFTWARE INTERRUPT INSTRUCTION

INT n (Software Interrupt) activates the interrupt service routine that corresponds to the number coded within the instruction. Interrupt type 3 is reserved for internal software-generated interrupts. However, the INT instruction may specify any interrupt type to allow multiple types of internal interrupts or to test the operation of a service routine. The interrupt service routine terminates with an IRET instruction that returns control to the instruction that follows INT.

Example: INT 3. Transfers control to the interrupt service routine specified by a type 3 interrupt.

Example: INT 0. Transfers control to the interrupt service routine specified by a type 0 interrupt, which is reserved for a divide error.

INTO (Interrupt on Overflow) invokes a type 4 interrupt if OF is set when the INTO instruction executes. The type 4 interrupt is reserved for this purpose.

Example: INTO. If the result of a previous operation has set OF and no intervening operation has reset OF, then INTO invokes a type 4 interrupt. The interrupt service routine terminates with an IRET instruction, which returns control to the instruction following INTO.

3.7 CHARACTER TRANSLATION AND STRING INSTRUCTIONS

The instructions in this category operate on characters or string elements rather than on logical or numeric values.

3.7.1 Translate Instruction

XLAT (Translate) replaces a byte in the AL register with a byte from a user-coded translation table. When XLAT is executed, AL should have the unsigned index to the table addressed by BX. XLAT changes the contents of AL from table index to table entry. BX is unchanged. The XLAT instruction is useful for translating from one coding system to another, such as from ASCII to EBCDIC. The translate table may be up to 256 bytes long. The value placed in the AL register serves as an index to the location of the corresponding translation value. Used with a LOOP instruction, the XLAT instruction can translate a block of codes up to 64K bytes long.

Example: XLAT. Replaces the byte in AL with the byte from the translate table that is selected by the value in AL.

3.7.2 String Manipulation Instructions and Repeat Prefixes

The string instructions (also called primitives) operate on string elements to move, compare, and scan byte or word strings. One-byte repeat prefixes can cause the operation of a string primitive to be repeated to process strings as long as 64K bytes.

The repeated string primitives use the direction flag, DF, to specify left-to-right or right-to-left string processing, and use a count in CX to limit the processing operation. These instructions use the register pair DS:SI to point to the source string element and the register pair ES:DI to point to the destination.

One of two possible opcodes represent each string primitive, depending on whether it is operating on byte strings or word strings. The string primitives are generic and require one or more operands along with the primitive to determine the size of the string elements being processed. These operands do not determine the addresses of the strings; the addresses must already be present in the appropriate registers.

Each repetition of a string operation using the Repeat prefixes includes the following steps:

1.   Acknowledge pending interrupts.

2.   Check CX for zero and stop repeating if CX is zero.

3.   Perform the string operation once.

4. Adjust the memory pointers in DS:SI and ES:DI by incrementing SI and DI if DF is 0 or by decrementing SI and DI if DF is 1.

5. Decrement CX (this step does not affect the flags).

6. For SCAS (Scan String) and CMPS (Compare String), check ZF for a match with the repeat condition and stop repeating if the ZF fails to match.

The Load String and Store String instructions allow a program to perform arithmetic or logical operations on string characters (using AX for word strings and AL for byte strings). Repeated operations that include instructions other than string primitives must use the loop instructions rather than a repeat prefix.

3.7.2.1 STRING MOVEMENT INSTRUCTIONS

REP (Repeat While CX Not Zero) specifies a repeated operation of a string primitive. The REP prefix causes the hardware to automatically repeat the associated string primitive until CX=0. This form of iteration allows the CPU to process strings much faster than would be possible with a regular software loop.

When the REP prefix accompanies a MOVS instruction, it operates as a memory-to-memory block transfer. To set up for this operation, the program must initialize CX and the register pairs DS:SI and ES:DI. CX specifies the number of bytes or words in the block.

If DF=0, the program must point DS:SI to the first element of the source string and point ES:DI to the destination address for the first element. If DF=1, the program must point these two register pairs to the last element of the source string and to the destination address for the last element, respectively.

Example: REP MOVSW. The processor checks the value in CX for zero. If this value is not zero, the processor moves a word from the location pointed to by DS:SI to the location pointed to by ES:DI and increments SI and DI by two (if DF=0). Next, the processor decrements CX by one and returns to the beginning of the repeat cycle to check CX again. After CX decrements to zero, the processor executes the instruction that follows.

MOVS (Move String) moves the string character pointed to by the combination of DS and SI to the location pointed to by the combination of ES and DI. This is the only memory-to-memory transfer supported by the instruction set of the base architecture. MOVSB operates on byte elements. The destination segment register cannot be overridden by a segment override prefix while the source segment register can be overridden.

Example: MOVSW. Moves the contents of the memory byte pointed to by DS:SI to the location pointed to by ES:DI.

3.7.2.2 OTHER STRING OPERATIONS

CMPS (Compare Strings) subtracts the destination string element (ES:DI) from the source string element (DS:SI) and updates the flags AF, SF, PF, CF and OF. If the string elements are equal, ZF=1; otherwise, ZF=0. If DF=0, the processor increments the memory pointers (SI and DI) for the two strings. The segment register used for the source address can be changed with a segment override prefix, while the destination segment register cannot be overridden.

Example: CMPSB. Compares the source and destination string elements with each other and returns the result of the comparison to ZF.

SCAS (Scan String) subtracts the destination string element at ES:DI from AX or AL and updates the flags AF, SF, ZF, PF, CF and OF. If the values are equal, ZF=1; otherwise, ZF=0. If DF=0, the processor increments the memory pointer (DI) for the string. The segment register used for the source address can be changed with a segment override prefix while the destination segment register cannot be overridden.

Example: SCASW. Compares the value in AX with the destination string element.

REPE/REPZ (Repeat While CX Equal/Zero) and *REPNE/REPNZ (Repeat While CX Not Equal/ Not Zero)* are the prefixes that are used exclusively with the SCAS (ScanString) and CMPS (Compare String) primitives.

The difference between these two types of prefix bytes is that REPE/REPZ terminates when ZF=0 and REPNE/REPNZ terminates when ZF=1. ZF does not require initialization before execution of a repeated string instruction.

When these prefixes modify either the SCAS or CMPS primitives, the processor compares the value of the current string element with the value in AX for word elements or with the value in AL for byte elements. The resulting state of ZF can then limit the operation of the repeated operation as well as a zero value in CX.

Example: REPE SCASB. Causes the processor to scan the string pointed to by ES:DI until it encounters a match with the byte value in AL or until CX decrements to zero.

LODS (Load String) places the source string element at DS:SI into AX for word strings or into AL for byte strings.

Example: LODSW. Loads AX with the value pointed to by DS:SI.

3.8 ADDRESS MANIPULATION INSTRUCTIONS

The set of address manipulation instructions provide a way to perform address calculations or to move to a new data segment or extra segment.

LEA (Load Effective Address) transfers the offset of the source operand (rather than its value) to the destination operand. The source operand must be a memory operand, and the destination operand must be a 16-bit general register (AX, DX, BX, CX, BP, SP, SI, or DI).

LEA does not affect any flags. This instruction is useful for initializing the registers before the execution of the string primitives or the XLAT instruction.

Example: LEA BX EBCDIC_TABLE. Causes the processor to place the address of the starting location of the table labeled EBCDIC_TABLE into BX.

LDS (Load Pointer Using DS) transfers a 32-bit pointer variable from the source operand to DS and the destination register. The source operand must be a memory operand, and the destination operand must be a 16-bit general register (AX, DX, BX, CX, BP, SP, SI or DI). DS receives the high-order segment word of the pointer. The destination register receives the low-order word, which points to a specific location within the segment.

Example: LDS SI, STRING_X. Loads DS with the word identifying the segment pointed to by STRING_X, and loads the offset of STRING_X into SI. Specifying SI as the destination operand is a convenient way to prepare for a string operation on a source string that is not in the current data segment.

LES (Load Pointer Using ES) operates identically to LDS except that ES receives the offset word rather than DS.

Example: LES DI, DESTINATION_X. Loads ES with the word identifying the segment pointed to by DESTINATION_X, and loads the offset of DESTINATION_X into DI. This instruction provides a convenient way to select a destination for a string operation if the desired location is not in the current extra segment.

3.9 FLAG CONTROL INSTRUCTIONS

The flag control instructions provide a method of changing the state of bits in the flag register.

3.9.1 Carry Flag Control Instructions

The carry flag instructions are useful in conjunction with rotate-with-carry instructions RCL and RCR. They can initialize the carry flag, CF, to a known state before execution of a rotate that moves the carry bit into one end of the rotated operand.

STC (Set Carry Flag) sets the carry flag (CF) to 1.

Example: STC

CLC (Clear Carry Flag) zeros the carry flag (CF).

Example: CLC

CMC (Complement Carry Flag) reverses the current status of the carry flag (CF).

Example: CMC

3.9.2 Direction Flag Control Instructions

The direction flag control instructions are specifically included to set or clear the direction flag, DF, which controls the left-to-right or right-to-left direction of string processing. IF DF=0, the processor automatically increments the string memory pointers, SI and DI, after each execution of a string primitive. If DF=1, the processor decrements these pointer values. The initial state of DF is 0.

CLD (Clear Direction Flag) zeros DF, causing the string instructions to auto-increment SI and/or DI. CLD does not affect any other flags.

Example: CLD

STD (Set Direction Flag) sets DF to 1, causing the string instructions to auto-decrement SI and/or DI. STD does not affect any other flags.

Example: STD

3.9.3 Flag Transfer Instructions

Though specific instructions exist to alter CF and DF, there is no direct method of altering the other flags. The flag transfer instructions allow a program to alter the other flag bits with the bit manipulation instructions after transferring these flags to the stack or the AH register.

The PUSHF and POPF instructions are also useful for preserving the state of the flag register before executing a procedure.

LAHF (Load AH from Flags) copies SF, ZF, AF, PF, and CF to AH bits 7, 6, 4, 2, and 0, respectively (see figure 3-13). The contents of the remaining bits (5, 3, and 1) are undefined. The flags remain unaffected. This instruction can assist in converting 8080/8085 assembly language programs to run on the base architecture of the 8086, 8088, 80186, 80188, and 80286.

Example: LAHF

SAHF (Store AH into Flags) transfers bits 7, 6, 4, 2, and 0 from AH into SF, ZF, AF, PF, and CF, respectively (see figure 3-13). This instruction also provides 8080/8085 compatibility with the 8086, 8088, 80186, 80188, and 80286.

Example: SAHF

PUSHF (Push Flags) decrements SP by two and then transfers all flags to the word at the top of stack pointed to by SP (see figure 3-14). The flags remain unaffected. This instruction enables a procedure to save the state of the flag register for later use.

Example: PUSHF

POPF (Pop Flags) transfers specific bits from the word at the top of stack into the low-order byte of the flag register (see figure 3-14). The processor then increments SP by two.

Note that an application program in the protected virtual address mode may not alter IOPL (the I/O privilege level flag) unless the program is executing at privilege level 0. A program may alter IF (the interrupt flag) only when executing at a level that is at least as privileged as IOPL.

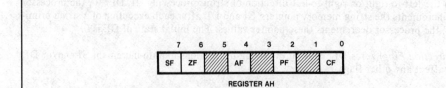

Figure 3-13. LAHF and SAHF

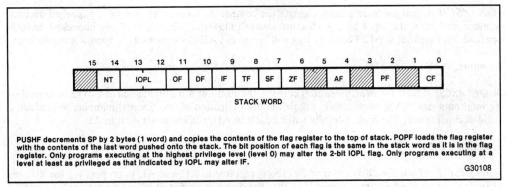

PUSHF decrements SP by 2 bytes (1 word) and copies the contents of the flag register to the top of stack. POPF loads the flag register with the contents of the last word pushed onto the stack. The bit position of each flag is the same in the stack word as it is in the flag register. Only programs executing at the highest privilege level (level 0) may alter the 2-bit IOPL flag. Only programs executing at a level at least as privileged as that indicated by IOPL may alter IF.

G30108

Figure 3-14. PUSHF and POPF

Procedures may use this instruction to restore the flag status from a previous value.

Example: POPF

3.10 BINARY-CODED DECIMAL ARITHMETIC INSTRUCTIONS

These instructions adjust the results of a previous arithmetic operation to produce a valid packed or unpacked decimal result. These instructions operate only on AL or AH registers.

3.10.1 Packed BCD Adjustment Instructions

DAA (Decimal Adjust) corrects the result of adding two valid packed decimal operands in AL. DAA must always follow the addition of two pairs of packed decimal numbers (one digit in each nibble) to obtain a pair of valid packed decimal digits as results. The carry flag will be set if carry was needed.

Example: DAA

DAS (Decimal Adjust for Subtraction) corrects the result of subtracting two valid packed decimal operands in AL. DAS must always follow the subtraction of one pair of packed decimal numbers (one digit in each nibble) from another to obtain a pair of valid packed decimal digits as results. The carry flag will be set if a borrow was needed.

Example: DAS

3.10.2 Unpacked BCD Adjustment Instructions

AAA (ASCII Adjust for Addition) changes the contents of register AL to a valid unpacked decimal number, and zeros the top 4 bits. AAA must always follow the addition of two unpacked decimal operands in AL. The carry flag will be set and AH will be incremented if a carry was necessary.

Example: AAA

AAS (ASCII Adjust for Subtraction) changes the contents of register AL to a valid unpacked decimal number, and zeros the top 4 bits. AAS must always follow the subtraction of one unpacked decimal operand from another in AL. The carry flag will be set and AH decremented if a borrow was necessary.

Example: AAS

AAM (ASCII Adjust for Multiplication) corrects the result of a multiplication of two valid unpacked decimal numbers. AAM must always follow the multiplication of two decimal numbers to produce a valid decimal result. The high order digit will be left in AH, the low order digit in AL.

Example: AAM

AAD (ASCII Adjust for Division) modifies the numerator in AH and AL to prepare for the division of two valid unpacked decimal operands so that the quotient produced by the division will be a valid unpacked decimal number. AH should contain the high-order digit and AL the low-order digit. This instruction will adjust the value and leave it in AL. AH will contain 0.

Example: AAD

3.11 TRUSTED INSTRUCTIONS

When operating in Protected Mode (Chapter 6 and following), the 80286 processor restricts the execution of trusted instructions according to the Current Privilege Level (CPL) and the current value of IOPL, the 2-bit I/O privilege flag. Only a program operating at the highest privilege level (level 0) may alter the value of IOPL. A program may execute trusted instructions only when executing at a level that is at least as privileged as that specified by IOPL.

Trusted instructions control I/O operations, interprocessor communications in a multiprocessor system, interrupt enabling, and the HLT instruction.

These protection considerations do not apply in the real address mode.

3.11.1 Trusted and Privileged Restrictions on POPF and IRET

POPF (POP Flags) and *IRET (Interrupt Return)* are not affected by IOPL unless they attempt to alter IF (flag register bit 9). To change IF, POPF must be part of a program that is executing at a privilege level greater than or equal to that specified by IOPL. Any attempt to change IF when CPL $\geq$ 0 will be ignored (i.e., the IF flag will be ignored). To change the IOPL field, CPL must be zero.

3.11.2 Machine State Instructions

These trusted instructions affect the machine state control interrupt response, the processor halt state, and the bus LOCK signal that regulates memory access in multiprocessor systems.

CLI (Clear Interrupt-Enable Flag) and *STI (Set Interrupt-Enable Flag)* alter bit 9 in the flag register. When IF=0, the processor responds only to internal interrupts and to non-maskable external interrupts. When IF=1, the processor responds to all interrupts. An interrupt service routine might use these instructions to avoid further interruption while it processes a previous interrupt request. As with the other flag bits, the processor clears IF during initialization. These instructions may be executed only if CPL $\leq$ IOPL. A protection exception will occur if they are executed when CPL $>$ IOPL.

Example: STI. Sets IF=1, which enables the processing of maskable external interrupts.

Example: CLI. Sets IF=0 to disable maskable interrupt processing.

HLT (Halt) causes the processor to suspend processing operations pending an interrupt or a system reset. This trusted instruction provides an alternative to an endless software loop in situations where a program must wait for an interrupt. The return address saved after the interrupt will point to the instruction immediately following HLT. This instruction may be executed only when CPL = 0.

Example: HLT

LOCK (Assert Bus Lock) is a *1-byte* prefix code that causes the processor to assert the bus LOCK signal during execution of the instruction that follows. LOCK does not affect any flags. LOCK may be used only when CPL ≤ IOPL. A protection exception will occur if LOCK is used when CPL > IOPL.

3.11.3 Input and Output Instructions

These trusted instructions provide access to the processor's I/O ports to transfer data to and from peripheral devices. In Protected Mode, these instructions may be executed only when CPL ≤ IOPL.

IN (Input from Port) transfers a byte or a word from an input port to AL or AX. If a program specifies AL with the IN instruction, the processor transfers 8 bits from the selected port to AL. Alternately, if a program specifies AX with the IN instruction, the processor transfers 16 bits from the port to AX.

The program can specify the number of the port in two ways. Using an immediate byte constant, the program can specify 256 8-bit ports numbered 0 through 255 or 128 16-bit ports numbered 0,2,4,...,252,254. Using the current value contained in DX, the program can specify 8-bit ports numbered 0 through 65,535, or 16-bit ports using even-numbered ports in the same range.

Example: IN AL,
        BYTE_PORT_NUMBER. Transfers 8 bits to AL from the port identified by the immediate
        constant BYTE_PORT_NUMBER.

OUT (Output to Port) transfers a byte or a word to an output port from AL or AX. The program can specify the number of the port using the same methods of the IN instruction.

Example: OUT AX, DX. Transfers 16 bits from AX to the port identified by the 16-bit number
        contained in DX.

INS and OUTS (Input String and Output String) cause block input or output operations using a Repeat prefix. See Chapter 4 for more information on INS and OUTS.

3.12 PROCESSOR EXTENSION INSTRUCTIONS

Processor Extension provides an extension to the instruction set of the base architecture (e.g., 80287). The NPX extends the instruction set of the CPU-based architecture to support high-precision integer and floating-point calculations. This extended instruction set includes arithmetic, comparison, transcendental, and data transfer instructions. The NPX also contains a set of useful constants to enhance the speed of numeric calculations.

A program contains instructions for the NPX in line with the instructions for the CPU. The system executes these instructions in the same order as they appear in the instruction stream. The NPX operates concurrently with the CPU to provide maximum throughput for numeric calculations.

The software emulation of the NPX is transparent to application software but requires more time for execution.

3.12.1 Processor Extension Synchronization Instructions

Escape and wait instructions allow a processor extension such as the 80287 NPX to obtain instructions and data from the system bus and to wait for the NPX to return a result.

ESC (Escape) identifies floating point numeric instructions and allows the 80286 to send the opcode to the NPX or to transfer a memory operand to the NPX. The 80287 NPX uses the Escape instructions to perform high-performance, high-precision floating point arithmetic that conforms to the IEEE floating point standard 754.

Example: ESC 6, ARRAY [SI]. The CPU sends the escape opcode 6 and the location of the array pointed to by SI to the NPX.

WAIT (Wait) suspends program execution until the 80286 CPU detects a signal on the $\overline{\text{BUSY}}$ pin. In a configuration that includes a numeric processor extension, the NPX activates the $\overline{\text{BUSY}}$ pin to signal that it has completed its processing task and that the CPU may obtain the results.

Example: WAIT

3.12.2 Numeric Data Processor Instructions

This section describes the categories of instructions available with Numeric Data Processor systems that include a Numeric Processor Extension or a software emulation of this processor extension.

3.12.2.1 ARITHMETIC INSTRUCTIONS

The extended instruction set includes not only the four arithmetic operations (add, subtract, multiply, and divide), but also subtract-reversed and divide-reversed instructions. The arithmetic functions include square root, modulus, absolute value, integer part, change sign, scale exponent, and extract exponent instructions.

3.12.2.2 COMPARISON INSTRUCTIONS

The comparison operations are the compare, examine, and test instructions. Special forms of the compare instruction can optimize algorithms by allowing comparisons of binary integers with real numbers in memory.

3.12.2.3 TRANSCENDENTAL INSTRUCTIONS

The instructions in this group perform the otherwise time-consuming calculations for all common trigonometric, inverse trigonometric, hyperbolic, inverse hyperbolic, logarithmic, and exponential functions. The transcendental instructions include tangent, arctangent, $2x - 1$, $Y . \log_2 X$, and $Y . \log_2 (X+1)$.

3.12.2.4 DATA TRANSFER INSTRUCTIONS

The data transfer instructions move operands among the registers and between a register and memory. This group includes the load, store, and exchange instructions.

3.12.2.5 CONSTANT INSTRUCTIONS

Each of the constant instructions loads a commonly used constant into an NPX register. The values have a real precision of 64 bits and are accurate to approximately 19 decimal places. The constants loaded by these instructions include 0, 1, Pi, $\log_e$ 10, $\log_2$ e, $\log_{10}$ 2, and log 2_e.

Extended Instruction Set

4

CHAPTER 4
EXTENDED INSTRUCTION SET

The instructions described in this chapter extend the capabilities of the base architecture instruction set described in Chapter 3. These extensions consist of new instructions and variations of some instructions that are not strictly part of the base architecture (in other words, not included on the 8086 and 8088). These instructions are also available on the 80186 and 80188. The instruction variations, described in Chapter 3, include the immediate forms of the PUSH and MUL instructions, PUSHA, POPA, and the privilege level restrictions on POPF.

New instructions described in this chapter include the string input and output instructions (INS and OUTS), the ENTER procedure and LEAVE procedure instructions, and the check index BOUND instruction.

4.1 BLOCK I/O INSTRUCTIONS

REP, the Repeat prefix, modifies INS and OUTS (the string I/O instructions) to provide a means of transferring blocks of data between an I/O port and Memory. These block I/O instructions are string primitives. They simplify programming and increase the speed of data transfer by eliminating the need to use a separate LOOP instruction or an intermediate register to hold the data.

INS and OUTS are trusted instructions. To use trusted instructions, a program must execute at a privilege level at least as privileged as that specified by the 2-bit IOPL flag (CPL ≤ IOPL). Any attempt by a less-privileged program to use a trusted instruction results in a protection exception. See Chapter 7 for information on protection concepts.

One of two possible opcodes represents each string primitive depending on whether it operates on byte strings or word strings. After each transfer, the memory address in SI or DI is updated by 1 for byte values and by 2 for word values. The value in the DF field determines if SI or DI is to be auto incremented (DF=0) or auto decremented (DF=1).

INS and OUTS use DX to specify I/O ports numbered 0 through 65,535 or 16-bit ports using only even port addresses in the same range.

INS (Input String from Port) transfers a byte or a word string element from an input port to memory. If a program specifies INSB, the processor transfers 8 bits from the selected port to the memory location indicated by ES:DI. Alternately, if a program specifies INSW, the processor transfers 16 bits from the port to the memory location indicated by ES:DI. The destination segment register choice (ES) cannot be changed for the INS instruction.

Combined with the REP prefix, INS moves a block of information from an input port to a series of consecutive memory locations.

Example: REP INSB. The processor repeatedly transfers 8 bits to the memory location indicated by ES:DI from the port selected by the 16-bit port number contained in DX. Following each byte transfer, the CPU decrements CX. The instruction terminates the block transfer when CX=0. After decrementing CX, the processor increments DI by one if DF=0. It decrements DI by one if DF=1.

OUTS (Output String to Port) transfers a byte or a word string element to an output port from memory. Combined with the REP prefix, OUTS moves a block of information from a series of consecutive memory locations indicated by DS:SI to an output port.

Example: REP OUTS WSTRING. Assuming that the program declares WSTRING to be a word-length string element, the assembler uses the 16-bit form of the OUTS instruction to create the object code for the program. The processor repeatedly transfers words from the memory locations indicated by DI to the output port selected by the 16-bit port number in DX.

Following each word transfer, the CPU decrements CX. The instruction terminates the block transfer when CX=0. After decrementing CX, the processor increments SI by two to point to the next word in memory if DF=0; it decrements SI by two if DF=1.

4.2 HIGH-LEVEL INSTRUCTIONS

The instructions in this section provide machine-language functions normally found only in high-level languages. These instructions include ENTER and LEAVE, which simplify the programming of procedures, and BOUND, which provides a simple method of testing an index against its predefined range.

ENTER (Enter Procedure) creates the stack frame required by most block-structured high-level languages. A LEAVE instruction at the end of a procedure complements an ENTER at the beginning of the procedure to simplify stack management and to control access to variables for nested procedures.

Example: ENTER 2048,3. Allocates 2048 bytes of dynamic storage on the stack and sets up pointers to two previous stack frames in the stack frame that ENTER creates for this procedure.

The ENTER instruction includes two parameters. The first parameter specifies the number of bytes of dynamic storage to be allocated on the stack for the routine being entered. The second parameter corresponds to the lexical nesting level (0-31) of the routine. (Note that the lexical level has no relationship to either the protection privilege levels or to the I/O privilege level.)

The specified lexical level determines how many sets of stack frame pointers the CPU copies into the new stack frame from the preceding frame. This list of stack frame pointers is sometimes called the "display." The first word of the display is a pointer to the last stack frame. This pointer enables a LEAVE instruction to reverse the action of the previous ENTER instruction by effectively discarding the last stack frame.

After ENTER creates the new display for a procedure, it allocates the dynamic storage space for that procedure by decrementing SP by the number of bytes specified in the first parameter. This new value of SP serves as a base for all PUSH and POP operations within that procedure.

To enable a procedure to address its display, ENTER leaves BP pointing to the beginning of the new stack frame. Data manipulation instructions that specify BP as a base register implicitly address locations within the stack segment instead of the data segment. Two forms of the ENTER instruction exist: nested and non-nested. If the lexical level is 0, the non-nested form is used. Since the second operand is 0, ENTER pushes BP, copies SP to BP and then subtracts the first operand from SP. The nested form of ENTER occurs when the second parameter (lexical level) is not 0. Figure 4-1 gives the formal definition of ENTER.

The Formal Definition Of The ENTER Instruction For All Cases Is Given By The Following Listing. LEVEL Denotes The Value Of The Second Operand.

```
Push BP
Set a temporary value FRAME_PTR := SP
If LEVEL > 0 then
    Repeat (LEVEL − 1) times:
        BP := BP −2
        Push the word pointed to by BP
    End repeat
    Push FRAME_PTR
End if
BP := FRAME_PTR
SP := SP − first operand.
```

Figure 4-1. Formal Definition of the ENTER Instruction

The main procedure (with other procedures nested within) operates at the highest lexical level, level 1. The first procedure it calls operates at the next deeper lexical level, level 2. A level 2 procedure can access the variables of the main program which are at fixed locations specified by the compiler. In the case of level 1, ENTER allocates only the requested dynamic storage on the stack because there is no previous display to copy.

A program operating at a higher lexical level calling a program at a lower lexical level requires that the called procedure should have access to the variables of the calling program. ENTER provides this access through a display that provides addressability to the calling program's stack frame.

A procedure calling another procedure at the same lexical level implies that they are parallel procedures and that the called procedure should not have access to the variables of the calling procedure. In this case, ENTER copies only that portion of the display from the calling procedure which refers to previously nested procedures operating at higher lexical levels. The new stack frame does not include the pointer for addressing the calling procedure's stack frame.

ENTER treats a reentrant procedure as a procedure calling another procedure at the same lexical level. In this case, each succeeding iteration of the reentrant procedure can address only its own variables and the variables of the calling procedures at higher lexical levels. A reentrant procedure can always address its own variables; it does not require pointers to the stack frames of previous iterations.

By copying only the stack frame pointers of procedures at higher lexical levels, ENTER makes sure that procedures access only those variables of higher lexical levels, not those at parallel lexical levels (see figure 4-2). Figures 4-2a through 4-2d demonstrate the actions of the ENTER instruction if the modules shown in figure 4-1 were to call one another in alphabetic order.

Block-structured high-level languages can use the lexical levels defined by ENTER to control access to the variables of previously nested procedures. For example, if PROCEDURE A calls PROCEDURE B which, in turn, calls PROCEDURE C, then PROCEDURE C will have access to the variables of MAIN and PROCEDURE A, but not PROCEDURE B because they operate at the same lexical level. Following is the complete definition of the variable access for figure 4-2.

1. MAIN PROGRAM has variables at fixed locations.

2. PROCEDURE A can access only the fixed variables of MAIN.

3. PROCEDURE B can access only the variables of PROCEDURE A and MAIN. PROCEDURE B cannot access the variables of PROCEDURE C or PROCEDURE D.

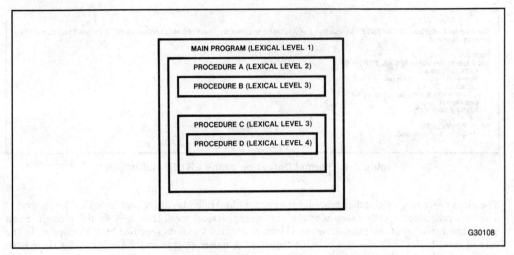

Figure 4-2. Variable Access in Nested Procedures

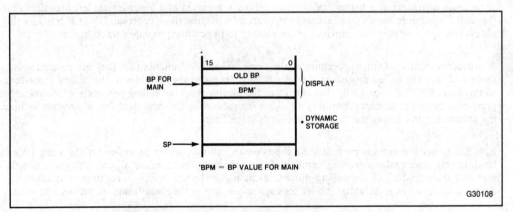

Figure 4-2a. Stack Frame for MAIN at Level 1

4. PROCEDURE C can access only the variables of PROCEDURE A and MAIN. PROCEDURE C cannot access the variables of PROCEDURE B or PROCEDURE D.

5. PROCEDURE D can access the variables of PROCEDURE C, PROCEDURE A, and MAIN. PROCEDURE D cannot access the variables of PROCEDURE B.

ENTER at the beginning of the MAIN PROGRAM creates dynamic storage space for MAIN but copies no pointers. The first and only word in the display points to itself because there is no previous value for LEAVE to return to BP. See figure 4-2a.

After MAIN calls PROCEDURE A, ENTER creates a new display for PROCEDURE A with the first word pointing to the previous value of BP (BPM for LEAVE to return to the MAIN stack frame) and the second word pointing to the current value of BP. Procedure A can access variables in MAIN since MAIN is at level 1. Therefore the base for the dynamic storage for MAIN is at [BP−2]. All dynamic variables for MAIN will be at a fixed offset from this value. See figure 4-2b.

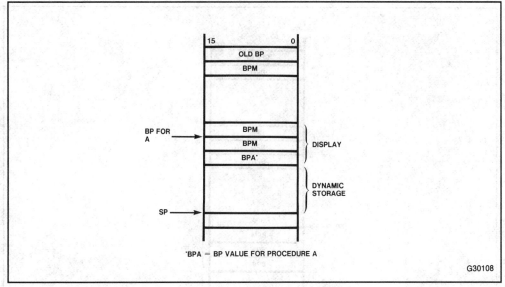

Figure 4-2b. Stack Frame for Procedure A

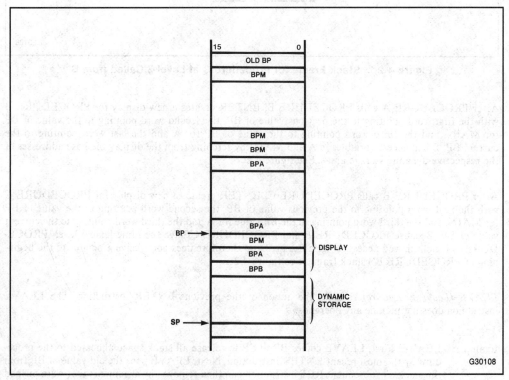

Figure 4-2c. Stack Frame for Procedure B at Level 3 Called from A

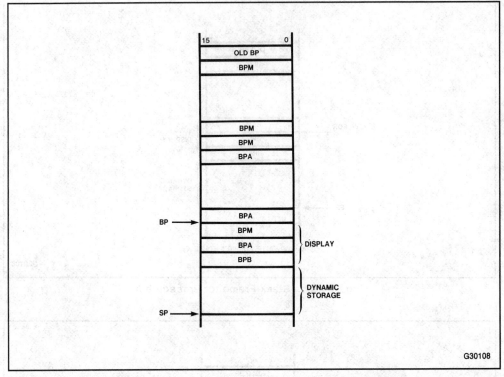

Figure 4-2d. Stack Frame for Procedure C at Level 3 Called from B

After PROCEDURE A calls PROCEDURE B, ENTER creates a new display for PROCEDURE B with the first word pointing to the previous value of BP, the second word pointing to the value of BP for MAIN, and the third word pointing to the value of BP for A and the last word pointing to the current BP. B can access variables in A and MAIN by fetching from the display the base addresses of the respective dynamic storage areas. See figure 4-2c.

After PROCEDURE B calls PROCEDURE C, ENTER creates a new display for PROCEDURE C with the first word pointing to the previous value of BP, the second word pointing to the value of BP for MAIN, and the third word pointing to the BP value for A and the third word pointing to the current value of BP. Because PROCEDURE B and PROCEDURE C have the same lexical level, PROCEDURE C is not allowed access to variables in B and therefore does not receive a pointer to the beginning of PROCEDURE B's stack frame. See figure 4-2d.

LEAVE (Leave Procedure) reverses the action of the previous ENTER instruction. The LEAVE instruction does not include any operands.

Example: LEAVE. First, LEAVE copies BP to SP to release all stack space allocated to the procedure by the most recent ENTER instruction. Next, LEAVE pops the old value of BP from the stack. A subsequent RET instruction can then remove any arguments that were pushed on the stack by the calling program for use by the called procedure.

BOUND (Detect Value Out of Range) verifies that the signed value contained in the specified register lies within specified limits. An interrupt (INT 5) occurs if the value contained in the register is less than the lower bound or greater than the upper bound.

The BOUND instruction includes two operands. The first operand specifies the register being tested. The second operand contains the effective relative address of the two signed BOUND limit values. The BOUND instruction assumes that it can obtain the upper limit from the memory word that immediately follows the lower limit. These limit values cannot be register operands; if they are, an invalid opcode exception occurs.

BOUND is useful for checking array bounds before using a new index value to access an element within the array. BOUND provides a simple way to check the value of an index register before the program overwrites information in a location beyond the limit of the array.

The two-word block of memory that specifies the lower and upper limits of an array might typically reside just before the array itself. This makes the array bounds accessible at a constant offset of −4 from the beginning of the array. Because the address of the array will already be present in a register, this practice avoids extra calculations to obtain the effective address of the array bounds.

Example: BOUND BX,ARRAY−4. Compares the value in BX with the lower limit at address ARRAY−4 and the upper limit at address ARRAY−2. If the signed value in BX is less than the lower bound or greater than the upper bound, the interrupt for this instruction (INT 5) occurs. Otherwise, this instruction has no effect.

Real Address Mode

5

CHAPTER 5
REAL ADDRESS MODE

The 80286 can be operated in either of two modes according to the status of the Protection Enabled bit of the MSW status register. In contrast to the "modes" and "mode bits" of some processors, however, the 80286 modes do not represent a radical transition between conflicting architectures. Instead, the setting of the Protection Enabled bit simply determines whether certain advanced features, in addition to the baseline architecture of the 80286, are to be made available to system designers and programmers.

If the Protection Enabled (PE) bit is set by the programmer, the processor changes into *Protected Virtual Address Mode*. In this mode of operation, memory addressing is performed in terms of virtual addresses, with on-chip mapping mechanisms performing the virtual-to-physical translation. Only in this mode can the system designer make use of the advanced architectural features of the 80286: virtual memory support, system-wide protection, and built-in multitasking mechanisms are among the new features provided in this mode of operation. Refer to Part II of this book (Chapters 6 through 11) for details on Protected Mode operation.

Initially, upon system reset, the processor starts up in *Real Address Mode*. In this mode of operation, all memory addressing is performed in terms of *real* physical addresses. In effect, the architecture of the 80286 in this mode is identical to that of the 8086 and other processors in the 8086 family. The principal features of this baseline architecture have already been discussed throughout Part I (Chapters 2 through 4) of this book. This chapter discusses certain additional topics—addressing, interrupt handling, and system initialization—that complete the system programmer's view of the 80286 in Real Address Mode.

5.1 ADDRESSING AND SEGMENTATION

Like other processors in the 8086 family, the 80286 provides a one-megabyte memory space (2^{20} bytes) when operated in Real Address Mode. Physical addresses are the 20-bit values that uniquely identify each byte location in this address space. Physical addresses, therefore, may range from 0 through FFFFFH. Address bits A20-A23 may not always be zero in Real Address Mode. A20-A23 should not be used by the system while the 80286 is operating in Real Address Mode.

An address is specified by a 32-bit pointer containing two components: (1) a 16-bit effective address offset that determines the displacement, in bytes, of a particular location within a segment; and (2) a 16-bit segment selector component that determines the starting address of the segment. Both components of an address may be referenced explicitly by an instruction (such as JMP, LES, LDS, or CALL); more often, however, the segment selector is simply the contents of a segment register.

The interpretation of the first component, the effective address offset, is straight-forward. Segments are at most 64K (2^{16}) bytes in length, so an unsigned 16-bit quantity is sufficient to address any arbitrary byte location with a segment. The lowest-addressed byte within a segment has an offset of 0, and the highest-addressed byte has an offset of FFFFH. Data operands must be completely contained within a segment and must be contiguous. (These rules apply in both modes.)

A segment selector is the second component of a logical address. This 16-bit quantity specifies the starting address of a segment within a physical address space of 2^{20} bytes.

Whenever the 80286 accesses memory in Real Address Mode, it generates a 20-bit physical address from a segment selector and offset value. The segment selector value is left-shifted four bit positions to form the segment base address. The offset is extended with 4 high order zeroes and added to the base to form the physical address (see figure 5-1).

Therefore, every segment is required to start at a byte address that is evenly divisible by 16; thus, each segment is positioned at a 20-bit physical address whose least significant four bits are zeroes. This arrangement allows the 80286 to interpret a segment selector as the high-order 16 bits of a 20-bit segment base address.

No limit or access checks are performed by the 80286 in the Real Address Mode. All segments are readable, writable, executable, and have a limit of 0FFFFH (65,535 bytes). To save physical memory, you can use unused portions of a segment as another segment by overlapping the two (see figure 5-2). The Intel 8086 software development tools support this feature via the segment override and group operators. *However, programs that access segment B from segment A become incompatible in the protected virtual address mode.*

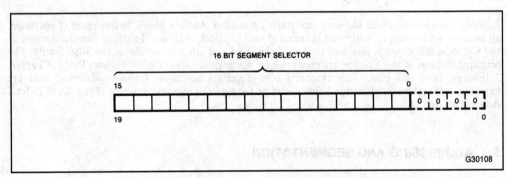

Figure 5-1a. Forming the Segment Base Address

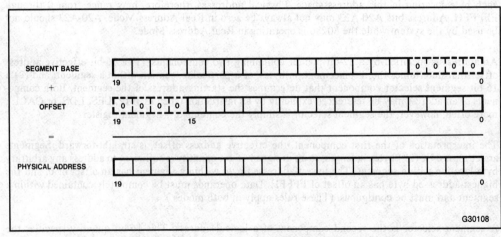

Figure 5-1b. Forming the 20-bit Physical Address in the Real Address Mode

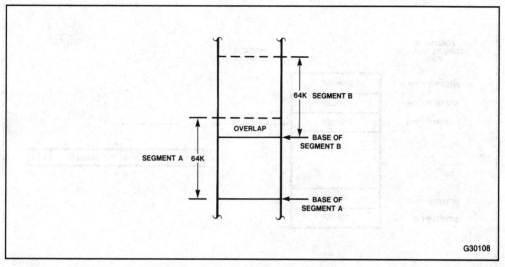

Figure 5-2. Overlapping Segments to Save Physical Memory

5.2 INTERRUPT HANDLING

Program interrupts may be generated in either of two distinct ways. An *internal* interrupt is caused directly by the currently executing program. The execution of a particular instruction results in the occurrence of an interrupt, whether intentionally (e.g., an INT n instruction) or as an unanticipated exception (e.g., invalid opcode). On the other hand, an *external* interrupt occurs asynchronously as the result of an event external to the processor, and bears no necessary relationship with the currently executing program. The INTR and NMI pins of the 80286 provide the means by which external hardware signals the occurrence of such events.

5.2.1 Interrupt Vector Table

Whatever its origin, whether internal or external, an interrupt demands immediate attention from an associated service routine. Control must be transferred, at least for the moment, from the currently executing program to the appropriate interrupt service routine. By means of interrupt vectors, the 80286 handles such control transfers uniformly for both kinds of interrupts.

An interrupt vector is an unsigned integer in the range of 0-255; every interrupt is assigned such a vector. In some cases, the assignment is predetermined and fixed: for example, an external NMI interrupt is invariably associated with vector 2, while an internal divide exception is always associated with vector 0. In most cases, however, the association of an interrupt and a vector is established dynamically. An external INTR interrupt, for example, supplies a vector in response to an interrupt acknowledge bus cycle, while the INT n instruction supplies a vector incorporated within the instruction itself. The vector is shifted two places left to form a byte address into the table (see figure 5-3).

In any case, the 80286 uses the interrupt vector as an index into a table in order to determine the address of the corresponding interrupt service routine. For Real Address Mode, this table is known as the Interrupt Vector Table. Its format is illustrated in figure 5-3.

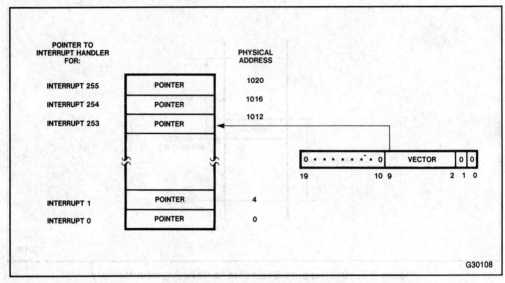

Figure 5-3. Interrupt Vector Table for Real Address Mode

Table 5-1. Interrupt Processing Order

Order	Interrupt
1.	Instruction exception
2.	Single step
3.	NMI
4.	Processor extension segment overrun
5.	INTR

The Interrupt Vector Table consists of as many as 256 consecutive entries, each four bytes long. Each entry defines the address of a service routine to be associated with the correspondingly numbered interrupt vector code. Within each entry, an address is specified by a full 32-bit pointer that consists of a 16-bit offset and a 16-bit segment selector. Interrupts 0-31 are reserved by Intel.

In Real Address Mode, the interrupt table can be accessed directly at physical memory location 0 through 1023. In the protected virtual address mode, however, the interrupt vector table has no fixed physical address and cannot be directly accessed. Therefore, *Real Address mode programs that directly manipulate the interrupt vector table will not work in the protected virtual address mode.*

5.2.1.1 INTERRUPT PRIORITIES

When simultaneous interrupt requests occur, they are processed in a fixed order as shown in table 5-1. Interrupt processing involves saving the flags, the return address, and setting CS:IP to point at the first instruction of the interrupt handler. If other interrupts remain enabled, they are processed before the first instruction of the current interrupt handler is executed. The last interrupt processed is therefore the first one serviced.

5.2.2 Interrupt Procedures

When an interrupt occurs in Real Address Mode, the 8086 performs the following sequence of steps. First, the FLAGS register, as well as the old values of CS and IP, are pushed onto the stack (see figure 5-4). The IF and TF flag bits are cleared. The vector number is then used to read the address of the interrupt service routine from the interrupt table. Execution begins at this address.

Thus, when control is passed to an interrupt service routine, the return linkage is placed on the stack, interrupts are disabled, and single-step trace (if in effect) is turned off. The IRET instruction at the end of the interrupt service routine will reverse these steps before transferring control to the program that was interrupted.

An interrupt service routine may affect registers other than other IP, CS, and FLAGS. It is the responsibility of an interrupt routine to save additional context information before proceeding so that the state of the machine can be restored upon completion of the interrupt service routine (PUSHA and POPA instructions are intended for these operations). Finally, execution of the IRET instruction pops the old IP, CS, and FLAGS from the stack and resumes the execution of the interrupted program.

5.2.3 Reserved and Dedicated Interrupt Vectors

In general, the system designer is free to use almost any interrupt vectors for any given purpose. Some of the lowest-numbered vectors, however, are reserved by Intel for dedicated functions; their use is specifically implied by certain types of exceptions. None of the first 32 vectors should be defined by the user; these vectors are either invoked by pre-defined exceptions or reserved by Intel for future expansion. Table 5-2 shows the dedicated and reserved vectors of the 80286 in Real Address Mode.

The purpose and function of the dedicated interrupt vectors may be summarized as follows (the saved value of CS:IP will include *all* leading prefixes):

- *Divide error (Interrupt 0)*. This exception will occur if the quotient is too large or an attempt is made to divide by zero using either the DIV or IDIV instruction. The saved CS:IP points at the first byte of the failing instruction. DX and AX are unchanged.

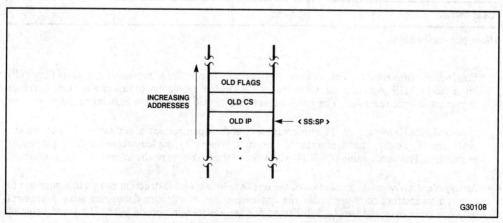

Figure 5-4. Stack Structure after Interrupt (Real Address Mode)

Table 5-2. Dedicated and Reserved Interrupt Vectors in Real Address Mode

Function	Interrupt Number	Related Instructions	Return Address Before Instruction Causing Exception?
Divide error exception	0	DIV, IDIV	Yes
Single step interrupt	1	All	N/A
NMI interrupt	2	All	N/A
Breakpoint interrupt	3	INT	N/A
INTO detected overflow exception	4	INTO	No
BOUND range exceeded exception	5	BOUND	Yes
Invalid opcode exception	6	Any undefined opcode	Yes
Processor extension not available exception	7	ESC or WAIT	Yes
Interrupt table limit too small	8	LIDT	Yes
Processor extension segment overrun interrupt	9	ESC	Yes
Segment overrun exception	13	Any memory reference instruction that attempts to reference 16-bit word at offset 0FFFFH.	Yes
Reserved	10-12, 14, 15		
Processor extension error interrupt	16	ESC or WAIT	N/A
Reserved	17-31		
User defined	32-255		

N/A = Not Applicable

- *Single-Step (Interrupt 1)*. This interrupt will occur after each instruction if the Trap Flag (TF) bit of the FLAGS register is set. Of course, TF is cleared upon entry to this or any other interrupt to prevent infinite recursion. The saved value of CS:IP will point to the next instruction.

- *Nonmaskable (Interrupt 2)*. This interrupt will occur upon receipt of an external signal on the NMI pin. Typically, the nonmaskable interrupt is used to implement power-fail/auto-restart procedures. The saved value of CS:IP will point to the first byte of the interrupted instruction.

- *Breakpoint (Interrupt 3)*. Execution of the one-byte breakpoint instruction causes this interrupt to occur. This instruction is useful for the implementation of software debuggers since it requires only one code byte and can be substituted for any instruction opcode byte. The saved value of CS:IP will point to the next instruction.

- *INTO Detected Overflow (Interrupt 4)*. Execution of the INTO conditional software interrupt instruction will cause this interrupt to occur if the overflow bit (OF) of the FLAGS register is set. The saved value of CS:IP will point to the next instruction.

- *BOUND Range Exceeded (Interrupt 5)*. Execution of the BOUND instruction will cause this interrupt to occur if the specified array index is found to be invalid with respect to the given array bounds. The saved value of CS:IP will point to the first byte of the BOUND instruction.

- *Invalid Opcode (Interrupt 6)*. This exception will occur if execution of an invalid opcode is attempted. (In Real Address Mode, most of the Protected Virtual Address Mode instructions are classified as invalid and should not be used). This interrupt can also occur if the effective address given by certain instructions, notably BOUND, LDS, LES, and LIDT, specifies a register rather than a memory location. The saved value of CS:IP will point to the first byte of the invalid instruction or opcode.

- *Processor Extension Not Available (Interrupt 7)*. Execution of the ESC instruction will cause this interrupt to occur if the status bits of the MSW indicate that processor extension functions are to be emulated in software. Refer to section 10.2.2 for more details. The saved value of CS:IP will point to the first byte of the ESC or the WAIT instruction.

- *Interrupt Table Limit Too Small (Interrupt 8)*. This interrupt will occur if the limit of the interrupt vector table was changed from 3FFH by the LIDT instruction and an interrupt whose vector is outside the limit occurs. The saved value of CS:IP will point to the first byte of the instruction that caused the interrupt or that was ready to execute before an external interrupt occurred. No error code is pushed.

- *Processor Extension Segment Overrun Interrupt (Interrupt 9)*. The interrupt will occur if a processor extension memory operand does not fit in a segment. The saved CS:IP will point at the first byte of the instruction that caused the interrupt.

- *Segment Overrun Exception (Interrupt 13)*. This interrupt will occur if a memory operand does not fit in a segment. In Real Mode this will occur only when a word operand begins at segment offset 0FFFFH. The saved CS:IP will point at the first byte of the instruction that caused the interrupt. No error code is pushed.

- *Processor Extension Error (Interrupt 16)*. This interrupt occurs after the numeric instruction that caused the error. It can only occur while executing a subsequent WAIT or ESC. The saved value of CS:IP will point to the first byte of the ESC or the WAIT instruction. The address of the failed numeric instruction is saved in the NPX.

5.3 SYSTEM INITIALIZATION

The 80286 provides an orderly way to start or restart an executing system. Upon receipt of the RESET signal, certain processor registers go into the determinate state shown in table 5-3.

Table 5-3. Processor State after RESET

Register	Contents
FLAGS	0002 (H)
MSW	FFF0 (H)
IP	FFF0 (H)
CS	F000 (H)
DS	0000 (H)
SS	0000 (H)
ES	0000 (H)

Since the CS register contains F000 (thus specifying a code segment starting at physical address F0000) and the instruction pointer contains FFF0, the processor will execute its first instruction at physical address FFFF0H. The uppermost 16 bytes of physical memory are therefore reserved for initial startup logic. Ordinarily, this location contains an intersegment direct JMP instruction whose target is the actual beginning of a system initialization or restart program.

Some of the steps normally performed by a system initialization routine are as follows:

- Allocate a stack.
- Load programs and data from secondary storage into memory.
- Initialize external devices.
- Enable interrupts (i.e., set the IF bit of the FLAGS register). Set any other desired FLAGS bit as well.
- Set the appropriate MSW flags if a processor extension is present, or if processor extension functions are to be emulated by software.
- Set other registers, as appropriate, to the desired initial values.
- Execute. (Ordinarily, this last step is performed as an intersegment JMP to the main system program.)

Memory Management and Virtual Addressing

6

CHAPTER 6
MEMORY MANAGEMENT AND VIRTUAL ADDRESSING

In Protected Virtual Address Mode, the 80286 provides an advanced architecture that retains substantial compatibility with the 8086 and other processors in the 8086 family. In many respects, the baseline architecture of the processor remains constant regardless of the mode of operation. Application programmers continue to use the same set of instructions, addressing modes, and data types in Protected Mode as in Real Address Mode.

The major difference between the two modes of operation is that the Protected Mode provides system programmers with additional architectural features, supplementary to the baseline architecture, that can be used to good advantage in the design and implementation of advanced systems. Especially noteworthy are the mechanisms provided for memory management, protection, and multitasking.

This chapter focuses on the memory management mechanisms of Protected Mode; the concept of a virtual address and the process of virtual-to-physical address translation are described in detail in this chapter. Subsequent chapters deal with other key aspects of Protected Mode operation. Chapter 7 discusses the issue of protection and the integrated mechanisms that support a system-wide protection policy. Chapter 8 discusses the notion of a task and its central role in the 80286 architecture. Chapters 9 through 11 discuss certain additional topics—interrupt handling, special instructions, system initialization, etc.—that complete the system programmer's view of 80286 Protected Mode.

6.1 MEMORY MANAGEMENT OVERVIEW

A memory management scheme interposes a mapping operation between logical addresses (i.e., addresses as they are viewed by programs) and physical addresses (i.e., actual addresses in real memory). Since the logical address spaces are independent of physical memory (dynamically relocatable), the mapping (the assignment of real address space to virtual address space) is transparent to software. This allows the program development tools (for static systems) or the system software (for reprogrammable systems) to control the allocation of space in real memory without regard to the specifics of individual programs.

Application programs may be translated and loaded independently since they deal strictly with virtual addresses. Any program can be relocated to use any available segments of physical memory.

The 80286, when operated in Protected Mode, provides an efficient on-chip memory management architecture. Moreover, as described in Chapter 11, the 80286 also supports the implementation of virtual memory systems—that is, systems that dynamically swap chunks of code and data between real memory and secondary storage devices (e.g., a disk) independent of and transparent to the executing application programs. Thus, a program-visible address is more aptly termed a virtual address rather than a logical address since it may actually refer to a location not currently present in real memory.

Memory management, then, consists of a mechanism for mapping the virtual addresses that are visible to the program onto the physical addresses of real memory. With the 80286, segmentation is the key to virtual memory addressing. Virtual memory is partitioned into a number of individual segments, which are the units of memory that are mapped into physical memory and swapped to and from secondary storage devices. Most of this chapter is devoted to a detailed discussion of the mapping and virtual memory mechanisms of the 80286.

The concept of a task also plays a significant role in memory management since distinct memory mappings may be assigned to the different tasks in a multitask or multi-user environment. A complete discussion of tasks is deferred until Chapter 8, "Tasks and State Transition." For present purposes, it is sufficient to think of a task as an ongoing process, or execution path, that is dedicated to a particular function. In a multi-user time-sharing environment, for example, the processing required to interact with a particular user may be considered as a single task, functionally independent of the other tasks (i.e., users) in the system.

6.2 VIRTUAL ADDRESSES

In Protected Mode, application programs deal exclusively with virtual addresses; programs have no access whatsoever to the actual physical addresses generated by the processor. As discussed in Chapter 2, an address is specified by a program in terms of two components: (1) a 16-bit effective address offset that determines the displacement, in bytes, of a location within a segment; and (2) a 16-bit segment selector that uniquely references a particular segment. Jointly, these two components constitute a complete 32-bit address (pointer data type), as shown in figure 6-1.

These 32-bit virtual addresses are manipulated by programs in exactly the same way as the two-component addresses of Real Address Mode. After a program loads the segment selector component of an address into a segment register, each subsequent reference to locations within the selected segment requires only a 16-bit offset be specified. Locality of reference will ordinarily insure that addresses can be specified very efficiently using only 16-bit offsets.

An important difference between Real Address Mode and Protected Mode, however, concerns the actual format and information content of segment selectors. In Real Address Mode, as with the 8086 and other processors in the 8086 family, a 16-bit selector is merely the upper bits of a segment's physical base address. By contrast, segment selectors in Protected Mode follow an entirely different format, as illustrated by figure 6-1.

Two of the selector bits, designated as the RPL field in figure 6-1, are not actually involved in the selection and specification of segments; their use is discussed in Chapter 7.

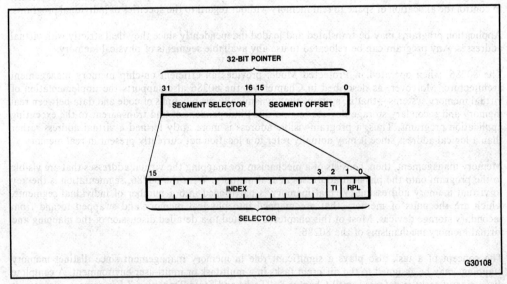

Figure 6-1. Format of the Segment Selector Component

The remaining 14 bits of the selector component uniquely designate a particular segment. The virtual address space of a program, therefore, may encompass as many as 16,384 (2^{14}) distinct segments. Segments themselves are of variable size, ranging from as small as a single byte to as large as 64K (2^{16}) bytes. Thus, a program's virtual address space may contain, altogether, up to a full gigabyte ($2^{30} = 2^{14} \times 2^{16}$) of individually addressable byte locations.

The entirety of a program's virtual address space is further subdivided into two separate halves, as distinguished by the TI ("table indicator") bit in the virtual address. These two halves are the global address space and the local address space.

The global address space is used for system-wide data and procedures including operating system software, library routines, runtime language support and other commonly shared system services. (To application programs, the operating system appears to be a set of service routines that are accessible to all tasks.) Global space is shared by all tasks to avoid unnecessary replication of system service routines and to facilitate shared data and interrupt handling. Global address space is defined by addresses with a zero in the TI bit position; it is identically mapped for all tasks in the system.

The other half of the virtual address space—comprising those addresses with the TI bit set—is separately mapped for each task in the system. Because such an address space is local to the task for which it is defined, it is referred to as a local address space. In general, code and data segments within a task's local address space are private to that particular task or user. Figure 6-2 illustrates the task isolation made possible by partitioning the virtual address spaces into local and global regions.

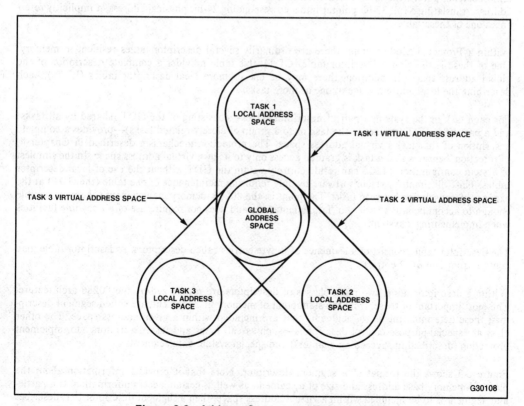

Figure 6-2. Address Spaces and Task Isolation

Within each of the two regions addressable by a program—either the global address space or a particular local address space—as many as 8,192 (2^{13}) distinct segments may be defined. The INDEX field of the segment selector allows for a unique specification of each of these segments. This 13-bit quantity acts as an index into a memory-resident table, called a descriptor table, that records the mapping between segment address and the physical locations allocated to each distinct segment. (These descriptor tables, and their role in virtual-to-physical address translation, are described in the sections that follow.)

In summary, a Protected Mode virtual address is a 32-bit pointer to a particular byte location within a one-gigabyte virtual address space. Each such pointer consists of a 16-bit selector component and a 16-bit offset component. The selector component, in turn, comprises a 13-bit table index, a 1-bit table indicator (local versus global), and a 2-bit RPL field; all but this last field serve to select a particular segment from among the 16K segments in a task's virtual address space. The offset component of a full pointer is an unsigned 16-bit integer that specifies the desired byte location within the selected segment.

6.3 DESCRIPTOR TABLES

A descriptor table is a memory-resident table either defined by program development tools in a static system or controlled by operating system software in systems that are reprogrammable. The descriptor table contents govern the interpretation of virtual addresses. Whenever the 80286 decodes a virtual address, translating a full 32-bit pointer into a corresponding 24-bit physical address, it implicitly references one of these tables.

Within a Protected Mode system, there are ordinarily several descriptor tables resident in memory. One of these is the global descriptor table (GDT); this table provides a complete description of the global address space. In addition, there may be one or more local descriptor tables (LDTs), each describing the local address space of one or more tasks.

For each task in the system, a pair of descriptor tables—consisting of the GDT (shared by all tasks) and a particular LDT (private to the task or to a group of closely related tasks)—provides a complete description of that task's virtual address space. The protection mechanism described in Chapter 7, "Protection," ensures that a task is granted access only to its own virtual address space. In the simplest of system configurations, tasks can reside entirely within the GDT without the use of local descriptor tables. This will simplify system software by only requiring maintenance of one table (the GDT) at the expense of no isolation between tasks. The point is: the 80286 memory management scheme is flexible enough to accommodate a variety of implementations and does not require use of all possible facilities when implementing a system.

The descriptor tables consist of a sequence of 8-byte entries called descriptors. A descriptor table may contain from 1 to 8192 entries.

Within a descriptor table, two main classes of descriptors are recognized by the 80286 architecture. The most important of these, from the standpoint of memory management, are called segment descriptors; these determine the set of segments that are included within a given address space. The other class are special-purpose control descriptors—such as call gates and task descriptors—to implement protection (described in succeeding chapters) and special system data segments.

Figure 6-3 shows the format of a segment descriptor. Note that it provides information about the physical-memory base address and size of a segment, as well as certain access information. If a particular segment is to be included within a virtual address space, then a segment descriptor that describes that segment must be included within the appropriate descriptor table. Thus, within the GDT, there

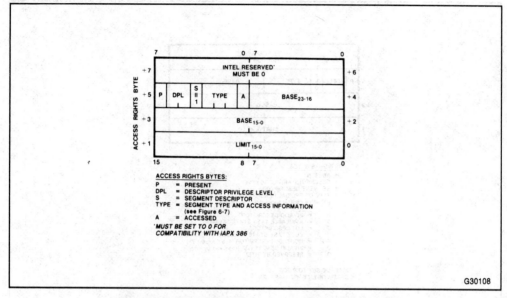

Figure 6-3. Code or Data Segment Descriptor (S = 1)

are segment descriptors for all of the segments that comprise a system's global address space. Similarly, within a task's LDT, there must be a descriptor for each of the segments that are to be included in that task's local address space.

Each local descriptor table is itself a special system segment, recognizable as such by the 80286 architecture and described by a specific type of segment descriptor (see figure 6-4). Because there is only a single GDT segment, it is not defined by a segment descriptor. Its base and size information is maintained in a dedicated register, GDTR, as described below (section 6.6.2).

Similarly, there is another dedicated register within the 80286, LDTR, that records the base and size of the current LDT segment (i.e., the LDT associated with the currently executing task). The LDTR register state, however, is volatile: its contents are automatically altered whenever a task switch is made from one task to another. An alternate specification independent of changeable register contents must therefore exist for each LDT in the system. This independent specification is accomplished by means of special system segment descriptors known as descriptor table descriptors or LDT descriptors.

Figure 6-4 shows the format of a descriptor table descriptor. (Note that it is distinguished from an ordinary segment descriptor by the contents of certain bits in the access byte.) This special type of descriptor is used to specify the physical base address and size of a local descriptor table that defines the virtual address space and address mapping for an individual user or task (figure 6-5).

Each LDT segment in a system must lie within that system's global address space. Thus, all of the descriptor table descriptors must be included among the entries in the global descriptor table (the GDT) of a system. In fact, these special descriptors may appear only in the GDT. Reference to an LDT descriptor within an LDT will cause a protection violation. Even though they are in the global address space available to all tasks, the descriptor table descriptors are protected from corruption within the GDT since they are special system segments and can only be accessed for loading into the LDTR register.

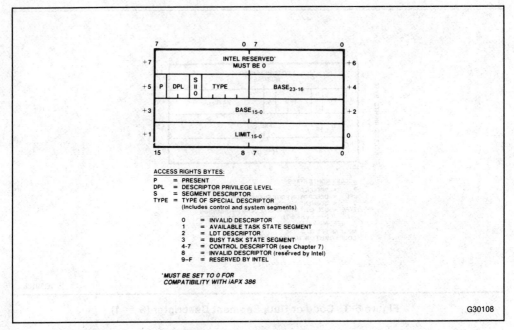

Figure 6-4. System Segment Descriptor or Gate Descriptor (S = 0)

6.4 VIRTUAL-TO-PHYSICAL ADDRESS TRANSLATION

The translation of a full 32-bit virtual address pointer into a real 24-bit physical address is shown by figure 6-6. When the segment's base address is determined as a result of the mapping process, the offset value is added to the result to obtain the physical address.

The actual mapping is performed on the selector component of the virtual address. The 16-bit segment selector is mapped to a 24-bit segment base address via a segment descriptor maintained in one of the descriptor tables.

The TI bit in the segment selector (see figure 6-1) determines which of two descriptor tables, either the GDT or the current LDT, is to be chosen for memory mapping. In either case, using the GDTR or LDTR register, the processor can readily determine the physical base address of the memory-resident table.

The INDEX field in the segment selector specifies a particular descriptor entry within the chosen table. The processor simply multiplies this index value by 8 (the length of a descriptor), and adds the result to the base address of the descriptor table in order to access the appropriate segment descriptor in the table.

Finally, the segment descriptor contains the physical base address of the target segment, as well as size (limit) and access information. The processor sums the 24-bit segment base and the specified 16-bit offset to generate the resulting 24-bit physical address.

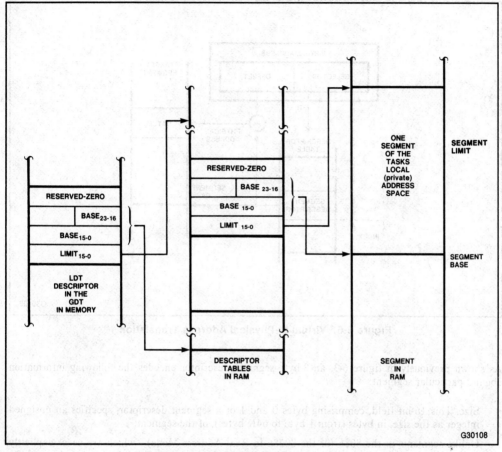

Figure 6-5. LDT Descriptor

6.5 SEGMENTS AND SEGMENT DESCRIPTORS

Segments are the basic units of 80286 memory management. In contrast to schemes based on fixed-size pages, segmentation allows for a very efficient implementation of software: variable-length segments can be tailored to the exact requirements of an application. Segmentation, moreover, is consistent with the way a programmer naturally deals with his virtual address space: programmers are encouraged to divide code and data into clearly defined modules and structures which are manipulated as consistent entities. This reduces (minimizes) the potential for virtual memory thrashing. Segmentation also eliminates the restrictions on data structures that span a page (e.g., a word that crosses page boundaries).

Each segment within an 80286 system is defined by an associated segment descriptor, which may appear in one or more descriptor tables. Its inclusion within a descriptor table represents the presence of its associated segment within the virtual address space defined by that table. Conversely, its ommission from a descriptor table means that the segment is absent from the corresponding address space.

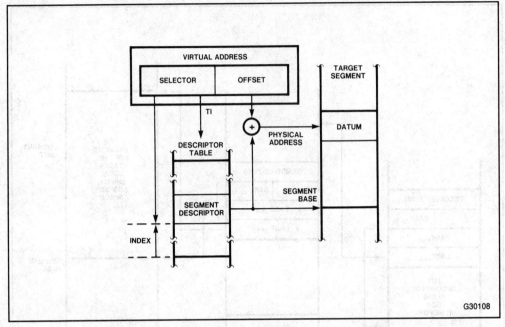

Figure 6-6. Virtual-to-Physical Address Translation

As shown previously in figure 6-3, an 8-byte segment descriptor encodes the following information about a particular segment:

- Size. This 16-bit field, comprising bytes 0 and 1 of a segment descriptor, specifies an unsigned integer as the size, in bytes (from 1 byte to 64K bytes), of the segment.

  Unlike segments in the 8086 (or the 80286 in Real Address Mode)—which are never explicitly limited to less than a full 64K bytes—Protected Mode segments are always assigned a specific size value. In conjunction with the protection features described in Chapter 7, this assigned size allows the enforcement of a very desirable and natural rule: inadvertent accesses to locations beyond a segment's actual boundaries are prohibited.

- Base. This 24-bit field, comprising bytes 2 through 4 of a segment descriptor, specifies the physical base address of the segment; it thus defines the actual location of the segment within the 16-megabyte real memory space. The base may be any byte address within the 16-megabyte real memory space.

- Access. This 8-bit field comprises byte 5 of a segment descriptor. This access byte specifies a variety of additional information about a segment, particularly in regard to the protection features of the 80286. For example, code segments are distinguished from data segments; and certain special access restrictions (such as Execute-Only or Read-Only) may be defined for segments of each type. Access byte values of 00H or 80H will always denote "invalid."

Figure 6-7 shows the access byte format for both code and data segment descriptors. Detailed discussion of the protection related fields within an access byte (Conforming, Execute-Only, Descriptor Privilege Level, Expand Down, and Write-Permitted), and their use in implementing protection policies, is deferred to Chapter 7. The two fields Accessed and Present are used for virtual memory implementations.

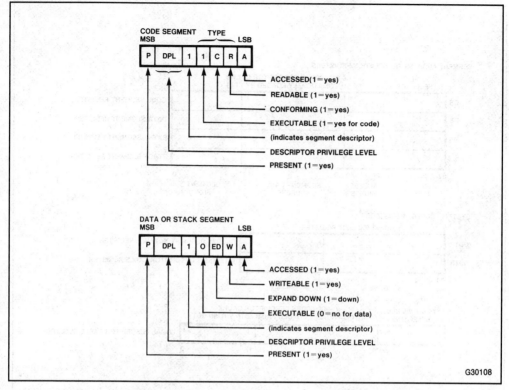

Figure 6-7. Segment Descriptor Access Bytes

6.6 MEMORY MANAGEMENT REGISTERS

The Protected Virtual Address Mode features of the 80286 operate at high performance due to extensions to the basic 8086 register set. Figure 6-8 illustrates that portion of the extended register structure that pertains to memory management. (For a complete summary of all Protected Mode registers, refer to section 10.1).

6.6.1 Segment Address Translation Registers

Figure 6-8 shows the segment registers CS,DS,ES, and SS. In contrast to their usual representation, however, these registers are now depicted as 64-bit registers, each with "visible" and "hidden" components.

The visible portions of these segment address translation registers are manipulated by programs exactly as if they were simply the 16-bit segment registers of Real Address Mode. By loading a segment selector into one of these registers, the program makes the associated segment one of its four currently addressable segments.

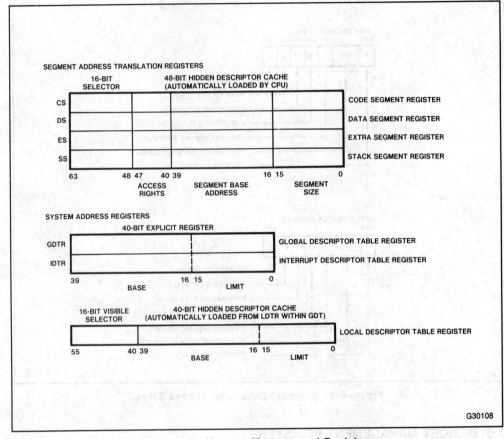

Figure 6-8. Memory Management Registers

The operations that load these registers—or, more exactly, those that load the visible portion of these registers—are normal program instructions. These instructions may be divided into two categories:

1. Direct segment-register load instructions. These instructions (such as LDS, LES, MOV, POP, etc.) can explicitly reference the SS, DS, or ES segment registers as the destination operand.

2. Implied segment-register load instructions. These instructions (such as intersegment CALL and JMP) implicitly reference the CS code segment register; as a result of these operations, the contents of CS are altered.

Using these instructions, a program loads the visible part of the segment register with a 16-bit selector (i.e., the high-order word of a virtual address pointer). Whenever this is done, the processor automatically uses the selector to reference the appropriate descriptor and loads the 48-bit hidden descriptor cache for that segment register.

The correspondence between selectors and descriptors has already been described. Remember that the selector's TI bit indicates one of the two descriptor tables, either the LDT or the GDT. Within the indicated table, a particular entry is chosen by the selector's 13-bit INDEX field. This index, scaled by a factor of 8, represents the relative displacement of the chosen table entry (a descriptor).

Thus, so long as a particular selector value is valid (i.e., it points to a valid segment descriptor within the bounds of the descriptor table), it can be readily associated with an 8-byte descriptor. When a selector value is loaded into the visible part of a segment register, the 80286 automatically loads 6 bytes of the associated descriptor into the hidden part of the register. These 6 bytes, therefore, contain the size, base, and access type of the selected segment. Figure 6-9 illustrates this transparent process of descriptor loading.

In effect, the hidden descriptor fields of the segment registers function as the memory management cache of the 80286. All the information required to address the current working set of segments—that is, the base address, size, and access rights of the currently addressable segments—is stored in this memory cache. Unlike the probabilistic caches of other architectures, however, the 80286 cache is completely deterministic: the caching of descriptors is explicitly controlled by the program.

Most memory references do not require the translation of a full 32-bit virtual address, or long pointer. Operands that are located within one of the currently addressable segments, as determined by the four segment registers, can be referenced very efficiently by means of a short pointer, which is simply a 16-bit offset.

In fact, most 80286 instructions reference memory locations in precisely this way, specifying only a 16-bit offset with respect to one of the currently addressable segments. The choice of segments (CS, DS, ES, or SS) is either implicit within the instruction itself, or explicitly specified by means of a segment-override prefix (as described in Chapter 2).

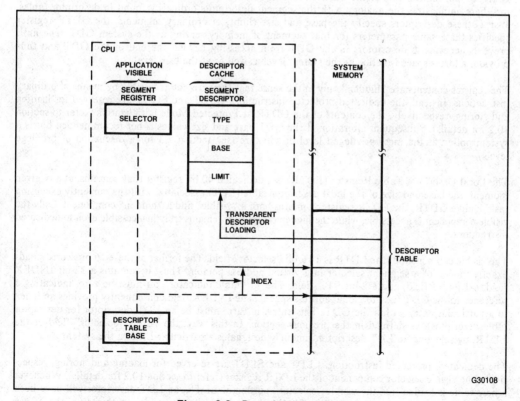

Figure 6-9. Descriptor Loading

Thus, in most cases, virtual-to-physical address translation is actually performed in two separate steps. First, when a program loads a new value into a segment register, the processor immediately performs a mapping operation; the physical base address of the selected segment (as well as certain additional information) is automatically loaded into the hidden portion of the register. The internal cache registers (virtual address translation hardware) are therefore dynamically shared among the 16K different segments potentially addressable within the user's virtual address space. No software overhead (either system or application) is required to perform this operation.

Subsequently, as the program utilizes a short pointer to reference a location within a segment, the processor generates a 24-bit physical address simply by adding the specified offset value to the previously cached segment base address. By encouraging the use of short pointers in this way, rather than requiring a full 32-bit virtual address for every memory reference, the 80286 provides a very efficient on-chip mechanism for address translation, with minimum overhead for references to memory-based tables or the need for external address-translation devices.

6.6.2 System Address Registers

The Global Descriptor Table Register (GDTR) is a dedicated 40-bit (5 byte) register used to record the base and size of a system's global descriptor table (GDT). Thus, two of these bytes define the size of the GDT, and three bytes define its base address.

In figure 6-8, the contents of the GDTR are referred to as a "hidden descriptor." The term "descriptor" here emphasizes the analogy with the segment descriptors ordinarily found in descriptor tables. Just as these descriptors specify the base and size (limit) of ordinary segments, the GDTR register specifies these same parameters for that segment of memory serving as the system GDT. The limit prevents accesses to descriptors in the GDT from accessing beyond the end of the GDT and thus provides address space isolation at the system level as well as at the task level.

The register contents are "hidden" only in the sense that they are not accessible by means of ordinary instructions. Instead, the dedicated protected instructions LGDT and SGDT are reserved for loading and storing, respectively, the contents of the GDTR at Protected Mode initialization (refer to section 10.2 for details). Subsequent alteration of the GDT base and size values is not recommended but is a system option at the most privileged level of software (see section 7.3 for a discussion of privilege levels).

The Local Descriptor Table Register (LDTR) is a dedicated 40-bit register that contains, at any given moment, the base and size of the local descriptor table (LDT) associated with the currently executing task. Unlike GDTR, the LDTR register contains both a "visible" and a "hidden" component. Only the visible component is accessible, while the hidden component remains truly inaccessible even to dedicated instructions.

The visible component of the LDTR is a 16-bit "selector" field. The format of these 16 bits corresponds exactly to that of a segment selector in a virtual address pointer. Thus, it contains a 13-bit INDEX field, a 1-bit TI field, and a 2-bit RPL field. The TI "table indicator" bit must be zero, indicating a reference to the GDT (i.e., to global address space). The INDEX field consequently provides an index to a particular entry within the GDT. This entry, in turn, must be an LDT descriptor (or descriptor table descriptor), as defined in the previous section. In this way, the visible "selector" field of the LDTR, by selecting an LDT descriptor, uniquely designates a particular LDT in the system.

The dedicated, protected instructions LLDT and SLDT are reserved for loading and storing, respectively, the visible selector component of the LDTR register (refer to section 10.2 for details). Whenever a new value is loaded into the visible "selector" portion of LDTR, an LDT descriptor will have been uniquely chosen (assuming, of course, that the "selector" value is valid). In this case, the 80286 automatically loads the hidden "descriptor" portion of LDTR with five bytes from the chosen LDT descriptor. Thus, size and base information about a particular LDT, as recorded in a memory-resident global descriptor table entry, is cached in the LDTR register.

New values may be loaded into the visible portion of the LDTR (and, thus, into the hidden portion as well) in either of two ways. The LLDT instruction, during system initialization, is used explicitly to set an initial value for the LDTR register; in this way, a local address space is provided for the first task in a multitasking environment. After system startup, explicit changes are not required since operations that automatically invoke a task switch (described in section 8.4) appropriately manage the LDTR.

At all times, the LDTR register thus records the physical base address (and size) of the current task's LDT; the descriptor table required for mapping the current local address space, therefore, is immediately accessible to the processor. Moreover, since GDTR always maintains the base address of the GDT, the table that maps the global address space is similarly accessible. The two system address registers, GDTR and LDTR, act as a special processor cache, maintaining current information about the two descriptor tables required, at any given time, for addressing the entire current virtual address space.

Protection 7

CHAPTER 7
PROTECTION

7.1 INTRODUCTION

In most microprocessor based products, the product's availability, quality, and reliability are determined by the software it contains. Software is often the key to a product's success. Protection is a tool used to shorten software development time, and improve software quality and reliability.

Program testing is an important step in developing software. A system with protection will detect software errors more quickly and accurately than a system without protection. Eliminating errors via protection reduces the development time for a product.

Testing software is difficult. Many errors occur only under complex circumstances which are difficult to anticipate. The result is that products are shipped with undetected errors. When such errors occur, products appear unreliable. The impact of a software error is multiplied if it introduces errors in other bug-free programs. Thus, the total system reliability reduces to that of the least reliable program running at any given time.

Protection improves the reliability of an entire system by preventing software errors in one program from affecting other programs. Protection can keep the system running even when some user program attempts an invalid or prohibited operation.

Hardware protection performs run-time checks in parallel with the execution of the program. But, hardware protection has traditionally resulted in a design that is more expensive and slower than a system without protection. However, the 80286 provides hardware-enforced protection without the performance or cost penalties normally associated with protection.

The protected mode 80286 implements extensive protection by integrating these functions on-chip. The 80286 protection is more comprehensive and flexible than comparable solutions. It can locate and isolate a large number of program errors and prevent the propagation of such errors to other tasks or programs. The protection of the total system detects and isolates bugs both during development and installed usage. Chapter 9 discusses exceptions in more detail.

The remaining sections of this chapter explain the protection model implemented in the 80286.

7.1.1 Types of Protection

Protection in the 80286 has three basic aspects:

1. Isolation of system software from user applications.

2. Isolation of users from each other (Inter-task protection).

3. Data-type checking.

The 80286 provides a four-level, ringed-type, increasingly-privileged protection mechanism to isolate applications software from various layers of system software. This is a major improvement and extension over the simpler two-level user/supervisor mechanism found in many systems. Software modules in a supervisor level are protected from modules in the application level and from software in less privileged supervisor levels.

Restricting the addressability of a software module enables an operating system to control system resources and priorities. This is especially important in an environment that supports multiple concurrent users. Multi-user, multi-tasking, and distributed processing systems require this complete control of system resources for efficient, reliable operation.

The second aspect of protection is isolating users from each other. Without such isolation an error in one user program could affect the operation of another error-free user program. Such subtle interactions are difficult to diagnose and repair. The reliability of applications programs is greatly enhanced by such isolation of users.

Within a system or application level program, the 80286 will ensure that all code and data segments are properly used (e.g., data cannot be executed, programs cannot be modified, and offset must be within defined limits, etc.). Such checks are performed on every memory access to provide full runtime error checking.

7.1.2 Protection Implementation

The protection hardware of the 80286 establishes constraints on memory and instruction usage. The number of possible interactions between instructions, memory, and I/O devices is practically unlimited. Out of this very large field the protection mechanism limits interactions to a controlled, understandable subset. Within this subset fall the list of "correct" operations. Any operation that does not fall into this subset is not allowed by the protection mechanism and is signalled as a protection violation.

To understand protection on the 80286, you must begin with its basic parts: segments and tasks. 80286 segments are the smallest region of memory which have unique protection attributes. Modular programming automatically produces separate regions of memory (segments) whose contents are treated as a whole. Segments reflect the natural construction of a program, e.g., code for module A, data for module A, stack for the task, etc. All parts of the segment are treated in the same way by the 80286. Logically separate regions of memory should be in separate segments.

The memory segmentation model (see figure 7-1) of the 80286 was designed to optimally execute code for software composed of independent modules. Modular programs are easier to construct and maintain. Compared to monolithic software systems, modular software systems have enhanced capabilities, and are typically easier to develop and test for proper operation.

Each segment in the system is defined by a memory-resident descriptor. The protection hardware prevents accesses outside the data areas and attempts to modify instructions, etc., as defined by the descriptors. Segmentation on the 80286 allows protection hardware to be integrated into the CPU for full data access control without any performance impact.

The segmented memory architecture of the 80286 provides unique capabilities for regulating the transfer of control between programs.

Programs are given direct but controlled access to other procedures and modules. This capability is the heart of isolating application and system programs. Since this access is provided and controlled directly by the 80286 hardware, there is no performance penalty. A system designer can take advantage of the 80286 access control to design high-performance modular systems with a high degree of confidence in the integrity of the system.

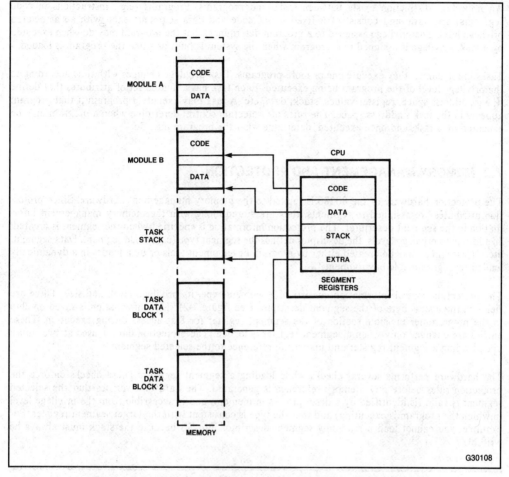

Figure 7-1. Addressing Segments of a Module within a Task

Access control between programs and the operating system is implemented via address space separation and a privilege mechanism. The address space control separates applications programs from each other while the privilege mechanism isolates system software from applications software. The privilege mechanism grants different capabilities to programs to access code, data, and I/O resources based on the associated protection level. Trusted software that controls the whole system is typically placed at the most privileged level. Ordinary application software does not have to deal with these control mechanisms. They come into play only when there is a transfer of control between tasks, or if the Operating System routines have to be invoked.

The protection features of multiple privilege levels extend to ensuring reliable I/O control. However, for a system designer to enable only one specific level to do I/O would excessively constrain subsequent extensions or application development. Instead, the 80286 permits each task to be assigned a separate minimum level where I/O is allowed. I/O privilege is discussed in section 10.3.

An important distinction exists between tasks and programs. Programs (e.g., instructions in code segments) are static and consist of a fixed set of code and data segments each with an associated privilege level. The privilege assigned to a program determines what the program may do when executed by a task. Privilege is assigned to a program when the system is built or when the program is loaded.

Tasks are dynamic; they execute one or more programs. Task privilege changes with time according to the privilege level of the program being executed. Each task has a unique set of attributes that define it, e.g., address space, register values, stack, data, etc. A task may execute a program if that program appears in the task's address space. The rules of protection control determine when a program may be executed by a task, and once executed, determine what the program may do.

7.2 MEMORY MANAGEMENT AND PROTECTION

The protection hardware of the 80286 is related to the memory management hardware. Since protection attributes are assigned to segments, they are stored along with the memory management information in the segment descriptor. The protection information is specified when the segment is created. In addition to privilege levels, the descriptor defines the segment type (e.g., Code segment, Data segment, etc.). Descriptors may be created either by program development tools or by a loader in a dynamically loaded reprogrammable environment.

The protection control information consists of a segment type, its privilege level, and size. These are fields in the access byte of the segment descriptor (see figure 7-2). This information is saved on-chip in the programmer invisible section of the segment register for fast access during execution. These entries are changed only when a segment register is loaded. The protection data is used at two times: upon loading a segment register and upon each reference to the selected segment.

The hardware performs several checks while loading a segment register. These checks enforce the protection rules before any memory reference is generated. The hardware verifies that the selected segment is valid (is identified by a descriptor, is in memory, and is accessible from the privilege level in which the program is executing) and that the type is consistent with the target segment register. For example, you cannot load a read-only segment descriptor into SS because the stack must always be writable.

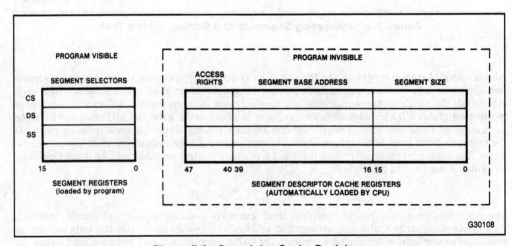

Figure 7-2. Descriptor Cache Registers

Each reference into the segment defined by a segment register is checked by the hardware to verify that it is within the defined limits of the segment and is of the proper type. For example, a code segment or read-only data segment cannot be written. All these checks are made before the memory cycle is started; any violation will prevent that cycle from starting and cause an exception to occur. Since the checks are performed concurrently with address formation, there is no performance penalty.

By controlling the access rights and privilege attributes of segments, the system designer can assure a program will not change its code or overwrite data belonging to another task. Such assurances are vital to maintaining system integrity in the face of error-prone programs.

7.2.1 Separation of Address Spaces

As described in Chapter 6, each task can address up to a gigabyte ($2^{14} - 2$ segments of up to 65,536 bytes each) of virtual memory defined by the task's LDT (Local Descriptor Table) and the system GDT. Up to one-half gigabyte (2^{13} segments of up to 65,536 bytes each) of the task's address space is defined by the LDT and represents the task's private address space. The remaining virtual address space is defined by the GDT and is common to all tasks in the system.

Each descriptor table is itself a special kind of segment recognized by the 80286 architecture. These tables are defined by descriptors in the GDT (Global Descriptor Table). The CPU has a set of base and limit registers that point to the GDT and the LDT of the currently running task. The local descriptor table register is loaded by a task switch operation.

An active task can only load selectors that reference segments defined by descriptors in either the GDT or its private LDT. Since a task cannot reference descriptors in other LDTs, and no descriptors in its LDT refer to data or code belonging to other tasks, it cannot gain access to another tasks' private code and data (see figure 7-3).

Since the GDT contains information that is accessible by all users (e.g., library routines, common data, Operating System services, etc.), the 80286 uses privilege levels and special descriptor types to control access (see section 7.2.2). Privilege levels protect more trusted data and code (in GDT and LDT) from less trusted access (WITHIN a task), while the private virtual address spaces defined by unique LDTs provide protection BETWEEN tasks (see figure 7-4).

7.2.2 LDT and GDT Access Checks

All descriptor tables have a limit used by the protection hardware to ensure address space separation of tasks. Each task's LDT can be a different size as defined by its descriptor in the GDT. The GDT may also contain less than 8191 descriptors as defined by the GDT limit value. The descriptor table limit identifies the last valid byte of the last descriptor in that table. Since each descriptor is eight bytes long, the limit value is $N \times 8 - 1$ for N descriptors.

Any attempt by a program to load a segment register, local descriptor table register (LDTR), or task register (TR) with a selector that refers to a descriptor outside the corresponding limit causes an exception with an error code identifying the invalid selector used (see figure 7-5).

Not all descriptor entries in the GDT or LDT need contain a valid descriptor. There can be holes, or "empty" descriptors, in the LDT and GDT. "Empty" descriptors allow dynamic allocation and deletion of segments or other system objects without changing the size of the GDT or LDT. Any descriptor with an access byte equal to zero is considered empty. Any attempt to load a segment register with a selector that refers to an empty descriptor will cause an exception with an error code identifying the invalid selection.

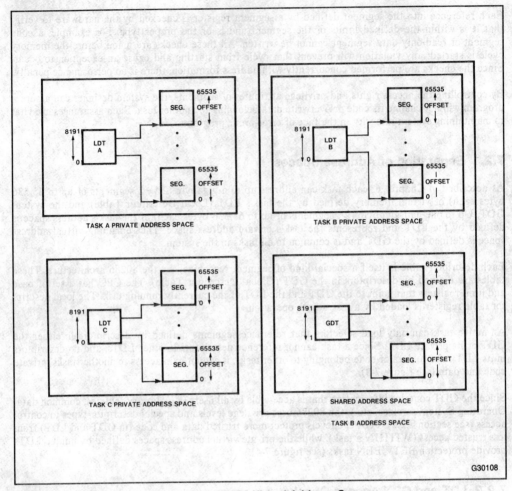

Figure 7-3. 80286 Virtual Address Space

7.2.3 Type Validation

After checking that a selector reference is within the bounds of a descriptor table and refers to a non-empty descriptor, the type of segment defined by the descriptor is checked against the destination register. Since each segment register has predefined functions, each must refer to certain types of segments (see section 7.4.1). An attempt to load a segment register in violation of the protection rules causes an exception.

The "null" selector is a special type of segment selector. It has an index field of all zeros and a table indicator of 0. The null selector appears to refer to GDT descriptor entry #0 (see GDT in figure 7-3). This selector value may be used as a place holder in the DS or ES segment registers; it may be loaded into them without causing an exception. However, any attempt to use the null segment registers to reference memory will cause an exception and prevent any memory cycle from occurring.

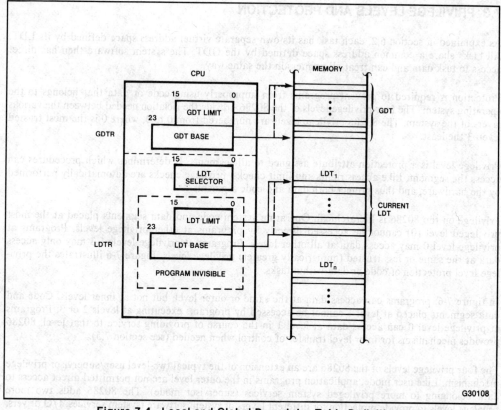

Figure 7-4. Local and Global Descriptor Table Definitions

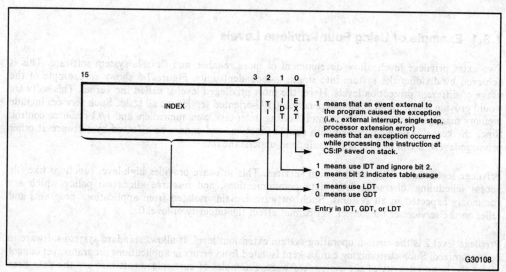

Figure 7-5. Error Code Format (on the stack)

7.3 PRIVILEGE LEVELS AND PROTECTION

As explained in section 6.2, each task has its own separate virtual address space defined by its LDT. All tasks share a common address space defined by the GDT. The system software then has direct access to task data and can treat all pointers in the same way.

Protection is required to prevent programs from improperly using code or data that belongs to the operating system. The four privilege levels of the 80286 provide the isolation needed between the various layers of the system. The 80286 privilege levels are numbered from 0 to 3, where 0 is the most trusted level, 3 the least.

Privilege level is a protection attribute assigned to all segments. It determines which procedures can access the segment. Like access rights and limit checks, privilege checks are automatically performed by the hardware, and thus protect both data and code segments.

Privilege on the 80286 is hierarchical. Operating system code and data segments placed at the most privileged level (0) cannot be accessed directly by programs at other privilege levels. Programs at privilege level 0 may access data at all other levels. Programs at privilege levels 1-3 may only access data at the same or less trusted (numerically greater) privilege levels. Figure 7-6 illustrates the privilege level protection of code or data within tasks.

In figure 7-6, programs can access data at the same or outer level, but not at inner levels. Code and data segments placed at level 1 cannot be accessed by programs executing at levels 2 or 3. Programs at privilege level 0 can access data at level 1 in the course of providing service to that level. 80286 provides mechanisms for inter-level transfer of control when needed (see section 7.5).

The four privilege levels of the 80286 are an extension of the typical two-level user/supervisor privilege mechanism. Like user mode, application programs in the outer level are not permitted direct access to data belonging to more privileged system services (supervisor mode). The 80286 adds two more privilege levels to provide protection for different layers of system software (system services, I/O drivers, etc.).

7.3.1 Example of Using Four Privilege Levels

Two extra privilege levels allow development of more reliable, and flexible system software. This is achieved by dividing the system into small, independent units. Figure 7-6 shows an example of the usage of different protection levels. Here, the most privileged level is called the kernel. This software would provide basic, application-independent, CPU-oriented services to all tasks. Such services include memory management, task isolation, multitasking, inter-task communication, and I/O resource control. Since the kernel is only concerned with simple functions and cannot be affected by software at other privilege levels, it can be kept small, safe, and understandable.

Privilege level one is designated system services. This software provides high-level functions like file access scheduling, character I/O, data communcations, and resource allocation policy which are commonly expected in all systems. Such software remains isolated from applications programs and relies on the services of the kernel, yet cannot affect the integrity of level 0.

Privilege level 2 is the custom operating system extensions level. It allows standard system software to be customized. Such customizing can be kept isolated from errors in applications programs, yet cannot affect the basic integrity of the system software. Examples of customized software are the data base manager, logical file access services, etc.

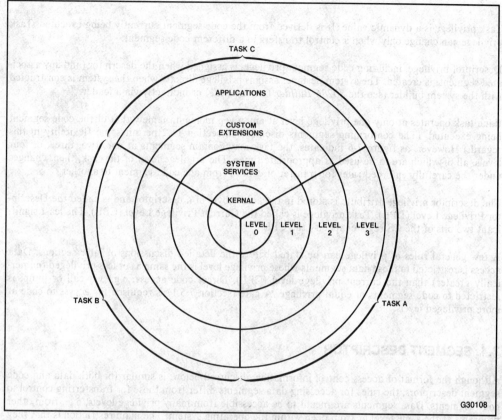

Figure 7-6. Code and Data Segments Assigned to a Privilege Level

This is just one example of protection mechanism usage. Levels 1 and 2 may be used in many different ways. The usage (or non-usage) is up to the system designer.

Programs at each privilege level are isolated from programs at outer layers, yet cannot affect programs in inner layers. Programs written for each privilege level can be smaller, easier to develop, and easier to maintain than a monolithic system where all system software can affect all other system software.

7.3.2 Privilege Usage

Privilege applies to tasks and three types of descriptors:

1. Main memory segments

2. Gates (control descriptors for state or task transitions, discussed in sections 7.5.1, 7.5.3, 8.3, 8.4 and 9.2)

3. Task state segments (discussed in Chapter 8).

Task privilege is a dynamic value. It is derived from the code segment currently being executed. Task privilege can change only when a control transfers to a different code segment.

Descriptor privilege, including code segment privilege, is assigned when the descriptor (and any associated segment) is created. The system designer assigns privilege directly when the system is constructed with the system builder (see the *80286 Builder User's Guide*) or indirectly via a loader.

Each task operates at only one privilege level at any given moment: namely that of the code segment being executed. (The conforming segments discussed in section 11.2 permit some flexibility in this regard.) However, as figure 7-6 indicates, the task may contain segments at one, two, three, or four levels, all of which are to be used at appropriate times. The privilege level of the task, then, changes under the carefully enforced rules for transfer of control from one code segment to another.

The descriptor privilege attribute is stored in the access byte of a descriptor and is called the Descriptor Privilege Level (DPL). Task privilege is called the Current Privilege Level (CPL). The least significant two bits of the CS register specify the CPL.

A few general rules of privilege can be stated before the detailed discussions of later sections. Data access is restricted to those data segments whose privilege level is the same as or less privileged (numerically greater) than the current privilege level (CPL). Direct code access, e.g., via call or jump, is restricted to code segments of equal privilege. A gate (section 7.5.1) is required for access to code at more privileged levels.

7.4 SEGMENT DESCRIPTOR

Although the format of access control information, discussed below, is similar for both data and code segment descriptors, the rules for accessing data segments differ from those for transferring control to code segments. Data segments are meant to be accessible from many privilege levels, e.g., from other programs at the same level or from deep within the operating system. The main restriction is that they cannot be accessed by less privileged code.

Code segments, on the other hand, are meant to be executed at a single privilege level. Transfers of control that cross privilege boundaries are tightly restricted, requiring the use of gates. Control transfers within a privilege level can also use gates, but they are not required. Control transfers are discussed in section 7.5.

Protection checks are automatically invoked at several points in selecting and using new segments. The process of addressing memory begins when the currently executing program attempts to load a selector into one of the segment registers. As discussed in Chapter 6, the selector has the form shown in figure 7-7.

When a new selector is loaded into a segment register, the processor accesses the associated descriptor to perform the necessary loading and privilege checks.

The protection mechanism verifies that the selector points to a valid descriptor type for the segment register (see section 7.4.1). After verifying the descriptor type, the CPU compares the privilege level of the task (CPL) to the privilege level in the descriptor (DPL) before loading the descriptor's information into the cache.

The general format of the eight bits in the segment descriptor's access rights byte is shown in table 7-1.

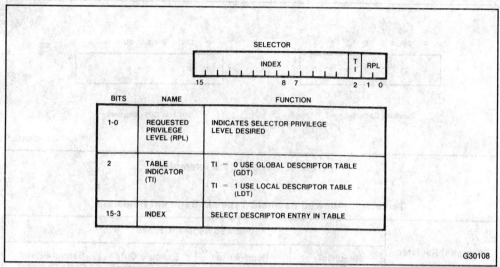

Figure 7-7. Selector Fields

Table 7-1. Segment Access Rights Byte Format

Bit	Name	Description
7	Present	1 means Present and addressable in real memory; 0 means not present. See section 11.3.
6,5	DPL	2-bit Descriptor Privilege Level, 0 to 3.
4	Segment	1 means Segment descriptor; 0 means control descriptor.
For Segment=1, the remaining bits have the following meanings:		
3	Executable	1 means code, 0 means data.
2	C or ED	If code, Conforming: 1 means yes, 0 no. If data, Expand Down: 1 yes, 0 no—normal case.
1	R or W	If code, Readable: 1 means readable, 0 not. If data, Writable: 1 means writable, 0 not.
0	Accessed	1 if segment descriptor has been Accessed, 0 if not.

NOTE: When the Segment bit (bit 4) is 0, the descriptor is for a gate, a task state segment, or a Local Descriptor Table, and the meanings of bits 0 through 3 change. Control transfers and descriptors are discussed in section 7.5.

For example, the access rights byte for a data and code segment present in real memory but not yet accessed (at the same privilege level) is shown in figure 7-8.

Whenever a segment descriptor is loaded into a segment register, the accessed bit in the descriptor table is set to 1. This bit is useful for determining the usage profile of the segment.

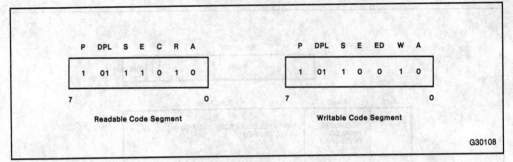

Figure 7-8. Access Byte Examples

Table 7-2. Allowed Segment Types in Segment Registers

Segment Register	Allowed Segment Types			
	Read Only Data Segment	Read-Write Data Segment	Execute Only Code Segment	Execute-Read Code Segment
DS	Yes	Yes	No	Yes
ES	Yes	Yes	No	Yes
SS	No	Yes	No	No
CS	No	No	Yes	Yes

NOTE

The Intel reserved bytes in the segment descriptor must be set to 0 for compatibility with the 80386.

7.4.1 Data Accesses

Data may be accessed in data segments or readable code segments. When DS or ES is loaded with a new selector, e.g., by an LDS, LES, or MOV to ES, SS, or DS instruction, the bits in the access byte are checked to verify legitimate descriptor type and access (see table 7-2). If any test fails, an error code is pushed onto the stack identifying the selector involved (see figure 7-5 for the error code format).

A privilege check is made when the segment register is loaded. In general, a data segment's DPL must be numerically greater than or equal to the CPL. The DPL of a descriptor loaded into the SS must equal the CPL. Conforming code segments are an exception to privilege checking rules (see section 11.2).

Once the segment descriptor and selector are loaded, the offset of subsequent accesses within the segment are checked against the limit given in the segment descriptor. Violating the segment size limit causes a General Protection exception with an error code of 0.

A normal data segment is addressed with offset values ranging from 0 to the size of the segment. When the ED bit of the access rights byte in the segment descriptor is 0, the allowed range of offsets is 0000H to the limit. If limit is 0FFFFH, the data segment contains 65,536 bytes.

Since stacks normally occupy different offset ranges (lower limit to 0FFFFH) than data segments, the limit field of a segment descriptor can be interpreted in two ways. The Expand Down (ED) bit in the access byte allows offsets for stack segments to be greater than the limit field. When ED is 1, the allowed range of offsets within the segment is limit + 1 to 0FFFFH. To allow a full stack segment, set ED to 1 and the limit to 0FFFFH. The ED bit of a data segment descriptor does not have to be set for use in SS (i.e., it will not cause an exception). Section 7.5.4 discusses stack segment usage in greater detail. An expand down (ED=1) segment can also be loaded into ES or DS.

Limit and access checks are performed before any memory reference is started. For stack push instructions (PUSH, PUSHA, ENTER, CALL, INT), a possible limit violation is identified before any internal registers are updated. Therefore, these instructions are fully restartable after a stack size violation.

7.4.2 Code Segment Access

Code segments are accessed via CS for execution. Segments that are execute-only can ONLY be executed; they cannot be accessed via DS or ES, nor read via CS with a CS override prefix. If a segment is executable (bit 3 = 1 in the access byte), access via DS or ES is possible only if it is also readable. Thus, any code segment that also contains data must be readable. (Refer to Chapter 2 for a discussion of segment override prefixes.)

An execute-only segment preserves the privacy of the code against any attempt to read it; such an attempt causes a general protection fault with an error code of 0. A code segment cannot be loaded into SS and is never writable. Any attempted write will cause a general protection fault with an error code of 0.

The limit field of a code segment descriptor identifies the last byte in the segment. Any offset greater than the limit value will cause a general protection fault. The prefetcher of the 80286 can never cause a code segment limit violation with an error code of 0. The program must actually attempt to execute an instruction beyond the end of the code segment to cause an exception.

If a readable non-conforming code segment is to be loaded into DS or ES, the privilege level requirements are the same as those stated for data segments in 7.4.1.

Code segments are subject to different privilege checks when executed. The normal privilege requirement for a jump or call to another code segment is that the current privilege level equal the descriptor privilege level of the new code segment. Jumps and calls within the current code segment automatically obey this rule.

Return instructions may pass control to code segments at the same or less (numerically greater) privileged level. Code segments at more privileged levels may only be reached via a call through a call gate as described in section 7.5.

An exception to this, previously stated, is the conforming code segment that allows the DPL of the requested code segment to be numerically less than (of greater privilege than) the CPL. Conforming code segments are discussed in section 11.2.

7.4.3 Data Access Restriction by Privilege Level

This section describes privilege verification when accessing either data segments (loading segment selectors into DS, ES, or SS) or readable code segments. Privilege verification when loading CS for transfer of control across privilege levels is described in the next section.

Three basic kinds of privilege level indicators are used when determining accessibility to a segment for reading and writing. They are termed Current Privilege Level (CPL), Descriptor Privilege Level (DPL), and Requested Privilege Level (RPL). The CPL is simply the privilege level of the code segment that is executing (except if the current code segment is conforming). The CPL is stored as bits 0 and 1 of the CS and SS registers. Bits 0 and 1 of DS and ES are not related to CPL.

DPL is the privilege level of the segment; it is stored in bits 5 and 6 of the access byte of a descriptor. For data access to data segments and non-conforming code segments, CPL must be numerically less than or equal to DPL (the task must be of equal or greater privilege) for access to be granted. Violation of this rule during segment load instruction causes a general protection exception with an error code identifying the selector.

While the enforcement of DPL protection rules provides the mechanism for the isolation of code and data at different privilege levels, it is conceivable that an erroneous pointer passed onto a more trusted program might result in the illegal modification of data with a higher privilege level. This possibility is prevented by the enforcement of effective privilege level protection rules and correct usage of the RPL value.

The RPL (requested privilege level) is used for pointer validation. It is the least significant two bits in the selector value loaded into any segment register. RPL is intended to indicate the privilege level of the originator of that selector. A selector may be passed down through several procedures at different levels. The RPL reflects the privilege level of the original supplier of the selector, not the privilege level of the intermediate supplier. The RPL must be numerically less than or equal to the DPL of the descriptor selected, thereby indicating greater or equal privilege of the supplier; otherwise, access is denied and a general protection violation occurs.

Pointer validity testing is required in any system concerned with preventing program errors from destroying system integrity. The 80286 provides hardware support for pointer validity testing. The RPL field indicates the privilege level of the originator of the pointer to the hardware. Access will be denied if the originator of the pointer did not have access to the selected segment even if the CPL is numerically less than or equal to the DPL. RPL can reduce the effective privilege of a task when using a particular selector. RPL *never* allows access to more privileged segments (CPL must always be numerically less than or equal to DPL).

A fourth term is sometimes used: the Effective Privilege Level (EPL). It is defined as the numeric maximum of the CPL and the RPL—meaning the one of lesser privilege. Access to a protected entity is granted only when the EPL is numerically less than or equal to the DPL of that entity. This is simply another way of saying that both CPL and RPL must be numerically less than or equal to DPL for access to be granted.

7.4.4 Pointer Privilege Stamping via ARPL

The ARPL instruction is provided in the 80286 to fill the RPL field of a selector with the minimum privilege (maximum numeric value) of the selector's current RPL and the caller's CPL (given in an instruction-specified register). A straight insertion of the caller's CPL would stamp the pointer with the privilege level of the caller, but not necessarily the ultimate originator of the selector (e.g., Level 3 supplies a selector to a level 2 routine that calls a level 0 routine with the same selector).

Figure 7-9 shows a program with an example of such a situation. The program at privilege level 3 calls a routine at level 2 via a gate. The routine at level 2 uses the ARPL instruction to assure that the selector's RPL is 3. When the level 2 routine calls a routine at level 0 and passes the selector, the ARPL instruction at level 0 leaves the RPL field unchanged.

```
Level 3        PUSH     SELECTOR          ; RPL value doesn't matter at level 3
               CALL     LEVEL_2

          Level_2:
               ENTER    4,0
               MOV      AX, [BP]+4        ; GET CS of return address, RPL=3
               ARPL     [BP]+6, AX        ; Put 3 in RPL field
Level 2          .
                 .
               PUSH     WORD PTR [BP]+6;  Pass selector
               CALL     Level_0

          Level_0:
               ENTER    6,0
Level 0        MOV      AX, [BP]+4        ; Get CS of return address, RPL=2
               ARPL     [BP]+6, AX        ; Leaves RPL unchanged
```

Figure 7-9. Pointer Privilege Stamping

Stamping a pointer with the originator's privilege eliminates the complex and time-consuming software typically associated with pointer validation in less comprehensive architectures. The 80286 hardware performs the pointer test automatically while loading the selector.

Privilege errors are trapped at the time the selector is loaded because pointers are commonly passed to other routines, and it may not be possible to identify a pointer's originator. To verify the access capabilities of a pointer, it should be tested when the pointer is first received from an untrusted source. The VERR (Verify Read), VERW (Verify Write), and LAR (Load Access Rights) instructions are provided for this purpose.

Although pointer validation is fully supported in the 80286, its use is an option of the system designer. To accommodate systems that do not require it, RPL can be ignored by setting selector RPLs to zero (except stack segment selectors) and not adjusting them with the ARPL instruction.

7.5 CONTROL TRANSFERS

Three kinds of control transfers can occur within a task:

1. Within a segment, causing no change of privilege level (a *short* jump, call, or return).

2. Between segments at the same privilege level (a *long* jump, call, or return).

3. Between segments at different privilege levels (a *long* call, or return). (NOTE: A JUMP to a different privilege level is not allowed.)

The first two types of control transfers need no special controls (with respect to privilege protection) beyond those discussed in section 7.4.

Inter-level transfers require special consideration to maintain system integrity. The protection hardware must check that:

• The task is currently allowed to access the destination address.

• The correct entry address is used.

To achieve control transfers, a special descriptor type called a gate is provided to mediate the change in privilege level. Control transfer instructions call the gate rather than transfer directly to a code segment. From the viewpoint of the program, a control transfer to a gate is the same as to another code segment.

Gates allow programs to use other programs at more privileged levels in the same manner as a program at the same privilege level. Programmers need never distinguish between programs or subroutines that are more privileged than the current program and those that are not. The system designer may, however, elect to use gates *only* for control transfers that cross privilege levels.

7.5.1 Gates

A gate is a four-word control descriptor used to redirect a control transfer to a different code segment in the same or more privileged level or to a different task. There are four types of gates: call, trap, interrupt, and task gates. The access rights byte distinguishes a gate from a segment descriptor, and determines which type of gate is involved. Figure 7-10 shows the format of a gate descriptor.

A key feature of a gate is the re-direction it provides. All four gate types define a new address which transfers control when invoked. This destination address normally cannot be accessed by a program. Loading the selector to a call gate into SS, DS, or ES will cause a general protection fault with an error code identifying the invalid selector.

Only the selector portion of an address is used to invoke a gate. The offset is ignored. All that a program need know about the desired function is the selector required to invoke the gate. The 80286 will automatically start the execution at the correct address stored within the gate.

A further advantage of a gate is that it provides a fixed address for any program to invoke another program. The calling program's address remains unaltered even if the entry address of the destination program changes. Thus, gates provide a fixed set of entry points that allow a task to access Operating System functions such as simple subroutines, yet the task is prohibited from simply jumping into the middle of the Operating System.

Call gates, as described in the next section, are used for control transfers within a task which must either be transparently redirected or which require an increase in privilege level. A call gate normally specifies a subroutine at a greater privilege level, and the called routine returns via a return instruction. Call gates also support delayed binding (resolution of target routine addresses at run-time rather than program-generation-time).

Trap and interrupt gates handle interrupt operations that are to be serviced within the current task. Interrupt gates cause interrupts to be disabled; trap gates do not. Trap and interrupt gates both require a return via the interrupt return instruction.

Task gates are used to control transfers between tasks and to make use of task state segments for task control and status information. Tasks are discussed in Chapter 8, interrupts in Chapter 9.

In the 80286 protection model, each privilege level has its own stack. Therefore, a control transfer (call or return) that changes the privilege level causes a new stack to be invoked.

Gate Descriptor Fields

Name	Value	Description
TYPE	4 5 6 7	Call Gate. Task Gate. Interrupt Gate. Trap Gate.
P	0 1	Descriptor Contents are not valid. Descriptor Contents are valid.
DPL	0-3	Descriptor Privilege Level.
WORD COUNT	0-31	Number of words to copy from caller's stack to called procedure's stack. Only used with call gate.
DESTINA-TION SELECTOR	16-bit selector	Selector to the target code segment (Call, Interrupt or Trap Gate). Selector to the target task state segment (Task Gate).
DESTINA-TION OFFSET	16-bit offset	Entry point within the target code segment.

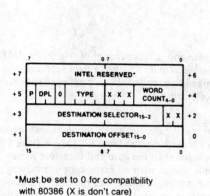

*Must be set to 0 for compatibility with 80386 (X is don't care)

G30108

Figure 7-10. Gate Descriptor Format

7.5.1.1 CALL GATES

Call gate descriptors are used by call and jump instructions in the same manner as a code segment descriptor. The hardware automatically recognizes that the destination selector refers to a gate descriptor. Then, the operation of the instruction is expanded as determined by the contents of the call gate. A jump instruction can access a call gate *only if* the target code segment is at the same privilege level. A call instruction uses a call gate for the same or more privileged access.

A call gate descriptor may reside in either the GDT or the LDT, but not in the IDT. Figure 7-10 gives the complete layout of a call gate descriptor.

A call gate can be referred to by either the long JMP or CALL instructions. From the viewpoint of the program executing a JMP or CALL instruction, the fact that the destination was reached via a call gate and not directly from the destination address of the instruction is not apparent.

The following is a description of the protection checks performed while transferring control (with the CALL instruction) through a call gate:

- Verifying that access to the call gate is allowed. One of the protection features provided by call gates is the access checks made to determine if the call gate may be used (i.e., checking if the privilege level of the calling program is adequate).

- Determining the destination address and whether a privilege transition is required. This feature makes privilege transitions transparent to the caller.

- Performing the privilege transition, if required.

Verifying access to a call gate is the same for any call gate and is independent of whether a JMP or CALL instruction was used. The rules of privilege used to determine whether a data segment may be accessed are employed to check if a call gate may be jumped-to or called. Thus, privileged subroutines can be hidden from untrusted programs by the absence of a call gate.

When an inter-segment CALL or JMP instruction selects a call gate, the gate's privilege and presence will be checked. The gate's DPL (in the access byte) is checked against the EPL (MAX (task CPL, selector RPL)). If EPL > CPL, the program is less privileged than the gate and therefore it may not make a transition. In this case, a general protection fault occurs with an error code identifying the gate. Otherwise, the gate is accessible from the program executing the call, and the control transfer is allowed to continue. After the privilege checks, the descriptor presence is checked. If the present bit of the gate access rights byte is 0 (i.e., the target code segment is not present), not present fault occurs with an error code identifying the gate.

The checks indicated in table 7-3 are applied to the contents of the call gate. Violating any of them causes the exception shown. The low order two bits of the error code are zero for these exceptions.

7.5.1.2 INTRA-LEVEL TRANSFERS VIA CALL GATE

The transfer is Intra-level if the destination code segment is at the same privilege level as CPL. Either the code segment is non-conforming with DPL = CPL, or it is conforming, with DPL ≤ CPL (see section 11.2 for this case). The 32-bit destination address in the gate is loaded into CS:IP.

Table 7-3. Call Gate Checks

Type of Check	Fault[1]	Error Code
Selector is not Null	GP	0
Selector is within Descriptor Table Limit	GP	Selector id
Descriptor is a Code Segment	GP	Code Segment id
Code Segment is Present	NP	Code Segment id
Nonconforming Code Segment DPL > CPL	GP	Code Segment id

NOTES:

[1] GP = General Protection, NP = Not-Present Exception.

The offset portion of the JMP or CALL destination address which refers to a call gate is always ignored.

If the IP value is not within the limit of the code segment, a general protection fault occurs with an error code of 0. If a CALL instruction is used, the return address is saved in the normal manner. The only effect of the call gate is to place a different address into CS:IP than that specified in the destination address of the JMP or CALL instruction. This feature is useful for systems which require that a fixed address be provided to programs, even though the entry address for the routine may change due to different functions, software changes, or segment relocation.

7.5.1.3 INTER-LEVEL CONTROL TRANSFER VIA CALL GATES

If the destination code segment of the call gate is at a different privilege level than the CPL, an inter-level transfer is being requested. However, if the destination code segment DPL > CPL, then a general protection fault occurs with an error code identifying the destination code segment.

The gate guarantees that all transitions to a more privileged level will go to a valid entry point rather than possibly into the middle of a procedure (or worse, into the middle of an instruction). See figure 7-11.

Calls to more privileged levels may be performed only through call gates. A JMP instruction can never cause a privilege change. Any attempt to use a call gate in this manner will cause a general protection fault with an error code identifying the gate. Returns to more privileged levels are also prohibited. Inter-level transitions due to interrupts use a different gate, as discussed in Chapter 9.

The RPL field of the CS selector saved as part of the return address will always identify the caller's CPL. This information is necessary to correctly return to the caller's privilege level during the return instruction. Since the CALL instruction places the CS value on the more privileged stack, and JMP instructions cannot change privilege levels, it is not possible for a program to maliciously place an invalid return address on the caller's stack.

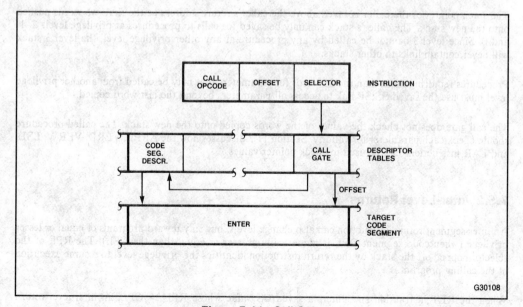

Figure 7-11. Call Gate

7.5.1.4 STACK CHANGES CAUSED BY CALL GATES

To maintain system integrity, each privilege level has a separate stack. Furthermore, each task normally uses separate stacks from other tasks for each privilege level. These stacks assure sufficient stack space to process calls from less privileged levels. Without them, trusted programs may not work correctly, especially if the calling program does not provide sufficient space on the caller's stack.

When a call gate is used to change privilege levels, a new stack is selected as determined by the new CPL. The new stack pointer value is loaded from the Task State Segment (TSS). The privilege level of the new stack data segment must equal the new CPL; if it does not, a task stack fault occurs with the saved machine state pointing at the CALL instruction and the error code identifying the invalid stack selector.

The new stack should contain enough space to hold the old SS:SP, the return address, and all parameters and local variables required to process the call. The initial stack pointers for privilege levels 0-2 in the TSS are strictly read only values. They are never changed during the course of execution.

The normal technique for passing parameters to a subroutine is to place them onto the stack. To make privilege transitions transparent to the called program, a call gate specifies that parameters are to be copied from the old stack to the new stack. The word count field in a call gate (see figure 7-10) specifies how many words (up to 31) are to be copied from the caller's stack to the new stack. If the word count is zero, no parameters are copied.

Before copying the parameters, the new stack is checked to assure that it is large enough to hold the parameters; if it is not, a stack fault occurs with an error code of 0. After the parameters are copied, the return link is on the new stack (i.e., a pointer to the old stack is placed in the new stack). In particular, the return address is pointed at by SS:SP. The call and return example of figure 7-12 illustrate the stack contents after a successful inter-level call.

The stack pointer of the caller is saved above the caller's return address as the first two words pushed onto the new stack. The caller's stack can only be saved for calls to procedures at privilege levels 2, 1, and 0. Since level 3 cannot be called by any procedure at any other privilege level, the level 3 stack will never contain links to other stacks.

Procedures requiring more than the 31 words for parameters that may be called from another privilege level must use the saved SS:SP link to access all parameters beyond the last word copied.

The call gate does not check the values of the words copied onto the new stack. The called procedure should check each parameter for validity. Section 11.3 discusses how the ARPL, VERR, VERW, LSL, and LAR instructions can be used to check pointer values.

7.5.2 Inter-Level Returns

An inter-segment return instruction can also change levels, but only toward programs of equal or lesser privilege (when code segment DPL is numerically greater or equal than the CPL). The RPL of the selector popped off the stack by the return instruction identifies the privilege level to resume execution of the calling program.

When the RET instruction encounters a saved CS value whose RPL > CPL, an inter-level return occurs. Checks shown in table 7-4 are made during such a return.

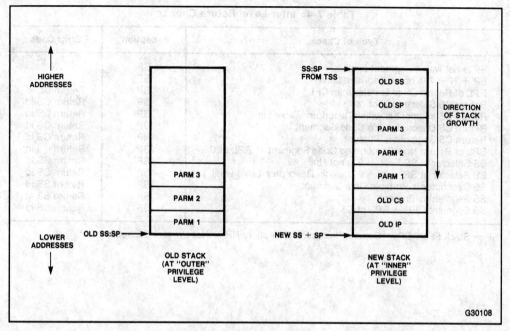

Figure 7-12. Stack Contents after an Inter-Level Call

The old SS:SP value is then adjusted by the number of bytes indicated in the RET instruction and loaded into SS:SP. The new SP value is not checked for validity. If SP is invalid it is not recognized until the first stack operation. The SS:SP value of the returning program is not saved. (Note: this value normally is the same as that saved in the TSS.)

The last step in the return is checking the contents of the DS and ES descriptor register. If DS or ES refer to segments whose DPL is greater than the new CPL (excluding conforming code segments), the segment registers are loaded with the null selector. Any subsequent memory reference that attempts to use the segment register containing the null selector will cause a general protection fault. This prevents less privileged code from accessing more privileged data previously accessed by the more privileged program.

Table 7-4. Inter-Level Return Checks

Type of Check	Exception*	Error Code
SP is not within Segment Limit	SF	0
SP + N + 7 is not in Segment Limit	SF	0
RPL of Return CS is Greater than CPL	GP	Return CS id
Return CS Selector is not null	GP	Return CS id
Return CS segment is within Descriptor Table Limit	GP	Return CS id
Return CS Descriptor is a Code Segment	GP	Return CS id
Return CS Segment is Present	NP	Return CS id
DPL of Return Non-Conforming Code Segment = RPL of CS	GP	Return CS id
SS Selector at SP + N + 6 is not Null	SF	Return SS id
SS Selector at SP + N + 6 is within Descriptor Table Limit	SF	Return SS id
SS Descriptor is Writable Data Segment	SF	Return SS id
SS Segment is Present	SF	Return SS id
SS Segment DPL = RPL of CS	SF	Return SS id

*SF = Stack Fault, GP = General Protection Exception, NP = Not-Present Exception

Tasks and State Transitions 8

CHAPTER 8
TASKS AND STATE TRANSITIONS

8.1 INTRODUCTION

An 80286 task is a single, sequential thread of execution. Each task can be isolated from all other tasks. There may be many tasks associated with an 80286 CPU, but only one task executes at any time. Switching the CPU from executing one task to executing another can occur as the result of either an interrupt or an inter-task CALL, JMP or IRET. A hardware-recognized data structure defines each task.

The 80286 provides a high performance task switch operation with complete isolation between tasks. A full task-switch operation takes only 22 microseconds at 8 MHz (18 microseconds at 10 MHz). High-performance, interrupt-driven, multi-application systems that need the benefits of protection are feasible with the 80286.

A performance advantage and system design advantage arise from the 80286 task switch:

- Faster task switch: A task switch is a single instruction performed by microcode. Such a scheme is 2-3 times faster than an explicit task switch instruction. A fast task switch translates to a significant performance boost for heavily multi-tasked systems over conventional methods.

- More reliable, flexible systems: The isolation between tasks and the high speed task switch allows interrupts to be handled by separate tasks rather than within the currently interrupted task. This isolation of interrupt handling code from normal programs prevents undesirable interactions between them. The interrupt system can become more flexible since adding an interrupt handler is as safe and easy as adding a new task.

- Every task is protected from all others via the separation of address spaces described in Chapter 7, including allocation of unique stacks to each active privilege level in each task (unless explicit sharing is planned in advance). If the address spaces of two tasks include no shared data, one task cannot affect the data of another task. Code sharing is always safe since code segments may never be written into.

8.2 TASK STATE SEGMENTS AND DESCRIPTORS

Tasks are defined by a special control segment called a Task State Segment (TSS). For each task, there must be an unique TSS. The definition of a task includes its address space and execution state. A task is invoked (made active) by inter-segment jump or call instructions whose destination address refers to a task state segment or a task gate.

The Task State Segment (TSS) has a special descriptor. The Task Register within the CPU contains a selector to that descriptor. Each TSS selector value is unique, providing an unambiguous "identifier" for each task. Thus, an operating system can use the value of the TSS selector to uniquely identify the task.

A TSS contains 22 words that define the contents of all registers and flags, the initial stacks for privilege levels 0-2, the LDT selector, and a link to the TSS of the previously executing task. Figure 8-1 shows the layout of the TSS. The TSS can not be written into like an ordinary data segment.

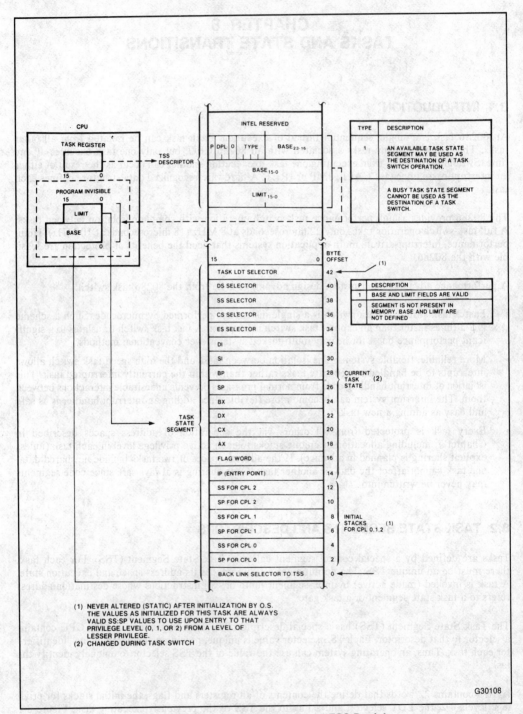

Figure 8-1. Task State Segment and TSS Registers

Each TSS consists of two parts, a static portion and a dynamic portion. The static entries are never changed by the 80286, while the dynamic entries are changed by each task switch out of this task. The static portions of this segment are the task LDT selector and the initial SS:SP stack pointer addresses for levels 0-2.

The modifiable or dynamic portion of the task state segment consists of all dynamically-variable and programmer-visible processor registers, including flags, segment registers, and the instruction pointer. It also includes the linkage word used to chain nested invocations of different tasks.

The link word provides a history of which tasks invoked others. The link word is important for restarting an interrupted task when the interrupt has been serviced. Placing the back link in the TSS protects the identity of the interrupted task from changes by the interrupt task, since the TSS is not writable by the interrupt task. (In most systems only the operating system has sufficient privilege to create or use a writable data segment "alias" descriptor for the TSS.)

The stack pointer entries in the TSS for privilege levels 0-2 are static (i.e., never written during a privilege or task switch). They define the stack to use upon entry to that privilege level. These stack entries are initialized by the operating system when the task is created. If a privilege level is never used, no stack need be allocated for it.

When entering a more privileged level, the caller's stack pointer is saved on the stack of the new privilege level, not in the TSS. Leaving the privilege level requires popping the caller's return address and stack pointer off the current stack. The stack pointer at that time will be the same as the initial value loaded from the TSS upon entry to the privilege level.

There is only one stack active at any time, the one defined by the SS and SP registers. The only other stacks that may be non-empty are those at outer (less privileged) levels that called the current level. Stacks for inner levels must be empty, since outward (to numerically larger privilege levels) calls from inner levels are not allowed.

The location of the stack pointer for an outer privilege level will always be found at the start of the stack of the inner privilege level called by that level. That stack may be the initial stack for this privilege level or an outer level. Look at the start of the stack for this privilege level. The TSS contains the starting stack address for levels 0-2. If the RPL of the saved SS selector is the privilege level required, then the stack pointer has been found. Otherwise, go to the beginning of the stack defined by that value and look at the saved SS:SP value there.

8.2.1 Task State Segment Descriptors

A special descriptor is used for task state segments. This descriptor must be accessible at all times; therefore, it can appear only in the GDT. The access byte distinguishes TSS descriptors from data or code segment descriptors. When bits 0 through 4 of the access byte are 00001 or 00011, the descriptor is for a TSS.

The complete layout of a task state segment descriptor is shown in figure 8-2.

Like a data segment, the descriptor contains a base address and limit field. The limit must be at least 002BH (43) to contain the minimum amount of information required for a TSS. An invalid task exception will occur if an attempt is made to switch to a task whose TSS descriptor limit is less than 43. The error code will identify the bad TSS.

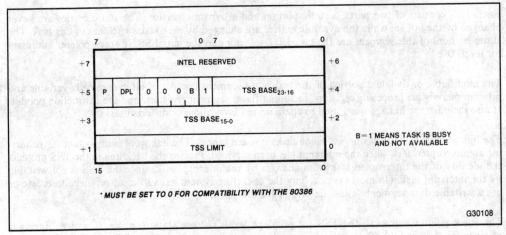

Figure 8-2. TSS Descriptor

The P-bit (Present) flag indicates whether this descriptor contains currently valid information: 1 means yes, 0 no. A task switch that attempts to reference a not-present TSS causes a not-present exception code identifying the task state segment selector.

The descriptor privilege level (DPL) controls use of the TSS by JMP or CALL instructions. By the same reasoning as that for call gates, DPL can prevent a program from calling the TSS and thereby cause a task switch. Section 8.3 discusses privilege considerations during a task switch in greater detail.

Bit 4 is always 0 since TSS is a control segment descriptor. Control segments cannot be accessed by SS, DS, or ES. Any attempt to load those segment registers with a selector that refers to a control segment causes general protection trap. This rule prevents the program from improperly changing the contents of a control segment.

TSS descriptors can have two states: idle and busy. Bit 1 of the access byte distinguishes them. The distinction is necessary since tasks are not re-entrant; a busy TSS may not be invoked.

8.3 TASK SWITCHING

A task switch may occur in one of four ways:

1. The destination selector of a long JMP or CALL instruction refers to a TSS descriptor. The offset portion of the destination address is ignored.

2. An IRET instruction is executed when the NT bit in the flag word = 1. The new task TSS selector is in the back link field of the current TSS.

3. The destination selector of a long JMP or CALL instruction refers to a task gate. The offset portion of the destination address is ignored. The new task TSS selector is in the gate. (See section 8.5 for more information on task gates.)

4. An interrupt occurs. This interrupt's vector refers to a task gate in the interrupt descriptor table. The new task TSS selector is in the gate. See section 9.4 for more information on interrupt tasks.

No new instructions are required for a task switch operation. The standard 8086 JMP, CALL, IRET, or interrupt operations perform this function. The distinction between the standard instruction and a task switch is made either by the type of descriptor referenced (for CALL, JMP, or INT) or by the NT bit (for IRET) in flag word.

Using the CALL or INT instruction to switch tasks implies a return is expected from the called task. The JMP and IRET instructions imply no return is expected from the new task.

When NT=1, the IRET instruction causes a return to the task that called the current one via CALL or INT instruction.

Access to TSS and task gate descriptors is restricted by the rules of privilege level. The data access rules are used, thereby allowing task switches to be restricted to programs of sufficient privilege. Address space separation does not apply to TSS descriptors since they must be in the GDT. The access rules for interrupts are discussed in section 9.4.

The task switch operation consists of the following eight steps:

1. Validate the requested task switch. For a task switch requested via a JMP, CALL, or an INT instruction, check that the current task is allowed to switch to the requested task. The DPL of the gate or the TSS descriptor for the requested task must be greater than or equal to both the CPL and the RPL of the requesting task. If it is not, the General Protection fault (#13) will occur with an error code identifying the descriptor (i.e , the gate selector if the task switch is requested via a task gate, or the selector for the TSS if the task switch is requested via a TSS descriptor).

    These checks are not performed if a task switch occurs due to an IRET instruction.

2. Check that the new TSS is present and that the new task is available (i.e. not Busy). A Not Present exception (#11) is signaled if the new TSS descriptor is marked 'Not Present' (P = 0). The General Protection exception (#13) is raised if the new TSS is marked 'Busy'.

    The task switch operation actually begins now and a detailed verification of the new TSS is carried out. Conditions which may disqualify the new TSS are listed in table 8-1 along with the exception raised and the error code pushed on the stack for each case. These tests are performed at different points during the course of the following remaining steps of the task switch operation.

3. Mark the new task to be BUSY by setting the 'BUSY' bit in the new TSS descriptor to 1.

4. Save the dynamic portion of the old TSS and load TR with the selector, base and limit for the new TSS. Set all CPU registers to corresponding values from the new TSS except DS, ES, CS, SS, and LDT.

5. If nesting tasks, set the Nested Task (NT) flag in the new TSS to 1. Also set the Task Switched flag (TS) of the CPU flag register to 1.

6. Validate the LDT selector and the LDT descriptor of the new TSS. Load the LDT cache (LDTR) with the LDT descriptor.

7. Validate the SS, CS, DS, and ES fields of the new TSS and load these values in their respective caches (i.e., SS, CS, DS, and ES registers).

8. Validate the IP field of the new TSS and then start executing the new task from CS:IP.

A more detailed explanation of steps 3-5 is given in Appendix B (80286 Instruction Set) under a pseudo procedure 'SWITCH_TASKS'. Notice how the exceptions described in table 8-1 may actually occur during a task switch. Similarly the exceptions that may occur during steps 1-2, and step 8 are explained in greater detail in the pseudo code description of the 286 instructions CALL, JMP, INT, and IRET in Appendix B. This information can be very helpful when debugging any protected mode code.

Note that the state of the outgoing task is always saved. If execution of that task is resumed, it will start after the instruction that caused the task switch. The values of the registers will be the same as that when the task stopped running.

Any task switch sets the Task Switched (TS) bit in the Machine Status Word (MSW). This flag is used when processor extensions such as the 80287 Numeric Processor Extension are present. The TS bit signals that the context of the processor extension may not belong to the current 80286 task. Chapter 11 discusses the TS bit and processor extensions in more detail.

Validity tests on a selector ensure that the selector is in the proper table (i.e., the LDT selector refers to GDT), lies within the bounds of the table, and refers to the proper type of descriptor (i.e., the LDT selector refers to the LDT descriptor).

Note that between steps 3 and 4 in table 8-1, all the registers of the new task are loaded. Several protection rule violations may exist in the new segment register contents. If an exception occurs in the context of the new task due to checks performed on the newly loaded descriptors, the DS and ES segments may not be accessible even though the segment registers contain non-zero values. These selector values must be saved for later reuse. When the exception handler reloads these segment registers, another protection exception may occur unless the exception handler pre-examines them and fixes any potential problems.

A task switch allows flexibility in the privilege level of the outgoing and incoming tasks. The privilege level at which execution resumes in the incoming task is not restricted by the privilege level of the outgoing task. This is reasonable, since both tasks are isolated from each other with separate address spaces and machine states. The privilege rules prevent improper access to a TSS. The only interaction between the tasks is to the extent that one started the other and the incoming task may restart the outgoing task by executing an IRET instruction.

Table 8-1. Checks Made during a Task Switch

	Test	Exception*	Error Code
1	Incoming TSS descriptor is present	NP	Incoming TSS selector
2	Incoming TSS is idle	GP	Incoming TSS selector
3	Limit of incoming TSS greater than 43	Invalid TSS	Incoming TSS selector
4	LDT selector of incoming TSS is valid	Invalid TSS	LDT selector
5	LDT of incoming TSS is present	Invalid TSS	LDT selector
6	CS selector is valid	Invalid TSS	Code segment selector
7	Code segment is present	NP	Code segment selector
8	Code segment DPL matches CS RPL	Invalid TSS	Code segment selector
9	Stack segment is valid	SF	Stack segment selector
10	Stack segment is writable data segment	GP	Stack segment selector
11	Stack segment is present	SF	Stack segment selector
12	Stack segment DPL = CPL	SF	Stack segment selector
13	DS/ES selectors are valid	GP	Segment selector
14	DS/ES segments are readable	GP	Segment selector
15	DS/ES segments are present	NP	Segment selector
16	DS/ES segment DPL ≥ CPL if not conform	GP	Segment selector

*NP = Not-Present Exception
GP = General Protection Fault
SF = Stack Fault

8.4 TASK LINKING

The TSS has a field called "back link" which contains the selector of the TSS of a task that should be restarted when the current task completes. The back link field of an interrupt-initiated task is automatically written with the TSS selector of the interrupted task.

A task switch initiated by a CALL instruction also points the back link at the outgoing task's TSS. Such task nesting is indicated to programs via the Nested Task (NT) bit in the flag word of the incoming task.

Task nesting is necessary for interrupt functions to be processed as separate tasks. The interrupt function is thereby isolated from all other tasks in the system. To restart the interrupted task, the interrupt handler executes an IRET instruction much in the same manner as an 8086 interrupt handler. The IRET instruction will then cause a task switch to the interrupted task.

Completion of a task occurs when the IRET instruction is executed with the NT bit in the flag word set. The NT bit is automatically set/reset by task switch operations as appropriate. Executing an IRET instruction with NT cleared causes the normal 8086 interrupt return function to be performed, and no task switch occurs.

Executing IRET with NT set causes a task switch to the task defined by the back link field of the current TSS. The selector value is fetched and verified as pointing to a valid, accessible TSS. The normal task switch operation described in section 8.3 then occurs. After the task switch is complete, the outgoing task is now idle and considered ready to process another interrupt.

Table 8-2 shows how the busy bit, NT bit, and link word of the incoming and outgoing task are affected by task switch operations caused by JMP, CALL, or IRETinstructions.

Violation of any of the busy bit requirements shown in table 8-2 causes a general protection fault with the saved machine state appearing as if the instruction had not executed. The error code identifies the selector of the TSS with the busy bit.

A bus lock is applied during the testing and setting of the TSS descriptor busy bit to ensure that two processors do not invoke the same task at the same time. See also section 11.4 for other multi-processor considerations.

Table 8-2. Effect of a Task Switch on BUSY and NT Bits and the Link Word

Affected Field	JMP Instruction Effect	CALL/INT Instruction Effect	IRET Instruction Effect
Busy bit of incoming task TSS descriptor	Set, must be 0 before	Set, must be 0 before	Unchanged, must be set
Busy bit of outgoing task TSS descriptor	Cleared	Unchanged (will already be 1)	Cleared
NT bit in incoming task flag word	Cleared	Set	Unchanged
NT bit in outgoing task flag word	Unchanged	Unchanged	Cleared
Back link in incoming task TSS	Unchanged	Set to outgoing task TSS selector	Unchanged
Back link of outgoing task TSS	Unchanged	Unchanged	Unchanged

The linking order of tasks may need to be changed to restart an interrupted task before the task that interrupted it completes. To remove a task from the list, trusted operating system software must change the backlink field in the TSS of the interrupting task first, then clear the busy bit in the TSS descriptor of the task removed from the list.

When trusted software deletes the link from one task to another, it should place a value in the backlink field, which will pass control to that trusted software when the task attempts to resume execution of another task via IRET.

8.5 TASK GATES

A task may be invoked by several different events. Task gates are provided to support this need. Task gates are used in the same way as call and interrupt gates. The ultimate effect of jumping to or calling a task gate is the same as jumping to or calling directly to the TSS in the task gate.

Figure 8-3 depicts the layout of a task gate.

A task gate is identified by the access byte field in bits 0 through 4 being 00101. The gate provides an extra level of indirection between the destination address and the TSS selector value. The offset portion of the JMP or CALL destination address is ignored.

Gate use provides flexibility in controlling access to tasks. Task gates can appear in the GDT, IDT, or LDT. The TSS descriptors for all tasks must be kept in the GDT. They are normally placed at level 0 to prevent any task from improperly invoking another task. Task gates placed in the LDT allow private access to selected tasks with full privilege control.

The data segment access rules apply to accessing a task gate via JMP, CALL, or INT instructions. The effective privilege level (EPL) of the destination selector must be numerically less than or equal to the DPL of the task gate descriptor. Any violation of this requirement causes a general protection fault with an error code identifying the task gate involved.

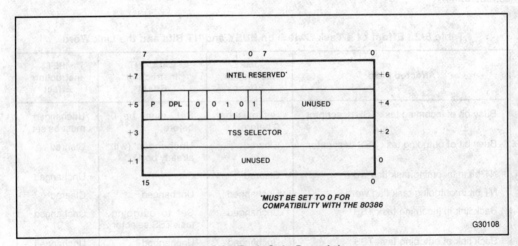

Figure 8-3. Task Gate Descriptor

Once access to the task gate has been verified, the TSS selector from the gate is read. The RPL of the TSS selector is ignored. From this point, all the checks and actions performed for a JMP or CALL to a TSS after access has been verified are performed (see section 8.4). Figure 8-4 illustrates an example of a task switch through a task gate.

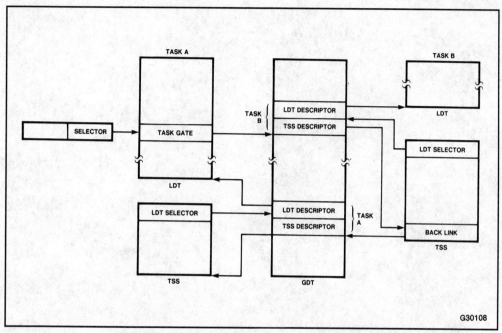

Figure 8-4. Task Switch Through a Task Gate

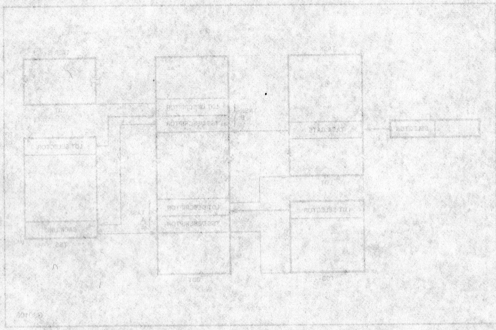

Interrupts and Exceptions

9

CHAPTER 9
INTERRUPTS AND EXCEPTIONS

Interrupts and exceptions are special cases of control transfer within a program. An interrupt occurs as a result of an event that is independent of the currently executing program, while exceptions are a direct result of the program currently being executed. Interrupts may be external or internal. External interrupts are generated by either the INTR or NMI input pins. Internal interrupts are caused by the INT instruction. Exceptions occur when an instruction cannot be completed normally. Although their causes differ, interrupts and exceptions use the same control transfer techniques and privilege rules; therefore, in the following discussions the term interrupt will also apply to exceptions.

The program used to service an interrupt may execute in the context of the task that caused the interrupt (i.e., used the same TSS, LDT, stacks, etc.) or may be a separate task. The choice depends on the function to be performed and the level of isolation required.

9.1 INTERRUPT DESCRIPTOR TABLE

Many different events may cause an interrupt. To allow the reason for an interrupt to be easily identified, each interrupt source is given a number called the interrupt vector. Up to 256 different interrupt vectors (numbers) are possible. See figure 9-1.

A table is used to define the handler for each interrupt vector. The Interrupt Descriptor Table (IDT) defines the interrupt handlers for up to 256 different interrupts. The IDT is in physical memory, pointed to by the contents of the on-chip IDT register that contains a 24-bit base and a 16-bit limit. The IDTR is normally loaded with the LIDT instruction by code that executes at privilege level 0 during system initialization. The IDT may be located anywhere in the physical address space of the 80286.

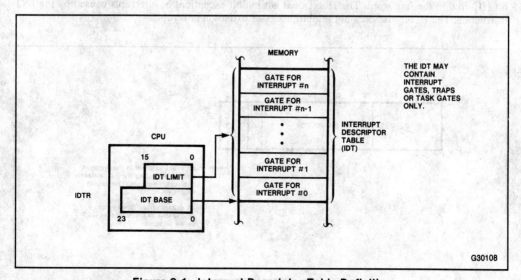

Figure 9-1. Interrupt Descriptor Table Definition

Each IDT entry is a 4-word gate descriptor that contains a pointer to the handler. The three types of gates permitted in the IDT are interrupt gates, trap gates (discussed in section 9.3), and task gates (discussed in section 9.5). Interrupt and task gates process interrupts in the same task, while task gates cause a task switch. Any other descriptor type in the IDT will cause an exception if it is referenced by an interrupt.

The IDT need not contain all 256 entries. A 16-bit limit register allows less than the full number of entries. Unused entries may be signaled by placing a zero in the access rights byte. If an attempt is made to access an entry outside the table limit, or if the wrong descriptor type is found, a general protection fault occurs with an error code pushed on the stack identifying the invalid interrupt vector (see figure 9-2).

Exception error codes that refer to an IDT entry can be identified by bit 1 of the error code that will be set. Bit 0 of the error code is 1 if the interrupt was caused by an event external to the program (i.e., an external interrupt, a single step, a processor extension error, or a processor extension not present).

Interrupts 0-31 are reserved for use by Intel. Some of the interrupts are used for instruction exceptions. The IDT limit must be at least 255 $(32 \times 8 - 1)$ to accommodate the minimum number of interrupts. The remaining 224 interrupts are available to the user.

9.2 HARDWARE INITIATED INTERRUPTS

Hardware-initiated interrupts are caused by some external event that activates either the INTR or NMI input pins of the processor. Events that use the INTR input are classified as maskable interrupts. Events that use the NMI input are classified as non-maskable interrupts.

All 224 user-defined interrupt sources share the INTR input, but each has the ability to use a separate interrupt handler. An 8-bit vector supplied by the interrupt controller identifies which interrupt is being signaled. To read the interrupt id, the processor performs the interrupt acknowledge bus sequence.

Maskable interrupts (from the INTR input) can be inhibited by software by setting the interrupt flag bit (IF) to 0 in the flag word. The IF bit does not inhibit exceptions or interrupts caused by the INT instruction. The IF bit also does not inhibit processor extension interrupts.

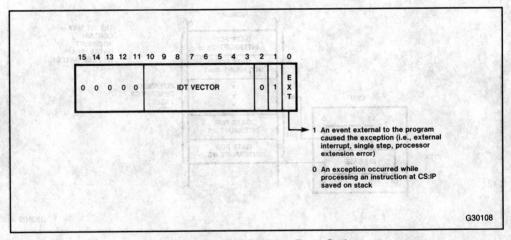

Figure 9-2. IDT Selector Error Code

The type of gate placed into the IDT for the interrupt vector will control whether other maskable interrupts remain enabled or not during the servicing of that interrupt. The flag word that was saved on the stack reflects the maskable interrupt enable status of the processor prior to the interrupt. The procedure servicing a maskable interrupt can also prevent further maskable interrupts during its work by resetting the IF flag.

Non-maskable interrupts are caused by the NMI input. They have a higher priority than the maskable interrupts (meaning that in case of simultaneous requests, the non-maskable interrupt will be serviced first). A non-maskable interrupt has a fixed vector (#2) and therefore does not require an interrupt acknowledge sequence on the bus. A typical use of an NMI is to invoke a procedure to handle a power failure or some other critical hardware exception.

A procedure servicing an NMI will not be further interrupted by other non-maskable interrupt requests until an IRET instruction is executed. A further NMI request is remembered by the hardware and will be serviced after the first IRET instruction. Only one NMI request can be remembered. To prevent a maskable interrupt from interrupting the NMI interrupt handler, the IF flag should be cleared either by using an interrupt gate in the IDT or by setting IF = 0 in the flag word of the task involved.

9.3 SOFTWARE INITIATED INTERRUPTS

Software initiated interrupts occur explicitly as interrupt instructions or may arise as the result of an exceptional condition that prevents the continuation of program execution. Software interrupts are not maskable. Two interrupt instructions exist which explicitly cause an interrupt: INT n and INT 3. The first allows specification of any interrupt vector; the second implies interrupt vector 3 (Breakpoint).

Other instructions like INTO, BOUND, DIV, and IDIV may cause an interrupt, depending on the overflow flag or values of the operands. These instructions have predefined vectors associated with them in the first 32 interrupts reserved by Intel.

A whole class of interrupts called exceptions are intended to detect faults or programming errors (in the use of operands or privilege levels). Exceptions cannot be masked. They also have fixed vectors within the first 32 interrupts. Many of these exceptions pass an error code on the stack, which is not the case with the other interrupt types discussed in section 9.2. Section 9.5 discusses these error codes as well as the priority among interrupts that can occur simultaneously.

9.4 INTERRUPT GATES AND TRAP GATES

Interrupt gates and trap gates are special types of descriptors that may only appear in the interrupt descriptor table. The difference between a trap and an interrupt gate is whether the interrupt enable flag is to be cleared or not. An interrupt gate specifies a procedure that enters with interrupts disabled (i.e., with the interrupt enable flag cleared); entry via a trap gate leaves the interrupt enable status unchanged. The NT flag is always cleared (after the old NT state is saved on the stack) when an interrupt uses these gates. Interrupts that have either gate in the associated IDT entry will be processed in the current task.

Interrupts and trap gates have the same structure as the call gates discussed in section 7.5.1. The selector and entry point for a code segment to handle the interrupt or exception is contained in the gate. See figure 9-3.

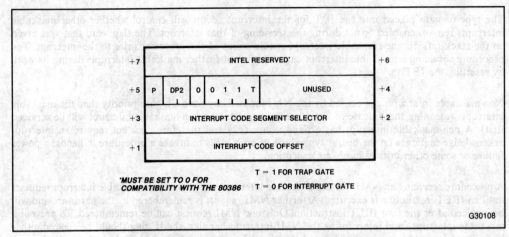

Figure 9-3. Trap/Interrupt Gate Descriptors

The access byte contains the Present bit, the descriptor privilege level, and the type identifier. Bits 0-4 of the access byte have a value of 00110 for interrupt gates, 00111 for trap gates. Byte 5 of the descriptor is not used by either of these gates; it is used only by the call gate, which uses it as the parameter word-count.

Trap and interrupt gates allow a privilege level transition to occur when passing control to a non-conforming code segment. Like a call gate, the DPL of the target code segment selected determines the new CPL. The DPL of the new non-conforming code segment must be numerically less than or equal to CPL.

No privilege transition occurs if the new code segment is conforming. If the DPL of the conforming code segment is greater than the CPL, a general protection exception will occur.

As with all descriptors, these gates in the IDT carry a privilege level. The DPL controls access to interrupts with the INT n and INT 3 instructions. For access, the CPL of the program must be less than or equal to the gate DPL. If the CPL is not, a general protection exception will result with an error code identifying the selected IDT gate. For exceptions and external interrupts, the CPL of the program is ignored while accessing the IDT.

Interrupts using a trap or an interrupt gate are handled in the same manner as an 8086 interrupt. The flags and return address of the interrupted program are saved on the stack of the interrupt handler. To return to the interrupted program, the interrupt handler executes an IRET instruction.

If an increase in privilege is required for handling the interrupt, a new stack will be loaded from the TSS. The stack pointer of the old privilege level will also be saved on the new stack in the same manner as a call gate. Figure 9-4 shows the stack contents after an exception with an error code (with and without a privilege level change).

If an *interrupt* or *trap* gate is used to handle an exception that passes an error code, the error code will be pushed onto the new stack after the return address (as shown in figure 9-4). If a *task* gate is used, the error code is pushed onto the stack of the new task. The return address is saved in the old TSS.

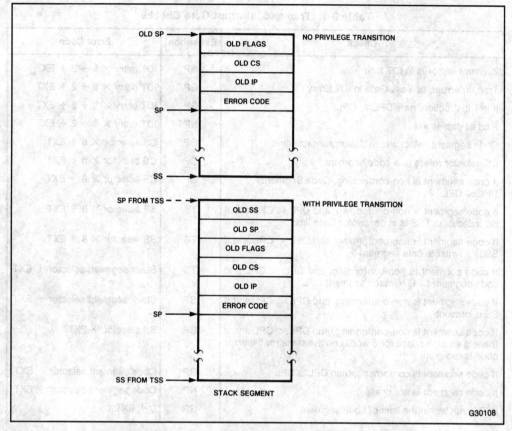

Figure 9-4. Stack Layout after an Exception with an Error Code

If an interrupt gate is used to handle an interrupt, it is assumed that the selected code segment has sufficient privilege to re-enable interrupts. The IRET instruction will not re-enable interrupts if CPL is numerically greater than IOPL.

Table 9-1 shows the checks performed during an interrupt operation that uses an interrupt or trap gate. EXT equals 1 when an event external to the program is involved; 0 otherwise. External events are maskable or non-maskable interrupts, single step interrupt, processor extension segment overrun interrupt, numeric processor not-present exception or numeric processor error. The EXT bit signals that the interrupt or exception is not related to the instruction at CS:IP. Each error code has bit 1 set to indicate an IDT entry is involved.

When the interrupt has been serviced, the service routine returns control via an IRET instruction to the routine that was interrupted. If an error code was passed, the exception handler must remove the error code from the stack before executing IRET.

The NT flag is cleared when an interrupt occurs which uses an interrupt or trap gate. Executing IRET with NT=0 causes the normal interrupt return function. Executing IRET with NT=1 causes a task switch (see section 8.4 for more details).

Table 9-1. Trap and Interrupt Gate Checks

Check	Exception*	Error Code
Interrupt vector is in IDT limit	GP	IDT entry × 8 + 2 + EXT
Trap, Interrupt, or Task Gate in IDT Entry	GP	IDT entry × 8 + 2 + EXT
If INT instruction, gate DPL ≥ CPL	GP	IDT entry × 8 + 2 + EXT
P bit of gate is set	NP	IDT entry × 8 + 2 + EXT
Code segment selector is in descriptor table limit	GP	CS selector × 8 + EXT
CS selector refers to a code segment	GP	CS selector × 8 + EXT
If code segment is non-conforming, Code Segment DPL ≤ CPL	GP	CS selector × 8 + EXT
If code segment is non-conforming, and DPL < CPL and if SS selector in TSS is in descriptor table limit	TS	SS selector × 8 + EXT
If code segment is non-conforming, and DPL < CPL and if SS is a writable data segment	TS	SS selector × 8 + EXT
If code segment is non-conforming, and DPL < CPL and code segment DPL = stack segment DPL	TS	Stack segment selector + EXT
If code segment is non-conforming, and DPL < CPL and if SS is present	SF	Stack segment selector + EXT
If code segment is non-conforming, and DPL < CPL and if there is enough space for 5 words on the stack (or 6 if error code is required)	SF	SS selector + EXT
If code segment is conforming, then DPL ≤ CPL	GP	Code segment selector + EXT
If code segment is not present	NP	Code segment selector + EXT
If IP is not within the limit of code segment	GP	0 + EXT

* GP = General Protection Exception
NP = Not Present Exception
SF = Stack Fault

Like the RET instruction, IRET is restricted to return to a level of equal or lesser privilege unless a task switch occurs. The IRET instruction works like the inter-segment RET instruction except that the flag word is popped and no stack pointer update for parameters is performed since no parameters are on the stack. See section 7.5.2 for information on inter-level returns.

To distinguish an inter-level IRET, the new CPL (which is the RPL of the return address CS selector) is compared with the current CPL. If they are the same, the IP and flags are popped and execution continues.

An inter-level return via IRET has all the same checks as shown in table 7-4. The only difference is the extra word on the stack for the old flag word.

Interrupt gates are typically associated with high-priority hardware interrupts for automatically disabling interrupts upon their invocation. Trap gates are typically software-invoked since they do not disable the maskable hardware interrupts. However, low-priority interrupts (e.g., a timer) are often invoked via a trap gate to allow other devices of higher priority to interrupt the handler of that lower priority interrupt.

Table 9-2 illustrates how the interrupt enable flag and interrupt type interact with the type of gate used.

9.5 TASK GATES AND INTERRUPT TASKS

The 80286 allows interrupts to directly cause a task switch. When an interrupt vector selects an entry in the IDT which is a task gate, a task switch occurs. The format of a task gate is described in section 8.5. If a task gate is used to handle an exception that passes an error code, the error code will be pushed onto the new task's stack.

A task gate offers two advantages over interrupt gates:

1. It automatically saves all of the processor registers as part of the task-switch operation, whereas an interrupt gate saves only the flag register and CS:IP.
2. The new task is completely isolated from the task that was interrupted. Address spaces are isolated and the interrupt-handling task is unaffected by the privilege level of the interrupted task.

An interrupt task switch works like any other task switch once the TSS selector is fetched from the task gate. Like a trap or an interrupt gate, privilege and presence rules are applied to accessing a task gate during an interrupt.

Interrupts that cause a task switch set the NT bit in the flags of the new task. The TSS selector of the interrupted task is saved in the back link field of the new TSS. The interrupting task executes IRET to perform a task switch to return to the interrupted task because NT was previously set. The interrupt task state is saved in its TSS before returning control to the task that was interrupted; NT is restored to its original value in the interrupted task.

Since the interrupt handler state after executing IRET is saved, a re-entry of the interrupt service task will result in the execution of the instruction that follows IRET. Therefore, when the next interrupt occurs, the machine state will be the same as that when the IRET instruction was executed.

Note that an interrupt task *resumes* execution each time it is re-invoked, whereas an interrupt procedure starts executing at the beginning of the procedure each time. The interrupted task restarts execution at the point of interruption because interrupts occur before the execution of an instruction.

Table 9-2. Interrupt and Gate Interactions

Type of Interrupt	Type of Gate	Further NMIs?	Further INTRs?	Further Exceptions?	Further software Interrupts?
NMI	Trap	No	Yes	Yes	Yes
NMI	Interrupt	No	No	Yes	Yes
INTR	Trap	Yes	Yes	Yes	Yes
INTR	Interrupt	Yes	No	Yes	Yes
Software	Trap	Yes	Yes	Yes	Yes
Software	Interrupt	Yes	No	Yes	Yes
Exception	Trap	Yes	Yes	Yes	Yes
Exception	Interrupt	Yes	No	Yes	Yes

When an interrupt task is used, the task must be concerned with avoiding further interrupts while it is operating. A general protection exception will occur if a task gate referring to a busy TSS is used while processing an interrupt. If subsequent interrupts can occur while the task is executing, the IF bit in the flag word (saved in the TSS) must be zero.

9.5.1 Scheduling Considerations

A software-scheduled operating system must be designed to handle the fact that interrupts can come along in the middle of scheduled tasks and cause a task switch to other tasks. The interrupt-scheduled tasks may call the operating system and eventually the scheduler, which needs to recognize that the task that just called it is not the one the operating system last scheduled.

If the Task Register (TR) does not contain the TSS selector of the last scheduled task, an interrupt initiated task switch has occurred. More than one task may have been interrupt-scheduled since the scheduler last ran. The scheduler must find via the backlink fields in each TSS all tasks that have been interrupted. The scheduler can clear those links and reset the busy bit in the TSS descriptors, putting them back in the scheduling queue for a new analysis of execution priorities. Unless the interrupted tasks are placed back in the scheduling queue, they would have to await a later restart via the task that interrupted them.

To locate tasks that have been interrupt-scheduled, the scheduler looks into the current task's TSS backlink (word one of the TSS), which points at the interrupted task. If that task was not the last task scheduled, then it's backlink field in the TSS also points to an interrupted task.

The backlink field of each interrupt-scheduled task should be set by the scheduler to point to a scheduling task that will reschedule the highest priority task when the interrupt-scheduled task executes IRET.

9.5.2 Deciding Between Task, Trap, and Interrupt Gates

Interrupts and exceptions can be handled with either a trap/interrupt gate or a task gate. The advantages of a task gate are all the registers are saved and a new set is loaded with full isolation between the interrupted task and the interrupt handler. The advantages of a trap/interrupt gate are faster response to an interrupt for simple operations and easy access to pointers in the context of the interrupted task. All interrupt handlers use IRET to resume the interrupted program.

Trap/interrupt gates require that the interrupt handler be able to execute at the same or greater privilege level than the interrupted program. If any program executing at level 0 can be interrupted through a trap/task gate, the interrupt handler must also execute at level 0 to avoid general protection exception. All code, data, and stack segment descriptors must be in the GDT to allow access from any task. But, placing all system interrupt handlers at privilege level 0 may be in consistent with maintaining the integrity of level 0 programs.

Some exceptions require the use of a task gate. The invalid task state segment exception (#10) can arise from errors in the original TSS as well as in the target TSS. Handling the exception within the same task could lead to recursive interrupts or other undesirable effects that are difficult to trace. The double fault exception (#8) should also use a task gate to prevent shutdown from another protection violation occurring during the servicing of the exception.

9.6 PROTECTION EXCEPTIONS AND RESERVED VECTORS

A protection violation will cause an exception, i.e., a non-maskable interrupt. Such a fault can be handled by the task that caused it if an interrupt or trap gate is used, or by a different task if a task gate is used (in the IDT).

Protection exceptions can be classified into program errors or implicit requests for service. The latter include stack overflow and not-present faults. Examples of program errors include attempting to write into a read-only segment, or violating segment limits.

Requests for service may use different interrupt vectors, but many diverse types of protection violation use the same general protection fault vector. Table 9-3 shows the reserved exceptions and interrupts. Interrupts 0-31 are reserved by Intel.

When simultaneous external interrupt requests occur, they are processed in the fixed order shown in table 9-4. For each interrupt serviced, the machine state is saved. The new CS:IP is loaded from the gate or TSS. If other interrupts remain enabled, they are processed before the first instruction of the current interrupt handler, i.e., the last interrupt processed is serviced first.

Table 9-3. Reserved Exceptions and Interrupts

Vector Number	Description	Restartable	Error Code on Stack
0	Divide Error Exception	Yes	No
1	Single Step Interrupt	Yes	No
2	NMI Interrupt	Yes	No
3	Breakpoint Interrupt	Yes	No
4	INTO Detected Overflow Exception	Yes	No
5	BOUND Range Exceeded Exception	Yes	No
6	Invalid Opcode Exception	Yes	No
7	Processor Extension Not Available Exception	Yes	No
8	Double Exception Detected	No	Yes (Always 0)
9	Processor Extension Segment Overrun Interrupt	No	No
10	Invalid Task State Segment	Yes	Yes
11	Segment Not Present	Yes	Yes
12	Stack Segment Overrun or Not Present	Yes	Yes
13	General Protection	Yes*	Yes

* Except for writes into read-only segments (see section 9.6)

Table 9-4. Interrupt Processing Order

Order	Interrupt
1	Instruction exception
2	Single step
3	NMI
4	Processor extension segment overrun
5	INTR

All but two exceptions are restartable after the exceptional condition is removed. The two non-restartable exceptions are the processor extension segment overrun and writing into read only segments with XCHG, ADC, SBB, RCL, and RCR instructions. The return address normally points to the failing instruction, including all leading prefixes.

The instruction and data addresses for the processor extension segment overrun are contained in the processor extension status registers.

Interrupt handlers for most exceptions receive an error code that identifies the selector involved, or a 0 in bits 15-3 of the error code field if there is no selector involved. The error code is pushed last, after the return address, on the stack that will be active when the trap handler begins execution. This ensures that the handler will not have to access another stack segment to find the error code.

The following sections describe the exceptions in greater detail.

9.6.1 Invalid OP-Code (Interrupt 6)

When an invalid opcode is detected by the execution unit, interrupt 6 is invoked. (It is not detected until an attempt is made to execute it, i.e., prefetching an invalid opcode does not cause this exception.) The saved CS:IP will point to the invalid opcode or any leading prefixes; no error code is pushed on the stack. The exception can be handled within the same task, and is restartable.

This exception will occur for all cases of an invalid operand. Examples include an inter-segment jump referencing a register operand, or an LES instruction with a register source operand.

9.6.2 Double Fault (Interrupt 8)

If two separate faults occur during a single instruction, end if the first fault is any of #0, #10, #11, #12, and #13, exception 8 (Double Fault) occurs (e.g., a general protection fault in level 3 is followed by a not-present fault due to a segment not-present). If another protection violation occurs during the processing of exception 8, the 80286 enters shutdown, during which time no further instructions or exceptions are processed.

Either NMI or RESET can force the CPU out of shutdown. An NMI input can bring the CPU out of shutdown if no errors occur while processing the NMI interrupt; otherwise, shutdown can only be exited via the RESET input. NMI causes the CPU to remain in protected mode, and RESET causes it to exit protected mode. Shutdown is signaled externally via a HALT bus operation with A1 LOW.

A task gate must be used for the double fault handler to assure a proper task state to respond to the exception. The back link field in the current TSS will identify the TSS of the task causing the exception. The saved address will point at the instruction that was being executed (or was ready to execute) when the error was detected. The error code will be null.

The "double fault" exception does not occur when detecting a new exception while trying to invoke handlers for the following exceptions: 1,2,3,4,5,6,7,9, and 16.

9.6.3 Processor Extension Segment Overrun (Interrupt 9)

Interrupt 9 signals that the processor extension (such as the 80287 numerics processor) has overrun the limit of a segment while attempting to read/write the second or subsequent words of an operand.

The interrupt is generated by the processor extension data channel within the 80286 during the limit test performed on each transfer of data between memory and the processor extension. This interrupt can be handled in the same task but is not restartable.

As with all external interrupts, Interrupt 9 is an asynchronous demand caused by the processor extension referencing something outside a segment boundary. Since Interrupt 9 can occur any time after the processor extension is started, the 80286 does not save any information that identifies what particular operation had been initiated in the processor extension. The processor extension maintains special registers that identify the last instruction it executed and the address of the desired operand.

After this interrupt occurs, no WAIT or escape instruction, except FNINIT, can be executed until the interrupt condition is cleared or the processor extension is reset. The interrupt signals that the processor extension is requesting an invalid data transfer. The processor extension will always be busy when waiting on data. Deadlock results if the CPU executes an instruction that causes it to wait for the processor extension before resetting the processor extension. Deadlock means the CPU is waiting for the processor extension to become idle while the processor extension waits for the CPU to service its data request.

The FNINIT instruction is guaranteed to reset the processor extension without causing deadlock. After the interrupt is cleared, this restriction is lifted. It is then possible to read the instruction and operand address via FSTENV or FSAVE, causing the segment overrun in the processor extension's special registers.

The task interrupted by interrupt 9 is not necessarily the task that executed the ESC instruction that caused the interrupt. The operating system should keep track of which task last used the NPX (see section 11.4). If the interrupted task did not execute the ESC instruction, it can be restarted. The task that executed the ESC instruction cannot.

9.6.4 Invalid Task State Segment (Interrupt 10)

Interrupt 10 is invoked if during a task switch the new TSS pointed to by the task gate is invalid. The EXT bit indicates whether the exception was caused by an event outside the control of the program.

A TSS is considered invalid in the cases shown in table 9-5.

Once the existence of the new TSS is verified, the task switch is considered complete, with the backlink set to the old task if necessary. All errors are handled in the context of the new task.

Exception 10 must be handled through a task gate to insure a proper TSS to process it. The handler must reset the busy bit in the new TSS.

9.6.5 Not Present (Interrupt 11)

Exception 11 occurs when an attempt is made to load a not-present segment or to use a control descriptor that is marked not-present. (If, however, the missing segment is an LDT that is needed in a task switch, exception 10 occurs.) This exception is fully restartable.

Any segment load instruction can cause this exception. Interrupt 11 is always processed in the context of the task in which it occurs.

Table 9-5. Conditions That Invalidate the TSS

Reason	Error Code
The limit in the TSS descriptor is less than 43	TSS id + EXT
Invalid LDT selector or LDT not present	LDT id + EXT
Stack segment selector is null	SS id + EXT
Stack segment selector is outside table limit	SS id + EXT
Stack segment is not a writable segment	SS id + EXT
Stack segment DPL does not match new CPL	SS id + EXT
Stack segment selector RPL ≠ CPL	SS id + EXT
Code segment selector is outside table limit	CS id + EXT
Code segment selector does not refer to code segment	CS id + EXT
Non-conforming code segment DPL ≠ CPL	CS id + EXT
Conforming code segment DPL > CPL	CS id + EXT
DS or ES segment selector is outside table limits	ES/DS id + EXT
DS or ES are not readable segments	ES/DS id + EXT

The error code has the form shown in Table 9-5. The EXT bit will be set if an event external to the program caused an interrupt that subsequently referenced a not-present segment. Bit 1 will be set if the error code refers to an IDT entry, e.g., an INT instruction referencing a not-present gate. The upper 14 bits are the upper 14 bits of the segment selector involved.

During a task switch, when a not-present exception occurs, the ES and DS segment registers may not be usable for referencing memory (the selector values are loaded before the descriptors are checked). The not-present handler should not rely on being able to use the values found in ES, SS, and DS without causing another exception. This is because the task switch itself may have changed the values in the registers. The exception occurs in the new task and the return pointer points to the first instruction of the new task. **Caution**: the loading of the DS or ES descriptors may not have been completed. The exception II handler should ensure that the DS and ES descriptors have been properly loaded before the execution of the first instruction of the new task.

9.6.6 Stack Fault (Interrupt 12)

Stack underflow or overflow causes exception 12, as does a not-present stack segment referenced during an inter-task or inter-level transition. This exception is fully restartable. A limit violation of the current stack results in an error code of 0. The EXT bit of the error code tells whether an interrupt external to the program caused the exception.

Any instruction that loads a selector to SS (e.g., POP SS, task switch) can cause this exception. This exception must use a task gate if there is a possibility that any level 0 stack may not be present.

When a stack fault occurs, the ES and DS segment registers may not be usable for referencing memory. During a task switch, the selector values are loaded before the descriptors are checked. The stack fault handler should check the saved values of SS, CS, DS, and ES to be sure that they refer to present segments before restoring them.

9.6.7 General Protection Fault (Interrupt 13)

If a protection violation occurs which is not covered in the preceding paragraphs, it is classed as Interrupt 13, a general protection fault. The error code is zero for limit violations, write to read-only segment violations, and accesses relative to DS or ES when they are zero or refer to a segment at a greater privilege level than CPL. Other access violations (e.g., a wrong descriptor type) push a non-zero error code that identifies the selector used on the stack. Error codes with bit 0 cleared and bits 15-2non-zero indicate a restartable condition.

Bit 1 of the error code identifies whether the selector is in the IDT or LDT/GDT. If bit 1=0 then bit 2 separates LDT from GDT. Bit 0 (EXT) indicates whether the exception was caused by the program or an event external to it (i.e., single stepping, an external interrupt, a processor extension not-present or a segment overrun). If bit 0 is set, the selector typically has nothing to do with the instruction that was interrupted. The selector refers instead to some step of servicing an interrupt that failed.

When bit 0 of the error code is set, the interrupted program can be restarted, except for processor extension segment overrun exceptions (see section 9.6.3). The exception with the bit 0 of the error code =1 indicates some interrupt has been lost due to a fault in the descriptor pointed to by the error code.

A non-zero error code with bit 0 cleared may be an operand of the interrupted instruction, an operand from a gate referenced by the instruction, or a field from the invalid TSS.

During a task switch, when a general protection exception occurs, the ES and DS segment registers may not be usable for referencing memory (the selector vaues are loaded before the descriptors are checked). The general protection handler should not rely on being able to use the values found in ES, SS, and DS without causing another exception. This is because the task switch itself may have changed the values in the registers. The exception occurs in the new task and the return pointer points to the first instruction of the new task. **Caution**: the loading of the DS or ES descriptors may not have been completed. The exception 13 handler should ensure that the DS and ES descriptors have been properly loaded before the execution of the first instruction of the new task.

In Real Address Mode, Interrupt 13 will occur if software attempts to read or write a 16-bit word at segment offset 0FFFFH.

9.7 ADDITIONAL EXCEPTIONS AND INTERRUPTS

Interrupts 0, 5, and 1 have not yet been discussed. Interrupt 0 is the divide-error exception, Interrupt 5 the bound-range exceeded exceptions, and Interrupt 1 the single step interrupt. The divide-error or bound-range exceptions make it appear as if that instruction had never executed: the registers are restored and the instruction can be restarted. The divide-error exception occurs during a DIV or an IDIV instruction when the quotient will be too large to be representable, or when the divisor is zero.

Interrupt 5 occurs when a value exceeds the limit set for it. A program can use the BOUND instruction to check a signed array index against signed limits defined in a two-word block of memory. The block can be located just before the array to simplify addressing. The block's first word specifies the array's lower limit, the second word specifies the array's upper limit, and a register specifies the array index to be tested.

9.7.1 Single Step Interrupt (Interrupt 1)

Interrupt 1 allows programs to execute one instruction at a time. This single-stepping is controlled by the TF bit in the flag word. Once this bit is set, an internal single step interrupt will occur after the next instruction has been executed. The interrupt saves the flags and return address on the stack, clears the TF bit, and uses an internally supplied vector of 1 to transfer control to the service routine via the IDT.

The IRET instruction or a task switch must be used to set the TF bit and to transfer control to the next instruction to be single stepped. If TF=1 in a TSS and that task is invoked, it will execute the first instruction and then be interrupted.

The single-step flag is normally not cleared by privilege changes inside a task. INT instructions, however, do clear TF. Therefore, software debuggers that single-step code must recognize and emulate INT n or INT 0 rather than executing them directly. System software should check the current execution privilege level after any single step interrupt to see whether single stepping should continue.

The interrupt priorities in hardware guarantee that if an external interrupt occurs, single stepping stops. When both an external interrupt and a single step interrupt occur together, the single step interrupt is processed first. This clears the TF bit. After saving the return address or switching tasks, the external interrupt input is examined before the first instruction of the single step handler executes. If the external interrupt is still pending, it is then serviced. The external interrupt handler is not single-stepped. Therefore, to single step an interrupt handler, just single step an interrupt instruction that refers to the interrupt handler.

System Control and Initialization

10

CHAPTER 10
SYSTEM CONTROL AND INITIALIZATION

Special flags, registers, and instructions provide contol of the critical processes and interaction in 80286 operations. The flag register includes 3 bits that represent the current I/O privilege level (IOPL: 2 bits) and the nested task bit (NT). Four additional registers support the virtual addressing and memory protection features, one points to the current Task State Segment and the other three point to the memory-based descriptor tables: GDT, LDT, and IDT. These flags and registers are discussed in the next section. The machine status word, (which indicates processor configuration and status) and the instructions that load and store it are discussed in section 10.2.2.

Similar instructions pertaining to the other registers are the subject of sections 10.2 and 10.3. A detailed description of initialization states and processes, which appears in section 10.4, is supplemented by the extensive example in Appendix A. Instructions that validate descriptors and pointers are covered in section 11.3.

10.1 SYSTEM FLAGS AND REGISTERS

The IOPL flag (bits 12 and 13 of the flags word) controls access to I/O operations and interrupt control instructions. These two bits represent the maximum privilege level (highest numerical CPL) at which the task is permitted to perform I/O instructions. Alteration of the IOPL flags is restricted to programs at level 0 or to a task switch.

IRET uses the NT flag to select the proper return: if NT=0, the normal return within a task is performed. As discussed in Chapter 8, the nested task flag (bit 14 of flags) is set when a task initiates a task switch via a CALL or INT instruction. The old and new task state segments are marked busy and the backlink field of the new TSS is set to the old TSS selector. An interrupt that does not cause a task switch will clear NT after the old NT state is saved. To prevent a program from causing an illegal task switch by setting NT and then executing IRET, a zero selector should be placed in the backlink field of the TSS. An illegal task switch using IRET will then cause exception 13. The instructions POPF and IRET can also set or clear NT when flags are restored from the stack. POPF and IRET can also change the interrupt enable flag. If CPL ≤ IOPL, then the Interrupt Flag (IF) can be changed by POPF and IRET. Otherwise, the state of the IF bit in the new flag word is ignored by these instructions. Note that the CLI and STI instructions are valid only when CPL ≤ IOPL; otherwise exception 13 occurs.

10.1.1 Descriptor Table Registers

The three descriptor tables used for all memory accesses are based at addresses supplied by (stored in) three registers: the global descriptor table register (GDTR), the interrupt descriptor table register (IDTR), and the local descriptor table register (LDTR). Each register contains a 24-bit base field and a 16-bit limit field. The base field gives the real memory address of the beginning of the table; the limit field tells the maximum offset permitted in accessing table entries. See figures 10-1 thru 10-3.

The LDTR also contains a selector field that identifies the descriptor for that table. LDT descriptors must reside in the GDT.

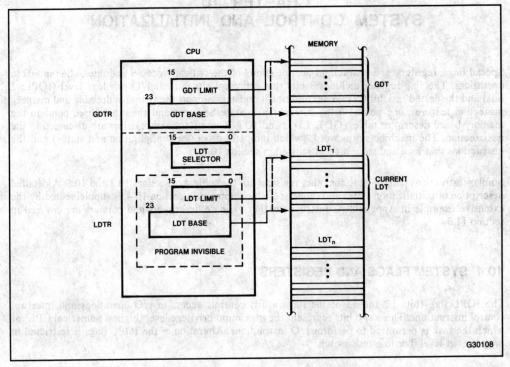

Figure 10-1. Local and Global Descriptor Table Definition

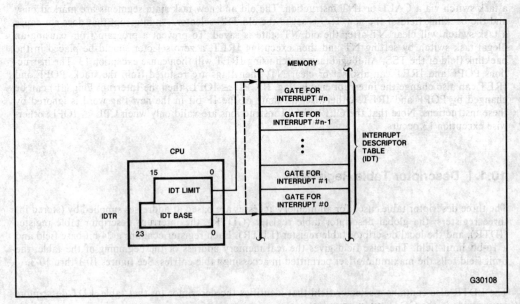

Figure 10-2. Interrupt Descriptor Table Definition

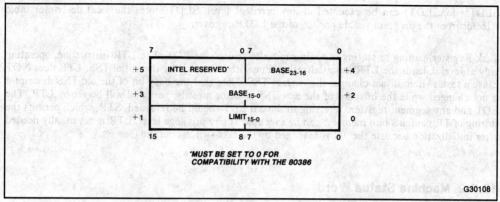

Figure 10-3. Data Type for Global Descriptor Table and Interrupt Descriptor Table

The task register (TR) points to the task state segment for the currently active task. It is similar to a segment register, with selector, base, and limit fields, of which only the selector field is readable under normal circumstances. Each such selector serves as a unique identifier for its task. The uses of the TR are described in Chapter 8.

The instructions controlling these special registers are described in the next section.

10.2 SYSTEM CONTROL INSTRUCTIONS

The instructions that load the GDTR and IDTR from memory can only be executed in real address mode or at privilege level 0; otherwise exception 13 occurs. The store instructions for GDTR and IDTR may be executed at any privilege level. The four instructions are LIDT, LGDT, SIDT, and SGDT. The instructions move 3 words between the indicated descriptor table register and the effective real memory address supplied (see figure 10-3). The format of the 3 words is: a 2-byte limit, a 3-byte real base address, followed by an unused byte. These instructions are normally used during system initialization.

The LLDT instruction loads the LDT registers from a descriptor in the GDT. LLDT uses a selector operand to that descriptor rather than referencing the descriptor directly. LLDT is only executable at privilege level 0; otherwise exception 13 occurs. LLDT is normally required only during system initial- ization because the processor automatically exchanges the LDTR contents as part of the task-switch operation.

Executing an LLDT instruction does not automatically update the TSS or the register caches. To properly change the LDT of the currently running task so that the change holds across task switches, you must perform, in order, the following three steps:

1. Store the new LDT selector into the appropriate word of TSS.

2. Load the new LDT selector into LDTR.

3. Reload the DS and ES registers if they refer to LDT-based descriptors.

Note that the current code segment and stack segment descriptors should reside in the GDT or be copied to the same location in the new LDT.

SLDT (store LDT) can be executed at any privilege level. SLDT stores the local descriptor table selector from the program visible portion of the LDTR register.

Task Register loading or storing is again similar to that of the LDT. The LTR instruction, operating only at level 0, loads the LTR at initialization time with a selector for the initial TSS. LTR does NOT cause a task switch; it just changes the current TSS. Note that the busy bit of the old TSS descriptor is not changed while the busy bit of the new TSS selector must be zero and will be set by LTR. The LDT and any segment registers referring to the old LDT should be reloaded. STR, which permits the storing of TR contents into memory, can be executed at any privilege level. LTR is not usually needed after initialization because the TR is managed by the task-switch operation.

10.2.2 Machine Status Word

The Machine Status Word (MSW) indicates the 80286 configuration and status. It is not part of a task's state. The MSW word is loaded by the LMSW instruction executed in real address mode or at privilege level 0 only, or is stored by the SMSW instruction executing at any privilege level. MSW is a 16-bit register, the lower four bits of which are used by the 80286. These bits have the meanings shown in table 10-1. Bits 15-4 of the MSW will be used by the 80386. 80286 software should not change these bits. If the bits are changed by the 286 software, compatibility with the 80386 will be destroyed.

The TS flag is set under hardware control and reset under software control. Once the TS flag is set, the next instruction using a processor extension causes a processor extension not-present exception (#7). This feature allows software to test whether the current processor extension state belongs to the current task as discussed in section 11.4. If the current processor extension state belongs to a different task, the software can save the state of any processor extension with the state of the task that uses it. Thus, the TS bit protects a task from processor extension errors that result from the actions of a previous task.

The CLTS instruction is used to reset the TS flag after the exception handler has set up the proper processor extension state. The CLTS instruction can be executed at privilege level 0 only.

Table 10-1. MSW Bit Functions

Bit Position	Name	Function
0	PE	Protected mode enable places the 80286 into protected mode and cannot be cleared except by RESET.
1	MP	Monitor processor extension allows WAIT instructions to cause a processor extension not-present exception (number 7) if TS is also set.
2	EM	Emulate processor extension causes a processor extension not-present exception (number 7) on ESC instructions to allow a processor extension to be emulated.
3	TS	Task switched indicates the next instruction using a processor extension will cause exception 7, allowing software to test whether the current processor extension context belongs to the current task.

The EM flag indicates a processor extension function is to be emulated by software. If EM=1 and MP=0, all ESCAPE instructions will be trapped via the processor extension not-present exception (#7).

MP flag tells whether a processor extension is present. If MP=1 and TS=1, escape and wait instructions will cause exception 7.

If ESC instructions are to be used, either the MP or the EM bit must be set, but not both.

The PE flag indicates that the 80286 is in the protected virtual address mode. Once the PE flag is set, it can be cleared only by a reset, which then puts the system in real address mode emulating the 8086.

Table 10-2 shows the recommended usage of the MSW. Other encodings of these bits are not recommended.

10.2.3 Other Instructions

Instructions that verify or adjust access rights, segment limits, or privilege levels can be used to avoid exceptions or faults that are correctable. Section 10.3 describes such instructions.

10.3 PRIVILEGED AND TRUSTED INSTRUCTIONS

Instructions that execute only at CPL=0 are called "privileged." An attempt to execute the privileged instructions at any other privilege level causes a general protection exception (#13) with an error code of zero. The privileged instructions manipulate descriptor tables or system registers. Incorrect use of these instructions can produce unrecoverable conditions. Some of these instructions (LGDT, LLDT, and LTR) are discussed in section 10.2.

Table 10-2. Recommended MSW Encodings for Processor Extension Control

TS	MP	EM	Recommended Use	Instructions Causing Exception 7
0	0	0	Initial encoding after RESET. 80286 operation is identical to 8086, 8088. Use this encoding only if no ESC instructions are to be executed.	None
0	0	1	No processor extension is available. Software will emulate its function. Wait instructions do not cause exception 7.	ESC
1	0	1	No processor extension is available. Software will emulate its function. The current processor extension context may belong to another task.	ESC
0	1	0	A processor extension exists.	WAIT (if TS=1)
1	1	0	A processor extension exists. The current processor extension context may belong to another task. The exception 7 on WAIT allows software to test for an error pending from a previous processor extension operation.	ESC or WAIT (if TS=1)

Other *privileged* instructions are:

- LIDT—Load interrupt descriptor table register
- LMSW—Load machine status word
- CLTS—Clear task switch flag
- HALT—Halt processor execution
- POPF (POP flags) or IRET can change the IF value only if the user is operating at a trusted privilege level. POPF does not change IOPL except at Level 0.

"Trusted" instructions are restricted to execution at a privilege level of CPL ≥ IOPL. For each task, the operating system defines a privilege level below which these instructions cannot be used. Most of these instructions deal with input/output or interrupt management. The IOPL field in the flag word that holds the privilege level limit can be changed only when CPL=0. The trusted instructions are:

- Input/Output—Block I/O, Input, and Output: IN, INW, OUT, OUTW, INSB, INSW, OUTSB, OUTSW
- Interrupts—Enable Interrupts, Disable Interrupts: STI, CLI
- Other—Lock Prefix

10.4 INITIALIZATION

Whenever the 80286 is initialized or reset, certain registers are set to predefined values. All additional desired initialization must be performed by user software. (See Appendix A for an example of a 286 initialization routine.) RESET forces the 80286 to terminate all execution and local bus activity; no instruction or bus action will occur as long as RESET is active. Execution in real address mode begins after RESET becomes inactive and an internal processing interval (3-4 clocks) occurs. The initial state at reset is:

```
FLAGS = 0002H
MSW  = FFF0H
IP   = FFF0H
CS Selector = F000H    CS.base = FF0000H   CS.limit = FFFFH
DS Selector = 0000H    DS.base = 000000H   DS.limit = FFFFH
ES Selector = 0000H    ES.base = 000000H   ES.limit = FFFFH
IDT base = 000000H     IDT.limit = 03FFH
```

Two fixed areas of memory are reserved: the system initialization area and the interrupt table area. The system initialization area begins at FFFFF0H (through FFFFFFH) and the interrupt table area begins at 000000H (through 0003FFH). The interrupt table area is not reserved.

At this point, segment registers are valid and protection bits are set to 0. The 80286 begins operation in real address mode, with PE=0. Maskable interrupts are disabled, and no processor extension is assumed or emulated (EM=MP=0).

DS, ES, and SS are initialized at reset to allow access to the first 64K of memory (exactly as in the 8086). The CS:IP combination specifies a starting address of FFFF0H. For real address mode, the four most significant bits are not used, providing the same FFF0H address as the 8086 reset location. Use of (or upgrade to) the protected mode can be supported by a bootstrap loader at the high end of the address space. As mentioned in Chapter 5, location FFFF0H ordinarily contains a JMP instruction whose target is the actual beginning of a system initialization or restart program.

After RESET, CS points to the top 64K bytes in the 16-Mbyte physical address space. Reloading CS register by a control transfer to a different code segment in real address mode will put zeros in the upper 4 bits. Since the initial IP is FFF0H, all of the upper 64K bytes of address space may be used for initialization.

Sections 10.4.1 and 10.4.2 describe the steps needed to initialize the 80286 in the real address mode and the protected mode, respectively.

10.4.1 Real Address Mode

1. Allocate a stack.

2. Load programs and data into memory from secondary storage.

3. Initialize external devices and the Interrupt Vector Table.

4. Set registers and MSW bits to desired values.

5. Set FLAG bits to desired values—including the IF bit to enable interrupts—after insuring that a valid interrupt handler exists for each possible interrupt.

6. Execute (usually via an inter-segment JMP to the main system program).

10.4.2 Protected Mode

The full 80286 virtual address mode initialization procedure requires additional steps to operate correctly:

1. Load programs and associated descriptor tables.

2. Load valid GDT and IDT descriptor tables, setting the GDTR and IDTR to their correct value.

3. Set the PE bit to enter protected mode.

4. Execute an intra-segment JMP to clear the processor queues.

5. Load or construct a valid task state segment for the initial task to be executed in protected mode.

6. Load the LDTR selector from the task's GDT or 0000H (null) if an LDT is not needed.

7. Set the stack pointer (SS, SP) to a valid location in a valid stack segment.

8. Mark all items not in memory as not-present.

9. Set FLAGS and MSW bits to correct values for the desired system configuation.

10. Initialize external devices.

11. Ensure that a valid interrupt handler exists for each possible interrupt.

12. Enable interrupts.

13. Execute.

The example in Appendix A shows the steps necessary to load all the required tables and registers that permit execution of the first task of a protected mode system. The program in Appendix A assumes that Intel development tools have been used to construct a prototype GDT, IDT, LDT, TSS, and all the data segments necessary to start up that first task. Typically, these items are stored on EPROM; on most systems it is necessary to copy them all into RAM to get going. Otherwise, the 80286 will attempt to write into the EPROM to set the accessed or busy bits.

The example in Appendix A also illustrates the ability to allocate unused entries in descriptor tables to grow the tables dynamically during execution. Using suitable naming conventions, the builder can allocate alias data segments that are larger than the prototype EPROM version. The code in the example will zero out the extra entries to permit later dynamic usage.

Advanced Topics

11

CHAPTER 11
ADVANCED TOPICS

This chapter describes some of the advanced topics as virtual memory management, restartable instructions, special segment attributes, and the validation of descriptors and pointers.

11.1 VIRTUAL MEMORY MANAGEMENT

When access to a segment is requested and the access byte in its descriptor indicates the segment is not present in real memory, the not-present fault occurs (exception 11, or 12 for stacks). The handler for this fault can be set up to bring the absent segment into real memory (swapping or overwriting another segment if necessary), or to terminate execution of the requesting program if this is not possible.

The accessed bit (bit 0) of the access byte is provided in both executable and data segment descriptors to support segment usage profiling. Whenever the descriptor is accessed by the 80286 hardware, the A-bit will be set in memory. This applies to selector test instructions (described below) as well as to the loading of a segment register. The reading of the access byte and the restoration of it with the A-bit set is an indivisible operation, i.e., it is performed as a read-modify-write with bus lock. If an operating system develops a profile of segment usage over time, it can recognize segments of low or zero access and choose among these candidates for replacement.

When a not-present segment is brought into real memory, the task that requested access to it can continue its execution because all instructions that load a segment register are restartable.

Not-present exceptions occur only on segment register load operations, gate accesses, and task switches. The saved instruction pointer refers to the first byte of the violating instruction. All other aspects of the saved machine state are exactly as they were before execution of the violating instruction began. After the fault handler clears up the fault condition and performs an IRET, the program continues to execute. The only external indication of a segment swap is the additional execution time.

11.2 SPECIAL SEGMENT ATTRIBUTES

11.2.1 Conforming Code Segments

Code segments intended for use at potentially different privilege levels need an attribute that permits them to emulate the privilege level of the calling task. Such segments are termed "conforming" segments. Conforming segments are also useful for interrupt-driven error routines that need only be as privileged as the routine that caused the error.

A conforming code segment has bit 2 of its access byte set to 1. This means it can be referenced by a CALL or JMP instruction in a task of equal or lesser privilege, i.e., CPL of the task is numerically greater than or equal to DPL of this segment. CPL does not change when executing the conforming code segment. A conforming segment continues to use the stack from the CPL. This is the only case in which the DPL of a code segment can be numerically less than the CPL. If bit 2 is a 0, the segment is not conforming and can be referenced only by a task of CPL=DPL.

Inter-segment Returns that refer to conforming code segments use the RPL field of the code selector of the return address to determine the new CPL. The RPL becomes the new CPL if the conforming code segment DPL≤RPL.

If a conforming segment is readable, it can be read from any privilege level without restriction. This is the only exception to the protection rules. This allows constants to be stored with conforming code. For example, a read-only look-up table can be embedded in a conforming code segment that can be used to convert system-wide logical ID's into character strings that represent those logical entities.

11.2.2 Expand-Down Data Segments

If bit 2 in the access byte of a data segment is 1, the segment is an expand-down segment. All the offsets that reference such a segment must be strictly greater than the segment limit, as opposed to normal data segments (bit 2=0) where all offsets must be less than or equal to the segment limit. Figure 11-1 shows an expand-down segment.

The size of the expand down segment can be changed by changing either the base or the limit. An expand down segment with Limit=0 will have a size of $2^{16}-1$ bytes. With a limit value of FFFFH, the expand down segment will have a size of 0 bytes. In an expand down segment, the base + offset value should always be greater than the base + limit value. Therefore, a full size segment (2^{16} bytes) can only be obtained by using an expand up segment.

The operating system should check the Expand-Down bit when a protection fault indicates that the limit of a data segment has been reached. If the Expand-Down bit is not set, the operating system should increase the segment limit; if it is set, the limit should be lowered. This supplies more room in either case (assuming the segment is not write-protected, i.e., that bit 1 is not 0). In some cases, if the operating system can ascertain that there is not enough room to expand the data segment to meet the need that caused the fault, it can move the data segment to a region of memory where there is enough room. See figure 11-2.

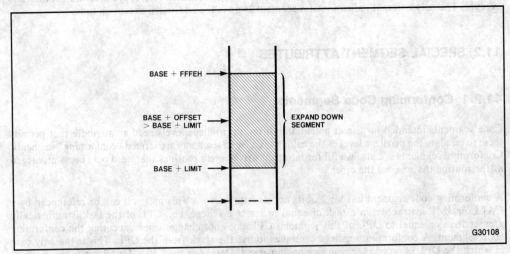

Figure 11-1. Expand-Down Segment

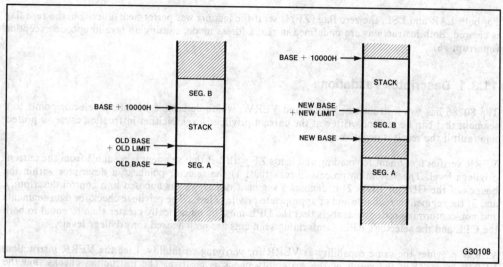

Figure 11-2. Dynamic Segment Relocation and Expansion of Segment Limit

11.3 POINTER VALIDATION

Pointer validation is an important part of locating programming errors. Pointer validation is necessary for maintaining isolation between the privilege levels. Pointer validation consists of the following steps:

1. Check if the supplier of the pointer is entitled to access the segment.
2. Check if the segment type is appropriate to its intended use.
3. Check if the pointer violates the segment limit.

The 80286 hardware automatically performs checks 2 and 3 during instruction execution, while software must assist in performing the first check. This point is discussed in section 11.3.2. Software can explicitly perform steps 2 and 3 to check for potential violations (rather than causing an exception). The unprivileged instructions LSL, LAR, VERR, and VERW are provided for this purpose.

The load access rights (LAR) instruction obtains the access rights byte of a descriptor pointed to by the selector used in the instruction. If that selector is visible at the CPL, the instruction loads the access byte into the specified destination register as the higher byte (the low byte is zero) and the zero flag is set. Once loaded, the access bits can be tested. System segments such as a task state segment or a descriptor table cannot be read or modified. This instruction is used to verify that a pointer refers to a segment of the proper privilege level and type. If the RPL or CPL is greater than DPL, or the selector is outside the table limit, no access value is returned and the zero flag is cleared. Conforming code segments may be accessed from any RPL or CPL.

Additional parameter checking can be performed via the load segment limit (LSL) instruction. If the descriptor denoted by the given selector (in memory or a register) is visible at the CPL, LSL loads the specified register with a word that consists of the limit field of that descriptor. This can only be done for segments, task state segments, and local descriptor tables (i.e., words from control descriptors are inaccessible). Interpreting the limit is a function of the segment type. For example, downward expandable data segments treat the limit differently than code segments do.

For both LAR and LSL, the zero flag (ZF) is set if the loading was performed; otherwise, the zero flag is cleared. Both instructions are undefined in real address mode, causing an invalid opcode exception (interrupt #6).

11.3.1 Descriptor Validation

The 80286 has two instructions, VERR and VERW, which determine whether a selector points to a segment that can be read or written at the current privilege level. Neither instruction causes a protection fault if the result is negative.

VERR verifies a segment for reading and loads ZF with 1 if that segment is readable from the current privilege level. The validation process checks that: 1) the selector points to a descriptor within the bounds of the GDT or LDT, 2) it denotes a segment descriptor (as opposed to a control descriptor), and 3) the segment is readable and of appropriate privilege level. The privilege check for data segments and non-conforming code segments is that the DPL must be numerically greater than or equal to both the CPL and the selector's RPL. Conforming segments are not checked for privilege level.

VERW provides the same capability as VERR for verifying writability. Like the VERR instruction, VERW loads ZF if the result of the writability check is positive. The instruction checks that the descriptor is within bounds, is a segment descriptor, is writable, and that its DPL is numerically greater than or equal to both the CPL and the selector's RPL. Code segments are never writable, conforming or not.

11.3.2 Pointer Integrity: RPL and the "Trojan Horse Problem"

The Requested Privilege Level (RPL) feature can prevent inappropriate use of pointers that could corrupt the operation of more privileged code or data from a less privileged level.

A common example is a file system procedure, FREAD (file_id, nybytes, buffer-ptr). This hypothetical procedure reads data from a file into a buffer, overwriting whatever is there. Normally, FREAD would be available at the user level, supplying only pointers to the file system procedures and data located and operating at a privileged level. Normally, such a procedure prevents user-level procedures from directly changing the file tables. However, in the absence of a standard protocol for checking pointer validity, a user-level procedure could supply a pointer into the file tables in place of its buffer pointer, causing the FREAD procedure to corrupt them unwittingly.

By using the RPL, you can avoid such problems. The RPL field allows a privilege attribute to be assigned to a selector. This privilege attribute would normally indicate the privilege level of the code which generated the selector. The 80286 hardware will automatically check the RPL of any selector loaded into a segment register or a control register to see if the RPL allows access.

To guard against invalid pointers, the called procedure need only ensure that all selectors passed to it have an RPL at least as high (numerically) as the original caller's CPL. This indicates that the selectors were not more trusted than their supplier. If one of the selectors is used to access a segment that the caller would not be able to access directly, i.e., the RPL is numerically greater than the DPL, then a protection fault will result when loaded into a segment or control register.

The caller's CPL is available in the CS selector that was pushed on the stack as the return address. A special instruction, ARPL, can be used to appropriately adjust the RPL field of the pointer. ARPL (Adjust RPL field of selector instruction) adjusts the RPL field of a selector to become the larger of its original value and the value of the RPL field in a specified register. The latter is normally loaded from the caller's CS register which can be found on the stack. If the adjustment changes the selector's RPL, ZF is set; otherwise, the zero flag is cleared.

11.4 NPX CONTEXT SWITCHING

The context of a processor extension (such as the 80287 numerics processor) is not changed by the task switch operation. A processor extension context need only be changed when a different task attempts to use the processor extension (which still contains the context of a previous task). The 80286 detects the first use of a processor extension after a task switch by causing the processor extension not-present exception (#7) if the TS bit is set. The interrupt handler may then decide whether a context change is necessary.

The 286 services numeric errors only when it executes wait or escape instructions because the processor extension is running independently. Therefore, the numerics error from one task may not be recorded until the 286 is running a different task. If the 286 task has changed, it makes sense to defer handling that error until the original task is restored. For example, interrupt handlers that use the NPX should not have their timing upset by a numeric error interrupt that pertains to some earlier process. It is of little value to service someone else's error.

If the task switch bit is set (bit 3 of MSW) when the CPU begins to execute a wait or escape instruction, the processor-extension not-present exception results (#7). The handler for this interrupt must know who currently "owns" the NPX, i.e., the handler must know the last task to issue a command to the NPX. If the owner is the same as the current task, then it was merely interrupted and the interrupt handler has since returned; the handler for interrupt 7 simply clears the TS bit, restores the working registers, and returns (restoring interrupts if enabled).

If the recorded owner is different from the current task, the handler must first save the existing NPX context in the save area of the old task. It can then re-establish the correct NPX context from the current task's save area.

The code example in figure 11-3 relies on the convention that each TSS entry in the GDT is followed by an alias entry for a data segment that points to the same physical region of memory that contains the TSS. The alias segment also contains an area for saving the NPX context, the kernel stack, and certain kernel data. That is, the first 44 bytes in that segment are the 286 context, followed by 94 bytes for the processor extension context, followed in some cases by the kernel stack and kernel private data areas.

The implied convention is that the stack segment selector points to this data segment alias so that whenever there is an interrupt at level zero and SS is automatically loaded, all of the above information is immediately addressable.

It is assumed that the program example knows about only one data segment that points to a global data area in which it can find the one word NPX owner to begin the processing described. The specific operations needed, and shown in the figure, are listed in table 11-1.

11.5 MULTIPROCESSOR CONSIDERATIONS

As mentioned in Chapter 8, a bus lock is applied during the testing and setting of the task busy bit to ensure that two processors do not invoke the same task at the same time. However, protection traps and conflicting use of dynamically varying segments or descriptors must be addressed by an inter-processor synchronization protocol. The protocol can use the indivisible semaphore operation of the base instruction set. Coordination of interrupt and trap vectoring must also be addressed when multiple concurrent processors are operating.

The interrupt bus cycles are locked so no interleaving occurs on those cycles. Descriptor caching is locked so that a descriptor reference cannot be altered while it is being fetched.

```
ASSEMBLER INVOKED BY:  ASM286,86 :F5:SWNPX.A86

LOC  OBJ                LINE    SOURCE
                          1 +1   $title('Switch the NPX Context on First Use After a Task Switch')
                          2
                          3              name     switch_npx_context
                          4
                          5              public   switch_NPX_context
                          6              extrn    last_npx_task:word
                          7      ;
                          8      ;         This interrupt handler will switch the NPX context if a new task
                          9      ;      is attempting to use the NPX context of another task after a task
                         10      ;      switch.  If the NPX context belongs to the current task, nothing happens.
                         11      ;
                         12      ;      A trap gate should be placed in IDT entry 7 referring to this routine.
                         13      ;      The DPL of the gate should be 0 to prevent spoofing.  The code segment
                         14      ;      must be at privilege level 0.
                         15      ;
                         16      ;      The kernel stack is assumed to overlay the TSS and the NPX save area
                         17      ;      is placed at the end of the TSS area.
                         18      ;
                         19      ;      A global word variable LAST_NPX_TASK identifies the TSS selector of
                         20      ;      the last task to use the NPX.
                         21      ;
  002C                   22      npx_save_area              equ      word ptr 44     ; Offset of NPX save area in TSS
                         23 +1   $eject
  ....                   24      kernel_code                segment er public
                         25
  0000                   26      switch_npx_context    proc    far wc(0)
                         27
  0000 50                28              push    ax                                  ; Save working registers
  0001 1E                29              push    ds
  0002 B8----        E   30              mov     ax,seg last_npx_task                ; Get address of id of last NPX task
  0005 8ED8             31              mov     ds,ax
  0007 0F00C8           32              str     ax                                  ; Get id of this task
  000A 24FC             33              and     al,not 3                            ; Remove RPL field
  000C 0F06             34              clts                                        ; Clear task switched flag
  000E FA               35              cli                                         ; No interrupts allowed!
                         36      ;
                         37      ;      Last_npx_word cannot change due to other interrupts after this point.
                         38      ;
  000F 3B060000      E   39              cmp     ax,ds:last_npx_task                 ; See if same task
  0013 7412             40              je      same_task
                         41
  0015 87060000      E   42              xchg    ax,ds:last_npx_task                 ; Set new task id and get old one
  0019 050800           43              add     ax,8                                ; Go to TSS alias
  001C 8ED8             44              mov     ds,ax                               ; Address TSS of previous NPX task
  001E DD362C00         45              fsave   ds:npx_save_area                    ; Save old NPX state
  0022 36DD262C00       46              frstor  ss:npx_save_area                    ; Get current NPX state
  0027                   47      same_task:
  0027 1F               48              pop     ds                                  ; Return to interrupted program
  0028 58               49              pop     ax
  0029 CF               50              iret
                         51
                         52      switch_npx_context         endp
                         53
  ....                   54      kernel_code                ends
*** WARNING #160, LINE #54, SEGMENT CONTAINS PRIVILEGED INSTRUCTIONS
                         55              end
```

Figure 11-3. Example of NPX Context Switching

When a program changes a descriptor that is shared with other processors, it should broadcast this fact to the other processors. This broadcasting can be done with an inter-processor interrupt. The handler for this interrupt must ensure that the segment registers, the LDTR and the TR, are re-loaded. This happens automatically if the interrupt is serviced by a task switch.

Modification of descriptors of shared segments in multi-processor systems may require that the on-chip descriptors also be updated. For example, one processor may attempt to mark the descriptor of a shared segment as not-present while another is using it. Software has to ensure that the descriptors in the segment register caches are updated with the new information. The segment register caches can be

Table 11-1. NPX Context Switching

Step	Operation	Lines (Figure 11-3)
1.	Save the working registers	28, 29
2.	Set up address for kernel work area	30, 31
3.	Get current task ID from Task Register	32
4.	Clear Task Switch flag to allow NPX work	34
5.	Inhibit interrupts	35
6.	Compare owner with current task ID	37
If same owner:		
7a.	Restore working registers	48, 49
7b.	and return	50
If owner is not current task:		
8a.	Use owner ID to save old context in its TSS	42, 43, 44
8b.	Restore context of current task;	45
	restore working registers;	46
	and return	52

updated by a re-entrant procedure that is invoked by an inter-processor interrupt. The handler must ensure that the segment registers, the LDTR and the TR, are re-loaded. This happens automatically if the interrupt is serviced by a task switch.

11.6 SHUTDOWN

Shutdown occurs when a severe error condition prevents further processing. Shutdown is very similar to HLT in that the 80286 stops executing instructions. The 80286 externally signals shutdown as a Halt bus cycle with A1=0. The NMI or RESET input will force the 80286 out of shutdown. The INTR input is ignored during shutdown.

Appendix
80286 System Initialization

A

APPENDIX A
80286 SYSTEM INITIALIZATION

```
$title('Switch the 80286 from Real Address Mode to Protected Mode')
            name    switch 80286_modes
            public  idt_desc,gdt_desc
;
;         Switch the 80286 from real address mode into protected mode.
;    The initial EPROM GDT, IDT, TSS, and LDT (if any) constructed by BLD286
;    will be copied from EPROM into RAM. The RAM areas are defined by data
;    segments allocated as fixed entries in the GDT. The CPU registers for
;    the GDT, IDT, TSS, and LDT will be set to point at the RAM-based
;    segments. The base fields in the RAM-based GDT will also be updated to
;    point at the RAM-based segments.
;
;         This code is used by adding it to the list of object modules given
;    to BLD286. BLD286 must then be told to place the segment
;    init_code at address FFFE10H. Execution of the mode switch code begins
;    after RESET. This happens because the mode switch code will start at
;    physical address FFFFF0H, which is the power up address. This code then
;    sets up RAM copies of the EPROM-based segments before jumping to the
;    initial task placed at a fixed GDT entry. After the jump, the CPU
;    executes in the state of the first task defined by BLD286.
;
;         This code will not use any of the EPROM-based tables directly.
;    Such use would result in the 80286 writing into EPROM to set
;    the A bit. Any use of a GDT or TSS will always be in the RAM copy.
;    The limit and size of the EPROM-based GDT and IDT must be stored at
;    the public symbols idt_desc and gdt_desc. The location commands of BLD286
;    provide this function
;
;         Interrupts are disabled during this mode switching code. Full error
;    checking is made of the EPROM-based GDT, IDT, TSS, and LDT to assure
;    they are valid before copying them to RAM. If any of the RAM-based
;    alias segments are smaller than the EPROM segments they are to hold,
;    halt or shutdown will occur. In general, any exception or NMI will
;    cause shutdown to occur until the first task is invoked.
;
;         If the RAM segment is larger than the EPROM segment, the RAM segment
;    will be expanded with zeros. If the initial TSS specifies an LDT,
;    the LDT will also be copied into ldt_alias with zero fill if needed.
;    The EPROM-based or RAM-based GDT, IDT, TSS, and LDT segments may be located
;    anywhere in physical memory.
;
```

```
;
;              Define layout of a descriptor.
;
desc            struc
limit           dw        0               ; Offset of last byte in segment
base_low        dw        0               ; Low 16 bits of 24-bit address
base_high       db        0               ; High 8 bits of 24-bit address
access          db        0               ; Access rights byte
res             dw        0               ; Reserved word
desc            ends
;
;              Define the fixed GDT selector values for the descriptors that
;                  define the EPROM-based tables. BLD286 must be instructed to place the
;                  appropriate descriptors into the GDT.
;
gdt_alias       equ       1*size desc     ; GDT(1) is data segment in RAM for GDT
idt_alias       equ       2*size desc     ; GDT(2) is data segment in RAM for IDT
start_TSS_alias equ       3*size desc     ; GDT(3) is data segment in RAM for TSS
start_task      equ       4*size desc     ; GDT(4) is TSS for starting task
start_LDT_alias equ       5*size desc     ; GDT(5) is data segment in RAM for LDT
;
;              Define machine status word bit positions.
;
PE              equ       1               ; Protection enable
MP              equ       2               ; Monitor processor extension
EM              equ       4               ; Emulate processor extension
;
;              Define particular values of descriptor access rights byte.
;
DT_ACCESS       equ       82H             ; Access byte value for an LDT
DS_ACCESS       equ       92H             ; Access byte value for data segment
                                          ;   which is grow up, at level 0, writeable
TSS_ACCESS      equ       81H             ; Access byte value for an idle TSS
DPL             equ       60H             ; Privilege level field of access rights
ACCESSED        equ       1               ; Define accessed bit
TI              equ       4               ; Position of TI bit
TSS_SIZE        equ       44              ; Size of a TSS
LDT_OFFSET      equ       42              ; Position of LDT in TSS
TIRPL_MASK      equ       size desc-1     ; TI and RPL field mask
;
;              Pass control from the power-up address to the mode switch code.
;                  The segment containing this code must be at physical address FFFE10H
;                  to place the JMP instruction at physical address FFFFF0H. The base
;                  address is chosen according to the size of this segment.
;
init_code       segment er

cs_offset       equ       0FE10H          ; Low 16 bits of starting address
                org       0FFFF0H-cs_offset; Start at address FFFFF0H
                jmp       reset_startup   ; Do not change CS!
```

```
;
;            Define the template for a temporary GDT used to locate the initial
;        GDT and stack. This data will be copied to location 0.
;        This space is also used for a temporary stack and finally serves
;        as the TSS written into when entering the initial TSS.
;
                    org      0                 ; Place remaining code below power_up

initial_gdt         desc     <>               ; Filler and null IDT descriptor
gdt_desc            desc     <>               ; Descriptor for EPROM GDT
idt_desc            desc     <>               ; Descriptor for EPROM IDT
temp_desc           desc     <>               ; Temporary descriptor

;            Define a descriptor that will point the GDT at location 0.
;        This descriptor will also be loaded into SS to define the initial
;        protected mode stack segment.
;
temp_stack          desc     <end_gdt-initial_gdt-1,0,0,DS_ACCESS,0>
;
;            Define the TSS descriptor used to allow the task switch to the
;        first task to overwrite this region of memory. The TSS will overlay
;        the initial GDT and stack at location 0.
;
save_tss            desc     <end_gdt-initial_gdt-1,0,0,TSS_ACCESS,0>
;
;            Define the initial stack space and filler for the end of the TSS.
;
                    dw       8 dup (0)
end_gdt             label    word

start_pointer       label    dword
                    dw       0,start_task      ; Pointer to initial task
;
;            Define template for the task definition list.
;
task_entry          struc                      ; Define layout of task description
TSS_sel             dw       ?                 ; Selector for TSS
TSS_alias           dw       ?                 ; Data segment alias for TSS
LDT_alias           dw       ?                 ; Data segment alias for LDT if any
task_entry          ends

task_list           task_entry    <start_task,start_TSS_alias,start_LDT_alias>
                    dw       0                 ; Terminate list

reset_startup:
        cli                                    ; No interrupts allowed!
        cld                                    ; Use autoincrement mode
        xor      di,di                         ; Point ES:DI at physical address 000000H
        mov      ds,di
        mov      es,di
        mov      ss,di                         ; Set stack at end of reserved area
        mov      sp,end_gdt-initial_gdt
```

```
;
;          Form an adjustment factor from the real CS base of FF0000H to the
;       segment base address assumed by ASM286. Any data reference made
;       into CS must add an indexing term [BP] to compensate for the difference
;       between the offset generated by ASM286 and the offset required from
;       the base of FF0000H.
;
start   proc                            ; The value of IP at run time will not be
                                        ;  the same as the one used by ASM286!
        call    start1                  ; Get true offset of start1
start1:
        pop     bp
        sub     bp,offset start1        ; Subtract ASM286 offset of start1
                                        ;  leaving adjustment factor in BP
        lidt    initial_gdt[bp]         ; Setup null IDT to force shutdown
                                        ;  on any protection error or interrupt
;
;          Copy the EPROM-based temporary GDT into RAM.
;
        lea     si,initial_gdt[bp]      ; Setup pointer to temporary GDT
                                        ;  template in EPROM
        mov     cx,(end_gdt-initial_gdt)/2  ; Set length
  rep   movs    es:word ptr [di],cs:[si]; Put into reserved RAM area
;
;          Look for 80287 processor extension. Assume all ones will be read
;       if an 80287 is not present.
;
        fninit                          ; Initialize 80287 if present
        mov     bx,EM                   ; Assume no 80287
        fstsw   ax                      ; Look at status of 80287
        or      al,al                   ; No errors should be present
        jnz     set_mode                ; Jump if no 80287

        fsetpm                          ; Put 80287 into protected mode
        mov     bx,MP
;
;          Switch to protected mode and setup a stack, GDT, and LDT.
;
set_mode:
        smsw    ax                      ; Get current MSW
        or      ax,PE                   ; Set PE bit
        or      ax,bx                   ; Set NPX status flags
        lmsw    ax                      ; Enter protected mode!
        jmp     $+2                     ; Clear queue of instructions decoded
                                        ;  while in Real Address Mode
                                        ; CPL is now 0, CS still points at
                                        ; FFFE10 in physical memory
```

```
        lgdt      temp_stack[bp]              ; Use initial GDT in RAM area
        mov       ax,temp_stack-initial_gdt   ; Setup SS with valid protected mode
        mov       ss,ax                       ;   selector to the RAM GDT and stack
        xor       ax,ax                       ; Set the current LDT to null
        lldt      ax                          ; Any references to it will cause
                                              ;   an exception causing shutdown
        mov       ax,save_tss-initial_gdt     ; Set initial TSS into the low RAM
        ltr       ax                          ; The task switch needs a valid TSS
;
;       Copy the EPROM-based GDT into the RAM data segment alias.
;       First the descriptor for the RAM data segment must be copied into
;       the temporary GDT.
;
        mov       ax,gdt_desc[bp].limit       ; Get size of GDT
        cmp       ax,6*size desc-1            ; Be sure the last entry expected by
                                              ;   this code is inside the GDT
        jb        bad_gdt                     ; Jump if GDT is not big enough

        mov       bx,gdt_desc-initial_gdt     ; Form selector to EPROM GDT
        mov       si,gdt_alias                ; Get selector of GDT alias
        call      copy_EPROM_dt               ; Copy into EPROM
        mov       si,idt_alias                ; Get selector of IDT alias
        mov       bx,idt_desc-initial_gdt     ; Indicate EPROM IDT
        call      copy_EPROM_dt
        mov       ax,gdt_desc-initial_gdt     ; Setup addressing into EPROM GDT
        mov       ds,ax
        mov       bx,gdt_alias                ; Get GDT alias data segment selector
        lgdt      [bx]                        ; Set GDT to RAM GDT
                                              ; SS and TR remain in low RAM
;
;       Copy all task's TSS and LDT segments into RAM
;
        lea       bx,task_list[bp]            ; Define list of tasks to setup
copy_task_loop:
        call      copy_tasks                  ; Copy them into RAM
        add       bx,size task_entry          ; Go to next entry
        mov       ax,cs:[bx].tss_sel          ; See if there is another entry
        or        ax,ax
        jnz       copy_task_loop
;
;       With TSS, GDT, and LDT set, startup the initial task!
;
        mov       bx,gdt_alias                ; Point DS at GDT
        mov       ds,bx
        mov       bx,idt_alias                ; Get IDT alias data segment selector
        lidt      [bx]                        ; Set IDT for errors and interrupts
        jmp       start_pointer[bp]           ; Start the first task!
                                              ; The low RAM area is overwritten with
                                              ;   the current CPU context
bad_gdt:
        hlt                                   ; Halt here if GDT is not big enough
```

```
start     endp
;
;            Copy the TSS and LDT for the task pointed at by CS:BX.
;            If the task has an LDT it will also be copied down.
;            BX and BP are transparent.
;
bad_tss:
          hlt                                    ; Halt here if TSS is invalid
copy_tasks        proc

          mov       si,gdt_alias                 ; Get addressability to GDT
          mov       ds,si
          mov       si,cs:[bx].tss_alias         ; Get selector for TSS alias
          mov       es,si                        ; Point ES at alias data segment
          lsl       ax,si                        ; Get length of TSS alias
          mov       si,cs:[bx].tss_sel           ; Get TSS selector
          lar       dx,si                        ; Get alias access rights
          jnz       bad_tss                      ; Jump if invalid reference

          mov       dl,dh                        ; Save TSS descriptor access byte
          and       dh,not DPL                   ; Ignore privilege
          cmp       dh,TSS_ACCESS                ; See if TSS
          jnz       bad_tss                      ; Jump if not

          lsl       cx,si                        ; Get length of EPROM based TSS
          cmp       cx,TSS_SIZE-1                ; Verify it is of proper size
          jb        bad_tss                      ; Jump if it is not big enough
;
;         Setup for moving the EPROM-based TSS to RAM
;         DS points at GDT
;
          mov       [si].access,DS_ACCESS        ; Make TSS into data segment
          mov       ds,si                        ; Point DS at EPROM TSS
          call      copy_with_fill               ; Copy DS segment to ES with zero fill
                                                 ;   CX has copy count, AX-CX fill count
;
;         Set the GDT TSS limit and base address to the RAM values.
;
          mov       ax,gdt_alias                 ; Restore GDT addressing
          mov       ds,ax
          mov       es,ax
          mov       di,cs:[bx].tss_sel           ; Get TSS selector
          mov       si,cs:[bx].tss_alias         ; Get RAM alias selector
          movsw                                  ; Copy limit
          movsw                                  ; Copy low 16 bits of address
          lodsw                                  ; Get high 8 bits of address
          mov       ah,dl                        ; Mark as TSS descriptor
          stosw                                  ; Fill in high address and access bytes
          movsw                                  ; Copy reserved word
```

```
;
;       See if a valid LDT is specified for the startup task
;       If so then copy the EPROM version into the RAM alias.
;

        mov     ds,cs:[bx].tss_alias    ; Address TSS to get LDT
        mov     si,ds:word ptr LDT_OFFSET
        and     si,not TIRPL_MASK       ; Ignore TI and RPL
        jz      no_ldt                  ; Skip this if no LDT used

        push    si                      ; Save LDT selector
        lar     dx,si                   ; Test descriptor
        jnz     bad_ldt                 ; Jump if invalid selector

        mov     dl,dh                   ; Save LDT descriptor access byte
        and     dh,not DPL              ; Ignore privilege
        cmp     dh, DT_ACCESS           ; Be sure it is an LDT descriptor
        jne     bad_ldt                 ; Jump if invalid

        mov     es:[si].access,DS_ACCESS; Mark LDT as data segment
        mov     ds,si                   ; Point DS at EPROM LDT
        lsl     ax,si                   ; Get LDT limit
        call    test_dt_limit           ; Verify it is valid
        mov     cx,ax                   ; Save for later
;
;       Examine the LDT alias segment and, if good, copy to RAM
;
        mov     si,cs:[bx].ldt_alias    ; Get ldt alias selector
        mov     es,si                   ; Point ES at alias segment
        lsl     ax,si                   ; Get length of alias segment
        call    test_dt_limit           ; Verify it is valid
        call    copy_with_fill          ; Copy LDT into RAM alias segment
;
;       Set the LDT limit and base address to the RAM copy of the LDT.
;
        mov     si,cs:[bx].ldt_alias    ; Restore LDT alias selector
        pop     di                      ; Restore LDT selector
        mov     ax,gdt_alias            ; Restore GDT addressing
        mov     ds,ax
        mov     es,ax
        movsw                           ; Move the RAM LDT limit
        movsw                           ; Move the low 16 bits across
        lodsw                           ; Get the high 8 bits
        mov     ah,dl                   ; Mark as LDT descriptor
        stosw                           ; Set high address and access rights
        movsw                           ; Copy reserved word
no_ldt:
        ret                             ; All done
bad_ldt:
        hlt                             ; Halt here if LDT is invalid

copy_tasks      endp
```

```
;
;          Test the descriptor table size in AX to verify that it is an
;       even number of descriptors in length.
;
test_dt_limit    proc

        push        ax                          ; Save length
        and         al,7                        ; Look at low order bits
        cmp         al,7                        ; Must be all ones
        pop         ax                          ; Restore length
        jne         bad_dt_limit

        ret                                     ; All OK
bad_dt_limit:
        hlt                                     ; Die!

test_dt_limit    endp


;
;          Copy the EPROM DT at selector BX in the temporary GDT to the alias
;       data segment at selector SI. Any improper descriptors or limits
;       will cause shutdown!
;
copy_EPROM_dt    proc

        mov         ax,ss                       ; Point ES:DI at temporary descriptor
        mov         es,ax
        mov         es:[bx].access,DS_ACCESS; Mark descriptor as a data segment
        mov         es:[bx].res,0               ; Clear reserved word
        lsl         ax,bx                       ; Get limit of EPROM DT
        mov         cx,ax                       ; Save for later
        call        test_dt_limit               ; Verify it is a proper limit
        mov         di,gdt_desc-initial_gdt     ; Address EPROM GDT in DS
        mov         ds,di
        mov         di,temp_desc-initial_gdt; Get selector for temporary descriptor
        push        di                          ; Save offset for later use as selector
        lodsw                                   ; Get alias segment size
        call        test_dt_limit               ; Verify it is an even multiple of
                                                ;   descriptors in length
        stosw                                   ; Put length into temporary
        movsw                                   ; Copy remaining entries into temporary
        movsw
        movsw
        pop         es                          ; ES now points at the GDT alias area
        mov         ds,bx                       ; DS now points at EPROM DT as data
                                                ; Copy segment to alias with zero fill
                                                ; CX is copy count, AX-CX is fill count
                                                ; Fall into copy_with_fill


copy_EPROM_dt    endp
```

```
;
;          Copy the segment at DS to the segment at ES for length CX.
;          Fill the end with AX-CX zeros. Use word operations for speed but
;          allow odd byte operations.
;
copy_with_fill   proc

            xor      si,si              ; Start at beginning of segments
            xor      di,di
            sub      ax,cx              ; Form fill count
            add      cx,1               ; Convert limit to count
            rcr      cx,1               ; Allow full 64K move
     rep    movsw                       ; Copy DT into alias area
            xchg     ax,cx              ; Get fill count and zero AX
            jnc      even_copy          ; Jump if even byte count on copy

            movsb                       ; Copy odd byte
            or       cx,cx
            jz       exit_copy          ; Exit if no fill

            stosb                       ; Even out the segment offset
            dec      cx                 ; Adjust remaining fill count
even_copy:
            shr      cx,1               ; Form word count on fill
     rep    stosw                       ; Clear unused words at end
            jnc      exit_copy          ; Exit if no odd byte remains

            stosb                       ; Clear last odd byte
exit_copy:
            ret

copy_with_fill   endp

init_code        ends
                 end


$B
```

Appendix
The 80286 Instruction Set

B

APPENDIX B
THE 80286 INSTRUCTION SET

This section presents the 80286 instruction set using Intel's ASM286 notation. All possible operand types are shown. Instructions are organized alphabetically according to generic operations. Within each operation, many different instructions are possible depending on the operand. The pages are presented in a standardized format, the elements of which are described in the following paragraphs.

Opcode

This column gives the complete object code produced for each form of the instruction. Where possible, the codes are given as hexadecimal bytes, presented in the order in which they will appear in memory. Several shorthand conventions are used for the parts of instructions which specify operands. These conventions are as follows:

/n: (*n* is a digit from 0 through 7) A ModRM byte, plus a possible immediate and displacement field follow the opcode. See figure B-1 for the encoding of the fields. The digit *n* is the value of the REG field of the ModRM byte. To obtain the possible hexadecimal values for /*n*, refer to column *n* of table B-1. Each row gives a possible value for the effective address operand to the instruction. The entry at the end of the row indicates whether the effective address operand is a register or memory; if memory, the entry indicates what kind of indexing and/or displacement is used. Entries with D8 or D16 signify that a one-byte or two-byte displacement quantity immediately follows the ModRM and optional immediate field bytes. The signed displacement is added to the effective address offset.

/r: A ModRM byte that contains both a register operand and an effective address operand, followed by a possible immediate and displacement field. See figure B-2 for the encoding of the fields. The ModRM byte could be any value appearing in table B-1. The column determines which register operand was selected; the row determines the form of effective address. If the row entry mentions D8 or D16, then a one-byte or two-byte displacement follows, as described in the previous paragraph.

cb: A one-byte signed displacement in the range of −128 to +127 follows the opcode. The displacement is sign-extended to 16 bits, and added modulo 65536 to the offset of the instruction FOLLOWING this instruction to obtain the new IP value.

cw: A two-byte displacement is added modulo 65536 to the offset of the instruction FOLLOWING this instruction to obtain the new IP value.

cd: A two-word pointer which will be the new CS:IP value. The offset is given first, followed by the selector.

db: An immediate byte operand to the instruction which follows the opcode and ModRM bytes. The opcode determines if it is a signed value.

dw: An immediate word operand to the instruction which follows the opcode and ModRM bytes. All words are given in the 80286 with the low-order byte first.

+rb: A register code from 0 through 7 which is added to the hexadecimal byte given at the left of the plus sign to form a single opcode byte. The codes are: AL=0, CL=1, DL=2, BL=3, AH=4, CH=5, DH=6, and BH=7.

pp/n Instruction Byte Format

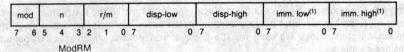

mod	n	r/m	disp-low	disp-high	imm. low[1]	imm. high[1]
7 6 5	4 3 2	1 0	7 0	7 0	7 0	7 0

ModRM

"mod" Field Bit Assignments

mod	Displacement
00	DISP = 0[2], disp-low and disp-high are absent
01	DISP = disp-low sign-extended to 16-bits, disp-high is absent
10	DISP = disp-high: disp-low
11	r/m is treated as a "reg" field

"r/m" Field Bit Assignments

r/m	Operand Address
000	(BX) + (SI) + DISP
001	(BX) + (DI) + DISP
010	(BP) + (SI) + DISP
011	(BP) + (DI) + DISP
100	(SI) + DISP
101	(DI) + DISP
110	(BP) + DISP[2]
111	(BX) + DISP

DISP follows 2nd byte of instruction (before data if required).

NOTES:

1. Opcode indicates presence and size of immediate value.
2. Except if mod=00 and r/m=110 then EA=disp-high: disp-low.

Figure B-1. /n Instruction Byte Format

Table B-1. ModRM Values

Rb =	AL	CL	DL	BL	AH	CH	DH	BH	
Rw =	AX	CX	DX	BX	SP	BP	SI	DI	
REG =	0	1	2	3	4	5	6	7	
	ModRM values								Effective address
mod=00	00	08	10	18	20	28	30	38	[BX + SI]
	01	09	11	19	21	29	31	39	[BX + DI]
	02	0A	12	1A	22	2A	32	3A	[BP + SI]
	03	0B	13	1B	23	2B	33	3B	[BP + DI]
	04	0C	14	1C	24	2C	34	3C	[SI]
	05	0D	15	1D	25	2D	35	3D	[DI]
	06	0E	16	1E	26	2E	36	3E	D16 (simple var)
	07	0F	17	1F	27	2F	37	3F	[BX]
mod=01	40	48	50	58	60	68	70	78	[BX + SI] + D8[1]
	41	49	51	59	61	69	71	79	[BX + DI] + D8
	42	4A	52	5A	62	6A	72	7A	[BP + SI] + D8
	43	4B	53	5B	63	6B	73	7B	[BP + DI] + D8
	44	4C	54	5C	64	6C	74	7C	[SI] + D8
	45	4D	55	5D	65	6D	75	7D	[DI] + D8
	46	4E	56	5E	66	6E	76	7E	[BP] + D8[2]
	47	4F	57	5F	67	6F	77	7F	[BX] + D8
mod=10	80	88	90	98	A0	A8	B0	B8	[BX + SI] + D16[3]
	81	89	91	99	A1	A9	B1	B9	[BX + DI] + D16
	82	8A	92	9A	A2	AA	B2	BA	[BP +SI] + D16
	83	8B	93	9B	A3	AB	B3	BB	[BP + DI] + D16
	84	8C	94	9C	A4	AC	B4	BC	[SI] + D16
	85	8D	95	9D	A5	AD	B5	BD	[DI] + D16
	86	8E	96	9E	A6	AE	B6	BE	[BP] + D16[2]
	87	8F	97	9F	A7	AF	B7	BF	[BX] + D16
mod=11	C0	C8	D0	D8	E0	E8	F0	F8	Ew=AX　Eb=AL
	C1	C9	D1	D9	E1	E9	F1	F9	Ew=CX　Eb=CL
	C2	CA	D2	DA	E2	EA	F2	FA	Ew=DX　Eb=DL
	C3	CB	D3	DB	E3	EB	F3	FB	Ew=BX　Eb=BL
	C4	CC	D4	DC	E4	EC	F4	FC	Ew=SP　Eb=AH
	C5	CD	D5	DD	E5	ED	F5	FD	Ew=BP　Eb=CH
	C6	CE	D6	DE	E6	EE	F6	FE	Ew=SI　Eb=DH
	C7	CF	D7	DF	E7	EF	F7	FF	Ew=DI　Eb=BH

NOTES:

1. D8 denotes an 8-bit displacement following the ModRM byte that is sign-extended and added to the index.

2. Default segment register is SS for effective addresses containing a BP index; DS is for other memory effective addresses.

3. D16 denotes the 16-bit displacement following the ModRM byte that is added to the index.

/r Instruction Byte Format

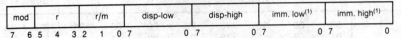

mod	r	r/m	disp-low	disp-high	imm. low[1]	imm. high[1]

7 6 5 4 3 2 1 0 7   0 7   0 7   0 7   0

"mod" Field Bit Assignments

mod	Displacement
00	DISP = 0[2], disp-low and disp-high are absent
01	DISP = disp-low sign-extended to 16-bits, disp-high is absent
10	DISP = disp-high; disp-low
11	r/m is treated as a "reg" field

"r" Field Bit Assignments

16-Bit (w = 1)	8-Bit (w = 0)	Segment
000 AX	000 AL	00 ES
001 CX	001 CL	01 CS
010 DX	010 DL	10 SS
011 BX	011 BL	11 DS
100 SP	100 AH	
101 BP	101 CH	
110 SI	110 DH	
111 DI	111 BH	

"r/m" Field Bit Assignments

r/m	Operand Address
000	(BX) + (SI) + DISP
001	(BX) + (DI) + DISP
010	(BP) + (SI) + DISP
011	(BP) + (DI) + DISP
100	(SI) + DISP
101	(DI) + DISP
110	(BP) + DISP[2]
111	(BX) + DISP

DISP follows 2nd byte of instruction (before data if required).

NOTES:

1. Opcode indicates presence and size of immediate field.
2. Except if mod=00 and r/m=110 then EA=disp-high: disp-low.

Figure B-2. /r Instruction Byte Format

+rw: A register code from 0 through 7 which is added to the hexadecimal byte given at the left of the plus sign to form a single opcode byte. The codes are: AX=0, CX=1, DX=2, BX=3, SP=4, BP=5, SI=6, and DI=7.

Instruction

This column gives the instruction mnemonic and possible operands. The type of operand used will determine the opcode and operand encodings. The following entries list the type of operand which can be encoded in the format shown in the instruction column. The Intel convention is to place the destination operand as the left hand operand. Source-only operands follow the destination operand.

In many cases, the same instruction can be encoded several ways. It is recommended that you use the shortest encoding. The short encodings are provided to save memory space.

cb: a destination instruction offset in the range of 128 bytes before the end of this instruction to 127 bytes after the end of this instruction.

cw: a destination offset within the same code segment as this instruction. Some instructions allow a short form of destination offset. See *cb* type for more information.

cd: a destination address, typically in a different code segment from this instruction. Using the *cd:* address form with call instructions saves the code segment selector.

db: a signed value between −128 and +127 inclusive which is an operand of the instruction. For instructions in which the *db* is to be combined in some way with a word operand, the immediate value is sign-extended to form a word. The upper byte of the word is filled with the topmost bit of the immediate value.

dw: an immediate word value which is an operand of the instruction.

eb: a byte-sized operand. This is either a byte register or a (possibly indexed) byte memory variable. Either operand location may be encoded in the ModRM field. Any memory addressing mode may be used.

ed: a memory-based pointer operand. Any memory addressing mode may be used. Use of a register addressing mode will cause exception 6.

ew: a word-sized operand. This is either a word register or a (possibly indexed) word memory variable. Either operand location may be encoded in the ModRM field. Any memory addressing mode may be used.

m: a memory location. Operands in registers do not have a memory address. Any memory addressing mode may be used. Use of a register addressing mode will cause exception 6.

mb: a memory-based byte-sized operand. Any memory addressing mode may be used.

mw: a memory-based word operand. Any memory addressing mode may be used.

rb: one of the byte registers AL, CL, DL, BL, AH, CH, DH, or BH; *rb* has the value 0,1,2,3,4,5,6, and 7, respectively.

rw: one of the word registers AX, CX, DX, BX, SP, BP, SI, or DI; *rw* has the value 0,1,2,3,4,5,6, and 7, respectively.

xb: a simple byte memory variable without a base or index register. MOV instructions between AL and memory have this optimized form if no indexing is required.

xw: a simple word memory variable without a base or index register. MOV instructions between AX and memory have this optimized form if no indexing is required.

Clocks

This column gives the number of clock cycles that this form of the instruction takes to execute. The amount of time for each clock cycle is computed by dividing one microsecond by the number of MHz at which the 80286 is running. For example, a 10-MHz 80286 (with the CLK pin connected to a 20-MHz crystal) takes 100 nanoseconds for each clock cycle.

Add one clock to instructions that use the base plus index plus displacement form of addressing. Add two clocks for each 16-bit memory based operand reference located on an odd physical address. Add one clock for each wait state added to each memory read. Wait states inserted in memory writes or instruction fetches do not necessarily increase execution time.

The clock counts establish the maximum execution rate of the 80286. With no delays in bus cycles, the actual clock count of an 80286 program will average 5-10% more than the calculated clock count due to instruction sequences that execute faster than they can be fetched from memory.

Some instruction forms give two clock counts, one unlabelled and one labelled. These counts indicate that the instruction has two different clock times for two different circumstances. Following are the circumstances for each possible label:

mem: The instruction has an operand that can either be a register or a memory variable. The unlabelled time is for the register; the *mem* time is for the memory variable. Also, one additional clock cycle is taken for indexed memory variables for which all three possible indices (base register, index register, and displacement) must be added.

noj: The instruction involves a conditional jump or interrupt. The unlabelled time holds when the jump is made; the noj time holds when the jump is not made.

pm: If the instruction takes more time to execute when the 80286 is in Protected Mode. The unlabelled time is for Real Address Mode; the pm time is for Protected Mode.

Description

This is a concise description of the operation performed for this form of the instruction. More details are given in the "Operation" section that appears later in this chapter.

Flags Modified

This is a list of the flags that are set to a meaningful value by the instruction. If a flag is always set to the same value by the instruction, the value is given ("=0" or "=1") after the flag name.

Flags Undefined

This is a list of the flags that have an undefined (meaningless) setting after the instruction is executed.

All flags not mentioned under "Flags Modified" or "Flags Undefined" are unchanged by the instruction.

Operation

This section fully describes the operation performed by the instruction. For some of the more complicated instructions, suggested usage is also indicated.

Protected Mode Exceptions

The possible exceptions involved with this instruction when running under the 80286 Protected Mode are listed below. These exceptions are abbreviated with a pound sign (#) followed by two capital letters and an optional error code in parenthesis. For example, #GP(0) denotes the general protection exception with an error code of zero. The next section describes all of the 80286 exceptions and the machine state upon entry to the exception.

If you are an applications programmer, consult the documentation provided with your operating system to determine what actions are taken by the system when exceptions occur.

Real Address Mode Exceptions

Since less error checking is performed by the 80286 when it is in Real Address Mode, there are fewer exceptions in this mode. One exception that is possible in many instructions is #GP(0). Exception 13 is generated whenever a word operand is accessed from effective address 0FFFFH in a segment. This happens because the second byte of the word is considered located at location 10000H, not at location 0, and thus exceeds the segment's addressability limit.

Protection Exceptions

In parallel with the execution of instructions, the protected-mode 80286 checks all memory references for validity of addressing and type of access. Violation of the memory protection rules built into the processor will cause a transfer of program control to one of the interrupt procedures described in this section. The interrupts have dedicated positions within the Interrupt Descriptor Table, which is shown in table B-2. The interrupts are referenced within the instruction set pages by a pound sign (#) followed by a two-letter mnemonic and the optional error code in parenthesis.

Error Codes

Some exceptions cause the 80286 to pass a 16-bit error code to the interrupt procedure. When this happens, the error code is the last item pushed onto the stack before control is tranferred to the interrupt procedure. If stacks were switched as a result of the interrupt (causing a privilege change or task switch), the error code appears on the interrupt procedure's stack, not on the stack of the task that was interrupted.

Table B-2. Protection Exceptions of the 80286

Abbreviation	Interrupt Number	Description
#UD	6	Undefined Opcode
#NM	7	No Math Unit Available
#DF	8	Double Fault
#MP	9	Math Unit Protection Fault
#TS	10	Invalid Task State Segment
#NP	11	Not Present
#SS	12	Stack Fault
#GP	13	General Protection
#MF	16	Math Fault

The error code generally contains the selector of the segment that caused the protection violation. The RPL field (bottom two bits) of the error code does not, however, contain the privilege level. Instead, it contains the following information:

- Bit 0 contains the value 1 if the exception was detected during an interrupt caused by an event external to the program (i.e., an external interrupt, a single step, a processor extension not-present exception, or a processor extension segment overrun). Bit 0 is 0 if the exception was detected while processing the regular instruction stream, even if the instruction stream is part of an external interrupt handling procedure or task. If bit 0 is set, the instruction pointed to by the saved CS:IP address is not responsible for the error. The current task can be restarted unless this is exception 9.

- Bit 1 is 1 if the selector points to the Interrupt Descriptor Table. In this case, bit 2 can be ignored, and bits 3-10 contain the index into the IDT.

- Bit 1 is 0 if the selector points to the Global or Local Descriptor Tables. In this case, bits 2-15 have their usual selector interpretation: bit 2 selects the table (1=Local, 0=Global), and bits 3-15 are the index into the table.

In some cases the 80286 chooses to pass an error code with no information in it. In these cases, all 16 bits of the error code are zero.

The existence and type of error codes are described under each of the following individual exceptions.

#DF 8 Double Fault (Zero Error Code)

This exception is generated when a second exception is detected while the processor is attempting to transfer control to the handler for an exception. For instance, it is generated if the code segment containing the exception handler is marked not present. It is also generated if invoking the exception handler causes a stack overflow.

This exception is not generated during the execution of an exeception handler. Faults detected within the instruction stream are handled by regular exceptions.

The error code is normally zero. The saved CS:IP will point at the instruction that was attempting to execute when the double fault occurred. Since the error code is normally zero, no information on the source of the exception is available. Restart is not possible.

The "double fault" exception does not occur when detecting a new exception while trying to invoke handlers for the following exceptions: 1, 2, 3, 4, 5, 6, 7, 9, and 16.

If another exception is detected while attempting to perform the double fault exception, the 80286 will enter shutdown (see section 11.5).

#GP 13 General Protection (Selector or Zero Error Code)

This exception is generated for all protection violations not covered by the other exceptions in this section. Examples of this include:

1. An attempt to address a memory location by using an offset that exceeds the limit for the segment involved.
2. An attempt to jump to a data segment.
3. An attempt to load SS with a selector for a read-only segment.
4. An attempt to write to a read-only segment.
5. Exceeding the maximum instruction length of 10 bytes.

If #GP occurred while loading a descriptor, the error code passed contains the selector involved. Otherwise, the error code is zero.

If the error code is not zero, the instruction can be restarted if the erroneous condition is rectified. If the error code is zero either a limit violation, a write protect violation, or an illegal use of invalid segment register occurred. An invalid segment register contains the values 0-3. A write protect fault on ADC, SBB, RCL, RCR, or XCHG is not restartable.

#MF 16 Math Fault (No Error Code)

This exception is generated when the numeric processor extension (the 80287) detects an error signalled by the ERROR input pin leading from the 80287 to the 80286. The ERROR pin is tested at the beginning of most floating point instructions, and when a WAIT instruction is executed with the EM bit of the Machine Status Word set to 0 (i.e., no emulation of the math unit). The floating point instructions that do not cause the ERROR pin to be tested are FNCLEX, FNINIT, FSETPM, FNSTCW, FNSTSW, FNSAVE, and FNSTENV.

If the handler corrects the error condition causing the exception, the floating point instruction that caused #MF can be restarted. This is not accomplished by IRET, however, since the fault occurs at the floating point instruction that follows the offending instruction. Before restarting the numeric instruction, the handler must obtain from the 80287 the address of the offending instruction and the address of the optional numeric operand.

#MP 9 Math Unit Protection Fault (No Error Code)

This exception is generated if the numeric operand is larger than one word and has the second or subsequent words outside the segment's limit. Not all math addressing errors cause exception 9. If the effective address of an ESCAPE instruction is not in the segment's limit, or if a write is attempted on a read-only segment, or if a one-word operand violates a segment limit, exception 13 will occur.

The #MP exception occurs during the execution of the numeric instruction by the 80287. Thus, the 80286 may be in an unrelated instruction stream at the time. Exception 9 may occur in a task unrelated to the task that executed the ESC instruction. The operating system should keep track of which task last used the NPX (see section 11.4).

The offending floating point instruction cannot be restarted; the task which attempted to execute the offending numeric instruction must be aborted. However, if exception 9 interrupted another task, the interrupted task may be restarted.

The exception 9 handler *must* execute FNINIT before executing any ESCAPE or WAIT instruction.

#NM 7 No Math Unit Available (No Error Code)

This exception occurs when any floating point instruction is executed while the EM bit or the TS bit of the Machine Status Word is 1. It also occurs when a WAIT instruction is encountered and both the MP and TS bits of the Machine Status Word are 1.

Depending on the setting of the MSW bits that caused this exception, the exception handler could provide emulation of the 80287, or it could perform a context switch of the math processor to prepare it for use by another task.

The instruction causing #NM can be restarted if the handler performs a numeric context switch. If the handler provided emulation of the math unit, it should advance the return pointer beyond the floating point instruction that caused NM.

#NP 11 Not Present (Selector Error Code)

This exception occurs when CS, DS, ES, or the Task Register is loaded with a descriptor that is marked not present but is otherwise valid. It can occur in an LLDT instruction, but the #NP exception will not occur if the processor attempts to load the LDT register during a task switch. A not-present LDT encountered during a task switch causes the #TS exception.

The error code passed is the selector of the descriptor that is marked not present.

Typically, the Not Present exception handler is used to implement a virtual memory system. The operating system can swap inactive memory segments to a mass-storage device such as a disk. Applications programs need not be told about this; the next time they attempt to access the swapped-out memory segment, the Not Present handler will be invoked, the segment will be brought back into memory, and the offending instruction within the applications program will be restarted.

If #NP is detected on loading CS, DS, or ES in a task switch, the exception occurs in the new task, and the IRET from the exception handler jumps directly to the next instruction in the new task.

The Not Present exception handler must contain special code to complete the loading of segment registers when #NP is detected in loading the CS or DS registers in a task switch and a trap or interrupt gate was used. The DS and ES registers have been loaded but their descriptors have not been loaded. Any memory reference using the segment register may cause exception 13. The #NP exception handler should execute code such as the following to ensure full loading of the segment registers:

```
MOV AX,DS
MOV DS,AX
MOV AX,ES
MOV ES,AX
```

#SS 12 Stack Fault (Selector or Zero Error Code)

This exception is generated when a limit violation is detected in addressing through the SS register. It can occur on stack-oriented instructions such as PUSH or POP, as well as other types of memory references using SS such as MOV AX,[BP+28]. It also can occur on an ENTER instruction when there is not enough space on the stack for the indicated local variable space, even if the stack exception is not triggered by pushing BP or copying the display stack. A stack exception can therefore indicate a stack overflow, a stack underflow or a wild offset. The error code will be zero.

#SS is also generated on an attempt to load SS with a descriptor that is marked not present but is otherwise valid. This can occur in a task switch, an inter-level call, an inter-level return, a move to the SS instruction or a pop to the SS instruction. The error code will be non-zero.

#SS is never generated when addressing through the DS or ES registers even if the offending register points to the same segment as the SS register.

The #SS exception handler must contain special code to complete the loading of segment registers. The DS and ES registers will not be fully loaded if a not-present condition is detected while loading the SS register. Therefore, the #SS exception handler should execute code such as the following to insure full loading of the segment registers:

```
MOV AX,DS
MOV DS,AX
MOV AX,ES
MOV ES,AX
```

Generally, the instruction causing #SS can be restarted, but there is one special case when it cannot: when a PUSHA or POPA instruction attempts to wrap around the 64K boundary of a stack segment. This condition is identified by the value of the saved SP, which can be either 0000H, 0001H, 0FFFEH, or 0FFFFH.

#TS 10 Invalid Task State Segment (Selector Error Code)

This exception is generated during a task switch when the new task state segment is invalid, that is, when a task state segment is too small; when the LDT indicated in a TSS is invalid or not present; when the SS, CS, DS, or ES indicated in a TSS are invalid (task switch); when the back link in a TSS is invalid (inter-task IRET).

#TS is not generated when the SS, CS, DS, or ES back link or privileged stack selectors point to a descriptor that is not present but otherwise is valid. #NP is generated in these cases.

The error code passed to the exception handler contains the selector of the offending segment, which can either be the Task State Segment itself, or a selector found within the Task State Segment.

The instruction causing #TS can be restarted.

#TS must be handled through a task gate.

The exception handler must reset the busy bit in the new TSS.

#UD 6 Undefined Opcode (No Error Code)

This exception is generated when an invalid operation code is detected in the instruction stream. Following are the cases in which #UD can occur:

1. The first byte of an instruction is completely invalid (e.g., 64H).
2. The first byte indicates a 2-byte opcode and the second byte is invalid (e.g., 0FH followed by 0FFH).
3. An invalid register is used with an otherwise valid opcode (e.g., MOV CS,AX).
4. An invalid opcode extension is given in the REG field of the ModRM byte (e.g., 0F6H /1).
5. A register operand is given in an instruction that requires a memory operand (e.g., LGDT AX).

Since the offending opcode will always be invalid, it cannot be restarted. However, the #UD handler might be coded to implement an extension of the 80286 instruction set. In that case, the handler could advance the return pointer beyond the extended instruction and return control to the program after the extended instruction is emulated. *Any such extensions may be incompatible with the 80386.*

Privilege Level and Task Switching on the 80286

The 80286 supports many of the functions necessary to implement a protected, multi-tasking operating system in hardware. This support is provided not by additional instructions, but by extension of the semantics of 8086/8088 instructions that change the value of CS:IP.

Whenever the 80286 performs an inter-segment jump, call, interrupt, or return, it consults the Access Rights (AR) byte found in the descriptor table entry of the selector associated with the new CS value. The AR byte determines whether the long jump being made is through a gate, or is a task switch, or is a simple long jump to the same privilege level. Table B-3 lists the possible values of the AR byte. The "privilege" headings at the top of the table give the Descriptor Privilege Level, which is referred to as the DPL within the instruction descriptions.

Each of the CALL, INT, IRET, JMP, and RET instructions contains on its instruction set pages a listing of the access rights checking and actions taken to implement the instruction. Instructions involving task switches contain the symbol SWITCH_TASKS, which is an abbreviation for the following list of checks and actions:

```
SWITCH_TASKS:
    Locked set AR byte of new TSS descriptor to Busy TSS (Bit 1 = 1)
    Current TSS cache must be valid with limit ≥ 41 else #TS (error code will be new TSS, but back link
    points at old TSS)
    Save machine state in current TSS
    If nesting tasks, set the new TSS link to the current TSS selector
    Any exception will be in new context Else set the AR byte of current TSS
    descriptor to Available TSS (Bit 1 = 0)
    Set the current TR to selector, base, and limit of new TSS
    New TSS limit ≥ 43 else #TS (new TSS)
    Set all machine registers to values from new TSS without loading descriptors for DS, ES, CS, SS, LDT
    Clear valid flags for LDT,SS,CS,DS,ES (not valid yet)
    If nesting tasks, set the Nested Task flag to 1
    Set the Task Switched flag to 1
    LDT from the new TSS must be within GDT table limits else #TS(LDT)
    AR byte from LDT descriptor must specify LDT segment else #TS(LDT)
    AR byte from LDT descriptor must indicate PRESENT else #TS(LDT)
    Load LDT cache with new LDT descriptor and set valid bit
```

Set CPL to the RPL of the CS selector in the new TSS
If new stack selector is null #TS(SS)
SS selector must be within its descriptor table limits else #TS(SS)
SS selector RPL must be equal to CPL else #TS(SS)
DPL of SS descriptor must equal CPL else #TS(SS)
SS descriptor AR byte must indicate writable data segment else #TS(SS)
SS descriptor AR byte must indicate PRESENT else #SS(SS)
Load SS cache with new stack segment and set valid bit
New CS selector must not be null else #TS(CS)
CS selector must be within its descriptor table limits else #TS(CS)
CS descriptor AR byte must indicate code segment else #TS(CS)
If non-conforming then DPL must equal CPL else #TS(CS)
If conforming then DPL must be ≤ CPL else #TS(CS)
CS descriptor AR byte must indicate PRESENT else #NP(CS)
Load CS cache with new code segment descriptor and set valid bit
For DS and ES:
If new selector is not null then perform following checks:
    Index must be within its descriptor table limits else #TS(segment selector)
    AR byte must indicate data or readable code else #TS(segment selector)
    If data or non-conforming code then:
        DPL must be ≥ CPL else #TS(segment selector)
        DPL must be ≥ RPL else #TS(segment selector)
    AR byte must indicate PRESENT else #NP(segment selector)
    Load cache with new segment descriptor and set valid bit

Table B-3. Hexadecimal Values for the Access Rights Byte

Not present, privilege =				Present, privilege =				Descriptor Type
0	1	2	3	0	1	2	3	
00	20	40	60	80	A0	C0	E0	Illegal
01	21	41	61	81	A1	C1	E1	Available Task State Segment
02	22	42	62	82	A2	C2	E2	Local Descriptor Table Segment
03	23	43	63	83	A3	C3	E3	Busy Task State Segment
04	24	44	64	84	A4	C4	E4	Call Gate
05	25	45	65	85	A5	C5	E5	Task Gate
06	26	46	66	86	A6	C6	E6	Interrupt Gate
07	27	47	67	87	A7	C7	E7	Trap Gate
08	28	48	68	88	A8	C8	E8	Illegal
09	29	49	69	89	A9	C9	E9	Illegal
0A	2A	4A	6A	8A	AA	CA	EA	Illegal
0B	2B	4B	6B	8B	AB	CB	EB	Illegal
0C	2C	4C	6C	8C	AC	CC	EC	Illegal
0D	2D	4D	6D	8D	AD	CD	ED	Illegal
0E	2E	4E	6E	8E	AE	CE	EE	Illegal
0F	2F	4F	6F	8F	AF	CF	EF	Illegal
10	30	50	70	90	B0	D0	F0	Expand-up, read only, ignored Data Segment
11	31	51	71	91	B1	D1	F1	Expand-up, read only, accessed Data Segment
12	32	52	72	92	B2	D2	F2	Expand-up, writable, ignored Data Segment
13	33	53	73	93	B3	D3	F3	Expand-up, writable, accessed Data Segment
14	34	54	74	94	B4	D4	F4	Expand-down, read only, ignored Data Segment
15	35	55	75	95	B5	D5	F5	Expand-down, read only, accessed Data Segment
16	36	56	76	96	B6	D6	F6	Expand-down, writable, ignored Data Segment
17	37	57	77	97	B7	D7	F7	Expand-down, writable, accessed Data Segment
18	38	58	78	98	B8	D8	F8	Non-conform, no read, ignored Code Segment
19	39	59	79	99	B9	D9	F9	Non-conform, no read, accessed Code Segment
1A	3A	5A	7A	9A	BA	DA	FA	Non-conform, readable, ignored Code Segment
1B	3B	5B	7B	9B	BB	DB	FB	Non-conform, readable, accessed Code Segment
1C	3C	5C	7C	9C	BC	DC	FC	Conforming, no read, ignored Code Segment
1D	3D	5D	7D	9D	BD	DD	FD	Conforming, no read, accessed Code Segment
1E	3E	5E	7E	9E	BE	DE	FE	Conforming, readable, ignored Code Segment
1F	3F	5F	7F	9F	BF	DF	FF	Conforming, readable, accessed Code Segment

AAA—ASCII Adjust AL After Addition

Opcode	Instruction	Clocks	Description
37	AAA	3	ASCII adjust AL after addition

FLAGS MODIFIED

Auxiliary carry, carry

FLAGS UNDEFINED

Overflow, sign, zero, parity

OPERATION

AAA should be executed only after an ADD instruction which leaves a byte result in the AL register. The lower nibbles of the operands to the ADD instruction should be in the range 0 through 9 (BCD digits). In this case, the AAA instruction will adjust AL to contain the correct decimal digit result. If the addition produced a decimal carry, the AH register is incremented, and the carry and auxiliary carry flags are set to 1. If there was no decimal carry, the carry and auxiliary carry flags are set to 0, and AH is unchanged. In any case, AL is left with its top nibble set to 0. To convert AL to an ASCII result, you can follow the AAA instruction with OR AL,30H.

The precise definition of AAA is as follows: if the lower 4 bits of AL are greater than nine, or if the auxiliary carry flag is 1, then increment AL by 6, AH by 1, and set the carry and auxiliary carry flags. Otherwise, reset the carry and auxiliary carry flags. In any case, conclude the AAA operation by setting the upper four bits of AL to zero.

PROTECTED MODE EXCEPTIONS

None

REAL ADDRESS MODE EXCEPTIONS

None

AAD—ASCII Adjust AX Before Division

Opcode	Instruction	Clocks	Description
D5 0A	AAD	14	ASCII adjust AX before division

FLAGS MODIFIED

Sign, zero, parity

FLAGS UNDEFINED

Overflow, auxiliary carry, carry

OPERATION

AAD is used to prepare two unpacked BCD digits (least significant in AL, most significant in AH) for a division operation which will yield an unpacked result. This is accomplished by setting AL to AL + (10 × AH), and then setting AH to 0. This leaves AX equal to the binary equivalent of the original unpacked 2-digit number.

PROTECTED MODE EXCEPTIONS

None

REAL ADDRESS MODE EXCEPTIONS

None

AAM—ASCII Adjust AX After Multiply

Opcode	Instruction	Clocks	Description
D4 0A	AAM	16	ASCII adjust AX after multiply

FLAGS MODIFIED

Sign, zero, parity

FLAGS UNDEFINED

Overflow, auxiliary carry, carry

OPERATION

AAM should be used only after executing a MUL instruction between two unpacked BCD digits, leaving the result in the AX register. Since the result is less than one hundred, it is contained entirely in the AL register. AAM unpacks the AL result by dividing AL by ten, leaving the quotient (most significant digit) in AH, and the remainder (least significant digit) in AL.

PROTECTED MODE EXCEPTIONS

None

REAL ADDRESS MODE EXCEPTIONS

None

AAS—ASCII Adjust AL After Subtraction

Opcode	Instruction	Clocks	Description
3F	AAS	3	ASCII adjust AL after subtraction

FLAGS MODIFIED

Auxiliary carry, carry

FLAGS UNDEFINED

Overflow, sign, zero, parity

OPERATION

AAS should be executed only after a subtraction instruction which left the byte result in the AL register. The lower nibbles of the operands to the SUB instruction should have been in the range 0 through 9 (BCD digits). In this case, the AAS instruction will adjust AL to contain the correct decimal digit result. If the subtraction produced a decimal carry, the AH register is decremented, and the carry and auxiliary carry flags are set to 1. If there was no decimal carry, the carry and auxiliary carry flags are set to 0, and AH is unchanged. In any case, AL is left with its top nibble set to 0. To convert AL to an ASCII result, you can follow the AAS instruction with OR AL,30H.

The precise definition of AAS is as follows: if the lower four bits of AL are greater than 9, or if the auxiliary carry flag is 1, then decrement AL by 6, AH by 1, and set the carry and auxiliary carry flags. Otherwise, reset the carry and auxiliary carry flags. In any case, conclude the AAS operation by setting the upper four bits of AL to zero.

PROTECTED MODE EXCEPTIONS

None

REAL ADDRESS MODE EXCEPTIONS

None

ADC/ADD—Integer Addition

Opcode			Instruction	Clocks	Description
10	/r		ADC eb,rb	2,mem=7	Add with carry byte register into EA byte
11	/r		ADC ew,rw	2,mem=7	Add with carry word register into EA word
12	/r		ADC rb,eb	2,mem=7	Add with carry EA byte into byte register
13	/r		ADC rw,ew	2,mem=7	Add with carry EA word into word register
14	db		ADC AL,db	3	Add with carry immediate byte into AL
15	dw		ADC AX,dw	3	Add with carry immediate word into AX
80	/2	db	ADC eb,db	3,mem=7	Add with carry immediate byte into EA byte
81	/2	dw	ADC ew,dw	3,mem=7	Add with carry immediate word into EA word
83	/2	db	ADC ew,db	3,mem=7	Add with carry immediate byte into EA word
00	/r		ADD eb,rb	2,mem=7	Add byte register into EA byte
01	/r		ADD ew,rw	2,mem=7	Add word register into EA word
02	/r		ADD rb,eb	2,mem=7	Add EA byte into byte register
03	/r		ADD rw,ew	2,mem=7	Add EA word into word register
04	db		ADD AL,db	3	Add immediate byte into AL
05	dw		ADD AX,dw	3	Add immediate word into AX
80	/0	db	ADD eb,db	3,mem=7	Add immediate byte into EA byte
81	/0	dw	ADD ew,dw	3,mem=7	Add immediate word into EA word
83	/0	db	ADD ew,db	3,mem=7	Add immediate byte into EA word

FLAGS MODIFIED

Overflow, sign, zero, auxiliary carry, parity, carry

FLAGS UNDEFINED

None

OPERATION

ADD and ADC perform an integer addition on the two operands. The ADC instruction also adds in the initial state of the carry flag. The result of the addition goes to the first operand. ADC is usually executed as part of a multi-byte or multi-word addition operation.

When a byte immediate value is added to a word operand, the immediate value is first sign-extended.

PROTECTED MODE EXCEPTIONS

#GP(0) if the result is in a non-writable segment. #GP(0) for an illegal memory operand effective address in the CS, DS, or ES segments; #SS(0) for an illegal address in the SS segment.

REAL ADDRESS MODE EXCEPTIONS

Interrupt 13 for a word operand at offset 0FFFFH.

AND—Logical AND

Opcode			Instruction	Clocks	Description
20	/r		AND eb,rb	2,mem=7	Logical-AND byte register into EA byte
21	/r		AND ew,rw	2,mem=7	Logical-AND word register into EA word
22	/r		AND rb,eb	2,mem=7	Logical-AND EA byte into byte register
23	/r		AND rw,ew	2,mem=7	Logical-AND EA word into word register
24	db		AND AL,db	3	Logical-AND immediate byte into AL
25	dw		AND AX,dw	3	Logical-AND immediate word into AX
80	/4	db	AND eb,db	3,mem=7	Logical-AND immediate byte into EA byte
81	/4	dw	AND ew,dw	3,mem=7	Logical-AND immediate word into EA word

FLAGS MODIFIED

Overflow=0, sign, zero, parity, carry=0

FLAGS UNDEFINED

Auxiliary carry

OPERATION

Each bit of the result is a 1 if both corresponding bits of the operands were 1; it is 0 otherwise.

PROTECTED MODE EXCEPTIONS

#GP(0) if the result is in a non-writable segment. #GP(0) for an illegal memory operand effective address in the CS, DS, or ES segments; #SS(0) for an illegal address in the SS segment.

REAL ADDRESS MODE EXCEPTIONS

Interrupt 13 for a word operand at offset 0FFFFH.

ARPL — Adjust RPL Field of Selector

Opcode	Instruction	Clocks	Description
63 /r	ARPL ew,rw	10,mem=11	Adjust RPL of EA word not less than RPL of rw

FLAGS MODIFIED

Zero

FLAGS UNDEFINED

None

OPERATION

The ARPL instruction has two operands. The first operand is a 16-bit memory variable or word register that contains the value of a selector. The second operand is a word register. If the RPL field (bottom two bits) of the first operand is less than the RPL field of the second operand, then the zero flag is set to 1 and the RPL field of the first operand is increased to match the second RPL. Otherwise, the zero flag is set to 0 and no change is made to the first operand.

ARPL appears in operating systems software, not in applications programs. It is used to guarantee that a selector parameter to a subroutine does not request more privilege than the caller was entitled to. The second operand used by ARPL would normally be a register that contains the CS selector value of the caller.

PROTECTED MODE EXCEPTIONS

#GP(0) if the result is in a non-writable segment. #GP(0) for an illegal memory operand effective address in the CS, DS, or ES segments; #SS(0) for an illegal address in the SS segment.

REAL ADDRESS MODE EXCEPTIONS

Interrupt 6. ARPL is not recognized in Real Address mode.

BOUND—Check Array Index Against Bounds

Opcode	Instruction	Clocks	Description
62 /r	BOUND rw,md	noj=13	INT 5 if rw not within bounds

FLAGS MODIFIED

None

FLAGS UNDEFINED

None

OPERATION

BOUND is used to ensure that a signed array index is within the limits defined by a two-word block of memory. The first operand (a register) must be greater than or equal to the first word in memory, and less than or equal to the second word in memory. If the register is not within the bounds, an INTERRUPT 5 occurs.

The two-word block might typically be found just before the array itself and therefore would be accessible at a constant offset of −4 from the array, simplifying the addressing.

PROTECTED MODE EXCEPTIONS

INTERRUPT 5 if the bounds test fails, as described above. #GP(0) for an illegal memory operand effective address in the CS, DS, or ES segments; #SS(0) for an illegal address in the SS segment.

The second operand must be a memory operand, not a register. If the BOUND instruction is executed with a ModRM byte representing a register second operand, then fault #UD will occur.

REAL ADDRESS MODE EXCEPTIONS

INTERRUPT 5 if the bounds test fails, as described above. Interrupt 13 for a second operand at offset 0FFFDH or higher. Interrupt 6 if the second operand is a register, as described in the paragraph above.

CALL—Call Procedure

Opcode		Instruction	Clocks*	Description
E8	cw	CALL cw	7	Call near, offset relative to next instruction
FF	/2	CALL ew	7,mem=11	Call near, offset absolute at EA word
9A	cd	CALL cd	13,pm=26	Call inter-segment, immediate 4-byte address
9A	cd	CALL cd	41	Call gate, same privilege
9A	cd	CALL cd	82	Call gate, more privilege, no parameters
9A	cd	CALL cd	86+4X	Call gate, more privilege, X parameters
9A	cd	CALL cd	177	Call via Task State Segment
9A	cd	CALL cd	182	Call via task gate
FF	/3	CALL ed	16,mem=29	Call inter-segment, address at EA doubleword
FF	/3	CALL ed	44	Call gate, same privilege
FF	/3	CALL ed	83	Call gate, more privilege, no parameters
FF	/3	CALL ed	90+4X	Call gate, more privilege, X parameters
FF	/3	CALL ed	180	Call via Task State Segment
FF	/3	CALL ed	185	Call via task gate

*Add one clock for each byte in the next instruction executed.

FLAGS MODIFIED

None, except when a task switch occurs

FLAGS UNDEFINED

None

OPERATION

The CALL instruction causes the procedure named in the operand to be executed. When the procedure is complete (a return instruction is executed within the procedure), execution continues at the instruction that follows the CALL instruction.

The CALL cw form of the instruction adds modulo 65536 (the 2-byte operand) to the offset of the instruction following the CALL and sets IP to the resulting offset. The 2-byte offset of the instruction that follows the CALL is pushed onto the stack. It will be popped by a near RET instruction within the procedure. The CS register is not changed by this form.

The CALL ew form of the instruction is the same as CALL cw except that the operand specifies a memory location from which the absolute 2-byte offset for the procedure is fetched.

The CALL cd form of the instruction uses the 4-byte operand as a pointer to the procedure called. The CALL ed form fetches the long pointer from the memory location specified. Both long pointer forms consult the AR byte in the descriptor indexed by the selector part of the long pointer. The AR byte can indicate one of the following descriptor types:

1. Code Segment—The access rights are checked, the return pointer is pushed onto the stack, and the procedure is jumped to.

2. Call Gate—The offset part of the pointer is ignored. Instead, the entire address of the procedure is taken from the call gate descriptor entry. If the routine being entered is more privileged, then a new stack (both SS and SP) is loaded from the task state segment for the new privilege level, and parameters determined by the wordcount field of the call gate are copied from the old stack to the new stack.

3. Task Gate—The current task's context is saved in its Task State Segment (TSS), and the TSS named in the task-gate is used to load the new context. The selector for the outgoing task (from TR) is stored into the new TSS's link field, and the new task's Nested Task flag is set. The outgoing task is left marked busy, the new TSS is marked busy, and execution resumes at the point at which the new task was last suspended.

4. Task State Segment—The current task is suspended and the new task initiated as in 3 above except that there is no intervening gate.

For long calls involving no task switch, the return link is the pointer of the instruction that follows the CALL, i.e., the caller's CS and updated IP. Task switches invoked by CALLs are linked by storing the outgoing task's TSS selector in the incoming TSS's link field and setting the Nested Task flag in the new task. Nested tasks must be terminated by an IRET. IRET releases the nested task and follows the back link to the calling task if the NT flag is set.

A precise list of the protection checks made and the actions taken is given by the following list:

CALL FAR:
    If indirect then check access of EA doubleword #GP(0) if limit violation
    New CS selector must not be null else #GP(0)
    Check that new CS selector index is within its descriptor table limits; else #GP (new CS selector)
    Examine AR byte of selected descriptor for various legal values:

        CALL CONFORMING CODE SEGMENT:
            DPL must be ≤ CPL else #GP (code segment selector)
            Segment must be PRESENT else #NP (code segment selector)
            Stack must be big enough for return address else #SS(0)
            IP must be in code segment limit else #GP(0)
            Load code segment descriptor into CS cache
            Load CS with new code segment selector
            Load IP with new offset

        CALL NONCONFORMING CODE SEGMENT:
            RPL must be ≤ CPL else #GP (code segment selector)
            DPL must be = CPL else #GP (code segment selector)
            Segment must be PRESENT else #NP (code segment selector)
            Stack must be big enough for return address else #SS(0)
            IP must be in code segment limit else #GP(0)
            Load code segment descriptor into CS cache
            Load CS with new code segment selector
            Set RPL of CS to CPL
            Load IP with new offset

        CALL TO CALL GATE:
            Call gate DPL must be ≥ CPL else #GP (call gate selector)
            Call gate DPL must be ≥ RPL else #GP (call gate selector)
            Call gate must be PRESENT else #NP (call gate selector)
            Examine code segment selector in call gate descriptor:
                Selector must not be null else #GP(0)
                Selector must be within its descriptor table limits else #GP (code segment selector)
                AR byte of selected descriptor must indicate code segment else #GP (code segment selector)
                DPL of selected descriptor must be ≤ CPL else #GP(code segment selector)
                If non-conforming code segment and DPL < CPL then

CALL GATE TO MORE PRIVILEGE:
Get new SS selector for new privilege level from TSS
Check selector and descriptor for new SS:
    Selector must not be null else #TS(0)
    Selector index must be within its descriptor table limits else #TS (SS selector)
    Selector's RPL must equal DPL of code segment else #TS (SS selector)
    Stack segment DPL must equal DPL of code segment else #TS (SS selector)
    Descriptor must indicate writable data segment else #TS (SS selector)
    Segment PRESENT else #SS (SS selector)
        New stack must have room for parameters plus 8 bytes else #SS(0)
        IP must be in code segment limit else #GP(0)
        Load new SS:SP value from TSS
        Load new CS:IP value from gate
        Load CS descriptor
        Load SS descriptor
        Push long pointer of old stack onto new stack
        Get word count from call gate, mask to 5 bits
        Copy parameters from old stack onto new stack
        Push return address onto new stack
        Set CPL to stack segment DPL
        Set RPL of CS to CPL
Else
    CALL GATE TO SAME PRIVILEGE:
    Stack must have room for 4-byte return address else #SS(0)
    IP must be in code segment limit else #GP(0)
    Load CS:IP from gate
    Push return address onto stack
    Load code segment descriptor into CS-cache
    Set RPL of CS to CPL

CALL TASK GATE:
    Task gate DPL must be ≥ CPL else #GP (gate selector)
    Task gate DPL must be ≥ RPL else #GP (gate selector)
    Task Gate must be PRESENT else #NP (gate selector)
    Examine selector to TSS, given in Task Gate descriptor:
        Must specify global in the local/global bit else #GP (TSS selector)
        Index must be within GDT limits else #GP (TSS selector)
        TSS descriptor AR byte must specify available TSS (bottom bits 00001) else #GP (TSS selector)
        Task State Segment must be PRESENT else #NP (TSS selector)
    SWITCH_TASKS with nesting to TSS
    IP must be in code segment limit else #GP(0)

TASK STATE SEGMENT:
    TSS DPL must be ≥ CPL else #GP (TSS selector)
    TSS DPL must be ≥ RPL else #GP (TSS selector)
    TSS descriptor AR byte must specify available TSS else #GP (TSS selector)
    Task State Segment must be PRESENT else #NP (TSS selector)
    SWITCH_TASKS with nesting to TSS
    IP must be in code segment limit else #GP(0)

    ELSE #GP (code segment selector)

PROTECTED MODE EXCEPTIONS

FAR calls: #GP, #NP, #SS, and #TS, as indicated in the list above.

NEAR direct calls: #GP(0) if procedure location is beyond the code segment limits.

NEAR indirect CALL: #GP(0) for an illegal memory operand effective address in the CS, DS, or ES segments; #SS(0) for an illegal address in the SS segment. #GP if the indirect offset obtained is beyond the code segment limits.

REAL ADDRESS MODE EXCEPTIONS

Interrupt 13 for a word operand at offset 0FFFFH.

CBW—Convert Byte into Word

Opcode	Instruction	Clocks	Description
98	CBW	2	Convert byte into word (AH = top bit of AL)

FLAGS MODIFIED

None

FLAGS UNDEFINED

None

OPERATION

CBW converts the signed byte in AL to a signed word in AX. It does so by extending the top bit of AL into all of the bits of AH.

PROTECTED MODE EXCEPTIONS

None

REAL ADDRESS MODE EXCEPTIONS

None

CLD—Clear Direction Flag

Opcode	Instruction	Clocks	Description
FC	CLD	2	Clear direction flag, SI and DI will increment

FLAGS MODIFIED

Direction=0

FLAGS UNDEFINED

None

OPERATION

CLD clears the direction flag. No other flags or registers are affected. After CLD is executed, string operations will increment the index registers (SI and/or DI) that they use.

PROTECTED MODE EXCEPTIONS

None

REAL ADDRESS MODE EXCEPTIONS

None

CLI—Clear Interrupt Flag

Opcode	Instruction	Clocks	Description
FA	CLI	3	Clear interrupt flag; interrupts disabled

FLAGS MODIFIED

Interrupt=0

FLAGS UNDEFINED

None

OPERATION

CLI clears the interrupt enable flag if the current privilege level is at least as privileged as IOPL. No other flags are affected. External interrupts will not be recognized at the end of the CLI instruction or thereafter until the interrupt flag is set.

PROTECTED MODE EXCEPTIONS

#GP(0) if the current privilege level is bigger (has less privilege) than the IOPL in the flags register. IOPL specifies the least privileged level at which I/O may be performed.

REAL ADDRESS MODE EXCEPTIONS

None

CLTS—Clear Task Switched Flag

Opcode	Instruction	Clocks	Description
0F 06	CLTS	2	Clear task switched flag

FLAGS MODIFIED

Task switched=0

FLAGS UNDEFINED

None

OPERATION

CLTS clears the task switched flag in the Machine Status Word. This flag is set by the 80286 every time a task switch occurs. The TS flag is used to manage processor extensions as follows: every execution of a WAIT or an ESC instruction will be trapped if the MP flag of MSW is set and the task switched flag is set. Thus, if a processor extension is present and a task switch has been made since the last ESC instruction was begun, the processor extension's context must be saved before a new instruction can be issued. The fault routine will save the context and reset the task switched flag or place the task requesting the processor extension into a queue until the current processor extension instruction is completed.

CLTS appears in operating systems software, not in applications programs. It is a privileged instruction that can only be executed at level 0.

PROTECTED MODE EXCEPTIONS

#GP(0) if CLTS is executed with a current privilege level other than 0.

REAL ADDRESS MODE EXCEPTIONS

None (valid in REAL ADDRESS MODE to allow power-up initialization for Protected Mode)

CMC—Complement Carry Flag

Opcode	Instruction	Clocks	Description
F5	CMC	2	Complement carry flag

FLAGS MODIFIED

Carry

FLAGS UNDEFINED

None

OPERATION

CMC reverses the setting of the carry flag. No other flags are affected.

PROTECTED MODE EXCEPTIONS

None

REAL ADDRESS MODE EXCEPTIONS

None

CMP—Compare Two Operands

Opcode			Instruction	Clocks	Description
3C	db		CMP AL,db	3	Compare immediate byte from AL
3D	dw		CMP AX,dw	3	Compare immediate word from AX
80	/7	db	CMP eb,db	3,mem=6	Compare immediate byte from EA byte
38	/r		CMP eb,rb	2,mem=7	Compare byte register from EA byte
83	/7	db	CMP ew,db	3,mem=6	Compare immediate byte from EA word
81	/7	dw	CMP ew,dw	3,mem=6	Compare immediate word from EA word
39	/r		CMP ew,rw	2,mem=7	Compare word register from EA word
3A	/r		CMP rb,eb	2,mem=6	Compare EA byte from byte register
3B	/r		CMP rw,ew	2,mem=6	Compare EA word from word register

FLAGS MODIFIED

Overflow, sign, zero, auxiliary carry, parity, carry

FLAGS UNDEFINED

None

OPERATION

CMP subtracts the second operand from the first operand, but it does not place the result anywhere. Only the flags are changed by this instruction. CMP is usually followed by a conditional jump instruction. See the "Jcond" instructions in this chapter for the list of signed and unsigned flag tests provided by the 80286.

If a word operand is compared to an immediate byte value, the byte value is first sign-extended.

PROTECTED MODE EXCEPTIONS

#GP(0) for an illegal memory operand effective address in the CS, DS, or ES segments; #SS(0) for an illegal address in the SS segment.

REAL ADDRESS MODE EXCEPTIONS

Interrupt 13 for a word operand at offset 0FFFFH.

CMPS/CMPSB/CMPSW—Compare string operands

Opcode	Instruction	Clocks	Description
A6	CMPS *mb,mb*	8	Compare bytes ES:[DI] from [SI]
A6	CMPSB	8	Compare bytes ES:[DI] from DS:[SI]
A7	CMPSW	8	Compare words ES:[DI] from DS:[SI]

FLAGS MODIFIED

Overflow, sign, zero, auxiliary carry, parity, carry

FLAGS UNDEFINED

None

OPERATION

CMPS compares the byte or word pointed to by SI with the byte or word pointed to by DI by performing the subtraction [SI] − [DI]. The result is not placed anywhere; only the flags reflect the result of the subtraction. The types of the operands to CMPS determine whether bytes or words are compared. The segment addressability of the first (SI) operand determines whether a segment override byte will be produced or whether the default segment register DS is used. The second (DI) operand must be addressible from the ES register; no segment override is possible.

After the comparison is made, both SI and DI are automatically advanced. If the direction flag is 0 (CLD was executed), the registers increment; if the direction flag is 1 (STD was executed), the registers decrement. The registers increment or decrement by 1 if a byte was moved; by 2 if a word was moved.

CMPS can be preceded by the REPE or REPNE prefix for block comparison of CX bytes or words. Refer to the REP instruction for details of this operation.

PROTECTED MODE EXCEPTIONS

#GP(0) for an illegal memory operand effective address in the CS, DS, or ES segments; #SS(0) for an illegal address in the SS segment.

REAL ADDRESS MODE EXCEPTIONS

Interrupt 13 for a word operand at offset 0FFFFH.

CWD—Convert Word to Doubleword

Opcode	Instruction	Clocks	Description
99	CWD	2	Convert word to doubleword (DX:AX = AX)

FLAGS MODIFIED

None

FLAGS UNDEFINED

None

OPERATION

CWD converts the signed word in AX to a signed doubleword in DX:AX. It does so by extending the top bit of AX into all the bits of DX.

PROTECTED MODE EXCEPTIONS

None

REAL ADDRESS MODE EXCEPTIONS

None

DAA—Decimal Adjust AL After Addition

Opcode	Instruction	Clocks	Description
27	DAA	3	Decimal adjust AL after addition

FLAGS MODIFIED

Sign, zero, auxiliary carry, parity, carry

FLAGS UNDEFINED

Overflow

OPERATION

DAA should be executed only after an ADD instruction which leaves a two-BCD-digit byte result in the AL register. The ADD operands should consist of two packed BCD digits. In this case, the DAA instruction will adjust AL to contain the correct two-digit packed decimal result.

The precise definition of DAA is as follows:

1. If the lower 4 bits of AL are greater than nine, or if the auxiliary carry flag is 1, then increment AL by 6, and set the auxiliary carry flag. Otherwise, reset the auxiliary carry flag.

2. If AL is now greater than 9FH, or if the carry flag is set, then increment AL by 60H, and set the carry flag. Otherwise, clear the carry flag.

PROTECTED MODE EXCEPTIONS

None

REAL ADDRESS MODE EXCEPTIONS

None

DAS—Decimal Adjust AL After Subtraction

Opcode	Instruction	Clocks	Description
2F	DAS	3	Decimal adjust AL after subtraction

FLAGS MODIFIED

Sign, zero, auxiliary carry, parity, carry

FLAGS UNDEFINED

Overflow

OPERATION

DAS should be executed only after a subtraction instruction which leaves a two-BCD-digit byte result in the AL register. The operands should consist of two packed BCD digits. In this case, the DAS instruction will adjust AL to contain the correct packed two-digit decimal result.

The precise definition of DAS is as follows:

1. If the lower four bits of AL are greater than 9, or if the auxiliary carry flag is 1, then decrement AL by 6, and set the auxiliary carry flag. Otherwise, reset the auxiliary carry flag.

2. If AL is now greater than 9FH, or if the carry flag is set, then decrement AL by 60H, and set the carry flag. Otherwise, clear the carry flag.

PROTECTED MODE EXCEPTIONS

None

REAL ADDRESS MODE EXCEPTIONS

None

DEC—Decrement by 1

Opcode	Instruction	Clocks	Description
FE /1	DEC *eb*	2,mem=7	Decrement EA byte by 1
FF /1	DEC *ew*	2,mem=7	Decrement EA word by 1
48+ *rw*	DEC *rw*	2	Decrement word register by 1

FLAGS MODIFIED

Overflow, sign, zero, auxiliary carry, parity

FLAGS UNDEFINED

None

OPERATION

1 is subtracted from the operand. Note that the carry flag is not changed by this instruction. If you want the carry flag set, use the SUB instruction with a second operand of 1.

PROTECTED MODE EXCEPTIONS

#GP(0) if the operand is in a non-writable segment. #GP(0) for an illegal memory operand effective address in the CS, DS, or ES segments; #SS(0) for an illegal address in the SS segment.

REAL ADDRESS MODE EXCEPTIONS

Interrupt 13 for a word operand at offset 0FFFFH.

DIV—Unsigned Divide

Opcode	Instruction	Clocks	Description
F6 /6	DIV *eb*	14,mem=17	Unsigned divide AX by EA byte
F7 /6	DIV *ew*	22,mem=25	Unsigned divide DX:AX by EA word

FLAGS MODIFIED

None

FLAGS UNDEFINED

Overflow, sign, zero, auxiliary carry, parity, carry

OPERATION

DIV performs an unsigned divide. The dividend is implicit; only the divisor is given as an operand. If the source operand is a BYTE operand, divide AX by the byte. The quotient is stored in AL, and the remainder is stored in AH. If the source operand is a WORD operand, divide DX:AX by the word. The high-order 16 bits of the dividend are kept in DX. The quotient is stored in AX, and the remainder is stored in DX. Non-integral quotients are truncated towards 0. The remainder is always less than the dividend.

PROTECTED MODE EXCEPTIONS

Interrupt 0 if the quotient is too big to fit in the designated register (AL or AX), or if the divisor is zero. #GP(0) for an illegal memory operand effective address in the CS, DS, or ES segments; #SS(0) for an illegal address in the SS segment.

REAL ADDRESS MODE EXCEPTIONS

Interrupt 0 if the quotient is too big to fit in the designated register (AL or AX), or if the divisor is zero. Interrupt 13 for a word operand at offset 0FFFFH.

ENTER—Make Stack Frame for Procedure Parameters

Opcode			Instruction	Clocks	Description
C8	dw	00	ENTER dw,0	11	Make stack frame for procedure parameters
C8	dw	01	ENTER dw,1	15	Make stack frame for procedure parameters
C8	dw	db	ENTER dw,db	12+4db	Make stack frame for procedure parameters

FLAGS MODIFIED

None

FLAGS UNDEFINED

None

OPERATION

ENTER is used to create the stack frame required by most block-structured high-level languages. The first operand specifies how many bytes of dynamic storage are to be allocated on the stack for the routine being entered. The second operand gives the lexical nesting level of the routine within the high-level-language source code. It determines how many stack frame pointers are copied into the new stack frame from the preceding frame. BP is used as the current stack frame pointer.

If the second operand is 0, ENTER pushes BP, sets BP to SP, and subtracts the first operand from SP.

For example, a procedure with 12 bytes of local variables would have an ENTER 12,0 instruction at its entry point and a LEAVE instruction before every RET. The 12 local bytes would be addressed as negative offsets from [BP]. See also section 4.2.

The formal definition of the ENTER instruction for all cases is given by the following listing. LEVEL denotes the value of the second operand.

```
LEVEL:=LEVEL MOD 32
Push BP
Set a temporary value FRAME_PTR := SP
If LEVEL > 0 then
    Repeat (LEVEL-1) times:
        BP := BP - 2
        Push the word pointed to by BP
    End repeat
    Push FRAME_PTR
End if
BP := FRAME_PTR
SP := SP - first operand.
```

PROTECTED MODE EXCEPTIONS

#SS(0) if SP were to go outside of the stack limit within any part of the instruction execution.

REAL ADDRESS MODE EXCEPTIONS

None

HLT—Halt

Opcode	Instruction	Clocks	Description
F4	HLT	2	Halt

FLAGS MODIFIED

None

FLAGS UNDEFINED

None

OPERATION

Successful execution of HLT causes the 80286 to cease executing instructions and to enter a HALT state. Execution resumes only upon receipt of an enabled interrupt or a reset. If an interrupt is used to resume program execution after HLT, the saved CS:IP value will point to the instruction that follows HLT.

PROTECTED MODE EXCEPTIONS

HLT is a privileged instruction. #GP(0) if the current privilege level is not 0.

REAL ADDRESS MODE EXCEPTIONS

None

IDIV — Signed Divide

Opcode	Instruction	Clocks	Description
F6 /7	IDIV *eb*	17,mem=20	Signed divide AX by EA byte (AL=Quo, AH=Rem)
F7 /7	IDIV *ew*	25,mem=28	Signed divide DX:AX by EA word (AX=Quo, DX=Rem)

FLAGS MODIFIED

None

FLAGS UNDEFINED

Overflow, sign, zero, auxiliary carry, parity, carry

OPERATION

IDIV performs a signed divide. The dividend is implicit; only the divisor is given as an operand. If the source operand is a BYTE operand, divide AX by the byte. The quotient is stored in AL, and the remainder is stored in AH. If the source operand is a WORD operand, divide DX:AX by the word. The high-order 16 bits of the dividend are in DX. The quotient is stored in AX, and the remainder is stored in DX. Non-integral quotients are truncated towards 0. The remainder has the same sign as the dividend and always has less magnitude than the dividend.

PROTECTED MODE EXCEPTIONS

Interrupt 0 if the quotient is too big to fit in the designated register (AL or AX), or if the divisor is 0. #GP(0) for an illegal memory operand effective address in the CS, DS, or ES segments; #SS(0) for an illegal address in the SS segment.

REAL ADDRESS MODE EXCEPTIONS

Interrupt 0 if the quotient is too big to fit in the designated register (AL or AX), or if the divisor is 0. Interrupt 13 for a word operand at offset 0FFFFH.

IMUL — Signed Multiply

Opcode			Instruction	Clocks	Description
F6	/5		IMUL *eb*	13,mem=16	Signed multiply (AX = AL × EA byte)
F7	/5		IMUL *ew*	21,mem=24	Signed multiply (DXAX = AX × EA word)
6B	/r	*db*	IMUL *rw,db*	21,mem=24	Signed multiply imm. byte into word reg.
69	/r	*dw*	IMUL *rw,ew,dw*	21,mem=24	Signed multiply (rw = EA word × imm. word)
6B	/r	*db*	IMUL *rw,ew,db*	21,mem=24	Signed multiply (rw = EA word × imm. byte)

FLAGS MODIFIED

Overflow, carry

FLAGS UNDEFINED

Sign, zero, auxiliary carry, parity

OPERATION

IMUL performs signed multiplication. If IMUL has a single byte source operand, then the source is multiplied by AL and the 16-bit signed result is left in AX. Carry and overflow are set to 0 if AH is a sign extension of AL; they are set to 1 otherwise.

If IMUL has a single word source operand, then the source operand is multiplied by AX and the 32-bit signed result is left in DX:AX. DX contains the high-order 16 bits of the product. Carry and overflow are set to 0 if DX is a sign extension of AX; they are set to 1 otherwise.

If IMUL has three operands, then the second operand (an effective address word) is multiplied by the third operand (an immediate word), and the 16 bits of the result are placed in the first operand (a word register). Carry and overflow are set to 0 if the result fits in a signed word (between −32768 and +32767, inclusive); they are set to 1 otherwise.

NOTE

The low 16 bits of the product of a 16-bit signed multiply are the same as those of an unsigned multiply. The three operand IMUL instruction can be used for unsigned operands as well.

PROTECTED MODE EXCEPTIONS

#GP(0) for an illegal memory operand effective address in the CS, DS, or ES segments; #SS(0) for an illegal address in the SS segment.

REAL ADDRESS MODE EXCEPTIONS

Interrupt 13 for a word operand at offset 0FFFFH.

IN—Input from Port

Opcode		Instruction	Clocks	Description
E4	db	IN AL,db	5	Input byte from immediate port into AL
EC		IN AL,DX	5	Input byte from port DX into AL
E5	db	IN AX,db	5	Input word from immediate port into AX
ED		IN AX,DX	5	Input word from port DX into AX

FLAGS MODIFIED

None

FLAGS UNDEFINED

None

OPERATION

IN transfers a data byte or data word from the port numbered by the second operand into the register (AL or AX) given as the first operand. You can access any port from 0 to 65535 by placing the port number in the DX register then using an IN instruction with DX as the second parameter. These I/O instructions can be shortened by using an 8-bit port I/O in the instruction. The upper 8 bits of the port address will be zero when an 8-bit port I/O is used.

Intel has reserved I/O port addresses 00F8H through 00FFH; they should not be used.

PROTECTED MODE EXCEPTIONS

#GP(0) if the current privilege level is bigger (has less privilege) than IOPL, which is the privilege level found in the flags register.

REAL ADDRESS MODE EXCEPTIONS

None

INC—Increment by 1

Opcode	Instruction	Clocks	Description
FE /0	INC eb	2,mem=7	Increment EA byte by 1
FF /0	INC ew	2,mem=7	Increment EA word by 1
40+rw	INC rw	2	Increment word register by 1

FLAGS MODIFIED

Overflow, sign, zero, auxiliary carry, parity

FLAGS UNDEFINED

None

OPERATION

1 is added to the operand. Note that the carry flag is not changed by this instruction. If you want the carry flag set, use the ADD instruction with a second operand of 1.

PROTECTED MODE EXCEPTIONS

#GP(0) if the operand is in a non-writable segment. #GP(0) for an illegal memory operand effective address in the CS, DS, or ES segments; #SS(0) for an illegal address in the SS segment.

REAL ADDRESS MODE EXCEPTIONS

Interrupt 13 for a word operand at offset 0FFFFH.

INS/INSB/INSW—Input from Port to String

Opcode	Instruction	Clocks	Description
6C	INS *eb*,DX	5	Input byte from port DX into ES:[DI]
6D	INS *ew*,DX	5	Input word from port DX into ES:[DI]
6C	INSB	5	Input byte from port DX into ES:[DI]
6D	INSW	5	Input word from port DX into ES:[DI]

FLAGS MODIFIED

None

FLAGS UNDEFINED

None

OPERATION

INS transfers data from the input port numbered by the DX register to the memory byte or word at ES:DI. The memory operand must be addressable from the ES register; no segment override is possible.

INS does not allow the specification of the port number as an immediate value. The port must be addressed through the DX register.

After the transfer is made, DI is automatically advanced. If the direction flag is 0 (CLD was executed), DI increments; if the direction flag is 1 (STD was executed), DI decrements. DI increments or decrements by 1 if a byte was moved; by 2 if a word was moved.

INS can be preceded by the REP prefix for block input of CX bytes or words. Refer to the REP instruction for details of this operation.

Intel has reserved I/O port addresses 00F8H through 00FFH; they should not be used.

NOTE

Not all input port devices can handle the rate at which this instruction transfers input data to memory.

PROTECTED MODE EXCEPTIONS

#GP(0) if CPL > IOPL. #GP(0) if the destination is in a non-writable segment. #GP(0) for an illegal memory operand effective address in the CS, DS, or ES segments; #SS(0) for an illegal address in the SS segment.

REAL ADDRESS MODE EXCEPTIONS

Interrupt 13 for a word operand at offset 0FFFFH.

INT/INTO—Call to Interrupt Procedure

Opcode	Instruction	Clocks[1]	Description
CC	INT 3	23[2]	Interrupt 3 (trap to debugger)
CC	INT 3	40	Interrupt 3, protected mode, same privilege
CC	INT 3	78	Interrupt 3, protected mode, more privilege
CC	INT 3	167	Interrupt 3, protected mode, via task gate
CD db	INT db	23[2]	Interrupt numbered by immediate byte
CD db	INT db	40	Interrupt, protected mode, same privilege
CD db	INT db	78	Interrupt, protected mode, more privilege
CD db	INT db	167	Interrupt, protected mode, via task gate
CE	INTO	24,noj=3[2]	Interrupt 4 if overflow flag is 1

[1] = Add one clock for each byte of the next instruction executed.
[2] = (real mode)

FLAGS MODIFIED

All if a task switch takes place; Trap Flag reset if no task switch takes place. Interrupt Flag is always reset in Real Mode, and reset in Protected Mode when INT references an interrupt gate.

FLAGS UNDEFINED

None

OPERATION

The INT instruction generates via software a call to an interrupt procedure. The immediate operand, from 0 to 255, gives the index number into the Interrupt Descriptor Table of the interrupt routine to be called. In protected mode, the IDT consists of 8-byte descriptors; the descriptor for the interrupt invoked must indicate an interrupt gate, a trap gate, or a task gate. In real address mode, the IDT is an array of 4-byte long pointers at the fixed location 00000H.

The INTO instruction is identical to the INT instruction except that the interrupt number is implicitly 4, and the interrupt is made only if the overflow flag of the 80286 is on. The clock counts for the four forms of INT db are valid for INTO, with the number of clocks increased by 1 for the overflow flag test.

The first 32 interrupts are reserved by Intel for systems use. Some of these interrupts are exception handlers for internally-generated faults. Most of these exception handlers should not be invoked with the INT instruction.

Generally, interrupts behave like far CALLs except that the flags register is pushed onto the stack before the return address. Interrupt procedures return via the IRET instruction, which pops the flags from the stack.

In Real Address mode, INT pushes the flags, CS and the return IP onto the stack in that order, then resets the Trap Flag, then jumps to the long pointer indexed by the interrupt number, in the interrupt vector table.

In Protected mode, INT also resets the Trap Flag. In Protected mode, the precise semantics of the INT instruction are given by the following:

INTERRUPT
    Interrupt vector must be within IDT table limits else #GP (vector number × 8+2+EXT)
    Descriptor AR byte must indicate interrupt gate, trap gate, or task gate else #GP (vector number × 8+2+EXT)
    If INT instruction then gate descriptor DPL must be ≥ CPL else #GP (vector number × 8+2+EXT)
    Gate must be PRESENT else #NP (vector number × 8+2+EXT)
    If TRAP GATE or INTERRUPT GATE:
    Examine CS selector and descriptor given in the gate descriptor:
        Selector must be non-null else #GP (EXT)
        Selector must be within its descriptor table limits else #GP (selector+EXT)
        Descriptor AR byte must indicate code segment else #GP (selector + EXT)
        Segment must be PRESENT else #NP (selector+EXT)
    If code segment is non-conforming and DPL < CPL then
        INTERRUPT TO INNER PRIVILEGE:
            Check selector and descriptor for new stack in current Task State Segment:
                Selector must be non-null else #TS(EXT)
                Selector index must be within its descriptor table limits else #TS (SS selector+EXT)
                Selector's RPL must equal DPL of code segment else #TS (SS selector+EXT)
                Stack segment DPL must equal DPL of code segment else #TS (SS selector+EXT)
                Descriptor must indicate writable data segment else #TS (SS selector+EXT)
                Segment must be PRESENT else #SS (SS selector+EXT)
            New stack must have room for 10 bytes else #SS(0)
            IP must be in CS limit else #GP(0)
            Load new SS and SP value from TSS
            Load new CS and IP value from gate
            Load CS descriptor
            Load SS descriptor
            Push long pointer to old stack onto new stack
            Push return address onto new stack
            Set CPL to new code segment DPL
            Set RPL of CS to CPL
            If INTERRUPT GATE then set the Interrupts Enabled Flag to 0 (disabled)
            Set the Trap Flag to 0
            Set the Nested Task Flag to 0
    If code segment is conforming or code segment DPL = CPL then
        INTERRUPT TO SAME PRIVILEGE LEVEL:
            Current stack limits must allow pushing 6 bytes else #SS(0)
            If interrupt was caused by fault with error code then
                Stack limits must allow push of two more bytes else #SS(0)
            IP must be in CS limit else #GP(0)
            Push flags onto stack
            Push current CS selector onto stack
            Push return offset onto stack
            Load CS:IP from gate
            Load CS descriptor
            Set the RPL field of CS to CPL
            Push error code (if any) onto stack
            If INTERRUPT GATE then set the Interrupts Enabled Flag to 0 (disabled)
            Set the Trap Flag to 0
            Set the Nested Task Flag to 0

Else #GP (CS selector + EXT)

If TASK GATE:
    Examine selector to TSS, given in Task Gate descriptor:
        Must specify global in the local/global bit else #GP (TSS selector)

```
        Index must be within GDT limits else #GP (TSS selector)
        AR byte must specify available TSS (bottom bits 00001) else #GP (TSS selector)
        Task State Segment must be PRESENT else #NP (TSS selector)
    SWITCH_TASKS with nesting to TSS
    If interrupt was caused by fault with error code then
        Stack limits must allow push of two more bytes else #SS(0)
        Push error code onto stack
    IP must be in CS limit else #GP(0)
```

NOTE

EXT is 1 if an external event (i.e., a single step, an external interrupt, an MF exception, or an MP exception) caused the interrupt; 0 if not (i.e., an INT instruction or other exceptions).

PROTECTED MODE EXCEPTIONS

#GP, #NP, #SS, and #TS, as indicated in the list above.

REAL ADDRESS MODE EXCEPTIONS

None; the 80286 will shut down if the SP = 1, 3, or 5 before executing the INT or INTO instruction—due to lack of stack space.

IRET—Interrupt Return

Opcode	Instruction	Clocks*	Description
CF	IRET	17,pm=31	Interrupt return (far return and pop flags)
CF	IRET	55	Interrupt return, lesser privilege
CF	IRET	169	Interrupt return, different task (NT=1)

*Add one clock for each byte in the next instruction executed.

FLAGS MODIFIED

Entire flags register popped from stack

FLAGS UNDEFINED

None

OPERATION

In real address mode, IRET pops IP, CS, and FLAGS from the stack in that order, and resumes the interrupted routine.

In protected mode, the action of IRET depends on the setting of the Nested Task Flag (NT) bit in the flag register. When popping the new flag image from the stack, note that the IOPL bits in the flag register are changed only when CPL=0.

If NT=0, IRET returns from an interrupt procedure without a task switch. The code returned to must be equally or less privileged than the interrupt routine as indicated by the RPL bits of the CS selector popped from the stack. If the destination code is of less privilege, IRET then also pops SP and SS from the stack.

If NT=1, IRET reverses the operation of a CALL or INT that caused a task switch. The task executing IRET has its updated state saved in its Task State Segment. This means that if the task is re-entered, the code that follows IRET will be executed.

The exact checks and actions performed by IRET in protected mode are given on the following page.

INTERRUPT RETURN:
    If Nested Task Flag=1 then
        RETURN FROM NESTED TASK:
            Examine Back Link Selector in TSS addressed by the current Task Register:
                Must specify global in the local/global bit else #TS (new TSS selector)
                Index must be within GDT limits else #TS (new TSS selector)
                AR byte must specify TSS else #TS (new TSS selector)
                New TSS must be busy else #TS (new TSS selector)
                Task State Segment must be PRESENT else #NP (new TSS selector)
            SWITCH_TASKS without nesting to TSS specified by back link selector
            Mark the task just abandoned as NOT BUSY
            IP must be in code segment limit else #GP(0)

If Nested Task Flag=0 then
    INTERRUPT RETURN ON STACK:
        Second word on stack must be within stack limits else #SS(0)
        Return CS selector RPL must be ≥ CPL else #GP (Return selector)
        If return selector RPL = CPL then
            INTERRUPT RETURN TO SAME LEVEL:
            Top 6 bytes on stack must be within limits else #SS(0)
            Return CS selector (at SP+2) must be non-null else #GP(0)
            Selector index must be within its descriptor table limits else #GP(Return selector)
            AR byte must indicate code segment else #GP (Return selector)
            If non-conforming then code segment DPL must = CPL else #GP (Return selector)
            If conforming then code segment DPL must be ≤ CPL else #GP (Return selector)
            Segment must be PRESENT else #NP (Return selector)
            IP must be in code segment limit else #GP(0)
            Load CS:IP from stack
            Load CS-cache with new code segment descriptor
            Load flags with third word on stack
            Increment SP by 6
    Else
    INTERRUPT RETURN TO OUTER PRIVILEGE LEVEL:
    Top 10 bytes on stack must be within limits else #SS(0)
    Examine return CS selector (at SP+2) and associated descriptor:
        Selector must be non-null else #GP(0)
        Selector index must be within its descriptor table limits else #GP (Return selector)
        AR byte must indicate code segment else #GP (Return selector)
        If non-conforming then code segment DPL must = CS selector RPL else #GP (Return selector)
        If conforming then code segment DPL must be > CPL else #GP (Return selector)
        Segment must be PRESENT else #NP (Return selector)
    Examine return SS selector (at SP+8) and associated descriptor:
        Selector must be non-null else #GP(0)
        Selector index must be within its descriptor table limits else #GP (SS selector)
        Selector RPL must equal the RPL of the return CS selector else #GP (SS selector)
        AR byte must indicate a writable data segment else #GP (SS selector)
        Stack segment DPL must equal the RPL of the return CS selector else #GP (SS selector)
        SS must be PRESENT else #SS (SS selector)
    IP must be in code segment limit else #GP(0)
    Load CS:IP from stack
    Load flags with values at (SP+4)
    Load SS:SP from stack
    Set CPL to the RPL of the return CS selector
    Load the CS-cache with the CS descriptor
    Load the SS-cache with the SS descriptor
    For each of ES and DS:
        If the current register setting is not valid for the outer level, then zero the register and
          clear the valid flag
        To be valid, the register setting must satisfy the following properties:
          Selector index must be within descriptor table limits
          AR byte must indicate data or readable code segment
          If segment is data or non-conforming code, then:
          DPL must be ≥ CPL, or
          DPL must be ≥ RPL.

PROTECTED MODE EXCEPTIONS

#GP, #NP, or #SS, as indicated in the above listing.

REAL ADDRESS MODE EXCEPTIONS

Interrupt 13 if the stack is popped when it has offset 0FFFFH.

Jcond—Jump Short If Condition Met

Opcode		Instruction	Clocks*	Description
77	cb	JA cb	7,noj=3	Jump short if above (CF=0 and ZF=0)
73	cb	JAE cb	7,noj=3	Jump short if above or equal (CF=0)
72	cb	JB cb	7,noj=3	Jump short if below (CF=1)
76	cb	JBE cb	7,noj=3	Jump short if below or equal (CF=1 or ZF=1)
72	cb	JC cb	7,noj=3	Jump short if carry (CF=1)
E3	cb	JCXZ cb	8,noj=4	Jump short if CX register is zero
74	cb	JE cb	7,noj=3	Jump short if equal (ZF=1)
7F	cb	JG cb	7,noj=3	Jump short if greater (ZF=0 and SF=OF)
7D	cb	JGE cb	7,noj=3	Jump short if greater or equal (SF=OF)
7C	cb	JL cb	7,noj=3	Jump short if less (SF/=OF)
7E	cb	JLE cb	7,noj=3	Jump short if less or equal (ZF=1 or SF/=OF)
76	cb	JNA cb	7,noj=3	Jump short if not above (CF=1 or ZF=1)
72	cb	JNAE cb	7,noj=3	Jump short if not above/equal (CF=1)
73	cb	JNB cb	7,noj=3	Jump short if not below (CF=0)
77	cb	JNBE cb	7,noj=3	Jump short if not below/equal (CF=0 and ZF=0)
73	cb	JNC cb	7,noj=3	Jump short if not carry (CF=0)
75	cb	JNE cb	7,noj=3	Jump short if not equal (ZF=0)
7E	cb	JNG cb	7,noj=3	Jump short if not greater (ZF=1 or SF/=OF)
7C	cb	JNGE cb	7,noj=3	Jump short if not greater/equal (SF/=OF)
7D	cb	JNL cb	7,noj=3	Jump short if not less (SF=OF)
7F	cb	JNLE cb	7,noj=3	Jump short if not less/equal (ZF=0 and SF=OF)
71	cb	JNO cb	7,noj=3	Jump short if not overflow (OF=0)
7B	cb	JNP cb	7,noj=3	Jump short if not parity (PF=0)
79	cb	JNS cb	7,noj=3	Jump short if not sign (SF=0)
75	cb	JNZ cb	7,noj=3	Jump short if not zero (ZF=0)
70	cb	JO cb	7,noj=3	Jump short if overflow (OF=1)
7A	cb	JP cb	7,noj=3	Jump short if parity (PF=1)
7A	cb	JPE cb	7,noj=3	Jump short if parity even (PF=1)
7B	cb	JPO cb	7,noj=3	Jump short if parity odd (PF=0)
78	cb	JS cb	7,noj=3	Jump short if sign (SF=1)
74	cb	JZ cb	7,noj=3	Jump short if zero (ZF=1)

*When a jump is taken, add one clock for every byte of the next instruction executed.

FLAGS MODIFIED

None

FLAGS UNDEFINED

None

OPERATION

Conditional jumps (except for JCXZ, explained below) test the flags, which presumably have been set in some meaningful way by a previous instruction. The conditions for each mnemonic are given in parentheses after each description above. The terms "less" and "greater" are used for comparing signed integers; "above" and "below" are used for unsigned integers.

If the given condition is true, then a short jump is made to the label provided as the operand. Instruction encoding is most efficient when the target for the conditional jump is in the current code segment and within −128 to +127 bytes of the first byte of the next instruction. Alternatively, the opposite sense (e.g., JNZ has opposite sense to that of JZ) of the conditional jump can skip around an unconditional jump to the destination.

This range is necessary for the assembler to construct a one-byte signed displacement from the end of the current instruction. If the label is out-of-range, or if the label is a FAR label, then you must perform a jump with the opposite condition around an unconditional jump to the non-short label.

Because there are, in many instances, several ways to interpret a particular state of the flags, ASM286 provides more than one mnemonic for most of the conditional jump opcodes. For example, consider that a programmer who has just compared a character to another in AL might wish to jump if the two were equal (JE), while another programmer who had just ANDed AX with a bit field mask would prefer to consider only whether the result was zero or not (he would use JZ, a synonym for JE).

JCXZ differs from the other conditional jumps in that it actually tests the contents of the CX register for zero, rather than interrogating the flags. This instruction is useful following a conditionally repeated string operation (REPE SCASB, for example) or a conditional loop instruction (such as LOOPNE TARGETLABEL). These instructions implicitly use a limiting count in the CX register. Looping (repeating) ends when either the CX register goes to zero or the condition specified in the instruction (flags indicating equals in both of the above cases) occurs. JCXZ is useful when the terminations must be handled differently.

PROTECTED MODE EXCEPTIONS

#GP(0) if the offset jumped to is beyond the limits of the code segment.

REAL ADDRESS MODE EXCEPTIONS

None

JMP—Jump

Opcode		Instruction	Clocks*	Description
EB	cb	JMP cb	7	Jump short
EA	cd	JMP cd	180	Jump to task gate
E9	cw	JMP cw	7	Jump near
EA	cd	JMP cd	11,pm=23	Jump far (4-byte immediate address)
EA	cd	JMP cd	38	Jump to call gate, same privilege
EA	cd	JMP cd	175	Jump via Task State Segment
FF	/4	JMP ew	7,mem=11	Jump near to EA word (absolute offset)
FF	/5	JMP ed	15,pm=26	Jump far (4-byte effective address in memory doubleword)
FF	/5	JMP ed	41	Jump to call gate, same privilege
FF	/5	JMP ed	178	Jump via Task State Segment
FF	/5	JMP ed	183	Jump to task gate

*Add one clock for every byte of the next instruction executed.

FLAGS MODIFIED

All if a task switch takes place; none if no task switch occurs.

FLAGS UNDEFINED

None

OPERATION

The JMP instruction transfers program control to a different instruction stream without recording any return information.

For inter-segment jumps, the destination can be a code segment, a call gate, a task gate, or a Task State Segment. The latter two destinations cause a complete task switch to take place.

Control transfers within a segment use the JMP cw or JMP cb forms. The operand is a relative offset added modulo 65536 to the offset of the instruction that follows the JMP. The result is the new value of IP; the value of CS is unchanged. The byte operand is sign-extended before it is added; it can therefore be used to address labels within 128 bytes in either direction from the next instruction.

Indirect jumps within a segment use the JMP ew form. The contents of the register or memory operand is an absolute offset, which becomes the new value of IP. Again, CS is unchanged.

Inter-segment jumps in real address mode simply set IP to the offset part of the long pointer and set CS to the selector part of the pointer.

In protected mode, inter-segment jumps cause the 80286 to consult the descriptor addressed by the selector part of the long pointer. The AR byte of the descriptor determines the type of the destination. (See table B-3 for possible values of the AR byte.) Following are the possible destinations:

1. Code segment—The addressability and visibility of the destination are verified, and CS and IP are loaded with the destination pointer values.

2. Call gate—The offset part of the destination pointer is ignored. After checking for validity, the processor jumps to the location stored in the call gate descriptor.

3. Task gate—The current task's state is saved in its Task State Segment (TSS), and the TSS named in the task gate is used to load a new context. The outgoing task is marked not busy, the new TSS is marked busy, and execution resumes at the point at which the new task was last suspended.

4. TSS—The current task is suspended and the new task is initiated as in 3 above except that there is no intervening gate.

Following is the list of checks and actions taken for long jumps in protected mode:

JUMP FAR:
    If indirect then check access of EA doubleword #GP(0) or #SS(0) if limit violation
    Destination selector is not null else #GP(0)
    Destination selector index is within its descriptor table limits else #GP (selector)
    Examine AR byte of destination selector for legal values:

        JUMP CONFORMING CODE SEGMENT:
            Descriptor DPL must be ≤ CPL else #GP (selector)
            Segment must be PRESENT else #NP (selector)
            IP must be in code segment limit else #GP(0)
            Load CS:IP from destination pointer
            Load CS-cache with new segment descriptor

        JUMP NONCONFORMING CODE SEGMENT:
            RPL of destination selector must be ≤ CPL else #GP (selector)
            Descriptor DPL must = CPL else #GP (selector)
            Segment must be PRESENT else #NP (selector)
            IP must be in code segment limit else #GP(0)
            Load CS:IP from destination pointer
            Load CS-cache with new segment descriptor
            Set RPL field of CS register to CPL

        JUMP TO CALL GATE:
            Descriptor DPL must be ≥ CPL else #GP (gate selector)
            Descriptor DPL must be ≥ gate selector RPL else #GP (gate selector)
            Gate must be PRESENT else #NP (gate selector)
            Examine selector to code segment given in call gate descriptor:
            Selector must not be null else #GP(0)
            Selector must be within its descriptor table limits else #GP (CS selector)
            Descriptor AR byte must indicate code segment else #GP (CS selector)
            If non-conforming, code segment descriptor DPL must = CPL else #GP (CS selector)
            If conforming, then code segment descriptor DPL must be ≤ CPL else #GP (CS selector)
            Code Segment must be PRESENT else #NP (CS selector)
            IP must be in code segment limit else #GP(0)
            Load CS:IP from call gate
            Load CS-cache with new code segment
            Set RPL of CS to CPL

        JUMP TASK GATE:
            Gate descriptor DPL must be ≥ CPL else #GP (gate selector)
            Gate descriptor DPL must be ≥ gate selector RPL else #GP (gate selector)
            Task Gate must be PRESENT else #NP (gate selector)
            Examine selector to TSS, given in Task Gate descriptor:
            Must specify global in the local/global bit else #GP (TSS selector)
            Index must be within GDT limits else #GP (TSS selector)
            Descriptor AR byte must specify available TSS (bottom bits 00001) else #GP (TSS selector)
            Task State Segment must be PRESENT else #NP (TSS selector)
            SWITCH_TASKS without nesting to TSS
            IP must be in code segment limit else #GP(0)

JUMP TASK STATE SEGMENT:
   TSS DPL must be ≥ CPL else #GP (TSS selector)
   TSS DPL must be ≥ TSS selector RPL else #GP (TSS selector)
   Descriptor AR byte must specify available TSS (bottom bits 00001) else #GP (TSS selector)
   Task State Segment must be PRESENT else #NP (TSS selector)
   SWITCH_TASKS with nesting to TS.
   IP must be in code segment limit else #GP(0)

   Else GP (selector)

PROTECTED MODE EXCEPTIONS

For NEAR jumps, #GP(0) if the destination offset is beyond the limits of the current code segment. For FAR jumps, #GP, #NP, #SS, and #TS, as indicated above. #UD if indirect inter-segment jump operand is a register.

REAL ADDRESS MODE EXCEPTIONS

#UD if indirect inter-segment jump operand is a register.

LAHF—Load Flags into AH Register

Opcode	Instruction	Clocks	Description
9F	LAHF	2	Load: AH = flags SF ZF xx AF xx PF xx CF

FLAGS MODIFIED

None

FLAGS UNDEFINED

None

OPERATION

The low byte of the flags word is transferred to AH. The bits, from MSB to LSB, are as follows: sign, zero, indeterminate, auxiliary carry, indeterminate, parity, indeterminate, and carry. See figure 3-5.

PROTECTED MODE EXCEPTIONS

None

REAL ADDRESS MODE EXCEPTIONS

None

LAR—Load Access Rights Byte

Opcode	Instruction	Clocks	Description
0F 02 /r	LAR rw,ew	14,mem=16	Load: high(rw)= Access Rights byte, selector ew

FLAGS MODIFIED
Zero

FLAGS UNDEFINED
None

OPERATION

LAR expects the second operand (memory or register word) to contain a selector. If the associated descriptor is visible at the current privilege level and at the selector RPL, then the access rights byte of the descriptor is loaded into the high byte of the first (register) operand, and the low byte is set to zero. The zero flag is set if the loading was performed (i.e., the selector index is within the table limit, descriptor DPL $\geq$ CPL, and descriptor DPL $\geq$ selector RPL); the zero flag is cleared otherwise.

Selector operands cannot cause protection exceptions.

PROTECTED MODE EXCEPTIONS

#GP(0) for an illegal memory operand effective address in the CS, DS, or ES segments; #SS(0) for an illegal address in the SS segment.

REAL ADDRESS MODE EXCEPTION

INTERRUPT 6; LAR is unrecognized in Real Address mode.

LDS/LES—Load Doubleword Pointer

Opcode	Instruction	Clocks	Description
C5 /r	LDS rw,ed	7,pm=21	Load EA doubleword into DS and word register
C4 /r	LES rw,ed	7,pm=21	Load EA doubleword into ES and word register

FLAGS MODIFIED

None

FLAGS UNDEFINED

None

OPERATION

The four-byte pointer at the memory location indicated by the second operand is loaded into a segment register and a word register. The first word of the pointer (the offset) is loaded into the register indicated by the first operand. The last word of the pointer (the selector) is loaded into the segment register (DS or ES) given by the instruction opcode.

When the segment register is loaded, its associated cache is also loaded. The data for the cache is obtained from the descriptor table entry for the selector given.

A null selector (values 0000-0003) can be loaded into DS or ES without a protection exception. Any memory reference using such a segment register value will cause a #GP(0) exception but will not result in a memory reference. The saved segment register value will be null.

Following is a list of checks and actions taken when loading the DS or ES registers:

If selector is non-null then:
    Selector index must be within its descriptor table limits else #GP (selector)
    Examine descriptor AR byte:

        Data segment or readable non-conforming code segment
            Descriptor DPL ≥ CPL else #GP (selector)
            Descriptor DPL ≥ selector RPL else #GP (selector)

        Readable conforming code segment
            No DPL, RPL, or CPL checks

        Else #GP (selector)

    Segment must be present else #NP (selector)
    Load registers from operand
    Load segment register descriptor cache

If selector is null then:
    Load registers from operand
    Mark segment register cache as invalid

PROTECTED MODE EXCEPTIONS

#GP or #NP, as indicated in the list above. #GP(0) or #SS(0) if operand lies outside segment limit. #UD if the source operand is a register.

REAL ADDRESS MODE EXCEPTIONS

Interrupt 13 for operand at offset 0FFFFH or 0FFFDH. #UD if the source operand is a register.

LEA—Load Effective Address Offset

Opcode	Instruction	Clocks	Description
8D /r	LEA rw,m	3	Calculate EA offset given by m, place in rw

FLAGS MODIFIED

None

FLAGS UNDEFINED

None

OPERATION

The effective address (offset part) of the second operand is placed in the first (register) operand.

PROTECTED MODE EXCEPTIONS

#UD if second operand is a register.

REAL ADDRESS MODE EXCEPTIONS

#UD if second operand is a register.

LEAVE—High Level Procedure Exit

Opcode	Instruction	Clocks	Description
C9	LEAVE	5	Set SP to BP, then POP BP

FLAGS MODIFIED

None

FLAGS UNDEFINED

None

OPERATION

LEAVE is the complementary operation to ENTER; it reverses the effects of that instruction. By copying BP to SP, LEAVE releases the stack space used by a procedure for its dynamics and display. The old frame pointer is now popped into BP, restoring the caller's frame, and a subsequent RET *nn* instruction will follow the back-link and remove any arguments pushed on the stack for the exiting procedure.

PROTECTED MODE EXCEPTIONS

#SS(0) if BP does not point to a location within the current stack segment.

REAL ADDRESS MODE EXCEPTIONS

Interrupt 13 for a word operand at offset 0FFFFH.

LGDT/LIDT—Load Global/Interrupt Descriptor Table Register

Opcode	Instruction	Clocks	Description
0F 01 /2	LGDT m	11	Load m into Global Descriptor Table reg
0F 01 /3	LIDT m	12	Load m into Interrupt Descriptor Table reg

FLAGS MODIFIED

None

FLAGS UNDEFINED

None

OPERATION

The Global or the Interrupt Descriptor Table Register is loaded from the six bytes of memory pointed to by the effective address operand (see figure 10.3). The LIMIT field of the descriptor table register loads from the first word; the next three bytes go to the BASE field of the register; the last byte is ignored.

LGDT and LIDT appear in operating systems software; they are not used in application programs. These are the only instructions that directly load a physical memory address in 80286 protected mode.

PROTECTED MODE EXCEPTIONS

#GP(0) if the current privilege level is not 0.

#UD if source operand is a register.

#GP(0) for an illegal memory operand effective address in the CS, DS, or ES segments; #SS(0) for an illegal address in the SS segment.

REAL ADDRESS MODE EXCEPTIONS

These instructions are valid in Real Address mode to allow the power-up initialization for Protected mode.

Interrupt 13 for a word operand at offset 0FFFFH. #UD if source operand is a register.

LLDT—Load Local Descriptor Table Register

Opcode	Instruction	Clocks	Description
0F 00 /2	LLDT ew	17,mem=19	Load selector ew into Local Descriptor Table register

FLAGS MODIFIED

None

FLAGS UNDEFINED

None

OPERATION

The word operand (memory or register) to LLDT should contain a selector pointing to the Global Descriptor Table. The GDT entry should be a Local Descriptor Table Descriptor. If so, then the Local Descriptor Table Register is loaded from the entry. The descriptor cache entries for DS, ES, SS, and CS are not affected. The LDT field in the TSS is not changed.

The selector operand is allowed to be zero. In that case, the Local Descriptor Table Register is marked invalid. All descriptor references (except by LAR, VERR, VERW or LSL instructions) will cause a #GP fault.

LLDT appears in operating systems software; it does not appear in applications programs.

PROTECTED MODE EXCEPTIONS

#GP(0) if the current privilege level is not 0. #GP (selector) if the selector operand does not point into the Global Descriptor Table, or if the entry in the GDT is not a Local Descriptor Table. #NP (selector) if LDT descriptor is not present. #GP(0) for an illegal memory operand effective address in the CS, DS, or ES segments; #SS(0) for an illegal address in the SS segment.

REAL ADDRESS MODE EXCEPTIONS

Interrupt 6; LLDT is not recognized in Real Address Mode.

LMSW—Load Machine Status Word

Opcode	Instruction	Clocks	Description
0F 01 /6	LMSW ew	3,mem=6	Load EA word into Machine Status Word

FLAGS MODIFIED

None

FLAGS UNDEFINED

None

OPERATION

The Machine Status Word is loaded from the source operand. This instruction may be used to switch to protected mode. If so, then it *must* be followed by an intra-segment jump to flush the instruction queue. LMSW will not switch back to Real Address Mode.

LMSW appears only in operating systems software. It does not appear in applications programs.

PROTECTED MODE EXCEPTIONS

#GP(0) if the current privilege level is not 0. #GP(0) for an illegal memory operand effective address in the CS, DS, or ES segments; #SS(0) for an illegal address in the SS segment.

REAL ADDRESS MODE EXCEPTIONS

Interrupt 13 for a word operand at offset 0FFFFH.

LOCK—Assert BUS LOCK Signal

Opcode	Instruction	Clocks	Description
F0	LOCK	0	Assert BUSLOCK signal for the next instruction

FLAGS MODIFIED

None

FLAGS UNDEFINED

None

OPERATION

LOCK is a prefix that will cause the BUS LOCK signal of the 80286 to be asserted for the duration of the instruction that it prefixes. In a multiprocessor environment, this signal should be used to ensure that the 80286 has exclusive use of any shared memory while BUS LOCK is asserted. The read-modify-write sequence typically used to implement TEST-AND-SET in the 80286 is the XCHG instruction.

The 80286 LOCK prefix activates the lock signal for the following instructions: MOVS, INS, and OUTS. XCHG always asserts BUS LOCK regardless of the presence or absence of the LOCK prefix.

PROTECTED MODE EXCEPTIONS

#GP(0) if the current privilege level is bigger (less privileged) than the I/O privilege level.

Other exceptions may be generated by the subsequent (locked) instruction.

REAL ADDRESS MODE EXCEPTIONS

None. Exceptions may still be generated by the subsequent (locked) instruction.

LODS/LODSB/LODSW—Load String Operand

Opcode	Instruction	Clocks	Description
AC	LODS *mb*	5	Load byte [SI] into AL
AD	LODS *mw*	5	Load word [SI] into AX
AC	LODSB	5	Load byte DS:[SI] into AL
AD	LODSW	5	Load word DS:[SI] into AX

FLAGS MODIFIED

None

FLAGS UNDEFINED

None

OPERATION

LODS loads the AL or AX register with the memory byte or word at SI. After the transfer is made, SI is automatically advanced. If the direction flag is 0 (CLD was executed), SI increments; if the direction flag is 1 (STD was executed), SI decrements. SI increments or decrements by 1 if a byte was moved; by 2 if a word was moved.

PROTECTED MODE EXCEPTIONS

#GP(0) for an illegal memory operand effective address in the CS, DS, or ES segments; #SS(0) for an illegal address in the SS segment.

REAL ADDRESS MODE EXCEPTIONS

Interrupt 13 for a word operand at offset 0FFFFH.

LOOP/LOOPcond—Loop Control with CX Counter

Opcode		Instruction	Clocks	Description
E2	cb	LOOP cb	8,noj=4	DEC CX; jump short if CX≠0
E1	cb	LOOPE cb	8,noj=4	DEC CX; jump short if CX≠0 and equal (ZF=1)
E0	cb	LOOPNE cb	8,noj=4	DEC CX; jump short if CX≠0 and not equal (ZF=0)
E0	cb	LOOPNZ cb	8,noj=4	DEC CX; jump short if CX≠0 and ZF=0
E1	cb	LOOPZ cb	8,noj=4	DEC CX; jump short if CX≠0 and zero (ZF=1)

FLAGS MODIFIED

None

FLAGS UNDEFINED

None

OPERATION

LOOP first decrements the CX register without changing any of the flags. Then, conditions are checked as given in the description above for the form of LOOP being used. If the conditions are met, then an intra-segment jump is made. The destination to LOOP is in the range from 126 (decimal) bytes before the instruction to 127 bytes beyond the instruction.

The LOOP instructions are intended to provide iteration control and to combine loop index management with conditional branching. To use the LOOP instruction you load an unsigned iteration count into CX, then code the LOOP at the end of a series of instructions to be iterated. The destination of LOOP is a label that points to the beginning of the iteration.

PROTECTED MODE EXCEPTIONS

#GP(0) if the offset jumped to is beyond the limits of the current code segment.

REAL ADDRESS MODE EXCEPTIONS

None

LSL—Load Segment Limit

Opcode	Instruction	Clocks	Description
0F 03 /r	LSL rw,ew	14,mem=16	Load: rw = Segment Limit, selector ew

FLAGS MODIFIED

Zero

FLAGS UNDEFINED

None

OPERATION

If the descriptor denoted by the selector in the second (memory or register) operand is visible at the CPL, a word that consists of the limit field of the descriptor is loaded into the left operand, which must be a register. The value is the limit field for that segment. The zero flag is set if the loading was performed (that is, if the selector is non-null, the selector index is within the descriptor table limits, the descriptor is a non-conforming segment descriptor with DPL ≥ CPL, and the descriptor DPL ≥ selector RPL); the zero flag is cleared otherwise.

The LSL instruction returns only the limit field of segments, task state segments, and local descriptor tables. The interpretation of the limit value depends on the type of segment.

The selector operand's value cannot result in a protection exception.

PROTECTED MODE EXCEPTIONS

#GP(0) for an illegal memory operand effective address in the CS, DS, or ES segments; #SS(0) for an illegal address in the SS segment.

REAL ADDRESS MODE EXCEPTIONS

Interrupt 6; LSL is not recognized in Real Address mode.

LTR—Load Task Register

Opcode	Instruction	Clocks	Description
0F 00 /3	LTR ew	17,mem=19	Load EA word into Task Register

FLAGS MODIFIED

None

FLAGS UNDEFINED

None

OPERATION

The Task Register is loaded from the source register or memory location given by the operand. The loaded TSS is marked busy. A task switch operation does not occur.

LTR appears only in operating systems software. It is not used in applications programs.

PROTECTED MODE EXCEPTIONS

#GP for an illegal memory operand effective address in the CS, DS, or ES segments; #SS for an illegal address in the SS segment.

#GP(0) if the current privilege level is not 0. #GP (selector) if the object named by the source selector is not a TSS or is already busy. #NP (selector) if the TSS is marked not present.

REAL ADDRESS MODE EXCEPTIONS

Interrupt 6; LTR is not recognized in Real Address mode.

MOV—Move Data

Opcode			Instruction		Clocks	Description
88	/r		MOV	eb,rb	2,mem=3	Move byte register into EA byte
89	/r		MOV	ew,rw	2,mem=3	Move word register into EA word
8A	/r		MOV	rb,eb	2,mem=5	Move EA byte into byte register
8B	/r		MOV	rw,ew	2,mem=5	Move EA word into word register
8C	/0		MOV	ew,ES	2,mem=3	Move ES into EA word
8C	/1		MOV	ew,CS	2,mem=3	Move CS into EA word
8C	/2		MOV	ew,SS	2,mem=3	Move SS into EA word
8C	/3		MOV	ew,DS	2,mem=3	Move DS into EA word
8E	/0		MOV	ES,mw	5,pm=19	Move memory word into ES
8E	/0		MOV	ES,rw	2,pm=17	Move word register into ES
8E	/2		MOV	SS,mw	5,pm=19	Move memory word into SS
8E	/2		MOV	SS,rw	2,pm=17	Move word register into SS
8E	/3		MOV	DS,mw	5,pm=19	Move memory word into DS
8E	/3		MOV	DS,rw	2,pm=17	Move word register into DS
A0	dw		MOV	AL,xb	5	Move byte variable (offset dw) into AL
A1	dw		MOV	AX,xw	5	Move word variable (offset dw) into AX
A2	dw		MOV	xb,AL	3	Move AL into byte variable (offset dw)
A3	dw		MOV	xw,AX	3	Move AX into word register (offset dw)
B0+	rb	db	MOV	rb,db	2	Move immediate byte into byte register
B8+	rw	dw	MOV	rw,dw	2	Move immediate word into word register
C6	/0	db	MOV	eb,db	2,mem=3	Move immediate byte into EA byte
C7	/0	dw	MOV	ew,dw	2,mem=3	Move immediate word into EA word

FLAGS MODIFIED

None

FLAGS UNDEFINED

None

OPERATION

The second operand is copied to the first operand.

If the destination operand is a segment register (DS, ES, or SS), then the associated segment register cache is also loaded. The data for the cache is obtained from the descriptor table entry for the selector given.

A null selector (values 0000-0003) can be loaded into DS and ES registers without causing a protection exception. Any use of a segment register with a null selector to address memory will cause #GP(0) exception. No memory reference will occur.

Any move into SS will inhibit all interrupts until after the execution of the next instruction.

Following is a listing of the protected-mode checks and actions taken in the loading of a segment register:

If SS is loaded:
    If selector is null then #GP(0)
    Selector index must be within its descriptor table limits else #GP (selector)
    Selector's RPL must equal CPL else #GP (selector)
    AR byte must indicate a writable data segment else #GP (selector)
    DPL in the AR byte must equal CPL else #GP (selector)
    Segment must be marked PRESENT else #SS (selector)
    Load SS with selector
    Load SS cache with descriptor
If ES or DS is loaded with non-null selector
    Selector index must be within its descriptor table limits else #GP (selector)
    AR byte must indicate data or readable code segment else #GP (selector)
    If data or non-conforming code, then both the RPL and the
        CPL must be less than or equal to DPL in AR byte else #GP (selector)
    Segment must be marked PRESENT else #NP (selector)
Load segment register with selector
Load segment register cache with descriptor
If ES or DS is loaded with a null selector:
    Load segment register with selector
    Clear descriptor valid bit

PROTECTED MODE EXCEPTIONS

If a segment register is being loaded, #GP, #SS, and #NP, as described in the listing above.

Otherwise, #GP(0) if the destination is in a non-writable segment. #GP(0) for an illegal memory operand effective address in the CS, DS, or ES segments; #SS(0) for an illegal address in the SS segment.

REAL ADDRESS MODE EXCEPTIONS

Interrupt 13 for a word operand at offset 0FFFFH.

MOVS/MOVSB/MOVSW—Move Data from String to String

Opcode	Instruction	Clocks	Description
A4	MOVS *mb,mb*	5	Move byte [SI] to ES:[DI]
A5	MOVS *mw,mw*	5	Move word [SI] to ES:[DI]
A4	MOVSB	5	Move byte DS:[SI] to ES:[DI]
A5	MOVSW	5	Move word DS:[SI] to ES:[DI]

FLAGS MODIFIED

None

FLAGS UNDEFINED

None

OPERATION

MOVS copies the byte or word at [SI] to the byte or word at ES:[DI]. The destination operand must be addressable from the ES register; no segment override is possible. A segment override may be used for the source operand.

After the data movement is made, both SI and DI are automatically advanced. If the direction flag is 0 (CLD was executed), the registers increment; if the direction flag is 1 (STD was executed), the registers decrement. The registers increment or decrement by 1 if a byte was moved; by 2 if a word was moved.

MOVS can be preceded by the REP prefix for block movement of CX bytes or words. Refer to the REP instruction for details of this operation.

PROTECTED MODE EXCEPTIONS

#GP(0) if the destination is in a non-writable segment. #GP(0) for an illegal memory operand effective address in the CS, DS, or ES segments; #SS(0) for an illegal address in the SS segment.

REAL ADDRESS MODE EXCEPTIONS

Interrupt 13 for a word operand at offset 0FFFFH.

MUL—Unsigned Multiplication of AL or AX

Opcode	Instruction	Clocks	Description
F6 /4	MUL *eb*	13,mem=16	Unsigned multiply (AX = AL × EA byte)
F7 /4	MUL *ew*	21,mem=24	Unsigned multiply (DXAX = AX × EA word)

FLAGS MODIFIED

Overflow, carry

FLAGS UNDEFINED

Sign, zero, auxiliary carry, parity

OPERATION

If MUL has a byte operand, then the byte is multiplied by AL, and the result is left in AX. Carry and overflow are set to 0 if AH is 0; they are set to 1 otherwise.

If MUL has a word operand, then the word is multiplied by AX, and the result is left in DX:AX. DX contains the high order 16 bits of the product. Carry and overflow are set to 0 if DX is 0; they are set to 1 otherwise.

PROTECTED MODE EXCEPTIONS

#GP(0) for an illegal memory operand effective address in the CS, DS, or ES segments; #SS(0) for an illegal address in the SS segment.

REAL ADDRESS MODE EXCEPTIONS

Interrupt 13 for a word operand at offset 0FFFFH.

NEG—Two's Complement Negation

Opcode	Instruction	Clocks	Description
F6 /3	NEG eb	2,mem=7	Two's complement negate EA byte
F7 /3	NEG ew	2,mem=7	Two's complement negate EA word

FLAGS MODIFIED

Overflow, sign, zero, auxiliary carry, parity, carry

FLAGS UNDEFINED

None

OPERATION

The two's complement of the register or memory operand replaces the old operand value. Likewise, the operand is subtracted from zero, and the result is placed in the operand.

The carry flag is set to 1 except when the input operand is zero, in which case the carry flag is cleared to 0.

PROTECTED MODE EXCEPTIONS

#GP(0) if the result is in a non-writable segment. #GP(0) for an illegal memory operand effective address in the CS, DS, or ES segments; #SS(0) for an illegal address in the SS segment.

REAL ADDRESS MODE EXCEPTIONS

Interrupt 13 for a word operand at offset 0FFFFH.

NOP—No OPERATION

Opcode	Instruction	Clocks	Description
90	NOP	3	No OPERATION

FLAGS MODIFIED

None

FLAGS UNDEFINED

None

OPERATION

Performs no operation. NOP is a one-byte filler instruction that takes up space but affects none of the machine context except IP.

PROTECTED MODE EXCEPTIONS

None

REAL ADDRESS MODE EXCEPTIONS

None

NOT—One's Complement Negation

Opcode	Instruction	Clocks	Description
F6 /2	NOT *eb*	2,mem=7	Reverse each bit of EA byte
F7 /2	NOT *ew*	2,mem=7	Reverse each bit of EA word

FLAGS MODIFIED

None

FLAGS UNDEFINED

None

OPERATION

The operand is inverted; that is, every 1 becomes a 0 and vice versa.

PROTECTED MODE EXCEPTIONS

#GP(0) if the result is in a non-writable segment. #GP(0) for an illegal memory operand effective address in the CS, DS, or ES segments; #SS(0) for an illegal address in the SS segment.

REAL ADDRESS MODE EXCEPTIONS

Interrupt 13 for a word operand at offset 0FFFFH.

OR—Logical Inclusive OR

Opcode			Instruction	Clocks	Description
08	/r		OR eb,rb	2,mem=7	Logical-OR byte register into EA byte
09	/r		OR ew,rw	2,mem=7	Logical-OR word register into EA word
0A	/r		OR rb,eb	2,mem=7	Logical-OR EA byte into byte register
0B	/r		OR rw,ew	2,mem=7	Logical-OR EA word into word register
0C	db		OR AL,db	3	Logical-OR immediate byte into AL
0D	dw		OR AX,dw	3	Logical-OR immediate word into AX
80	/1	db	OR eb,db	3,mem=7	Logical-OR immediate byte into EA byte
81	/1	dw	OR ew,dw	3,mem=7	Logical-OR immediate word into EA word

FLAGS MODIFIED

Overflow=0, sign, zero, parity, carry=0

FLAGS UNDEFINED

Auxiliary carry

OPERATION

This instruction computes the inclusive OR of the two operands. Each bit of the result is 0 if both corresponding bits of the operands are 0; each bit is 1 otherwise. The result is placed in the first operand.

PROTECTED MODE EXCEPTIONS

#GP(0) if the result is in a non-writable segment. #GP(0) for an illegal memory operand effective address in the CS, DS, or ES segments; #SS(0) for an illegal address in the SS segment.

REAL ADDRESS MODE EXCEPTIONS

Interrupt 13 for a word operand at offset 0FFFFH.

OUT—Output to Port

Opcode		Instruction	Clocks	Description
E6	db	OUT db,AL	3	Output byte AL to immediate port number db
E7	db	OUT db,AX	3	Output word AX to immediate port number db
EE		OUT DX,AL	3	Output byte AL to port number DX
EF		OUT DX,AX	3	Output word AX to port number DX

FLAGS MODIFIED

None

FLAGS UNDEFINED

None

OPERATION

OUT transfers a data byte or data word from the register (AL or AX) given as the second operand to the output port numbered by the first operand. You can output to any port from 0-65535 by placing the port number in the DX register then using an OUT instruction with DX as the first operand. If the instruction contains an 8-bit port ID, that value is zero-extended to 16 bits.

Intel reserves I/O port addresses 00F8H through 00FFH; these addresses should not be used.

PROTECTED MODE EXCEPTIONS

#GP(0) if the current privilege level is bigger (has less privilege) than IOPL, which is the privilege level found in the flags register.

REAL ADDRESS MODE EXCEPTIONS

None

OUTS/OUTSB/OUTSW—Output String to Port

Opcode	Instruction	Clocks	Description
6E	OUTS DX,eb	5	Output byte [SI] to port number DX
6F	OUTS DX,ew	5	Output word [SI] to port number DX
6E	OUTSB	5	Output byte DS:[SI] to port number DX
6F	OUTSW	5	Output word DS:[SI] to port number DX

FLAGS MODIFIED

None

FLAGS UNDEFINED

None

OPERATION

OUTS transfers data from the memory byte or word at SI to the output port numbered by the DX register.

OUTS does not allow the specification of the port number as an immediate value. The port must be addressed through the DX register.

After the transfer is made, SI is automatically advanced. If the direction flag is 0 (CLD was executed), SI increments; if the direction flag is 1 (STD was executed), SI decrements. SI increments or decrements by 1 if a byte was moved; by 2 if a word was moved.

OUTS can be preceded by the REP prefix for block output of CX bytes or words. Refer to the REP instruction for details of this operation.

Intel reserves I/O port addresses 00F8H through 00FFH; these addresses should not be used.

NOTE

Not all output devices can handle the rate at which this instruction transfers data.

PROTECTED MODE EXCEPTIONS

#GP(0) if CPL > IOPL. #GP(0) for an illegal memory operand effective address in the CS, DS, or ES segments; #SS(0) for an illegal address in the SS segment.

REAL ADDRESS MODE EXCEPTIONS

Interrupt 13 for a word operand at offset 0FFFFH.

POP—Pop a Word from the Stack

Opcode	Instruction	Clocks	Description
1F	POP DS	5,pm=20	Pop top of stack into DS
07	POP ES	5,pm=20	Pop top of stack into ES
17	POP SS	5,pm=20	Pop top of stack into SS
8F /0	POP *mw*	5	Pop top of stack into memory word
58+*rw*	POP *rw*	5	Pop top of stack into word register

FLAGS MODIFIED

None

FLAGS UNDEFINED

None

OPERATION

The word on the top of the 80286 stack, addressed by SS:SP, replaces the previous contents of the memory, register, or segment register operand. The stack pointer SP is incremented by 2 to point to the new top of stack.

If the destination operand is another segment register (DS, ES, or SS), the value popped must be a selector. In protected mode, loading the selector initiates automatic loading of the descriptor information associated with that selector into the hidden part of the segment register; loading also initiates validation of both the selector and the descriptor information.

A null value (0000-0003) may be loaded into the DS or ES register without causing a protection exception. Attempts to reference memory using a segment register with a null value will cause #GP(0) exception. No memory reference will occur. The saved value of the segment register will be null.

A POP SS instruction will inhibit all interrupts, including NMI, until after the execution of the next instruction. This permits a POP SP instruction to be performed first.

Following is a listing of the protected-mode checks and actions taken in the loading of a segment register:

If SS is loaded:
    If selector is null then #GP(0)
    Selector index must be within its descriptor table limits else #GP (selector)
    Selector's RPL must equal CPL else #GP (selector)
    AR byte must indicate a writable data segment else #GP (selector)
    DPL in the AR byte must equal CPL else #GP (selector)
    Segment must be marked PRESENT else #SS (selector)
    Load SS register with selector
    Load SS cache with descriptor

If ES or DS is loaded with non-null selector:
    AR byte must indicate data or readable code segment else #GP (selector)
    If data or non-conforming code, then both the RPL and the
        CPL must be less than or equal to DPL in AR byte else #GP (selector)
    Segment must be marked PRESENT else #NP (selector)
    Load segment register with selector
    Load segment register cache with descriptor
If ES or DS is loaded with a null selector:
    Load segment register with selector
    Clear valid bit in cache

PROTECTED MODE EXCEPTIONS

If a segment register is being loaded, #GP, #SS, and #NP, as described in the listing above.

Otherwise, #SS(0) if the current top of stack is not within the stack segment.

#GP(0) if the destination is in a non-writable segment. #GP(0) for an illegal memory operand effective address in the CS, DS, or ES segments; #SS(0) for an illegal address in the SS segment.

REAL ADDRESS MODE EXCEPTIONS

Interrupt 13 for a word operand at offset 0FFFFH.

POPA—Pop All General Registers

Opcode	Instruction	Clocks	Description
61	POPA	19	Pop in order: DI,SI,BP,SP,BX,DX,CX,AX

FLAGS MODIFIED

None

FLAGS UNDEFINED

None

OPERATION

POPA pops the eight general registers given in the description above, except that the SP value is discarded instead of loaded into SP. POPA reverses a previous PUSHA, restoring the general registers to their values before PUSHA was executed. The first register popped is DI.

PROTECTED MODE EXCEPTIONS

#SS(0) if the starting or ending stack address is not within the stack segment.

REAL ADDRESS MODE EXCEPTIONS

Interrupt 13 for a word operand at offset 0FFFFH.

POPF—Pop from Stack into the Flags Register

Opcode	Instruction	Clocks	Description
9D	POPF	5	Pop top of stack into flags register

FLAGS MODIFIED

Entire flags register is popped from stack

FLAGS UNDEFINED

None

OPERATION

The top of the 80286 stack, pointed to by SS:SP, is copied into the 80286 flags register. The stack pointer SP is incremented by 2 to point to the new top of stack. The flags, from the top bit (bit 15) to the bottom (bit 0), are as follows: undefined, nested task, I/O privilege level (2 bits), overflow, direction, interrupts enabled, trap, sign, zero, undefined, auxiliary carry, undefined, parity, undefined, and carry.

The I/O privilege level will be altered only when executing at privilege level 0. The interrupt enable flag will be altered only when executing at a level at least as privileged as the I/O privilege level. If you execute a POPF instruction with insufficient privilege, there will be no exception nor will the privileged bits be changed.

PROTECTED MODE EXCEPTIONS

#SS(0) if the top of stack is not within the stack segment.

REAL ADDRESS MODE EXCEPTIONS

Interrupt 13 for a word operand at 0FFFFH.

In real mode the NT and IOPL bits will not be modified.

PUSH—Push a Word onto the Stack

Opcode	Instruction	Clocks	Description
06	PUSH ES	3	Push ES
0E	PUSH CS	3	Push CS
16	PUSH SS	3	Push SS
1E	PUSH DS	3	Push DS
50+ *rw*	PUSH *rw*	3	Push word register
FF /6	PUSH *mw*	5	Push memory word
68 *dw*	PUSH *dw*	3	Push immediate word
6A *db*	PUSH *db*	3	Push immediate sign-extended byte

FLAGS MODIFIED

None

FLAGS UNDEFINED

None

OPERATION

The stack pointer SP is decremented by 2, and the operand is placed on the new top of stack, which is pointed to by SS:SP.

The 80286 PUSH SP instruction pushes the value of SP as it existed before the instruction. This differs from the 8086, which pushes the new (decremented by 2) value.

PROTECTED MODE EXCEPTIONS

#SS(0) if the new value of SP is outside the stack segment limit.

#GP(0) for an illegal memory operand effective address in the CS, DS, or ES segments; #SS(0) for an illegal address in the SS segment.

REAL ADDRESS MODE EXCEPTIONS

None; the 80286 will shut down if SP = 1—due to lack of stack space.

PUSHA—Push All General Registers

Opcode	Instruction	Clocks	Description
60	PUSHA	17	Push in order: AX,CX,DX,BX,original SP,BP,SI,DI

FLAGS MODIFIED

None

FLAGS UNDEFINED

None

OPERATION

PUSHA saves the registers noted above on the 80286 stack. The stack pointer SP is decremented by 16 to hold the 8 word values. Since the registers are pushed onto the stack in the order in which they were given, they will appear in the 16 new stack bytes in the reverse order. The last register pushed is DI.

PROTECTED MODE EXCEPTIONS

#SS(0) if the starting or ending address is outside the stack segment limit.

REAL ADDRESS MODE EXCEPTIONS

The 80286 will shut down if SP = 1, 3, or 5 before executing PUSHA. If SP = 7, 9, 11, 13, or 15, exception 13 will occur.

PUSHF—Push Flags Register onto the Stack

Opcode	Instruction	Clocks	Description
9C	PUSHF	3	Push flags register

FLAGS MODIFIED

None

FLAGS UNDEFINED

None

OPERATION

The stack pointer SP is decremented by 2, and the 80286 flags register is copied to the new top of stack, which is pointed to by SS:SP. The flags, from the top bit (15) to the bottom bit (0), are as follows: undefined, nested task, I/O privilege level (2 bits), overflow, direction, interrupts enabled, trap, sign, zero, undefined, auxiliary carry, undefined, parity, undefined, and carry.

PROTECTED MODE EXCEPTIONS

#SS(0) if the new value of SP is outside the stack segment limit.

REAL ADDRESS MODE EXCEPTIONS

None; the 80286 will shut down if SP=1 due—to lack of stack space.

RCL/RCR/ROL/ROR—Rotate Instructions

Opcode			Instruction	Clocks-N*	Description
D0	/2		RCL eb,1	2,mem=7	Rotate 9-bits (CF, EA byte) left once
D2	/2		RCL eb,CL*	5,mem=8	Rotate 9-bits (CF, EA byte) left CL times
C0	/2	db	RCL eb,db*	5,mem=8	Rotate 9-bits (CF, EA byte) left db times
D1	/2		RCL ew,1	2,mem=7	Rotate 17-bits (CF, EA word) left once
D3	/2		RCL ew,CL*	5,mem=8	Rotate 17-bits (CF, EA word) left CL times
C1	/2	db	RCL ew,db*	5,mem=8	Rotate 17-bits (CF, EA word) left db times
D0	/3		RCR eb,1	2,mem=7	Rotate 9-bits (CF, EA byte) right once
D2	/3		RCR eb,CL*	5,mem=8	Rotate 9-bits (CF, EA byte) right CL times
C0	/3	db	RCR eb,db*	5,mem=8	Rotate 9-bits (CF, EA byte) right db times
D1	/3		RCR ew,1	2,mem=7	Rotate 17-bits (CF, EA word) right once
D3	/3		RCR ew,CL*	5,mem=8	Rotate 17-bits (CF, EA word) right CL times
C1	/3	db	RCR ew,db*	5,mem=8	Rotate 17-bits (CF, EA word) right db times
D0	/0		ROL eb,1	2,mem=7	Rotate 8-bit EA byte left once
D2	/0		ROL eb,CL*	5,mem=8	Rotate 8-bit EA byte left CL times
C0	/0	db	ROL eb,db*	5,mem=8	Rotate 8-bit EA byte left db times
D1	/0		ROL ew,1	2,mem=7	Rotate 16-bit EA word left once
D3	/0		ROL ew,CL*	5,mem=8	Rotate 16-bit EA word left CL times
C1	/0	db	ROL ew,db*	5,mem=8	Rotate 16-bit EA word left db times
D0	/1		ROR eb,1	2,mem=7	Rotate 8-bit EA byte right once
D2	/1		ROR eb,CL*	5,mem=8	Rotate 8-bit EA byte right CL times
C0	/1	db	ROR eb,db*	5,mem=8	Rotate 8-bit EA byte right db times
D1	/1		ROR ew,1	2,mem=7	Rotate 16-bit EA word right once
D3	/1		ROR ew,CL*	5,mem=8	Rotate 16-bit EA word right CL times
C1	/1	db	ROR ew,db*	5,mem=8	Rotate 16-bit EA word right db times

* Add 1 clock to the times shown for each rotate made

FLAGS MODIFIED

Overflow (only for single rotates), carry

FLAGS UNDEFINED

Overflow for multi-bit rotates

OPERATION

Each rotate instruction shifts the bits of the register or memory operand given. The left rotate instructions shift all of the bits upward, except for the top bit, which comes back around to the bottom. The right rotate instructions do the reverse: the bits shift downward, with the bottom bit coming around to the top.

For the RCL and RCR instructions, the carry flag is part of the rotated quantity. RCL shifts the carry flag into the bottom bit and shifts the top bit into the carry flag; RCR shifts the carry flag into the top bit and shifts the bottom bit into the carry flag. For the ROL and ROR instructions, the original value of the carry flag is not a part of the result; nonetheless, the carry flag receives a copy of the bit that was shifted from one end to the other.

The rotate is repeated the number of times indicated by the second operand, which is either an immediate number or the contents of the CL register. To reduce the maximum execution time, the 80286 does not allow rotation counts greater than 31. If a rotation count greater than 31 is attempted, only the bottom five bits of the rotation are used. The 8086 does not mask rotate counts.

The overflow flag is set only for the single-rotate (second operand = 1) forms of the instructions. The OF bit is set to be accurate if a shift of length 1 is done. Since it is undefined for all other values, including a zero shift, it can always be set for the count-of-1 case regardless of the actual count. For left shifts/rotates, the CF bit after the shift is XORed with the high-order result bit. For right shifts/rotates, the high-order two bits of the result are XORed to get OF. Neither flag bit is modified when the count value is zero.

PROTECTED MODE EXCEPTIONS

#GP(0) if the result is in a non-writable segment. #GP(0) for an illegal memory operand effective address in the CS, DS, or ES segments; #SS(0) for an illegal address in the SS segment.

REAL ADDRESS MODE EXCEPTIONS

Interrupt 13 for a word operand at offset 0FFFFH.

REP/REPE/REPNE—Repeat Following String Operation

Opcode		Instruction	Clocks*	Description
F3	6C	REP INS *eb*,DX	5+4*CX	Input CX bytes from port DX into ES:[DI]
F3	6D	REP INS *ew*,DX	5+4*CX	Input CX words from port DX into ES:[DI]
F3	6C	REP INSB	5+4*CX	Input CX bytes from port DX into ES:[DI]
F3	6D	REP INSW	5+4*CX	Input CX words from port DX into ES:[DI]
F3	A4	REP MOVS *mb,mb*	5+4*CX	Move CX bytes from [SI] to ES:[DI]
F3	A5	REP MOVS *mw,mw*	5+4*CX	Move CX words from [SI] to ES:[DI]
F3	A4	REP MOVSB	5+4*CX	Move CX bytes from DS:[SI] to ES:[DI]
F3	A5	REP MOVSW	5+4*CX	Move CX words from DS:[SI] to ES:[DI]
F3	6E	REP OUTS DX,*eb*	5+4*CX	Output CX bytes from [SI] to port DX
F3	6F	REP OUTS DX,*ew*	5+4*CX	Output CX words from [SI] to port DX
F3	6E	REP OUTSB	5+4*CX	Output CX bytes from DS:[SI] to port DX
F3	6F	REP OUTSW	5+4*CX	Output CX words from DS:[SI] to port DX
F3	AA	REP STOS *mb*	4+3*CX	Fill CX bytes at ES:[DI] with AL
F3	AB	REP STOS *mw*	4+3*CX	Fill CX words at ES:[DI] with AX
F3	AA	REP STOSB	4+3*CX	Fill CX bytes at ES:[DI] with AL
F3	AB	REP STOSW	4+3*CX	Fill CX words at ES:[DI] with AX
F3	A6	REPE CMPS *mb,mb*	5+9*N	Find nonmatching bytes in ES:[DI] and [SI]
F3	A7	REPE CMPS *mw,mw*	5+9*N	Find nonmatching words in ES:[DI] and [SI]
F3	A6	REPE CMPSB	5+9*N	Find nonmatching bytes in ES:[DI] and DS:[SI]
F3	A7	REPE CMPSW	5+9*N	Find nonmatching words in ES:[DI] and DS:[SI]
F3	AE	REPE SCAS *mb*	5+8*N	Find non-AL byte starting at ES:[DI]
F3	AF	REPE SCAS *mw*	5+8*N	Find non-AX word starting at ES:[DI]
F3	AE	REPE SCASB	5+8*N	Find non-AL byte starting at ES:[DI]
F3	AF	REPE SCASW	5+8*N	Find non-AX word starting at ES:[DI]
F2	A6	REPNE CMPS *mb,mb*	5+9*N	Find matching bytes in ES:[DI] and [SI]
F2	A7	REPNE CMPS *mw,mw*	5+9*N	Find matching words in ES:[DI] and [SI]
F2	A6	REPNE CMPSB	5+9*N	Find matching bytes in ES:[DI] and DS:[SI]
F2	A7	REPNE CMPSW	5+9*N	Find matching words in ES:[DI] and DS:[SI]
F2	AE	REPNE SCAS *mb*	5+8*N	Find AL, starting at ES:[DI]
F2	AF	REPNE SCAS *mw*	5+8*N	Find AX, starting at ES:[DI]
F2	AE	REPNE SCASB	5+8*N	Find AL, starting at ES:[DI]
F2	AF	REPNE SCASW	5+8*N	Find AX, starting at ES:[DI]

* N denotes the number of iterations actually executed.

FLAGS MODIFIED

By CMPS and SCAS, none by REP

FLAGS UNDEFINED

None

OPERATION

REP, REPE, and REPNE are prefix operations. These prefixes cause the string instruction that follows to be repeated CX times or (for REPE and REPNE) until the indicated condition in the zero flag is no longer met. Thus, REPE stands for "Repeat while equal," REPNE for "Repeat while not equal."

The REP prefixes make sense only in the contexts listed above. They cannot be applied to anything other than string operations.

Synonymous forms of REPE and REPNE are REPZ and REPNZ, respectively.

The REP prefixes apply only to one string instruction at a time. To repeat a block of instructions, use a LOOP construct.

The precise action for each iteration is as follows:

1. Check the CX register. If it is zero, exit the iteration and move to the next instruction.
2. Acknowledge any pending interrupts.
3. Perform the string operation once.
4. Decrement CX by 1; no flags are modified.
5. If the string operation is SCAS or CMPS, check the zero flag. If the repeat condition does not hold, then exit the iteration and move to the next instruction. Exit if the prefix is REPE and ZF=0 (the last comparison was not equal), or if the prefix is REPNE and ZF=1 (the last comparison was equal).
6. Go to step 1 for the next iteration.

As defined by the individual string-ops, the direction of movement through the block is determined by the direction flag. If the direction flag is 1 (STD was executed), SI and/or DI start at the end of the block and move backward; if the direction flag is 0 (CLD was executed), SI and/or DI start at the beginning of the block and move forward.

For repeated SCAS and CMPS operations the repeat can be exited for one of two different reasons: the CX count can be exhausted or the zero flag can fail the repeat condition. Your code will probably want to distinguish between the two cases. It can do so via either the JCXZ instruction or the conditional jumps that test the zero flag (JZ, JNZ, JE, and JNE).

NOTE

Not all input/output ports can handle the rate at which the repeated I/O instructions execute.

PROTECTED MODE EXCEPTIONS

None by REP; exceptions can be generated when the string-op is executed.

REAL ADDRESS MODE EXCEPTIONS

None by REP; exceptions can be generated when the string-op is executed.

RET—Return from Procedure

Opcode		Instruction	Clocks*	Description
CB		RET	15,pm=25	Return to far caller, same privilege
CB		RET	55	Return, lesser privilege, switch stacks
C3		RET	11	Return to near caller, same privilege
CA	dw	RET dw	15,pm=25	RET (far), same privilege, pop dw bytes
CA	dw	RET dw	55	RET (far), lesser privilege, pop dw bytes
C2	dw	RET dw	11	RET (near), same privilege, pop dw bytes pushed before Call

*Add 1 clock for each byte in the next instruction executed.

FLAGS MODIFIED

None

FLAGS UNDEFINED

None

OPERATION

RET transfers control to a return address located on the stack. The address is usually placed on the stack by a CALL instruction; in that case, the return is made to the instruction that follows the CALL.

There is an optional numeric parameter to RET. It gives the number of stack bytes to be released after the return address is popped. These bytes are typically used as input parameters to the procedure called.

For the intra-segment return, the address on the stack is a 2-byte quantity popped into IP. The CS register is unchanged.

For the inter-segment return, the address on the stack is a 4-byte-long pointer. The offset is popped first, followed by the selector. In real address mode, CS and IP are directly loaded.

In protected mode, an inter-segment return causes the processor to consult the descriptor addressed by the return selector. The AR byte of the descriptor must indicate a code segment of equal or less privilege (of greater or equal numeric value) than the current privilege level. Returns to a lesser privilege level cause the stack to be reloaded from the value saved beyond the parameter block.

The DS and ES segment registers may be set to zero by the inter-segment RET instruction. If these registers refer to segments which cannot be used by the new privilege level, they are set to zero to prevent unauthorized access.

The following list of checks and actions describes the protected-mode inter-segment return in detail.

Inter-segment RET:
    Second word on stack must be within stack limits else #SS(0)
    Return selector RPL must be ≥ CPL else #GP (return selector)
    If return selector RPL = CPL then

RETURN TO SAME LEVEL:
Return selector must be non-null else #GP(0)
Selector index must be within its descriptor table limits else #GP (selector)
Descriptor AR byte must indicate code segment else #GP (selector)
If non-conforming then code segment DPL must equal CPL else #GP (selector)
If conforming then code segment DPL must be ≤ CPL else #GP (selector)
Code segment must be PRESENT else #NP (selector)
Top word on stack must be within stack limits else #SS(0)
IP must be in code segment limit else #GP(0)
Load CS:IP from stack
Load CS-cache with descriptor
Increment SP by 4 plus the immediate offset if it exists
Else
  RETURN TO OUTER PRIVILEGE LEVEL:
Top (8+immediate) bytes on stack must be within stack limits else #SS(0)
Examine return CS selector (at SP+2) and associated descriptor:
    Selector must be non-null else #GP(0)
    Selector index must be within its descriptor table limits else #GP (selector)
    Descriptor AR byte must indicate code segment else #GP (selector)
    If non-conforming then code segment DPL must equal return selector RPL else #GP (selector)
    If conforming then code segment DPL must be ≤ return selector RPL else #GP (selector)
    Segment must be PRESENT else #NP (selector)
Examine return SS selector (at SP+6+imm) and associated descriptor:
    Selector must be non-null else #GP(0)
    Selector index must be within its descriptor table limits else #GP (selector)
    Selector RPL must equal the RPL of the return CS selector else #GP (selector)
    Descriptor AR byte must indicate a writable data segment else #GP (selector)
    Descriptor DPL must equal the RPL of the return CS selector else #GP (selector)
    Segment must be PRESENT else #SS (selector)
IP must be in code segment limit else # GP(0)
Set CPL to the RPL of the return CS selector
Load CS:IP from stack
Set CS RPL to CPL
Increment SP by 4 plus the immediate offset if it exists
Load SS:SP from stack
Load the CS-cache with the return CS descriptor
Load the SS-cache with the return SS descriptor
For each of ES and DS:
    If the current register setting is not valid for the outer level, set the
      register to null (selector = AR = 0)
    To be valid, the register setting must satisfy the following properties:
      Selector index must be within descriptor table limits
      Descriptor AR byte must indicate data or readable code segment
      If segment is data or non-conforming code, then:
        DPL must be ≥ CPL, or
        DPL must be ≥ RPL

PROTECTED MODE EXCEPTIONS

#GP, #NP, or #SS, as described in the above listing.

REAL ADDRESS MODE EXCEPTIONS

Interrupt 13 if the stack pop wraps around from 0FFFFH to 0.

SAHF—Store AH into Flags

Opcode	Instruction	Clocks	Description
9E	SAHF	2	Store AH into flags SF ZF xx AF xx PF xx CF

FLAGS MODIFIED

Sign, zero, auxiliary carry, parity, carry

FLAGS UNDEFINED

None

OPERATION

The flags listed above are loaded with values from the AH register, from bits 7, 6, 4, 2, and 0, respectively.

PROTECTED MODE EXCEPTIONS

None

REAL ADDRESS MODE EXCEPTIONS

None

SAL/SAR/SHL/SHR—Shift Instructions

Opcode		Instruction	Clocks-N*	Description
D0	/4	SAL eb,1	2,mem=7	Multiply EA byte by 2, once
D2	/4	SAL eb,CL	5,mem=8	Multiply EA byte by 2, CL times
C0	/4 db	SAL eb,db	5,mem=8	Multiply EA byte by 2, db times
D1	/4	SAL ew,1	2,mem=7	Multiply EA word by 2, once
D3	/4	SAL ew,CL	5,mem=8	Multiply EA word by 2, CL times
C1	/4 db	SAL ew,db	5,mem=8	Multiply EA word by 2, db times
D0	/7	SAR eb,1	2,mem=7	Signed divide EA byte by 2, once
D2	/7	SAR eb,CL	5,mem=8	Signed divide EA byte by 2, CL times
C0	/7 db	SAR eb,db	5,mem=8	Signed divide EA byte by 2, db times
D1	/7	SAR ew,1	2,mem=7	Signed divide EA word by 2, once
D3	/7	SAR ew,CL	5,mem=8	Signed divide EA word by 2, CL times
C1	/7 db	SAR ew,db	5,mem=8	Signed divide EA word by 2, db times
D0	/5	SHR eb,1	2,mem=7	Unsigned divide EA byte by 2, once
D2	/5	SHR eb,CL	5,mem=8	Unsigned divide EA byte by 2, CL times
C0	/5 db	SHR eb,db	5,mem=8	Unsigned divide EA byte by 2, db times
D1	/5	SHR ew,1	2,mem=7	Unsigned divide EA word by 2, once
D3	/5	SHR ew,CL	5,mem=8	Unsigned divide EA word by 2, CL times
C1	/5 db	SHR ew,db	5,mem=8	Unsigned divide EA word by 2, db times

* Add 1 clock to the times shown for each shift performed

FLAGS MODIFIED

Overflow (only for single-shift form), carry, zero, parity, sign

FLAGS UNDEFINED

Auxiliary carry; also overflow for multibit shifts (only).

OPERATION

SAL (or its synonym SHL) shifts the bits of the operand upward. The high-order bit is shifted into the carry flag, and the low-order bit is set to 0.

SAR and SHR shift the bits of the operand downward. The low-order bit is shifted into the carry flag. The effect is to divide the operand by 2. SAR performs a signed divide: the high-order bit remains the same. SHR performs an unsigned divide: the high-order bit is set to 0.

The shift is repeated the number of times indicated by the second operand, which is either an immediate number or the contents of the CL register. To reduce the maximum execution time, the 80286 does not allow shift counts greater than 31. If a shift count greater than 31 is attempted, only the bottom five bits of the shift count are used. The 8086 uses all 8 bits of the shift count.

The overflow flag is set only if the single-shift forms of the instructions are used. For left shifts, it is set to 0 if the high bit of the answer is the same as the result carry flag (i.e., the top two bits of the original operand were the same); it is set to 1 if they are different. For SAR it is set to 0 for all single shifts. For SHR, it is set to the high-order bit of the original operand. Neither flag bit is modified when the count value is zero.

PROTECTED MODE EXCEPTIONS

#GP(0) if the operand is in a non-writable segment. #GP(0) for an illegal memory operand effective address in the CS, DS, or ES segments; #SS(0) for an illegal address in the SS segment.

REAL ADDRESS MODE EXCEPTIONS

Interrupt 13 for a word operand at offset 0FFFFH.

SBB—Integer Subtraction With Borrow

Opcode			Instruction	Clocks	Description
18	/r		SBB eb,rb	2,mem=7	Subtract with borrow byte register from EA byte
19	/r		SBB ew,rw	2,mem=7	Subtract with borrow word register from EA word
1A	/r		SBB rb,eb	2,mem=7	Subtract with borrow EA byte from byte register
1B	/r		SBB rw,ew	2,mem=7	Subtract with borrow EA word from word register
1C	db		SBB AL,db	3	Subtract with borrow imm. byte from AL
1D	dw		SBB AX,dw	3	Subtract with borrow imm. word from AX
80	/3	db	SBB eb,db	3,mem=7	Subtract with borrow imm. byte from EA byte
81	/3	dw	SBB ew,dw	3,mem=7	Subtract with borrow imm. word from EA word
83	/3	db	SBB ew,db	3,mem=7	Subtract with borrow imm. byte from EA word

FLAGS MODIFIED

Overflow, sign, zero, auxiliary carry, parity, carry

FLAGS UNDEFINED

None

OPERATION

The second operand is added to the carry flag and the result is subtracted from the first operand. The first operand is replaced with the result of the subtraction, and the flags are set accordingly.

When a byte-immediate value is subtracted from a word operand, the immediate value is first sign-extended.

PROTECTED MODE EXCEPTIONS

#GP(0) if the result is in a non-writable segment. #GP(0) for an illegal memory operand effective address in the CS, DS, or ES segments; #SS(0) for an illegal address in the SS segment.

REAL ADDRESS MODE EXCEPTIONS

Interrupt 13 for a word operand at offset 0FFFFH.

SCAS / SCASB / SCASW — Compare String Data

Opcode	Instruction	Clocks	Description
AE	SCAS *mb*	7	Compare bytes AL - ES:[DI], advance DI
AF	SCAS *mw*	7	Compare words AX - ES:[DI], advance DI
AE	SCASB	7	Compare bytes AL - ES:[DI], advance DI
AF	SCASW	7	Compare words AX - ES:[DI], advance DI

FLAGS MODIFIED

Overflow, sign, zero, auxiliary carry, parity, carry

FLAGS UNDEFINED

None

OPERATION

SCAS subtracts the memory byte or word at ES:DI from the AL or AX register. The result is discarded; only the flags are set. The operand must be addressable from the ES register; no segment override is possible.

After the comparison is made, DI is automatically advanced. If the direction flag is 0 (CLD was executed), DI increments; if the direction flag is 1 (STD was executed), DI decrements. DI increments or decrements by 1 if bytes were compared; by 2 if words were compared.

SCAS can be preceded by the REPE or REPNE prefix for a block search of CX bytes or words. Refer to the REP instruction for details of this operation.

PROTECTED MODE EXCEPTIONS

#GP(0) for an illegal memory operand effective address in the CS, DS, or ES segments; #SS(0) for an illegal address in the SS segment.

REAL ADDRESS MODE EXCEPTIONS

Interrupt 13 for a word operand at offset 0FFFFH.

SGDT/SIDT—Store Global/Interrupt Descriptor Table Register

Opcode			Instruction	Clocks	Description
0F	01	/0	SGDT m	11	Store Global Descriptor Table register to m
0F	01	/1	SIDT m	12	Store Interrupt Descriptor Table register to m

FLAGS MODIFIED

None

FLAGS UNDEFINED

None

OPERATION

The contents of the descriptor table register are copied to six bytes of memory indicated by the operand. The LIMIT field of the register goes to the first word at the effective address; the next three bytes get the BASE field of the register; and the last byte is undefined.

SGDT and SIDT appear only in operating systems software; they are not used in applications programs.

PROTECTED MODE EXCEPTIONS

#UD if the destination operand is a register. #GP(0) if the destination is in a non-writable segment. #GP(0) for an illegal memory operand effective address in the CS, DS, or ES segments; #SS(0) for an illegal address in the SS segment.

REAL ADDRESS MODE EXCEPTIONS

These instructions are valid in Real Address mode to facilitate power-up or to reset initialization prior to entering Protected mode.

#UD if the destination operand is a register. Interrupt 13 for a word operand at offset 0FFFFH.

SLDT—Store Local Descriptor Table Register

Opcode	Instruction	Clocks	Description
0F 00 /0	SLDT ew	2,mem=3	Store Local Descriptor Table register to EA word

FLAGS MODIFIED

None

FLAGS UNDEFINED

None

OPERATION

The Local Descriptor Table register is stored in the 2-byte register or memory location indicated by the effective address operand. This register is a selector that points into the Global Descriptor Table.

SLDT appears only in operating systems software. It is not used in applications programs.

PROTECTED MODE EXCEPTIONS

#GP(0) if the destination is in a non-writable segment. #GP(0) for an illegal memory operand effective address in the CS, DS, or ES segments; #SS(0) for an illegal address in the SS segment.

REAL ADDRESS MODE EXCEPTIONS

Interrupt 6; SLDT is not recognized in Real Address mode.

SMSW—Store Machine Status Word

Opcode	Instruction	Clocks	Description
0F 01 /4	SMSW *ew*	2,mem=3	Store Machine Status Word to EA word

FLAGS MODIFIED

None

FLAGS UNDEFINED

None

OPERATION

The Machine Status Word is stored in the 2-byte register or memory location indicated by the effective address operand.

PROTECTED MODE EXCEPTIONS

#GP(0) if the destination is in a non-writable segment. #GP(0) for an illegal memory operand effective address in the CS, DS, or ES segments; #SS(0) for an illegal address in the SS segment.

REAL ADDRESS MODE EXCEPTIONS

Interrupt 13 for a word operand at offset 0FFFFH.

STC—Set Carry Flag

Opcode	Instruction	Clocks	Description
F9	STC	2	Set carry flag

FLAGS MODIFIED

Carry=1

FLAGS UNDEFINED

None

OPERATION

The carry flag is set to 1.

PROTECTED MODE EXCEPTIONS

None

REAL ADDRESS MODE EXCEPTIONS

None

STD—Set Direction Flag

Opcode	Instruction	Clocks	Description
FD	STD	2	Set direction flag so SI and DI will decrement

FLAGS MODIFIED

Direction = 1

FLAGS UNDEFINED

None

OPERATION

The direction flag is set to 1. This causes all subsequent string operations to decrement the index registers (SI and/or DI) on which they operate.

PROTECTED MODE EXCEPTIONS

None

REAL ADDRESS MODE EXCEPTIONS

None

STI—Set Interrupt Enable Flag

Opcode	Instruction	Clocks	Description
FB	STI	2	Set interrupt enable flag, interrupts enabled

FLAGS MODIFIED

Interrupt = 1 (enabled)

FLAGS UNDEFINED

None

OPERATION

The interrupts-enabled flag is set to 1. The 80286 will now respond to external interrupts after executing the STI instruction.

PROTECTED MODE EXCEPTIONS

#GP(0) if the current privilege level is bigger (has less privilege) than the I/O privilege level.

REAL ADDRESS MODE EXCEPTIONS

None

STOS/STOSB/STOSW—Store String Data

Opcode	Instruction	Clocks	Description
AA	STOS *mb*	3	Store AL to byte ES:[DI], advance DI
AB	STOS *mw*	3	Store AX to word ES:[DI], advance DI
AA	STOSB	3	Store AL to byte ES:[DI], advance DI
AB	STOSW	3	Store AX to word ES:[DI], advance DI

FLAGS MODIFIED

None

FLAGS UNDEFINED

None

OPERATION

STOS transfers the contents the AL or AX register to the memory byte or word at ES:DI. The operand must be addressable from the ES register; no segment override is possible.

After the transfer is made, DI is automatically advanced. If the direction flag is 0 (CLD was executed), DI increments; if the direction flag is 1 (STD was executed), DI decrements. DI increments or decrements by 1 if a byte was moved; by 2 if a word was moved.

STOS can be preceded by the REP prefix for a block fill of CX bytes or words. Refer to the REP instruction for details of this operation.

PROTECTED MODE EXCEPTIONS

#GP(0) if the destination is in a non-writable segment. #GP(0) for an illegal memory operand effective address in the CS, DS, or ES segments; #SS(0) for an illegal address in the SS segment.

REAL ADDRESS MODE EXCEPTIONS

Interrupt 13 for a word operand at offset 0FFFFH.

STR—Store Task Register

Opcode	Instruction	Clocks	Description
0F 00 /1	STR ew	2,mem=3	Store Task Register to EA word

FLAGS MODIFIED

None

FLAGS UNDEFINED

None

OPERATION

The contents of the Task Register are copied to the 2-byte register or memory location indicated by the effective address operand.

PROTECTED MODE EXCEPTIONS

#GP(0) if the destination is in a non-writable segment. #GP(0) for an illegal memory operand effective address in the CS, DS, or ES segments; #SS(0) for an illegal address in the SS segment.

REAL ADDRESS MODE EXCEPTIONS

Interrupt 6; STR is not recognized in Real Address mode.

SUB—Integer Subtraction

Opcode			Instruction	Clocks	Description
28	/r		SUB eb,rb	2,mem=7	Subtract byte register from EA byte
29	/r		SUB ew,rw	2,mem=7	Subtract word register from EA word
2A	/r		SUB rb,eb	2,mem=7	Subtract EA byte from byte register
2B	/r		SUB rw,ew	2,mem=7	Subtract EA word from word register
2C	db		SUB AL,db	3	Subtract immediate byte from AL
2D	dw		SUB AX,dw	3	Subtract immediate word from AX
80	/5	db	SUB eb,db	3,mem=7	Subtract immediate byte from EA byte
81	/5	dw	SUB ew,dw	3,mem=7	Subtract immediate word from EA word
83	/5	db	SUB ew,db	3,mem=7	Subtract immediate byte from EA word

FLAGS MODIFIED

Overflow, sign, zero, auxiliary carry, parity, carry

FLAGS UNDEFINED

None

OPERATION

The second operand is subtracted from the first operand, and the first operand is replaced with the result.

When a byte-immediate value is subtracted from a word operand, the immediate value is first sign-extended.

PROTECTED MODE EXCEPTIONS

#GP(0) if the result is in a non-writable segment. #GP(0) for an illegal memory operand effective address in the CS, DS, or ES segments; #SS(0) for an illegal address in the SS segment.

REAL ADDRESS MODE EXCEPTIONS

Interrupt 13 for a word operand at offset 0FFFFH.

TEST—Logical Compare

Opcode		Instruction	Clocks	Description
84	/r	TEST eb,rb	2,mem=6	AND byte register into EA byte for flags only
84	/r	TEST rb,eb	2,mem=6	AND EA byte into byte register for flags only
85	/r	TEST ew,rw	2,mem=6	AND word register into EA word for flags only
85	/r	TEST rw,ew	2,mem=6	AND EA word into word register for flags only
A8	db	TEST AL,db	3	AND immediate byte into AL for flags only
A9	dw	TEST AX,dw	3	AND immediate word into AX for flags only
F6	/0 db	TEST eb,db	3,mem=6	AND immediate byte into EA byte for flags only
F7	/0 dw	TEST ew,dw	3,mem=6	AND immediate word into EA word for flags only

FLAGS MODIFIED

Overflow=0, sign, zero, parity, carry=0

FLAGS UNDEFINED

Auxiliary carry

OPERATION

TEST computes the bit-wise logical AND of the two operands given. Each bit of the result is 1 if both of the corresponding bits of the operands are 1; each bit is 0 otherwise. The result of the operation is discarded; only the flags are modified.

PROTECTED MODE EXCEPTIONS

#GP(0) for an illegal memory operand effective address in the CS, DS, or ES segments; #SS(0) for an illegal address in the SS segment.

REAL ADDRESS MODE EXCEPTIONS

Interrupt 13 for a word operand at offset 0FFFFH.

VERR, VERW — Verify a Segment for Reading or Writing

Opcode			Instruction	Clocks	Description
0F	00	/4	VERR *ew*	14,mem=16	Set ZF=1 if seg. can be read, selector *ew*
0F	00	/5	VERW *ew*	14,mem=16	Set ZF=1 if seg. can be written, selector *ew*

FLAGS MODIFIED

Zero

FLAGS UNDEFINED

None

OPERATION

VERR and VERW expect the 2-byte register or memory operand to contain the value of a selector. The instructions determine whether the segment denoted by the selector is reachable from the current privilege level; the instructions also determine whether it is readable or writable. If the segment is determined to be accessible, the zero flag is set to 1; if the segment is not accessible, it is set to 0. To set ZF, the following conditions must be met:

1. The selector must denote a descriptor within the bounds of the table (GDT or LDT); that is, the selector must be "defined."

2. The selector must denote the descriptor of a code or data segment.

3. If the instruction is VERR, the segment must be readable. If the instruction is VERW, the segment must be a writable data segment.

4. If the code segment is readable and conforming, the descriptor privilege level (DPL) can be any value for VERR. Otherwise, the DPL must be greater than or equal to (have less or the same privilege as) both the current privilege level and the selector's RPL.

The validation performed is the same as if the segment were loaded into DS or ES and the indicated access (read or write) were performed. The zero flag receives the result of the validation. The selector's value cannot result in a protection exception. This enables the software to anticipate possible segment access problems.

PROTECTED MODE EXCEPTIONS

The only faults that can occur are those generated by illegally addressing the memory operand which contains the selector. The selector is not loaded into any segment register, and no faults attributable to the selector operand are generated.

#GP(0) for an illegal memory operand effective address in the CS, DS, or ES segments; #SS(0) for an illegal address in the SS segment.

REAL ADDRESS MODE EXCEPTIONS

Interrupt 6; VERR and VERW are not recognized in Real Address Mode.

WAIT—Wait Until $\overline{\text{BUSY}}$ Pin Is Inactive (HIGH)

Opcode	Instruction	Clocks	Description
9B	WAIT	3	Wait until $\overline{\text{BUSY}}$ pin is inactive (HIGH)

FLAGS MODIFIED

None

FLAGS UNDEFINED

None

OPERATION

WAIT suspends execution of 80286 instructions until the $\overline{\text{BUSY}}$ pin is inactive (high). The $\overline{\text{BUSY}}$ pin is driven by the 80287 numeric processor extension. WAIT is issued to ensure that the numeric instruction being executed is complete, and to check for a possible numeric fault (see below).

PROTECTED MODE EXCEPTIONS

#NM if task switch flag in MSW is set. #MF if 80287 has detected an unmasked numeric error.

REAL ADDRESS MODE EXCEPTIONS

Same as Protected mode.

XCHG—Exchange Memory/Register with Register

Opcode	Instruction	Clocks	Description
86 /r	XCHG eb,rb	3,mem=5	Exchange byte register with EA byte
86 /r	XCHG rb,eb	3,mem=5	Exchange EA byte with byte register
87 /r	XCHG ew,rw	3,mem=5	Exchange word register with EA word
87 /r	XCHG rw,ew	3,mem=5	Exchange EA word with word register
90+ rw	XCHG AX,rw	3	Exchange word register with AX
90+ rw	XCHG rw,AX	3	Exchange with word register

FLAGS MODIFIED

None

FLAGS UNDEFINED

None

OPERATION

The two operands are exchanged. The order of the operands is immaterial. BUS LOCK is asserted for the duration of the exchange, regardless of the presence or absence of the LOCK prefix or IOPL.

PROTECTED MODE EXCEPTIONS

#GP(0) if either operand is in a non-writable segment. #GP(0) for an illegal memory operand effective address in the CS, DS, or ES segments; #SS(0) for an illegal address in the SS segment.

REAL ADDRESS MODE EXCEPTIONS

Interrupt 13 for a word operand at offset 0FFFFH.

XLAT—Table Look-up Translation

Opcode	Instruction	Clocks	Description
D7	XLAT *mb*	5	Set AL to memory byte DS:[BX + unsigned AL]
D7	XLATB	5	Set AL to memory byte DS:[BX + unsigned AL]

FLAGS MODIFIED

None

FLAGS UNDEFINED

None

OPERATION

When XLAT is executed, AL should be the unsigned index into a table addressed by DS:BX. XLAT changes the AL register from the table index into the table entry. BX is unchanged.

PROTECTED MODE EXCEPTIONS

#GP(0) for an illegal memory operand effective address in the CS, DS, or ES segments; #SS(0) for an illegal address in the SS segment.

REAL ADDRESS MODE EXCEPTIONS

Interrupt 13 for a word operand at offset 0FFFFH.

XOR—Logical Exclusive OR

Opcode			Instruction	Clocks	Description
30	/r		XOR eb,rb	2,mem=7	Exclusive-OR byte register into EA byte
31	/r		XOR ew,rw	2,mem=7	Exclusive-OR word register into EA word
32	/r		XOR rb,eb	2,mem=7	Exclusive-OR EA byte into byte register
33	/r		XOR rw,ew	2,mem=7	Exclusive-OR EA word into word register
34	db		XOR AL,db	3	Exclusive-OR immediate byte into AL
35	dw		XOR AX,dw	3	Exclusive-OR immediate word into AX
80	/6	db	XOR eb,db	3,mem=7	Exclusive-OR immediate byte into EA byte
81	/6	dw	XOR ew,dw	3,mem=7	Exclusive-OR immediate word into EA word

FLAGS MODIFIED

Overflow=0, sign, zero, parity, carry=0

FLAGS UNDEFINED

Auxiliary carry

OPERATION

XOR computes the exclusive OR of the two operands. Each bit of the result is 1 if the corresponding bits of the operands are different; each bit is 0 if the corresponding bits are the same. The answer replaces the first operand.

PROTECTED MODE EXCEPTIONS

#GP(0) if the result is in a non-writable segment. #GP(0) for an illegal memory operand effective address in the CS, DS, or ES segments; #SS(0) for an illegal address in the SS segment.

REAL ADDRESS MODE EXCEPTIONS

Interrupt 13 for a word operand at offset 0FFFFH.

Appendix C
8086/8088 Compatibility Considerations

APPENDIX C
8086/8088 COMPATIBILITY CONSIDERATIONS

SOFTWARE COMPATIBILITY CONSIDERATIONS

In general, the real address mode 80286 will correctly execute ROM-based 8086/8088 software. The following is a list of the minor differences between 8086 and 80286 (Real mode).

1. Add Six Interrupt Vectors.

   The 80286 adds six interrupts which arise only if the 8086 program has a hidden bug. These interrupts occur only for instructions which were undefined on the 8086/8088 or if a segment wraparound is attempted. It is recommended that you add an interrupt handler to the 8086 software that is to be run on the 80286, which will treat these interrupts as invalid operations.

   This additional software does not significantly effect the existing 8086 software because the interrupts do not normally occur and should not already have been used since they are in the interrupt group reserved by Intel. Table C-1 describes the new 80286 interrupts.

2. Do not Rely on 8086/8088 Instruction Clock Counts.

   The 80286 takes fewer clocks for most instructions than the 8086/8088. The areas to look into are delays between I/O operations, and assumed delays in 8086/8088 operating in parallel with an 8087.

3. Divide Exceptions Point at the DIV Instruction.

   Any interrupt on the 80286 will always leave the saved CS:IP value pointing at the beginning of the instruction that failed (including prefixes). On the 8086, the CS:IP value saved for a divide exception points at the next instruction.

Table C-1. New 80286 Interrupts

Interrupt Number	Function
5	A BOUND instruction was executed with a register value outside the two limit values.
6	An undefined opcode was encountered.
7	The EM bit in the MSW has been set and an ESC instruction was executed. This interrupt will also occur on WAIT instructions if TS is set.
8	The interrupt table limit was changed by the LIDT instruction to a value between 20H and 43H. The default limit after reset is 3FFH, enough for all 256 interrupts.
9	A processor extension data transfer exceeded offset OFFFFH in a segment. This interrupt handler *must* execute FNINIT before *any* ESC or WAIT instruction is executed.
13	Segment wraparound was attempted by a word operation at offset OFFFFH.
16	When 80286 attempted to execute a coprocessor instruction ERROR pin indicated an unmasked exception from previous coprocessor instruction.

4. Use Interrupt 16 for Numeric Exceptions.

Any 80287 system *must* use interrupt vector 16 for the numeric error interrupt. If an 8086/8087 or 8088/8087 system uses another vector for the 8087 interrupt, both vectors should point at the numeric error interrupt handler.

5. Numeric Exception Handlers Should allow Prefixes.

The saved CS:IP value in the NPX environment save area will point at any leading prefixes before an ESC instruction. On 8086/8088 systems, this value points only at the ESC instruction.

6. Do Not Attempt Undefined 8086/8088 Operations.

Instructions like POP CS or MOV CS,op will either cause exception 6 (undefined opcode) or perform a protection setup operation like LIDT on the 80286. Undefined bit encodings for bits 5-3 of the second byte of POP MEM or PUSH MEM will cause exception 13 on the 80286.

7. Place a Far JMP Instruction at FFFF0H.

After reset, CS:IP = F000:FFF0 on the 80286 (versus FFFF:0000 on the 8086/8088). This change was made to allow sufficient code space to enter protected mode without reloading CS. Placing a far JMP instruction at FFFF0H will avoid this difference. Note that the BOOTSTRAP option of LOC86 will automatically generate this jump instruction.

8. Do not Rely on the Value Written by PUSH SP.

The 80286 will push a different value on the stack for PUSH SP than the 8086/8088. If the value pushed is important, replace PUSH SP instructions with the following three instructions:

```
PUSH       BP
MOV        BP,SP
XCHG       BP,[BP]
```

This code functions as the 8086/8088 PUSH SP instruction on the 80286.

9. Do not Shift or Rotate by More than 31 Bits.

The 80286 masks all shift/rotate counts to the low 5 bits. This MOD 32 operation limits the count to a maximum of 31 bits. With this change, the longest shift/rotate instruction is 39 clocks. Without this change, the longest shift/rotate instruction would be 264 clocks, which delays interrupt response until the instruction completes execution.

10. Do not Duplicate Prefixes.

The 80286 sets an instruction length limit of 10 bytes. The only way to violate this limit is by duplicating a prefix two or more times before an instruction. Exception 6 occurs if the instruction length limit is violated. The 8086/8088 has no instruction length limit.

11. Do not Rely on Odd 8086/8088 LOCK Characteristics.

The LOCK prefix and its corresponding output signal should only be used to prevent other bus masters from interrupting a data movement operation. The 80286 will always assert LOCK during an XCHG instruction with memory (even if the LOCK prefix was not used). LOCK should only be used with the XCHG, MOV, MOVS, INS, and OUTS instructions.

The 80286 LOCK signal will *not* go active during an instruction prefetch.

12. Do not Single Step External Interrupt Handlers.

The priority of the 80286 single step interrupt is different from that of the 8086/8088. This change was made to prevent an external interrupt from being single-stepped if it occurs while single stepping through a program. The 80286 single step interrupt has higher priority than any external interrupt.

The 80286 will still single step through an interrupt handler invoked by INT instructions or an instruction exception.

13. Do not Rely on IDIV Exceptions for Quotients of 80H or 8000H.

   The 80286 can generate the largest negative number as a quotient for IDIV instructions. The 8086 will instead cause exception 0.

14. Do not Rely on NMI Interrupting NMI Handlers.

   After an NMI is recognized, the NMI input and processor extension limit error interrupt is masked until the first IRET instruction is executed.

15. The NPX error signal does not pass through an interrupt controller (an 8087 INT signal does). Any interrupt controller-oriented instructions for the 8087 may have to be deleted.

16. If any real-mode program relies on address space wrap-around (e.g., FFF0:0400=0000:0300), then external hardware should be used to force the upper 4 addresses to zero during real mode.

17. Do not use I/O ports 00F8-00FFH. These are reserved for controlling 80287 and future processor extensions.

HARDWARE COMPATIBILITY CONSIDERATIONS

1. Address after Reset

   8086 has CS:IP = ffff:0000 and physical address ffff0.
   80286 has CS:IP = f000:fff0 and physical address fffff0.

   Note: After 80286 reset, until the first 80286 far JMP or far CALL, the code segment base is ff0000. This means A20-A23 will be high for CS-relative bus cycles (code fetch or use of CS override prefix) after reset until the first far JMP or far CALL instruction is performed.

2. Physical Address Formation

   In real mode or protected mode, the 80286 always forms a physical address by adding a 16-bit offset with a 24-bit segment base value (8086 has 20-bit base value). Therefore, if the 80286 in real mode has a segment base within 64K of the top of the 1Mbyte address space, and the program adds an offset of ffffh to the segment base, the physical address will be slightly above 1Mbyte. Thus, to fully duplicate 1Mbyte wraparound that the 8086 has, it is always necessary to force A20 low externally when the 80286 is in real mode, but system hardware uses all 24 address lines.

3. LOCK signal

   On the 8086, LOCK asserted means this bus cycle is within a group of two or more locked bus cycles. On the 80286, the LOCK signal means lock this bus cycle to the NEXT bus cycle. Therefore, on the 80286, the LOCK signal is not asserted on the last locked bus cycle of the group of locked bus cycles.

4. Coprocessor Interface

   8086, synchronous to 8086, can become a bus master.
   80287, asynchronous to 80286 and 80287, cannot become a bus master.

   8087 pulls opcode and pointer information directly from data bus.
   80286 passes opcode and pointer information to 80287.

   8087 uses interrupt path to signal errors to 8086.
   80287 uses dedicated ERROR signal.

   8086 requires explicit WAIT opcode preceding all ESC instructions to synchronize with 8087.
   80286 has automatic instruction synchronization with 80287.

5. Bus Cycles

   8086 has four-clock minimum bus cycle, with a time-multiplexed address/data bus.
   80286 has two-clock minimum bus cycle, with separate buses for address and data.

Appendix D
80286/80386 Software Compatibility Considerations

APPENDIX D
80286/80386 SOFTWARE
COMPATIBILITY CONSIDERATIONS

This appendix describes the considerations required in designing an *Operating System* for the protected mode 80286 so that it will operate on an 80386. An 80286 Operating System running on the 80386 would not use any of the advanced features of the 80386 (i.e., paging or segments larger than 64K), but would run 80286 code faster. Use of the new 80386 features requires changes in the 80286 Operating System.

The 80386 is no different than any other software compatible processor in terms of requiring the same system environment to run the same software; the 80386 must have the same amount of physical memory and I/O devices in the system as the 80286 system to run the same software. Note that an 80386 system requires a different memory system to achieve the higher performance.

The 80286 design considerations can be generally characterized as avoiding use of functions or memory that the 80386 will use. The exception to this rule is initialization code executed after power up. Such code must be changed to configure the 80386 system to match that of the 80286 system.

The following are 80286/80386 software compatibility design considerations:

1. Isolate the protected mode initialization code.

   System initialization code will be required on the 80386 to program operating parameters before executing any significant amount of 80286 software. The 80286 initialization software should be isolated from the rest of the Operating System.

   The initialization code in Appendix A is an example of isolated initialization code. Such code can be extended to include programming of operating parameters before executing the initial protected mode task.

2. Avoid wraparound of 80286 24-bit physical address space.

   Since the 80386 has a larger physical address space, any segment whose base address is greater than FF0000 and whose limit is beyond FFFFFF will address the seventeenth megabyte of memory in the 80386 32-bit physical address space instead of the first megabyte on an 80286.

   No expand-down segments shouldhave a base address in the range FF00001–FFFFFF. No expand-up segments should wrap around the 80286 address space (the sum of their base and limit is in the range 000000–00FFFE).

3. Zero the last word of every 80286 descriptor.

   The 80386 uses the last word of each descriptor to expand the base address and limit fields of segments. Placing zeros in the descriptor will cause the 80386 to treat the segments the same way as an 80286 (except for address space wraparound as mentioned above).

4. Use only 80H or 00H for invalid descriptors.

   The 80386 uses more descriptor types than the 80286. Numeric values of 8–15 in bits 3–0 of the access byte for control descriptors will cause a protection exception on the 80286, but may be defined for other segment types on the 80386. Access byte values of 80H and 00H will remain undefined descriptors on both the 80286 and the 80386.

5. Put error interrupt handlers in reserved interrupts 14, 15, 17–31.

   Some of the unused, Intel-reserved interrupts of the 80286 will be used by the 80386 (i.e., page fault or bus error). These interrupts should not occur while executing an 80286 operating system on an 80386. However, it is safest to place an interrupt handler in these interrupts to print an error message and stop the system if they do occur.

6. Do not change bits 15–4 of MSW.

    The 80386 uses some of the undefined bits in the machine status word. 80286 software should ignore bits 15–4 of the MSW. To change the MSW on an 80286, read the old value first with LMSW, change bits 3–0 only, then write the new value with SMSW.

7. Use a restricted LOCK protocol for multiprocessor systems.

    The 80386 supports the 8086/80286 LOCK functions for simple instructions, but not the string move instructions. Any need for locked string moves can be satisfied by gaining control of a status semaphore before using the string move instruction. Any attempt to execute a locked string move will cause a protection exception on the 80386.

    The general 80286 LOCK protocol does not efficiently extend to large multiprocessor systems. If all the processors in the system frequently use the 8086/80286 LOCK, they will prevent other processors from accessing memory and thereby impact system performance.

Access to semaphores in the future, including current 80286 Operating Systems, should use a protocol with the following restrictions:

•   Be sure the semaphore starts at a physical memory address that is a multiple of 4.

•   Do not use string moves to access the variable.

•   All accesses by any instruction or I/O device (even simple reads or writes) must use the LOCK prefix or system LOCK signal.

INDEX

80287 Numeric Processor Extension (NPX)

8087 Numeric Processor Extension
(NPX)

PREFACE

AN INTRODUCTION TO THE 80286

This supplement describes the 80287 Numeric Processor Extension (NPX) for the 80286 microprocessor. Below is a brief overview of 80286 concepts, along with some of the nomenclature used throughout this and other Intel publications.

The 80286 Microsystem

The 80286 is a new VLSI microprocessor system with exceptional capabilities for supporting large-system applications. Based on a new-generation CPU (the Intel 80286), this powerful microsystem is designed to support multiuser reprogrammable and real-time multitasking applications. Its dedicated system support circuits simplify system hardware; sophisticated hardware and software tools reduce both the time and the cost of product development.

The 80286 is a virtual-memory microprocessor with on-chip memory management and protection. The 80286 microsystem offers a total-solution approach, enabling you to develop high-speed, interactive, multiuser, multitasking—and multiprocessor—systems more rapidly and at higher performance than ever before.

- Reliability and system up-time are becoming increasingly important in all applications. Information must be protected from misuse or accidental loss. The 80286 includes a sophisticated and flexible four-level protection mechanism that isolates layers of operating system programs from application programs to maintain a high degree of system integrity.

- The 80286 provides 16 megabytes of physical address space to support today's application requirements. This large physical memory enables the 80286 to keep many large programs and data structures simultaneously in memory for high-speed access.

- For applications with dynamically changing memory requirements, such as multiuser business systems, the 80286 CPU provides on-chip memory management and virtual memory support. On an 80286-based system, each user can have up to a gigabyte (2^{30} bytes) of virtual-address space. This large address space virtually eliminates restrictions on the number or size of programs that may be part of the system.

- Large multiuser or real-time multitasking systems are easily supported by the 80286. High-performance features, such as a very high-speed task switch, fast interrupt-response time, inter-task protection, and a quick and direct operating system interface, make the 80286 highly suited to multiuser/multitasking applications.

- The 80286 has two operating modes: Real-Address mode and Protected-Address mode. In Real-Address mode, the 80286 is fully compatible with the 8086, 8088, 80186, and 80188 microprocessors; all of the extensive libraries of 8086 and 8088 software execute four to six times faster on the 80286, without any modification.

- In Protected-Address mode, the advanced memory management and protection features of the 80286 become available, without any reduction in performance. Upgrading 8086 and 8088 application programs to use these new memory management and protection features usually requires only reassembly or recompilation (some programs may require minor modification). This compatibility between 80286 and 8086 processor families reduces both the time and the cost of software development.

The Organization of This Manual

This manual describes the 80287 Numeric Processor Extension (NPX) for the 80286 microprocessor. The material in this manual is presented from the perspective of software designers, both at an applications and at a systems software level.

- Chapter One, "Overview of Numeric Processing," gives an overview of the 80287 NPX and reviews the concepts of numeric computation using the 80287.

- Chapter Two, "Programming Numeric Applications," provides detailed information for software designers generating applications for systems containing an 80286 CPU with an 80287 NPX. The 80286/80287 instruction set mnemonics are explained in detail, along with a description of programming facilities for these systems. A comparative 80287 programming example is given.

- Chapter Three, "System-Level Numeric Programming," provides information of interest to systems software writers, including details of the 80287 architecture and operational characteristics.

- Chapter Four, "Numeric Programming Examples," provides several detailed programming examples for the 80287, including conditional branching, the conversion between floating-point values and their ASCII representations, and the calculation of several trigonometric functions. These examples illustrate assembly-language programming on the 80287 NPX.

- Appendix A, "Machine Instruction Encoding and Decoding," gives reference information on the encoding of NPX instructions.

- Appendix B, "Compatability between the 80287 NPX and the 8087," describes the differences between the 80287 and the 8087.

- Appendix C, "Implementing the IEEE P754 Standard," gives details of the IEEE P754 Standard.

- The Glossary defines 80287 and floating-point terminology. Refer to it as needed.

Related Publications

To best use the material in this manual, readers should be familiar with the operation and architecture of 80286 systems. The following manuals contain information related to the content of this supplement and of interest to programmers of 80287 systems:

- *Introduction to the 80286*, order number 210308
- *ASM286 Assembly Language Reference Manual*, order number 121924
- *80286 Operating System Writer's Guide*, order number 121960
- *80286 Hardware Reference Manual*, order number 210760
- *Microprocessor and Peripheral Handbook*, order number 210844
- *PL/M-286 User's Guide*, order number 121945
- *80287 Support Library Reference Manual*, order number 122129
- *8086 Software Toolbox Manual*, order number 122203 (includes information about 80287 Emulator Software)

TABLE OF CONTENTS

APPENDIX A
MACHINE INSTRUCTION ENCODING AND DECODING

APPENDIX B
COMPATIBILITY BETWEEN THE 80287 NPX AND THE 8087

APPENDIX C
IMPLEMENTING THE IEEE P754 STANDARD

GLOSSARY OF 80287 AND FLOATING-POINT TERMINOLOGY

INDEX

Figures

TABLE OF CONTENTS

Tables

Overview of Numeric Processing 1

CHAPTER 1
OVERVIEW OF NUMERIC PROCESSING

The 80287 NPX is a high-performance numerics processing element that extends the 80286 architecture by adding significant numeric capabilities and direct support for floating-point, extended-integer, and BCD data types. The 80286 CPU with 80287 NPX easily supports powerful and accurate numeric applications through its implementation of the proposed IEEE 754 Standard for Binary Floating-Point Arithmetic.

INTRODUCTION TO THE 80287 NUMERIC PROCESSOR EXTENSION

The 80287 Numeric Processor Extension (NPX) is highly compatible with its predecessor, the earlier Intel 8087 NPX.

The 8087 NPX was designed for use in 8086-family systems. The 8086 was the first microprocessor family to partition the processing unit to permit high-performance numeric capabilities. The 8087 NPX for this processor family implemented a complete numeric processing environment in compliance with the proposed IEEE 754 Floating-Point Standard.

With the 80287 Numeric Processor Extension, high-speed numeric computations have been extended to 80286 high-performance multi-tasking and multi-user systems. Multiple tasks using the numeric processor extension are afforded the full protection of the 80286 memory management and protection features.

Figure 1-1 illustrates the relative performance of 8-MHz 8086/8087 and 80286/80287 systems in executing numerics-oriented applications.

Performance

Table 1-1 compares the execution times of several 80287 instructions with the equivalent operations executed in software on an 8-MHz 80286. The software equivalents are highly-optimized assembly-language procedures from the 80287 emulator. As indicated in the table, the 80287 NPX provides about 50 to 100 times the performance of software numeric routines on the 80286 CPU. An 8-MHz 80287 multiplies 32-bit and 64-bit real numbers in about 11.9 and 16.9 microseconds, respectively. Of course, the actual performance of the NPX in a given system depends on the characteristics of the individual application.

Although the performance figures shown in table 1-1 refer to operations on real (floating-point) numbers, the 80287 also manipulates fixed-point binary and decimal integers of up to 64 bits or 18 digits, respectively. The 80287 can improve the speed of multiple-precision software algorithms for integer operations by 10 to 100 times.

Because the 80287 NPX is an extension of the 80286 CPU, no software overhead is incurred in setting up the NPX for computation. The 80287 and 80286 processors coordinate their activities in a manner transparent to software. Moreover, built-in coordination facilities allow the 80286 CPU to proceed with other instructions while the 80287 NPX is simultaneously executing numeric instructions. Programs can exploit this concurrency of execution to further increase system performance and throughput.

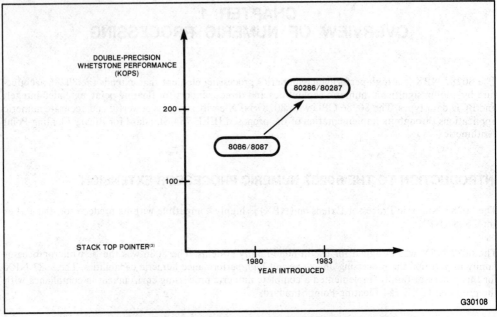

Figure 1-1. Evolution and Performance of Numeric Processors

Table 1-1. Numeric Processing Speed Comparisons

Floating-Point Instruction		Approximate Performance Ratios: 8 MHz 80287 to 8 MHz Protected Mode iAPX using E80287
FADD ST,ST (Temp Real)	Addition	1: 42
FDIV DWORD PTR (Single-Precision)	Division	1:266
FXAM (Stack(0) assumed)	Examine	1:139
FYL2X (Stack(0),(1) assumed)	Logarithm	1: 99
FPATAN (Stack(0) assumed)	Arctangent	1:153
F2XM1 (Stack(0) assumed)	Exponentiation	1: 41

Ease of Use

The 80287 NPX offers more than raw execution speed for computation-intensive tasks. The 80287 brings the functionality and power of accurate numeric computation into the hands of the general user.

Like the 8087 NPX that preceded it, the 80287 is explicitly designed to deliver stable, accurate results when programmed using straightforward "pencil and paper" algorithms. The IEEE 754 standard specifically addresses this issue, recognizing the fundamental importance of making numeric computations both easy and safe to use.

For example, most computers can overflow when two single-precision floating-point numbers are multiplied together and then divided by a third, even if the final result is a perfectly valid 32-bit number.

The 80287 delivers the correctly rounded result. Other typical examples of undesirable machine behavior in straightforward calculations occur when solving for the roots of a quadratic equation:

$$\frac{-b \pm \sqrt{b^2 - 4ac}}{2a}$$

or computing financial rate of return, which involves the expression: $(1+i)^n$. On most machines, straightforward algorithms will not deliver consistently correct results (and will not indicate when they are incorrect). To obtain correct results on traditional machines under all conditions usually requires sophisticated numerical techniques that are foreign to most programmers. General application programmers using straightforward algorithms will produce much more reliable programs using the 80287. This simple fact greatly reduces the software investment required to develop safe, accurate computation-based products.

Beyond traditional numerics support for scientific applications, the 80287 has built-in facilities for commercial computing. It can process decimal numbers of up to 18 digits without round-off errors, performing *exact arithmetic* on integers as large as 2^{64} or 10^{18}. Exact arithmetic is vital in accounting applications where rounding errors may introduce monetary losses that cannot be reconciled.

The NPX contains a number of optional facilities that can be invoked by sophisticated users. These advanced features include two models of infinity, directed rounding, gradual underflow, and either automatic or programmed exception-handling facilities.

These automatic exception-handling facilities permit a high degree of flexibility in numeric processing software, without burdening the programmer. While performing numeric calculations, the NPX automatically detects exception conditions that can potentially damage a calculation. By default, on-chip exception handlers may be invoked to field these exceptions so that a reasonable result is produced, and execution may proceed without program interruption. Alternatively, the NPX can signal the CPU, invoking a software exception handler whenever various types of exceptions are detected.

Applications

The NPX's versatility and performance make it appropriate to a broad array of numeric applications. In general, applications that exhibit any of the following characteristics can benefit by implementing numeric processing on the 80287:

- Numeric data vary over a wide range of values, or include nonintegral values.
- Algorithms produce very large or very small intermediate results.
- Computations must be very precise; i.e., a large number of significant digits must be maintained.
- Performance requirements exceed the capacity of traditional microprocessors.
- Consistently safe, reliable results must be delivered using a programming staff that is not expert in numerical techniques.

Note also that the 80287 can reduce software development costs and improve the performance of systems that use not only real numbers, but operate on multiprecision binary or decimal integer values as well.

A few examples, which show how the 80287 might be used in specific numerics applications, are described below. In many cases, these types of systems have been implemented in the past with minicomputers. The advent of the 80287 brings the size and cost savings of microprocessor technology to these applications for the first time.

- Business data processing—The NPX's ability to accept decimal operands and produce *exact* decimal results of up to 18 digits greatly simplifies accounting programming. Financial calculations that use power functions can take advantage of the 80287's exponentiation and logarithmic instructions.

- Process control—The 80287 solves dynamic range problems automatically, and its extended precision allows control functions to be fine-tuned for more accurate and efficient performance. Control algorithms implemented with the NPX also contribute to improved reliability and safety, while the 80287's speed can be exploited in real-time operations.

- Computer numerical control (CNC)—The 80287 can move and position machine tool heads with accuracy in real-time. Axis positioning also benefits from the hardware trigonometric support provided by the 80287.

- Robotics—Coupling small size and modest power requirements with powerful computational abilities, the NPX is ideal for on-board six-axis positioning.

- Navigation—Very small, lightweight, and accurate inertial guidance systems can be implemented with the 80287. Its built-in trigonometric functions can speed and simplify the calculation of position from bearing data.

- Graphics terminals—The 80287 can be used in graphics terminals to locally perform many functions that normally demand the attention of a main computer; these include rotation, scaling, and interpolation. By also using an 82720 Graphics Display Controller to perform high speed data transfers, very powerful and highly self-sufficient terminals can be built from a relatively small number of 80286 family parts.

- Data acquisition—The 80287 can be used to scan, scale, and reduce large quantities of data as it is collected, thereby lowering storage requirements and time required to process the data for analysis.

The preceding examples are oriented toward *traditional* numerics applications. There are, in addition, many other types of systems that do not appear to the end user as *computational*, but can employ the 80287 to advantage. Indeed, the 80287 presents the imaginative system designer with an opportunity similar to that created by the introduction of the microprocessor itself. Many applications can be viewed as numerically-based if sufficient computational power is available to support this view. This is analogous to the thousands of successful products that have been built around "buried" microprocessors, even though the products themselves bear little resemblance to computers.

Upgradability

The architecture of the 80286 CPU is specifically adapted to allow easy upgradability to use an 80287, simply by plugging in the 80287 NPX. For this reason, designers of 80286 systems may wish to incorporate the 80287 NPX into their designs in order to offer two levels of price and performance at little additional cost.

Two features of the 80286 CPU make the design and support of upgradable 80286 systems particularly simple:

- The 80286 can be programmed to recognize the presence of an 80287 NPX; that is, software can recognize whether it is running on an 80286 or an 80287 system.

- After determining whether the 80287 NPX is available, the 80286 CPU can be instructed to let the NPX execute all numeric instructions. If an 80287 NPX is not available, the 80286 CPU can emulate all 80287 numeric instructions in software. This emulation is completely transparent to the application software—the same object code may be used by both 80286 and 80287 systems. No relinking or recompiling of application software is necessary; the same code will simply execute faster on the 80287 than on the 80286 system.

To facilitate this design of upgradable 80286 systems, Intel provides a software emulator for the 80287 that provides the functional equivalent of the 80287 hardware, implemented in software on the 80286. Except for timing, the operation of this 80287 emulator (E80287) is the same as for the 80287 NPX hardware. When the emulator is combined as part of the systems software, the 80286 system with 80287 emulation and the 80286 with 80287 hardware are virtually indistinguishable to an application program. This capability makes it easy for software developers to maintain a single set of programs for both systems. System manufacturers can offer the NPX as a simple plug-in performance option without necessitating any changes in the user's software.

Programming Interface

The 80286/80287 pair is programmed as a single processor; all of the 80287 registers appear to a programmer as extensions of the basic 80286 register set. The 80286 has a class of instructions known as ESCAPE instructions, all having a common format. These ESC instructions are numeric instructions for the 80287 NPX. These numeric instructions for the 80287 are simply encoded into the instruction stream along with 80286 instructions.

All of the CPU memory-addressing modes may be used in programming the NPX, allowing convenient access to record structures, numeric arrays, and other memory-based data structures. All of the memory management and protection features of the CPU are extended to the NPX as well.

Numeric processing in the 80287 centers around the NPX register stack. Programmers can treat these eight 80-bit registers as either a fixed register set, with instructions operating on explicitly-designated registers, or a classical stack, with instructions operating on the top one or two stack elements.

Internally, the 80287 holds all numbers in a uniform 80-bit temporary-real format. Operands that may be represented in memory as 16-, 32-, or 64-bit integers, 32-, 64-, or 80-bit floating-point numbers, or 18-digit packed BCD numbers, are automatically converted into temporary-real format as they are loaded into the NPX registers. Computation results are subsequently converted back into one of these destination data formats when they are stored into memory from the NPX registers.

Table 1-2 lists each of the seven data types supported by the 80287, showing the data format for each type. All operands are stored in memory with the least significant digits starting at the initial (lowest) memory address. Numeric instructions access and store memory operands using only this initial address. For maximum system performance, all operands should start at even memory addresses.

Table 1-3 lists the 80287 instructions by class. No special programming tools are necessary to use the 80287, because all of the NPX instructions and data types are directly supported by the ASM286 Assembler and Intel's appropriate high-level languages.

Software routines for the 80287 may be written in ASM286 Assembler or any of the following higher-level languages:

PL/M-286
PASCAL-286
FORTRAN-286
C-286

Table 1-2. Numeric Data Types

Data Type	Bits	Significant Digits (Decimal)	Approximate Range (Decimal)
Word integer	16	4	$-32{,}768 \leq X \leq +32{,}767$
Short integer	32	9	$-2 \times 10^9 \leq X \leq +2 \times 10^9$
Long integer	64	18	$-9 \times 10^{18} \leq X \leq +9 \times 10^{18}$
Packed decimal	80	18	$-99...99 \leq X \leq +99...99$ (18 digits)
Short real*	32	6–7	$8.43 \times 10^{-37} \leq |X| \leq 3.37 \times 10^{38}$
Long real*	64	15–16	$4.19 \times 10^{-307} \leq |X| \leq 1.67 \times 10^{308}$
Temporary real	80	19	$3.4 \times 10^{-4932} \leq |X| \leq 1.2 \times 10^{4932}$

Table 1-3. Principal NPX Instructions

Class	Instruction Types
Data Transfer	Load (all data types), Store (all data types), Exchange
Arithmetic	Add, Subtract, Multiply, Divide, Subtract Reversed, Divide Reversed, Square Root, Scale, Remainder, Integer Part, Change Sign, Absolute Value, Extract
Comparison	Compare, Examine, Test
Transcendental	Tangent, Arctangent, $2^x - 1$, $Y \cdot Log_2(X + 1)$, $Y \cdot Log_2(X)$
Constants	0, 1, π, $Log_{10}2$, Log_e2, Log_210, Log_2e
Processor Control	Load Control Word, Store Control Word, Store Status Word, Load Environment, Store Environment, Save, Restore, Clear Exceptions, Initialize, Set Protected Mode

In addition, all of the development tools supporting the 8086 and 8087 can also be used to develop software for the 80286 and 80287 operating in Real-Address mode.

All of these high-level languages provide programmers with access to the computational power and speed of the 80287 without requiring an understanding of the architecture of the 80286 and 80287 chips. Such architectural considerations as concurrency and data synchronization are handled automatically by these high-level languages. For the ASM286 programmer, specific rules for handling these issues are discussed in a later section of this supplement.

Hardware Interface

As an extension of the 80286 processor, the 80287 is wired very much in parallel with the 80286 CPU. Four special status signals, PEREQ, $\overline{\text{PEACK}}$, BUSY, and $\overline{\text{ERROR}}$, permit the two processors to coordinate their activities. The 80287 NPX also monitors the 80286 $\overline{\text{S1}}$, $\overline{\text{S0}}$, COD/$\overline{\text{INTA}}$, READY, HLDA, and CLK pins to monitor the execution of ESC instructions (numeric instructions) by the 80286.

As shown in figure 1-2, the 80287 NPX is divided internally into two processing elements; the Bus Interface Unit (BIU) and the Numeric Execution Unit (NEU). The two units operate independently of one another: the BIU receives and decodes instructions, requests operand transfers with memory, and executes processor control instructions, whereas the NEU processes individual numeric instructions.

The BIU handles all of the status and signal lines between the 80287 and the 80286. The NEU executes all instructions that involve the register stack. These instructions include arithmetic, logical, transcendental, constant, and data transfer instructions. The data path in the NEU is 84 bits wide (68 fraction bits, 15 exponent bits, and a sign bit), allowing internal operand transfers to be performed at very high speeds.

The 80287 executes a single numeric instruction at a time. Before executing most ESC instructions, the 80286 tests the $\overline{BUSY}$ pin and, before initiating the command, waits until the 80287 indicates that it is not busy. Once initiated, the 80286 continues program execution, while the 80287 executes the numeric instruction. Unlike the 8087, which required a WAIT instruction to test the $\overline{BUSY}$ signal before each ESC opcode, these WAIT instructions are permissible, but not necessary, in 80287 programs.

In all cases, a WAIT or ESC instruction should be inserted after any 80287 store to memory (except FSTSW or FSTCW) or load from memory (except FLDENV, FLDCW, or FRSTOR) before the 80286 reads or changes the memory value.

When needed, all data transfers between memory and the 80287 NPX are performed by the 80286 CPU, using its Processor Extension Data Channel. Numeric data transfers performed by the 80286 use the same timing as any other bus cycle, and all such transfers come under the supervision of the

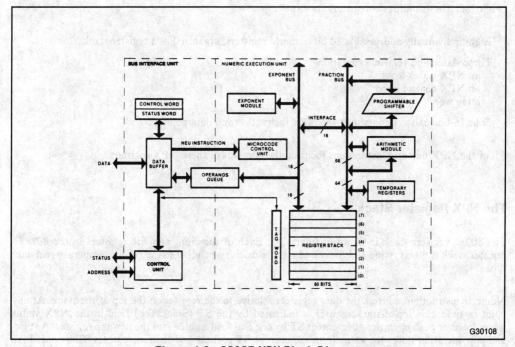

Figure 1-2. 80287 NPX Block Diagram

80286 memory management and protection mechanisms. The 80286 Processor Extension Data Channel and the hardware interface between the 80286 and 80287 processors are described in Chapter Six of the *80286 Hardware Reference Manual*.

From the programmer's perspective, the 80287 can be considered just an extension of the 80286 processor. All interaction between the 80286 and the 80287 processors on the hardware level is handled automatically by the 80286 and is transparent to the software.

To communicate with the 80287, the 80286 uses the reserved I/O port addresses 00F8H, 00FAH, and 00FCH (I/O ports numbered 00F8H through 00FFH are reserved for the 80286/80287 interface). These I/O operations are performed automatically by the 80286 and are distinct from I/O operations that result from program I/O instructions. I/O operations resulting from the execution of ESC instructions are completely transparent to software. Any program may execute ESCAPE (numeric) instructions, without regard to its current I/O Privilege Level (IOPL).

To guarantee correct operation of the 80287, programs must not perform any explicit I/O operations to any of the eight ports reserved for the 80287. The IOPL of the 80286 can be used to protect the integrity of 80287 computations in multiuser reprogrammable applications, preventing any accidental or other tampering with the 80287 (see Chapter Eight of the *80286 Operating System Writer's Guide*).

80287 NUMERIC PROCESSOR ARCHITECTURE

To the programmer, the 80287 NPX appears as a set of additional registers complementing those of the 80286. These additional registers consist of

- Eight individually-addressable 80-bit numeric registers, organized as a register stack

- Three sixteen-bit registers containing:
  an NPX status word
  an NPX control word
  a tag word

- Four 16-bit registers containing the NPX instruction and data pointers

All of the NPX numeric instructions focus on the contents of these NPX registers.

The NPX Register Stack

The 80287 register stack is shown in figure 1-3. Each of the eight numeric registers in the 80287's register stack is 80 bits wide and is divided into fields corresponding to the NPX's temporary-real data type.

Numeric instructions address the data registers relative to the register on the top of the stack. At any point in time, this top-of-stack register is indicated by the ST (Stack Top) field in the NPX status word. Load or push operations decrement ST by one and load a value into the new top register. A store-and-pop operation stores the value from the current ST register and then increments ST by one. Like 80286 stacks in memory, the 80287 register stack grows *down* toward lower-addressed registers.

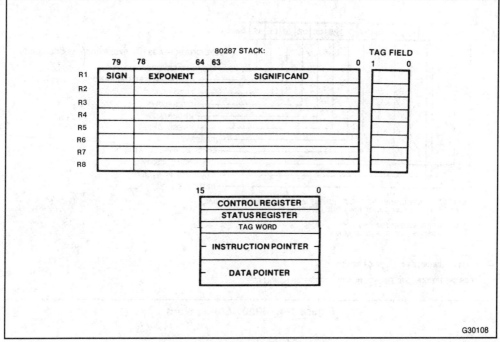

Figure 1-3. 80287 Register Set

Many numeric instructions have several addressing modes that permit the programmer to implicitly operate on the top of the stack, or to explicitly operate on specific registers relative to the ST. The ASM286 Assembler supports these register addressing modes, using the expression ST(0), or simply ST, to represent the current Stack Top and ST(i) to specify the ith register from ST in the stack ($0 \leq i \leq 7$). For example, if ST contains 011B (register 3 is the top of the stack), the following statement would add the contents of the top two registers on the stack (registers 3 and 5):

```
FADD     ST,ST(2)
```

The stack organization and top-relative addressing of the numeric registers simplify subroutine programming by allowing routines to pass parameters on the register stack. By using the stack to pass parameters rather than using "dedicated" registers, calling routines gain more flexibility in how they use the stack. As long as the stack is not full, each routine simply loads the parameters onto the stack before calling a particular subroutine to perform a numeric calculation. The subroutine then addresses its parameters as ST, ST(1), etc., even though ST may, for example, refer to physical register 3 in one invocation and physical register 5 in another.

The NPX Status Word

The 16-bit status word shown in figure 1-4 reflects the overall state of the 80287. This status word may be stored into memory using the FSTSW/FNSTSW, FSTENV/FNSTENV, and FSAVE/FNSAVE instructions, and can be transferred into the 80286 AX register with the FSTSW AX/FNSTSW AX instructions, allowing the NPX status to be inspected by the CPU.

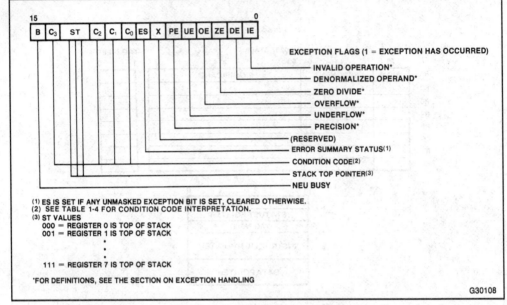

Figure 1-4. 80287 Status Word

The Busy bit (bit 15) and the $\overline{\text{BUSY}}$ pin indicate whether the 80287's execution unit is idle (B=0) or is executing a numeric instruction or signalling an exception (B=1). (The instructions FNSTSW, FNSTSW AX, FNSTENV, and FNSAVE do not set the Busy bit themselves, nor do they require the Busy bit to be clear in order to execute.)

The four NPX condition code bits (C_0-C_3) are similar to the flags in a CPU: the 80287 updates these bits to reflect the outcome of arithmetic operations. The effect of these instructions on the condition code bits is summarized in table 1-4. These condition code bits are used principally for conditional branching. The FSTWAX instruction stores the NPX status word directly into the CPU AX register, allowing these condition codes to be inspected efficiently by 80286 code.

Bits 12-14 of the status word point to the 80287 register that is the current Stack Top (ST). The significance of the stack top has been described in the section on the Register Stack.

Figure 1-4 shows the six error flags in bits 0-5 of the status word. Bit 7 is the error summary status (ES) bit. ES is set if any unmasked exception bits are set, and is cleared otherwise. If this bit is set, the $\overline{\text{ERROR}}$ signal is asserted. Bits 0-5 indicate whether the NPX has detected one of six possible exception conditions since these status bits were last cleared or reset.

Control Word

The NPX provides the programmer with several processing options, which are selected by loading a word from memory into the control word. Figure 1-5 shows the format and encoding of the fields in the control word.

Table 1-4. Interpreting the NPX Condition Codes

Instruction Type	C_3	C_2	C_1	C_0	Interpretation
Compare, Test	0	0	X	0	ST > Source or 0 (FTST)
	0	0	X	1	ST < Source or 0 (FTST)
	1	0	X	0	ST = Source or 0 (FTST)
	1	1	X	1	ST is not comparable
Remainder	Q_1	0	Q_0	Q_2	Complete reduction with three low bits of quotient in C_0, C_3, and C_1
	U	1	U	U	Incomplete Reduction
Examine	0	0	0	0	Valid, positive unnormalized
	0	0	0	1	Invalid, positive, exponent = 0
	0	0	1	0	Valid, negative, unnormalized
	0	0	1	1	Invalid, negative, exponent = 0
	0	1	0	0	Valid, positive, normalized
	0	1	0	1	Infinity, positive
	0	1	1	0	Valid, negative, normalized
	0	1	1	1	Infinity, negative
	1	0	0	0	Zero, positive
	1	0	0	1	Empty Register
	1	0	1	0	Zero, negative
	1	0	1	1	Empty Register
	1	1	0	0	Invalid, positive, exponent = 0
	1	1	0	1	Empty Register
	1	1	1	0	Invalid, negative, exponent = 0
	1	1	1	1	Empty Register

NOTES:
1. ST = Top of stack
2. X = value is not affected by instruction
3. U = value is undefined following instruction
4. Q_n = Quotient bit n following complete reduction (C_2=0)

The low-order byte of this control word configures the 80287 error and exception masking. Bits 0–5 of the control word contain individual masks for each of the six exception conditions recognized by the 80287. The high-order byte of the control word configures the 80287 processing options, including

- Precision control

- Rounding control

- Infinity control

The Precision control bits (bits 8-9) can be used to set the 80287 internal operating precision at less than the default precision (64-bit significand). These control bits can be used to provide compatibility with the earlier-generation arithmetic processors having less precision than the 80287, as required by the IEEE 754 standard. Setting a lower precision, however, will not affect the execution time of numeric calculations.

The rounding control bits (bits 10-11) provide for directed rounding and true chop as well as the unbiased round-to-nearest-even mode specified in the IEEE 754 standard.

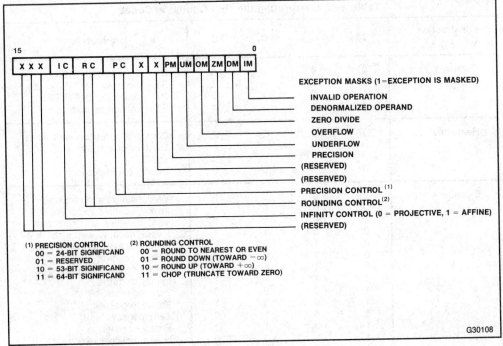

Figure 1-5. 80287 Control Word Format

The infinity control bit (bit 12) determines the manner in which the 80287 treats the special values of infinity. Either affine closure (where positive infinity is distinct from negative infinity) or projective closure (infinity is treated as a single unsigned quantity) may be specified. These two alternative views of infinity are discussed in the section on Computation Fundamentals.

The NPX Tag Word

The tag word indicates the contents of each register in the register stack, as shown in figure 1-6. The tag word is used by the NPX itself in order to track its numeric registers and optimize performance. Programmers may use this tag information to interpret the contents of the numeric registers. The tag values are stored in the tag word corresponding to the physical registers 0–7. Programmers must use the current Stack Top (ST) pointer stored in the NPX status word to associate these tag values with the relative stack registers ST(0) through ST(7).

The NPX Instruction and Data Pointers

The NPX instruction and data registers provide support for programmed exception-handlers. Whenever the 80287 executes a math instruction, the NPX internally saves the instruction address, the operand address (if present), and the instruction opcode. The 80287 FSTENV and FSAVE instructions store this data into memory, allowing exception handlers to determine the precise nature of any numeric exceptions that may be encountered.

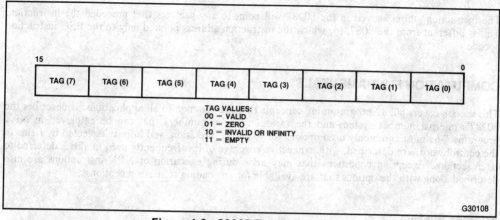

Figure 1-6. 80287 Tag Word Format

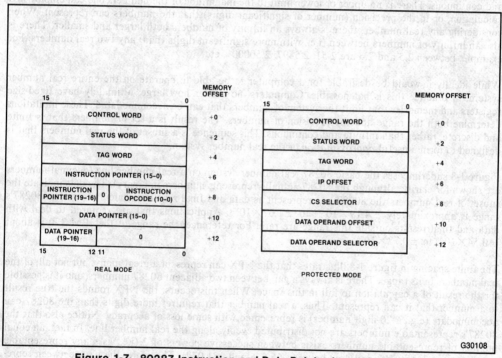

Figure 1-7. 80287 Instruction and Data Pointer Image in Memory

When stored in memory, the instruction and data pointers appear in one of two formats, depending on the operating mode of the 80287. Figure 1-7 shows these pointers as they are stored following an FSTENV instruction. In Real-Address mode, these values are the 20-bit physical address and 11-bit opcode formatted like the 8087. In Protected mode, these values are the 32-bit virtual addresses used by the program that executed the ESC instruction.

The instruction address saved in the 80287 will point to any prefixes that preceded the instruction. This is different from the 8087, for which the instruction address pointed only to the ESC instruction opcode.

COMPUTATION FUNDAMENTALS

This section covers 80287 programming concepts that are common to all applications. It describes the 80287's internal number system and the various types of numbers that can be employed in NPX programs. The most commonly used options for rounding, precision, and infinity (selected by fields in the control word) are described, with exhaustive coverage of less frequently used facilities deferred to later sections. Exception conditions that may arise during execution of NPX instructions are also described along with the options that are available for responding to these exceptions.

Number System

The system of real numbers that people use for pencil and paper calculations is conceptually infinite and continuous. There is no upper or lower limit to the magnitude of the numbers one can employ in a calculation, or to the precision (number of significant digits) that the numbers can represent. When considering any real number, there is always an infinity of numbers both larger and smaller. There is also an infinity of numbers between (i.e., with more significant digits than) any two real numbers. For example, between 2.5 and 2.6 are 2.51, 2.5897, 2.500001, etc.

While ideally it would be desirable for a computer to be able to operate on the entire real number system, in practice this is not possible. Computers, no matter how large, ultimately have fixed-size registers and memories that limit the system of numbers that can be accommodated. These limitations determine both the range and the precision of numbers. The result is a set of numbers that is finite and discrete, rather than infinite and continuous. This sequence is a subset of the real numbers that is designed to form a useful *approximation* of the real number system.

Figure 1-8 superimposes the basic 80287 real number system on a real number line (decimal numbers are shown for clarity, although the 80287 actually represents numbers in binary). The dots indicate the subset of real numbers the 80287 can represent as data and final results of calculations. The 80287's range is approximately $\pm 4.19 \times 10^{-307}$ to $\pm 1.67 \times 10^{308}$. Applications that are required to deal with data and final results outside this range are rare. For reference, the range of the IBM 370 is about $\pm 0.54 \times 10^{-78}$ to $\pm 0.72 \times 10^{76}$.

The finite spacing in figure 1-8 illustrates that the NPX can represent a great many, but not all, of the real numbers in its range. There is always a gap between two adjacent 80287 numbers, and it is possible for the result of a calculation to fall in this space. When this occurs, the NPX rounds the true result to a number that it can represent. Thus, a real number that requires more digits than the 80287 can accommodate (e.g., a 20-digit number) is represented with some loss of accuracy. Notice also that the 80287's representable numbers are not distributed evenly along the real number line. In fact, an equal number of representable numbers exists between successive powers of 2 (i.e., as many representable numbers exist between 2 and 4 as between 65,536 and 131,072). Therefore, the gaps between representable numbers are larger as the numbers increase in magnitude. All integers in the range $\pm 2^{64}$ (approximately $\pm 10^{18}$), however, are exactly representable.

In its internal operations, the 80287 actually employs a number system that is a substantial superset of that shown in figure 1-8. The internal format (called temporary real) extends the 80287's range to about $\pm 3.4 \times 10^{-4932}$ to $\pm 1.2 \times 10^{4932}$, and its precision to about 19 (equivalent decimal) digits. This format is designed to provide extra range and precision for constants and intermediate results, and is not normally intended for data or final results.

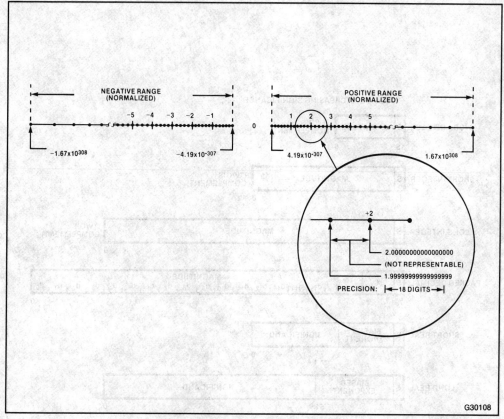

Figure 1-8. 80287 Number System

From a practical standpoint, the 80287's set of real numbers is sufficiently large and dense so as not to limit the vast majority of microprocessor applications. Compared to most computers, including mainframes, the NPX provides a very good approximation of the real number system. It is important to remember, however, that it is not an exact representation, and that arithmetic on real numbers is inherently approximate.

Conversely, and equally important, the 80287 *does* perform exact arithmetic on integer operands. That is, an operation on two integers returns an exact integral result, provided that the true result is an integer and is in range. For example, $4 \div 2$ yields an exact integer, $1 \div 3$ does not, and $2^{40} \times 2^{30} + 1$ does not, because the result requires greater than 64 bits of precision.

Data Types and Formats

The 80287 recognizes seven numeric data types, divided into three classes: binary integers, packed decimal integers, and binary reals. A later section describes how these formats are stored in memory (the sign is always located in the highest-addressed byte). Figure 1-9 summarizes the format of each data type. In the figure, the most significant digits of all numbers (and fields within numbers) are the leftmost digits. Table 1-5 provides the range and number of signficant (decimal) digits that each format can accommodate.

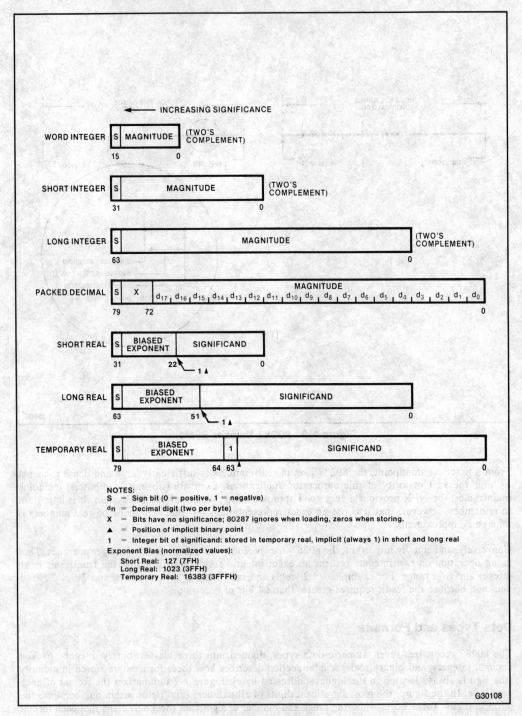

NOTES:

S = Sign bit (0 = positive, 1 = negative)

d_n = Decimal digit (two per byte)

X = Bits have no significance; 80287 ignores when loading, zeros when storing.

▲ = Position of implicit binary point

1 = Integer bit of significand: stored in temporary real, implicit (always 1) in short and long real

Exponent Bias (normalized values):

Short Real: 127 (7FH)

Long Real: 1023 (3FFH)

Temporary Real: 16383 (3FFFH)

Figure 1-9. Data Formats

Table 1-5. Real Number Notation

Notation	Value		
Ordinary Decimal	178.125		
Scientific Decimal	1△78125E2		
Scientific Binary	1△0110010001E111		
Scientific Binary (Biased Exponent)	1△0110010001E10000110		
80287 Short Real (Normalized)	**Sign**	**Biased Exponent**	**Significand**
	0	10000110	▲ 01100100010000000000000 └─1△ (implicit)

BINARY INTEGERS

The three binary integer formats are identical except for length, which governs the range that can be accommodated in each format. The leftmost bit is interpreted as the number's sign: 0=positive and 1=negative. Negative numbers are represented in standard two's complement notation (the binary integers are the only 80287 format to use two's complement). The quantity zero is represented with a positive sign (all bits are 0). The 80287 word integer format is identical to the 16-bit signed integer data type of the 80286.

DECIMAL INTEGERS

Decimal integers are stored in packed decimal notation, with two decimal digits "packed" into each byte, except the leftmost byte, which carries the sign bit (0=positive, 1=negative). Negative numbers are not stored in two's complement form and are distinguished from positive numbers only by the sign bit. The most significant digit of the number is the leftmost digit. All digits must be in the range 0H–9H.

REAL NUMBERS

The 80287 stores real numbers in a three-field binary format that resembles scientific, or exponential, notation. The number's significant digits are held in the *significand* field, the *exponent* field locates the binary point within the significant digits (and therefore determines the number's magnitude), and the *sign* field indicates whether the number is positive or negative. (The exponent and significand are analogous to the terms "characteristic" and "mantissa" used to describe floating point numbers on some computers.) Negative numbers differ from positive numbers only in the sign bits of their significands.

Table 1-5 shows how the real number 178.125 (decimal) is stored in the 80287 short real format. The table lists a progression of equivalent notations that express the same value to show how a number can be converted from one form to another. The ASM286 and PL/M-286 language translators perform a similar process when they encounter programmer-defined real number constants. Note that not every decimal fraction has an exact binary equivalent. The decimal number 1/10, for example, cannot be expressed exactly in binary (just as the number 1/3 cannot be expressed exactly in decimal). When a translator encounters such a value, it produces a rounded binary approximation of the decimal value.

The NPX usually carries the digits of the significand in normalized form. This means that, except for the value zero, the significand is an *integer* and a *fraction* as follows:

$1_\Delta fff...ff$

where Δ indicates an assumed binary point. The number of fraction bits varies according to the real format: 23 for short, 52 for long, and 63 for temporary real. By normalizing real numbers so that their integer bit is always a 1, the 80287 eliminates leading zeros in small values ($|X| < 1$). This technique maximizes the number of significant digits that can be accommodated in a significand of a given width. Note that, in the short and long real formats, the integer bit is *implicit* and is not actually stored; the integer bit is physically present in the temporary real format only.

If one were to examine only the signficand with its assumed binary point, all normalized real numbers would have values between 1 and 2. The exponent field locates the *actual* binary point in the significant digits. Just as in decimal scientific notation, a positive exponent has the effect of moving the binary point to the right, and a negative exponent effectively moves the binary point to the left, inserting leading zeros as necessary. An unbiased exponent of zero indicates that the position of the assumed binary point is also the position of the actual binary point. The exponent field, then, determines a real number's magnitude.

In order to simplify comparing real numbers (e.g., for sorting), the 80287 stores exponents in a biased form. This means that a constant is added to the *true exponent* described above. The value of this bias is different for each real format (see figure 1-9). It has been chosen so as to force the *biased exponent* to be a positive value. This allows two real numbers (of the same format and sign) to be compared as if they are unsigned binary integers. That is, when comparing them bitwise from left to right (beginning with the leftmost exponent bit), the first bit position that differs orders the numbers; there is no need to proceed further with the comparison. A number's true exponent can be determined simply by subtracting the bias value of its format.

The short and long real formats exist in memory only. If a number in one of these formats is loaded into an 80287 register, it is automatically converted to temporary real, the format used for all internal operations. Likewise, data in registers can be converted to short or long real for storage in memory. The temporary real format may be used in memory also, typically to store intermediate results that cannot be held in registers.

Most applications should use the long real form to store real number data and results; it provides sufficient range and precision to return correct results with a minimum of programmer attention. The short real format is appropriate for applications that are constrained by memory, but it should be recognized that this format provides a smaller margin of safety. It is also useful for debugging algorithms, because roundoff problems will manifest themselves more quickly in this format. The temporary real format should normally be reserved for holding intermediate results, loop accumulations, and constants. Its extra length is designed to shield final results from the effects of rounding and overflow/underflow in intermediate calculations. However, the range and precision of the long real form are adequate for most microcomputer applications.

Rounding Control

Internally, the 80287 employs three extra bits (guard, round, and sticky bits) that enable it to represent the infinitely precise true result of a computation; these bits are not accessible to programmers. Whenever the destination can represent the infinitely precise true result, the 80287 delivers it. Rounding occurs in arithmetic and store operations when the format of the destination cannot exactly represent the infinitely precise true result. For example, a real number may be rounded if it is stored in a shorter real format, or in an integer format. Or, the infinitely precise true result may be rounded when it is returned to a register.

The NPX has four rounding modes, selectable by the RC field in the control word (see figure 1-5). Given a true result b that cannot be represented by the target data type, the 80287 determines the two representable numbers a and c that most closely bracket b in value ($a < b < c$). The processor then rounds (changes) b to a or to c according to the mode selected by the RC field as shown in table 1-6. Round introduces an error in a result that is less than one unit in the last place to which the result is rounded. "Round to nearest" is the default mode and is suitable for most applications; it provides the most accurate and statistically unbiased estimate of the true result. The chop mode is provided for integer arithmetic applications.

"Round up" and "round down" are termed directed rounding and can be used to implement interval arithmetic. Interval arithmetic generates a certifiable result independent of the occurrence of rounding and other errors. The upper and lower bounds of an interval may be computed by executing an algorithm twice, rounding up in one pass and down in the other.

Precision Control

The 80287 allows results to be calculated with either 64, 53, or 24 bits of precision in the significand as selected by the precision control (PC) field of the control word. The default setting, and the one that is best suited for most applications, is the full 64 bits of significance provided by the temporary-real format. The other settings are required by the proposed IEEE standard, and are provided to obtain compatibility with the specifications of certain existing programming languages. Specifying less precision nullifies the advantages of the temporary real format's extended fraction length, and does not increase execution speed. When reduced precision is specified, the rounding of the fractional value clears the unused bits on the right to zeros.

Infinity Control

The 80287's system of real numbers may be closed by either of two models of infinity. These two means of closing the number system, projective and affine closure, are illustrated schematically in figure 1-10. The setting of the IC field in the control word selects one model or the other. The default

Table 1-6. Rounding Modes

RC Field	Rounding Mode	Rounding Action
00	Round to nearest	Closer to b of a or c; if equally close, select even number (the one whose least significant bit is zero).
01	Round down (toward $-\infty$)	a
10	Round up (toward $+\infty$)	c
11	Chop (toward 0)	Smaller in magnitude of a or c

NOTE: $a < b < c$; a and c are representable, b is not.

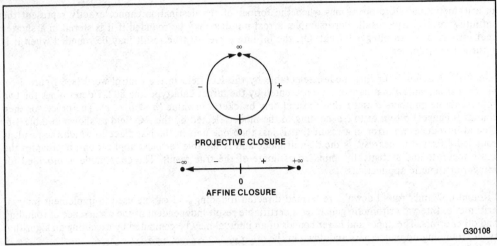

Figure 1-10. Projective versus Affine Closure

means of closure is projective, and this is recommended for most computations. When projective closure is selected, the NPX treats the special values $+\infty$ and $-\infty$ as a single unsigned infinity (similar to its treatment of signed zeros). In the affine mode the NPX respects the signs of $+\infty$ and $-\infty$.

While affine mode may provide more information than projective, there are occasions when the sign may in fact represent misinformation. For example, consider an algorithm that yields an intermediate result x of $+0$ and -0 (the same numeric value) in different executions. If $1/x$ were then computed in affine mode, two entirely different values ($+\infty$ and $-\infty$) would result from numerically identical values of x. Projective mode, on the other hand, provides less information but never returns misinformation. In general, then, projective mode should be used globally, with affine mode reserved for local computations where the programmer can take advantage of the sign and knows for certain that the nature of the computations will not produce a misleading result.

SPECIAL COMPUTATIONAL SITUATIONS

Besides being able to represent positive and negative numbers, the 80287 data formats may be used to describe other entities. These special values provide extra flexibility, but most users will not need to understand them in order to use the 80287 successfully. This section describes the special values that may occur in certain cases and the significance of each. The 80286 exceptions are also described, for writers of exception handlers and for those interested in probing the limits of computation using the 80287.

The material presented in this section is mainly of interest to programmers concerned with writing exception handlers. For many readers, this section can be browsed lightly.

Special Numeric Values

The 80287 data formats encompass encodings for a variety of special values in addition to the typical real or integer data values that result from normal calculations. These special values have significance and can express relevant information about the computations or operations that produced them. The various types of special values are

- Non-normal real numbers, including
  denormals
  unnormals
- Zeros and pseudo zeros
- Positive and negative infinity
- NaN (Not-a-Number)
- Indefinite

The following description explains the origins and significance of each of these special values. Tables 1-12 through 1-15 at the end of this section show how each of these special values is encoded for each of the numeric data types.

NONNORMAL REAL NUMBERS

As described previously, the 80287 generally stores nonzero real numbers in normalized floating-point form; that is, the integer (leading) bit of the significand is always a 1. This bit is explicitly stored in the temporary real format, and is implicitly assumed to be a one (1_Δ) in the short- and long-real formats. Since leading zeros are eliminated, normalized storage allows the maximum number of significant digits to be held in a significand of a given width.

When a floating-point numeric value becomes very close to zero, normalized storage cannot be used to express the value accurately. To accommodate these instances, the 80287 can store and operate on reals that are not normalized, i.e., whose significands contain one or more leading zeros. Nonnormals typically arise when the result of a calculation yields a value that is too small to be represented in normal form.

Nonnormal values can exist in one of two forms:

- The floating-point exponent may be stored at its most negative value (a *Denormal*),
- The integer bit (and perhaps other leading bits) of the significand may be zero (an *Unnormal*).

The leading zeros of nonnormals permit smaller numbers to be represented, at the cost of some lost precision (the number of significant bits is reduced by the leading zeros). In typical algorithms, extremely small values are most likely to be generated as intermediate, rather than final results. By using the NPX's temporary real format for holding intermediate, values as small as $\pm 3.4 \times 10^{-4932}$ can be represented; this makes the occurrence of nonnormal numbers a rare phenomenon in 80287 applications. Nevertheless, the NPX can load, store, and operate on nonnormalized real numbers when they do occur.

Denormals and Gradual Underflow

A denormal is the result of the NPX's response to an underflow exception when that exception has been masked by the programmer (see the 80287 control word, figure 1-5). Underflow occurs when the absolute value of a real number becomes too small to be represented in the destination format, that is, when the exponent of the true result is too negative to be represented in the destination format. For example, a true exponent of -130 will cause underflow if the destination is short real, because -126 is the smallest exponent this format can accommodate. No underflow would occur if the destination were long real or temporary real, since these formats can handle exponents down to -1023 and $-16,383$, respectively.

Most computers underflow "abruptly:" they simply return a zero result, which is likely to produce an unacceptable final result if computation continues. The 80287, on the other hand, underflows "gradually" when the underflow exception is masked. Gradual underflow is accomplished by denormalizing the result until it is just within the exponent range of the destination format. Denormalizing means incrementing the true result's exponent and inserting a corresponding leading zero in the significand, shifting the rest of the significand one place to the right. Denormal values may occur in any of the short-real, long-real, or temporary-real formats. Table 1-7 illustrates how a result might be denormalized to fit a short-real destination.

The intent of the 80287's masked response to underflow is to allow computation to continue without program intervention, while introducing an error that carries about the same risk of contaminating the final result as roundoff error. Roundoff (precision) errors occur frequently in real number calculations; sometimes they spoil the result of computation, but often they do not. Recognizing that roundoff errors are often nonfatal, computation usually proceeds, and the programmer inspects the final results to see if these errors have had a significant effect. The 80287's masked underflow response allows programmers to treat underflows in a similar manner; the computation continues and the programmer can examine the final result to determine if an underflow has had important consequences. (If the underflow has had a significant effect, an invalid operation will probably be signalled later in the computation.)

Denormalization produces a denormal or a zero. Denormals are readily identified by their exponents, which are always the minimum for their formats; in biased form, this is always the bit string: 00...00. This same exponent value is also assigned to the zeros, but a denormal has a nonzero significand. A denormal in a register is tagged special. Tables 1-14 and 1-15 later in this chapter show how denormal values are encoded in each of the real data formats.

The denormalization process may cause the loss of low-order significand bits as they are shifted off the right. In a severe case, *all* the significand bits of the true result are shifted out and replaced by the leading zeros. In this case, the result of denormalization is a true zero, and if the value is in a register, it is tagged as such. However, this is a comparatively rare occurrence and, in any case, is no worse than "abrupt" underflow.

Table 1-7. Denormalization Process

Operation	Sign	Exponent[1]	Significand
True Result	0	−129	1△01011100...00
Denormalize	0	−128	0△101011100...00
Denormalize	0	−127	0△0101011100...00
Denormalize	0	−126	0△00101011100...00
Denormal Result[2]	0	−126	0△00101011100...00

NOTES:

[1] Expressed as unbiased, decimal number.

[2] Before storing, significand is rounded to 24 bits, integer bit is dropped, and exponent is biased by adding 126.

Denormals are rarely encountered in most applications. Typical debugged algorithms generate extremely small results during the evaluation of intermediate subexpressions; the final result is usually of an appropriate magnitude for its short or long real destination. If intermediate results are held in temporary real, as is recommended, the great range of this format makes underflow very unlikely. Denormals are likely to arise only when an application generates a great many intermediates, so many that they cannot be held on the register stack or in temporary real memory variables. If storage limitations force the use of short or long reals for intermediates, and small values are produced, underflow may occur, and, if masked, may generate denormals.

Accessing a denormal may produce an exception as shown in table 1-8. (The denormalized exception signals that a denormal has been fetched.) Denormals may have reduced significance due to lost low-order bits, and an option of the proposed IEEE standard precludes operations on nonnormalized operands. This option may be implemented in the form of an exception handler that responds to unmasked denormalized exceptions. Most users will mask this exception so that computation may proceed; any loss of accuracy will be analyzed by the user when the final result is delivered.

As table 1-8 shows, the division and remainder operations do not accept denormal divisors and raise the invalid operation exception. Recall also that the transcendental instructions require normalized operands and do *not* check for exceptions. In all other cases, the NPX converts denormals to unnormals, and the rules governing unnormal arithmetic then apply (unnormals are described in the following section).

Unnormals—Descendents of Denormal Operands

An unnormal is the result of a computation using denormal operands and is therefore the descendent of the 80287's masked underflow response. An unnormal may exist only in the temporary real format; it may have any exponent that a normal value may have (that is, in biased form any nonzero value), but it is distinguished from a normal by the integer bit of its significand, which is always 0. An unnormal in a register is tagged valid. Unnormals are distinct from denormals, which have an exponent of 00...00 in biased form.

Unnormals allows arithmetic to continue following an underflow while still retaining their identity as numbers that may have reduced significance. That is, unnormal operands generate unnormal results, so long as their unnormality has a significant effect on the result. Unnormals are thus prevented from "masquerading" as normals, numbers that have full significance. On the other hand, if an unnormal has an insignificant effect on a calculation with a normal, the result will be normal. For example, adding a small unnormal to a large normal yields a normal result. The converse situation yields an unnormal.

Table 1-8. Exceptions Due to Denormal Operands

Operation	Exception	Masked Response
FLD (short/long real)	D	Load as equivalent unnormal
Arithmetic (except following)	D	Convert (in a work area) denormal to equivalent unnormal and proceed
Compare and test	D	Convert (in a work area) denormal to equivalent unnormal and proceed
Division or FPREM with denormal divisor	I	Return real *indefinite*

Table 1-9 shows how the instruction set deals with unnormal operands. Note that the unnormal may be the original operand or a temporary created by the 80287 from a denormal.

ZEROS AND PSEUDO ZEROS

The value *zero* in the real and decimal integer formats may be signed either positive or negative, although the sign of a binary integer zero is always positive. For computational purposes, the value of zero always behaves identically, regardless of sign, and typically the fact that a zero may be signed is transparent to the programmer. If necessary, the FXAM instruction may be used to determine a zero's sign.

The zeros discussed above are called true zeros; if one of them is loaded or generated in a register, the register is tagged zero. Table 1-10 lists the results of instructions executed with zero operands and also shows how a true zero may be created from nonzero operands.

Only the temporary real format may contain a special class of values called pseudo zeros. A pseudo zero is an unnormal whose significand is all zeros, but whose (biased) exponent is nonzero (true zeros have a zero exponent). Neither is a pseudo zero's exponent all ones, since this encoding is reserved for infinities and NANs. A pseudo zero result will be produced if two unnormals, containing a total of more than 64 leading zero bits in their significands, are multiplied together. This is a remote possibility in most applications, but it can happen.

Table 1-9. Unnormal Operands and Results

Operation	Result
Addition/subtraction	Normalization of operand with larger abosolute value determines normalization of result.
Multiplication	If either operand is unnormal, result is unnormal.
Division (unnormal dividend only)	Result is unnormal.
FPREM (unnormal dividend only)	Result if normalized.
Division/FPREM (unnormal divisor)	Signal invalid operation.
Compare/FTST	Normalize as much as possible before making comparison.
FRNDINT	Normalize as much as possible before rounding.
FSQRT	Signal invalid operation.
FST, FSTP (short/long real destination)	If value is above destination's underflow boundary, then signal invalid operation; else signal underflow.
FSTP (temporary real destination)	Store as usual.
FIST, FISTP, FBSTP	Signal invalid operation.
FLD	Load as usual.
FXCH	Exchange as usual.
Transcendental instructions	Undefined; operands must be normal and are not checked.

Pseudo zero operands behave like unnormals, except in the following cases where they produce the same results as true zeros:

- Compare and test instructions
- FRNDINT (round to integer)
- Division, where the dividend is either a true zero or a pseudo zero (the divisor is a pseudo zero)

In addition and subtraction of a pseudo zero and a true zero or another pseudo zero, the pseudo zero(s) behaves like unnormals, except for the determination of the result's sign. The sign is determined as shown in table 1-10 for two true zero operands.

INFINITY

The real formats support signed representations of infinities. These values are encoded with a biased exponent of all ones and a significand of $1_\triangle 00...00$; if the infinity is in a register, it is tagged special. The significand distinguishes infinities from NANs, including real *indefinite*.

A programmer may code an infinity, or it may be created by the NPX as its masked response to an overflow or a zero divide exception. Note that when rounding is up or down, the masked response may create the largest valid value representable in the destination rather than infinity. See table 1-11 for details. As operands, infinities behave somewhat differently depending on how the infinity control field in the control word is set (see table 1-12). When the projective model of infinity is selected, the infinities behave as a single unsigned representation; because of this, infinity cannot be compared with any value except infinity. In affine mode, the signs of the infinities are observed, and comparisons are possible.

NaN (NOT A NUMBER)

A NaN (Not a Number) is a member of a class of special values that exist in the real formats only. A NaN has an exponent of 11..11B, may have either sign, and may have any significand except $1_\triangle 00..00$B, which is assigned to the infinities. A NaN in a register is tagged special.

The 80287 will generate the special NaN, real *indefinite*, as its masked response to an invalid operation exception. This NaN is signed negative; its significand is encoded $1_\triangle 100..00$. All other NaNs represent programmer-created values.

Whenever the NPX uses an operand that is a NaN, it signals an invalid operation exception in its status word. If this exception is masked in the 80287 control word, the 80287's masked exception response is to return the NaN as the operation result. If both operands of an instruction are NaNs, the result is the NaN with the larger absolute value. In this way, a NaN that enters a computation propagates through the computation and will eventually be delivered as the final result. Note, however, that the transcendental instructions do not check their operands, and a NaN will produce an undefined result.

By unmasking the invalid operation exception, the programmer can use NaNs to trap to the exception handler. The generality of this approach and the large number of NaN values that are available provide the sophisticated programmer with a tool that can be applied to a variety of special situations.

For example, a compiler could use NaNs as references to uninitialized (real) array elements. The compiler could preinitialize each array element with a NaN whose significand contained the index (relative position) of the element. If an application program attempted to access an element that it had not initialized, it would use the NaN placed there by the compiler. If the invalid operation exception were unmasked, an interrupt would occur, and the exception handler would be invoked. The exception handler could determine which element had been accessed, since the operand address field of the exception pointers would point to the NaN, and the NaN would contain the index number of the array element.

Table 1-10. Zero Operands and Results

Operation/Operands	Result	Operation/Operands	Result
FLD, FBLD[1]		Division	
+0	+0	±0 ÷ ±0	Invalid operation
−0	−0	±X ÷ ±0	Zerodivide
FILD[2]		+0 ÷ +X, −0 ÷ −X	+0
+0	+0	+0 ÷ −X, −0 ÷ +X	−0
FST, FSTP		−X ÷ −Y, +X ÷ +Y	+0, underflow[8]
+0	+0	−X ÷ +Y, +X ÷ −Y	−0, underflow[8]
−0	−0		
+X[3]	+0	FPREM	
−X[3]	−0	±0 rem ±0	Invalid operation
FBSTP		±X rem ±0	Invalid operation
+0	+0	+0 rem +X, +0 rem −X	+0
−0	−0	−0 rem +X, −0 rem −X	−0
FIST, FISTP		+X rem +Y, +X rem −Y	+0[9]
+0	+0	−X rem −Y, −X rem +Y	−0[9]
−0	+0		
+X[4]	+0	FSQRT	
−X[4]	+0	−0	−0
		+0	+0
Addition			
+0 plus +0	+0	Compare	
−0 plus −0	−0	±0: +X	A < B
+0 plus −0, −0 plus +0	*0[5]	±0: ±0	A = B
−X plus +X, +X plus −X	*0[5]	±0: −X	A > B
±0 plus ±X, ±X plus ±0	†X[6]		
		FTST	
Subtraction		±0	Zero
+0 minus −0	+0	FCHS	
−0 minus +0	−0	+0	−0
+0 minus +0, −0 minus −0	*0[5]	−0	+0
+X minus +X, −X minus −X	*0[5]	FABS	
±0 minus ±X, ±X minus ±0	†X[6]	±0	+0
		F2XM1	
Multiplication		+0	+0
+0•+0, −0•−0	+0	−0	−0
+0•−0, −0•+0	−0	FRNDINT	
+0•+X, +X•+0	+0	+0	+0
+0•−X, −X•+0	−0	−0	−0
−0•+X, +X•−0	−0	FXTRACT	
−0•−X, −X•−0	+0	+0	Both +0
+X•+Y, −X•−Y	+0, underflow[7]	−0	Both −0
+X•−Y, −X•+Y	−0, underflow[7]		

NOTES:

[1] Arithmetic and compare operations with real memory operands interpret the memory operand signs in the same way.

[2] Arithmetic and compare operations with binary integers interpret the integer sign in the same manner.

(3) Severe underflows in storing to short or long real may generate zeros.

(4) Small values (|X| <1) stored into integers may round to zero.

(5) Sign is determined by round mode:
    * = + for nearest, up, or chop
    * = − for down

(6) † = sign of X.

(7) Very small values of X and Y may yield zeros, after rounding of true result. NPX signals underflow to warn that zero has been yielded by nonzero operands.

(8) Very small X and very large Y may yield zero, after rounding of true result. NPX signals underflow to warn that zero has been yielded from nonzero operands.

(9) When Y divides into X exactly.

NaNs could also be used to speed up debugging. In its early testing phase, a program often contains multiple errors. An exception handler could be written to save diagnostic information in memory whenever it was invoked. After storing the diagnostic data, it could supply a NaN as the result of the erroneous instruction, and that NaN could point to its associated diagnostic area in memory. The program would then continue, creating a different NaN for each error. When the program ended, the NaN results could be used to access the diagnostic data saved at the time the errors occurred. Many errors could thus be diagnosed and corrected in one test run.

Table 1-11. Masked Overflow Response with Directed Rounding

True Result		Rounding Mode	Result Delivered
Normalization	Sign		
Normal	+	Up	+∞
Normal	+	Down	Largest finite positive number[1]
Normal	−	Up	Largest finite negative number[1]
Normal	−	Down	−∞
Unnormal	+	Up	+∞
Unnormal	−	Down	Largest exponent, result's significand[2]
Unnormal	+	Up	Largest exponent, result's significand[2]
Unnormal	−	Down	−∞

NOTES:

(1) The largest valid representable reals are encoded:
    exponent: 11...10B
    significand: (1)△11...10B

(2) The significand retains its identity as an unnormal; the true result is rounded as usual (effectively chopped toward 0 in this case). The exponent is encoded 11...10B.

Table 1-12. Infinity Operands and Results

Operation	Projective Result	Affine Result
Addition		
$+\infty$ plus $+\infty$	Invalid operation	$+\infty$
$-\infty$ plus $-\infty$	Invalid operation	$-\infty$
$+\infty$ plus $-\infty$	Invalid operation	Invalid operation
$-\infty$ plus $+\infty$	Invalid operation	Invalid operation
$\pm\infty$ plus $\pm X$	*∞	*∞
$\pm X$ plus $\pm\infty$	*∞	*∞
Subtraction		
$+\infty$ minus $-\infty$	Invalid operation	$+\infty$
$-\infty$ minus $+\infty$	Invalid operation	$-\infty$
$+\infty$ minus $+\infty$	Invalid operation	Invalid operation
$-\infty$ minus $-\infty$	Invalid operation	Invalid operation
$\pm\infty$ minus $\pm X$	*∞	*∞
$\pm X$ minus $\pm\infty$	†∞	†∞
Multiplication		
$\pm\infty \cdot \pm\infty$	⊕	⊕
$\pm\infty \cdot \pm Y$	⊕	⊕
$\pm 0 \cdot \pm\infty, \pm\infty * \pm 0$	Invalid operation	Invalid operation
Division		
$\pm\infty \div \pm\infty$	Invalid operation	Invalid operation
$\pm\infty \div \pm X$	⊕	⊕
$\pm X \div \pm\infty$	⊕	⊕
FSQRT		
$-\infty$	Invalid operation	Invalid operation
$+\infty$	Invalid operation	$+\infty$
FPREM		
$\pm\infty$ rem $\pm\infty$	Invalid operation	Invalid operation
$\pm\infty$ rem $\pm X$	Invalid operation	Invalid operation
$\pm Y$ rem $\pm\infty$	*Y	*Y
± 0 rem $\pm\infty$	*0	*0
FRNDINT		
$\pm\infty$	*∞	*∞
FSCALE		
$\pm\infty$ scaled by $\pm\infty$	Invalid operation	Invalid operation
$\pm\infty$ scaled by $\pm X$	*∞	*∞
± 0 scaled by $\pm\infty$	*0	*0
$\pm Y$ scaled by $\pm\infty$	Invalid operation	Invalid operation
FXTRACT		
$\pm\infty$	Invalid operation	Invalid operation
Compare		
$\pm\infty: \pm\infty$	A = B	$-\infty < +\infty$
$\pm\infty: \pm Y$	A ? B (and) invalid operation	$-\infty < Y < +\infty$
$\pm\infty: \pm 0$	A ? B (and) invalid operation	$-\infty < 0 < +\infty$
FTST		
$\pm\infty$	A ? B (and) invalid operation	*∞

NOTES:

X = zero or nonzero operand

Y = nonzero operand

* = sign of original operand

† = sign is complement of original operand's sign

⊕ = sign is "exclusive or" original operand signs (+ if operands had same sign, − if operands had different signs)

INDEFINITE

For every 80287 numeric data type, one unique encoding is reserved for representing the special value *indefinite*. The 80287 produces this encoding as its response to a masked invalid-operation exception. In the case of reals, the indefinite value can be stored and loaded like any NaN, and it always retains its special identity; programmers are advised not to use this encoding for any other purpose. Packed decimal *indefinite* may be stored by the NPX in a FBSTP instruction; attempting to use this encoding in a FBLD instruction, however, will have an undefined result. In the binary integers, the same encoding may represent either *indefinite* or the largest negative number supported by the format (-2^{15}, -2^{31}, or -2^{63}). The 80287 will store this encoding as its masked response to an invalid operation, or when the value in a source register represents or rounds to the largest negative integer representable by the destination. In situations where its origin may be ambiguous, the invalid operation exception flag can be examined to see if the value was produced by an exception response. When this encoding is loaded, or used by an integer arithmetic or compare operation, it is always interpreted as a negative number; thus *indefinite* cannot be loaded from a packed decimal or binary integer.

ENCODING OF DATA TYPES

Tables 1-13 through 1-16 show how each of the special values just described is encoded for each of the numeric data types. In these tables, the least-significant bits are shown to the right and are stored in the lowest memory addresses. The sign bit is always the left-most bit of the highest-addressed byte.

Table 1-13. Binary Integer Encodings

	Class	Sign	Magnitude
Positives	(Largest)	0	11...11
		•	•
		•	•
		•	•
	(Smallest)	0	00...01
	Zero	0	00...00
Negatives	(Smallest)	1	11...11
		•	•
		•	•
		•	•
	(Largest/*Indefinite**)	1	00...00

Word:	◄———— 15 bits ————►
Short:	◄———— 31 bits ————►
Long:	◄———— 63 bits ————►

NOTES:

If this encoding is used as a source operand (as in an integer load or integer arithmetic instruction), the 80287 interprets it as the largest negative number representable in the format: -2^{15}, -2^{31}, or -2^{63}. The 80287 will deliver this encoding to an integer destination in two cases:

1) If the result is the largest negative number

2) As the response to a masked invalid operation exception, in which case it represents the special value *integer indefinite*.

Table 1-14. Packed Decimal Encodings

Class		Sign		Magnitude					
				digit	digit	digit	digit	. . .	digit
Positives	(Largest)	0	0000000	1 0 0 1	1 0 0 1	1 0 0 1	1 0 0 1	. . .	1 0 0 1
		•	•				•		
		•	•				•		
		•	•				•		
	(Smallest)	0	0000000	0 0 0 0	0 0 0 0	0 0 0 0	0 0 0 0	. . .	0 0 0 1
	Zero	0	0000000	0 0 0 0	0 0 0 0	0 0 0 0	0 0 0 0	. . .	0 0 0 0
Negatives	Zero	1	0000000	0 0 0 0	0 0 0 0	0 0 0 0	0 0 0 0	. . .	0 0 0 0
	(Smallest)	1	0000000	0 0 0 0	0 0 0 0	0 0 0 0	0 0 0 0	. . .	0 0 0 1
		•	•				•		
		•	•				•		
		•	•				•		
	(Largest)	1	0000000	1 0 0 1	1 0 0 1	1 0 0 1	1 0 0 1	. . .	1 0 0 1
Indefinite[1]		1	1111111	1 1 1 1	1 1 1 1	U U U U[2]	U U U U	. . .	U U U U

|◄— 1 byte —►| |◄————————————————— 9 bytes —————————————————►|

NOTES:

1. The *packed decimal indefinite* encoding is stored by FBSTP in response to a masked invalid operation exception. Attempting to load this value via FBLD produces an undefined result.

2. UUUU means bit values are undefined and may contain any value.

Table 1-15. Real and Long Real Encodings

	Class		Sign	Biased Exponent	Significand* $\triangle$ff...ff
Positives		NaNs	0 ⋮ 0	11...11 ⋮ 11...11	11...11 ⋮ 00...01
		∞	0	11...11	00...00
	Reals	Normals	0 ⋮ 0	11...10 ⋮ 00...01	11...11 ⋮ 00...00
		Denormals	0 ⋮ 0	00...00 ⋮ 00...00	11...11 ⋮ 00...01
		Zero	0	00...00	00...00
Negatives		Zero	1	00...00	00...00
		Denormals	1 ⋮ 1	00...00 ⋮ 00...00	00...01 ⋮ 11...11
		Normals	1 ⋮ 1	00...01 ⋮ 11...10	00...00 ⋮ 11...11
		∞	1	11...11	00...00
	NaNs		1 ⋮	11...11 ⋮	00...01 ⋮
		Indefinite	1	11...11	10...00
			⋮ 1	⋮ 11...11	⋮ 11...11

Short: ◄──── 8 bits ────► ◄──── 23 bits ────►
Long: ◄──── 11 bits ────► ◄──── 52 bits ────►

*Integer bit is implied and not stored.

Table 1-16. Temporary Real Encodings

Class			Sign	Biased Exponent	Significand* 1_Δff...ff
Positives	Reals	NaNs	0 • • • 0	11...11 • • • 11...11	111...11 • • • 100...01
		∞	0	11...11	100...00
			0 • • • • •	11...10 • • • •	Normals 111...11 • • • 100...00
			• • • • • 0	• • • • 00...01	Unnormals 011...11 • • 000...00
			0 • • • 0	00...00 • • • 00...00	Denormals 011...11 • • 000...01
		Zero	0	00...00	000...00
Negatives		Zero	1	00...00	000...00
			1 • • • 1	00...00 • • • 00...00	Denormals 000...01 • • 011...11
			1 • • • • •	00...01 • • • •	Unnormals 000...00 • • 011...11
			• • • • • 1	• • • • 11...10	Normals 100...00 • • • 111...11

Table 1-16. Temporary Real Encodings (Cont'd.)

Class			Sign	Biased Exponent	Significand* $\|_\triangle$ff...ff
Negatives		∞	1	11...11	100...00
	NaNs		1	11...11	100...00
			•	•	•
			•	•	•
			•	•	•
		Indefinite	1	11...11	110...00
			•	•	•
			•	•	•
			•	•	•
			1	11...11	111...11

← 15 bits → ← 64 bits →

Numeric Exceptions

Whenever the 80287 NPX attempts a numeric operation with invalid operands or produces a result that cannot be represented, the 80287 recognizes a numeric exception condition. Altogether, the 80287 checks for the following six classes of exceptions while executing numeric instructions:

1. Invalid operation
2. Divide-by-zero
3. Denormalized operand
4. Numeric overflow
5. Numeric underflow
6. Inexact result (precision)

INVALID OPERATION

The 80287 reports an invalid operation if any of the following occurs:

- An attempt to load a register that is not empty (stack overflow).
- An attempt to pop an operand from an empty register (stack underflow).
- An operand is a NaN.
- The operands cause the operation to be indeterminate (square root of a negative number, 0/0).

An invalid operation generally indicates a program error.

ZERO DIVISOR

If an instruction attempts to divide a finite nonzero operand by zero, the 80287 will report a zero divide exception.

DENORMALIZED OPERAND

If an instruction attempts to operate on a denormal, the NPX reports the denormalized operand exception. This exception allows users to implement in software an option of the proposed IEEE standard specifying that operands must be prenormalized before they are used.

NUMERIC OVERFLOW AND UNDERFLOW

If the exponent of a numeric result is too large for the destination real format, the 80287 signals a numeric overflow. Conversely, if the exponent of a result is too small to be represented in the destination format, a numeric underflow is signaled. If either of these exceptions occur, the result of the operation is outside the range of the destination real format.

Typical algorithms are most likely to produce extremely large and small numbers in the calculation of intermediate, rather than final, results. Because of the great range of the temporary real format (recommended as the destination format for intermediates), overflow and underflow are relatively rare events in most 80287 applications.

INEXACT RESULT

If the result of an operation is not exactly representable in the destination format, the 80287 rounds the number and reports the precision exception. For example, the fraction $1/3$ cannot be precisely represented in binary form. This exception occurs frequently and indicates that some (generally acceptable) accuracy has been lost; it is provided for applications that need to perform exact arithmetic only.

HANDLING NUMERIC ERRORS

When numeric errors occur, the NPX takes one of two possible courses of action:

- The NPX can itself handle the error, producing the most reasonable result and allowing numeric program execution to continue undisturbed.
- A software exception handler can be invoked by the CPU to handle the error.

Each of the six exception conditions described above has a corresponding flag bit in the 80287 status word and a mask bit in the 80287 control word. If an exception is masked (the corresponding mask bit in the control word = 1), the 80287 takes an appropriate default action and continues with the computation. If the exception is unmasked (mask=0), the 80287 asserts the $\overline{\text{ERROR}}$ output to the 80286 to signal the exception and invoke a software exception handler.

The NPX reports an exception by setting the corresponding flag in the NPX status word to 1. The NPX then checks the corresponding exception mask in the control word to determine if it should "field" the exception (mask=1), or if it should signal the exception to the CPU to invoke a software exception handler (mask=0).

If the mask is set, the exception is said to be *masked* (from user software), and the NPX executes its on-chip masked response for that exception. If the mask is not set (mask=0), the exception is *unmasked*, and the NPX performs its unmasked response. The masked response always produces a standard result, then proceeds with the instruction. The unmasked response always traps to a software exception handler, allowing the CPU to recognize and take action on the exception. Table 1-17 gives a complete description of all exception conditions and the NPX's masked response.

Table 1-17. Exception Conditions and Masked Responses

Condition	Masked Response
Invalid Operation	
Source register is tagged empty (usually due to stack underflow).	Return real *indefinite*.
Destination register is not tagged empty (usually due to stack overflow).	Return real *indefinite* (overwrite destination value).
One or both operands is a NaN.	Return NaN with larger absolute value (ignore signs).
(Compare and test operations only): one or both operands is a NaN.	Set condition codes "not comparable."
(Addition operations only): closure is affine and operands are opposite-signed infinities; or closure is projective and both operands are ∞ (signs immaterial).	Return real *indefinite*.
(Subtraction operations only): closure is affine and operands are like-signed infinities; or closure is projective and both operands are ∞ (signs immaterial).	Return real *indefinite*.
(Multiplication operations only): $\infty * 0$; or $0 * \infty$.	Return real *indefinite*.
(Division operations only): $\infty \div \infty$; or $0 \div 0$; or $0 \div$ pseudo zero; or divisor is denormal or unnormal.	Return real *indefinite*.
(FPREM instruction only): modulus (divisor) is unnormal or denormal; or dividend is ∞.	Return real *indefinite*, set condition code = "complete remainder."
(FSQRT instruction only): operand is nonzero and negative; or operand is denormal or unnormal; or closure is affine and operand is $-\infty$; or closure is projective and operand is ∞.	Return real *indefinite*.
(Compare operations only): closure is projective and ∞ is being compared with 0, a normal, or ∞.	Set condition code = "not comparable."
(FTST instruction only): closure is projective and operand is ∞.	Set condition code = "not comparable."
(FIST, FISTP instructions only): source register is empty, a NaN, denormal, unnormal, ∞, or exceeds representable range of destination.	Store integer *indefinite*.
(FBSTP instruction only): source register is empty, a NaN, denormal, unnormal, ∞, or exceeds 18 decimal digits.	Stored packed decimal *indefinite*.
(FST, FSTP instructions only): destination is short or long real and source register is an unnormal with exponent in range.	Store real *indefinite*.
(FXCH instruction only): one or both registers is tagged empty.	Change empty register(s) to real *indefinite* and then perform exchange.

Table 1-17. Exception Conditions and Masked Responses (Cont'd.)

Condition	Masked Response
Denormalized Operand	
(FLD instruction only): source operand is denormal.	No special action; load as usual.
(Arithmetic operations only): one or both operands is denormal.	Convert (in a work area) the operand to the equivalent unnormal and proceed.
(Compare and test operations only): one or both operands is denormal *or unnormal* (other than pseudo zero).	Convert (in a work area) any denormal to the equivalent unnormal; normalize as much as possible, and proceed with operation.
Zero Divide	
(Division operations only): divisor = 0.	Return ∞ signed with "exclusive or" of operand signs.
Overflow	
(Arithmetic operations only): rounding is nearest or chop, and exponent of true result $> 16,383$.	Return properly signed ∞ and signal precision exception.
(FST, FSTP instructions only): rounding is nearest or chop, and exponent of true result $> +127$ (short real destination) or $> +1023$ (long real destination).	Return properly signed ∞ and signal precision exception.
Underflow	
(Arithmetic operations only): exponent of true result $< -16,382$ (true).	Denormalize until exponent rises to $-16,382$ (true), round significand to 64 bits. If denormalized rounded significand = 0, then return true 0; else, return denormal (tag = special, biased exponent = 0).
(FST, FSTP instructions only): destination is short real and exponent of true result < -126 (true).	Denormalize until exponent rises to -126 (true), round significand to 24 bits, store true 0 if denormalized rounded significand = 0; else, store denormal (biased exponent = 0).
(FST, FSTP instructions only): destination is long real and exponent of true result < -1022 (true).	Denormalize until exponent rises to -1022 (true), round significand to 53 bits, store true 0 if rounded denormalized significand = 0; else, store denormal (biased exponent = 0).
Precision	
True rounding error occurs.	No special action.
Masked response to overflow exception earlier in instruction.	No special action.

Note that when exceptions are masked, the NPX may detect multiple exceptions in a single instruction, because it continues executing the instruction after performing its masked response. For example, the 80287 could detect a denormalized operand, perform its masked response to this exception, and then detect an underflow.

Automatic Exception Handling

As described in the previous section, when the 80287 NPX encounters an exception condition whose corresponding mask bit in the NPX control word is set, the NPX automatically performs an internal fix-up (masked-exception) response. The 80287 NPX has a default fix-up activity for every possible exception condition it may encounter. These masked-exception responses are designed to be safe and are generally acceptable for most numeric applications.

As an example of how even severe exceptions can be handled safely and automatically using the NPX's default exception responses, consider a calculation of the parallel resistance of several values using only the standard formula (figure 1-11). If R1 becomes zero, the circuit resistance becomes zero. With the divide-by-zero and precision exceptions masked, the 80287 NPX will produce the correct result.

By masking or unmasking specific numeric exceptions in the NPX control word, NPX programmers can delegate responsibility for most exceptions to the NPX, reserving the most severe exceptions for programmed exception handlers. Exception-handling software is often difficult to write, and the NPX's masked responses have been tailored to deliver the most reasonable result for each condition. For the majority of applications, programmers will find that masking all exceptions other than Invalid Operation will yield satisfactory results with the least programming effort. An Invalid Operation exception normally indicates a fatal error in a program that must be corrected; this exception should not normally be masked.

The exception flags in the NPX status word provide a cumulative record of exceptions that have occurred since these flags were last cleared. Once set, these flags can be cleared only by executing the FCLEX (clear exceptions) instruction, by reinitializing the NPX, or by overwriting the flags with an FRSTOR or FLDENV instruction. This allows a programmer to mask all exceptions (except invalid operation), run a calculation, and then inspect the status word to see if any exceptions were detected at any point in the calculation.

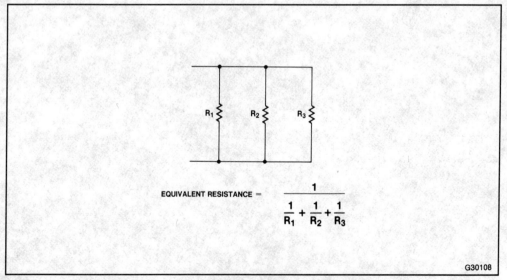

EQUIVALENT RESISTANCE $= \dfrac{1}{\dfrac{1}{R_1} + \dfrac{1}{R_2} + \dfrac{1}{R_3}}$

G30108

Figure 1-11. Arithmetic Example Using Infinity

Software Exception Handling

If the NPX encounters an unmasked exception condition, it signals the exception to the 80286 CPU using the $\overline{\text{ERROR}}$ status line between the two processors.

The next time the 80286 CPU encounters a WAIT or ESC instruction in its instruction stream, the 80286 will detect the active condition of the $\overline{\text{ERROR}}$ status line and automatically trap to an exception response routine using interrupt #16—the Processor Extension Error exception.

This exception response routine is typically a part of the systems software. Typical exception responses may include:

- Incrementing an exception counter for later display or printing
- Printing or displaying diagnostic information (e.g., the 80287 environment and registers)
- Aborting further execution
- Using the exception pointers to build an instruction that will run without exception and executing it

Application programmers on 80286 systems having systems software support for the 80287 NPX should consult their references for the appropriate system response to NPX exceptions. For systems programmers, specific details on writing software exception handlers are included in the section "System-Level Numeric Programming" later in this manual.

The 80287 NPX differs from the 8087 NPX in the manner in which numeric exceptions are signalled to the CPU; the 8087 requires an interrupt controller (8259A) to interrupt the CPU, while the 80287 does not. Programmers upgrading 8087 software to operate on an 80287 should be aware of these differences and any implications they might have on numeric exception-handling software. Appendix B explains the differences between the 80287 and the 8087 NPX in greater detail.

Programming Numeric Applications

2

CHAPTER 2
PROGRAMMING NUMERIC APPLICATIONS

Programmers developing applications for the 80287 have a wide range of instructions and programming alternatives from which to choose.

The following sections describe the 80287 instruction set in detail, and follow up with a discussion of several of the programming facilities that are available to programmers of 80287.

THE 80287 NPX INSTRUCTION SET

This section describes the operation of all 80287 instructions. Within this section, the instructions are divided into six functional classes:

- Data Transfer instructions
- Arithmetic instructions
- Comparison instructions
- Transcendental instructions
- Constant instructions
- Processor Control instructions

At the end of this section, each of the instructions is described in terms of its execution speed, bus transfers, and exceptions, as well as a coding example for each combination of operands accepted by the instruction. For easy reference, this information is concentrated into a table, organized alphabetically by instruction mnemonic.

Throughout this section, the instruction set is described as it appears to the ASM286 programmer who is coding a program. Appendix A covers the actual machine instruction encodings, which are principally of use to those reading unformatted memory dumps, monitoring instruction fetches on the bus, or writing exception handlers.

Compatibility with the 8087 NPX

The instruction set for the 80287 NPX is largely the same as that for the 8087 NPX used with 8086 and 8088 systems. Most object programs generated for the 8087 will execute without change on the 80287. Several instructions are new to the 80287, and several 8087 instructions perform no useful function on the 80287. Appendix B at the back of this manual gives details of these instruction set differences and of the differences in the ASM86 and ASM286 assemblers.

Numeric Operands

The typical NPX instruction accepts one or two operands as inputs, operates on these, and produces a result as an output. Operands are most often (the contents of) register or memory locations. The operands of some instructions are predefined; for example, FSQRT always takes the square root of the number in the top stack element. Others allow, or require, the programmer to explicitly code the operand(s) along with the instruction mnemonic. Still others accept one explicit operand and one implicit operand, which is usually the top stack element.

Whether supplied by the programmer or utilized automatically, the two basic types of operands are *sources* and *destinations*. A source operand simply supplies one of the inputs to an instruction; it is not altered by the instruction. Even when an instruction converts the source operand from one format to another (e.g., real to integer), the conversion is actually performed in an internal work area to avoid altering the source operand. A destination operand may also provide an input to an instruction. It is distinguished from a source operand, however, because its content may be altered when it receives the result produced by the operation; that is, the destination is replaced by the result.

Many instructions allow their operands to be coded in more than one way. For example, FADD (add real) may be written without operands, with only a source or with a destination and a source. The instruction descriptions in this section employ the simple convention of separating alternative operand forms with slashes; the slashes, however, are not coded. Consecutive slashes indicate an option of no explicit operands. The operands for FADD are thus described as

//source/destination, source

This means that FADD may be written in any of three ways:

F A D D
F A D D   *source*
F A D D   *destination, source*

When reading this section, it is important to bear in mind that memory operands may be coded with any of the CPU's memory addressing modes. To review these modes—direct, register indirect, based, indexed, based indexed—refer to the *80286 Programmer's Reference Manual*. Table 2-17 later in this chapter also provides several addressing mode examples.

Data Transfer Instructions

These instructions (summarized in table 2-1) move operands among elements of the register stack, and between the stack top and memory. Any of the seven data types can be converted to temporary real and loaded (pushed) onto the stack in a single operation; they can be stored to memory in the same manner. The data transfer instructions automatically update the 80287 tag word to reflect the register contents following the instruction.

FLD *source*

FLD (load real) loads (pushes) the source operand onto the top of the register stack. This is done by decrementing the stack pointer by one and then copying the content of the source to the new stack top. The source may be a register on the stack (ST(i)) or any of the real data types in memory. Short and long real source operands are converted to temporary real automatically. Coding FLD ST(0) duplicates the stack top.

FST *destination*

FST (store real) transfers the stack top to the destination, which may be another register on the stack or a short or long real memory operand. If the destination is short or long real, the significand is rounded to the width of the destination according to the RC field of the control word, and the exponent is converted to the width and bias of the destination format.

Table 2-1. Data Transfer Instructions

Real Transfers	
FLD	Load real
FST	Store real
FSTP	Store real and pop
FXCH	Exchange registers
Integer Transfers	
FILD	Integer load
FIST	Integer store
FISTP	Integer store and pop
Packed Decimal Transfers	
FBLD	Packed decimal (BCD) load
FBSTP	Packed decimal (BCD) store and pop

If, however, the stack top is tagged special (it contains ∞, a NaN, or a denormal) then the stack top's significand is not rounded but is chopped (on the right) to fit the destination. Neither is the exponent converted, but it also is chopped on the right and transferred "as is." This preserves the value's identification as ∞ or a NaN (exponent all ones) or a denormal (exponent all zeros) so that it can be properly loaded and tagged later in the program if desired.

FSTP destination

FSTP (store real and pop) operates identically to FST except that the stack is popped following the transfer. This is done by tagging the top stack element empty and then incrementing ST. FSTP permits storing to a temporary real memory variable, whereas FST does not. Coding FSTP ST(0) is equivalent to popping the stack with no data transfer.

FXCH//destination

FXCH (exchange registers) swaps the contents of the destination and the stack top registers. If the destination is not coded explicitly, ST(1) is used. Many 80287 instructions operate only on the stack top; FXCH provides a simple means of effectively using these instructions on lower stack elements. For example, the following sequence takes the square root of the third register from the top:

```
FXCH ST(3)
FSQRT
FXCH ST(3)
```


FILD source

FILD (integer load) converts the source memory operand from its binary integer format (word, short, or long) to temporary real and loads (pushes) the result onto the stack. The (new) stack top is tagged zero if all bits in the source were zero, and is tagged valid otherwise.

FIST *destination*

FIST (integer store) rounds the content of the stack top to an integer according to the RC field of the control word and transfers the result to the destination. The destination may define a word or short integer variable. Negative zero is stored in the same encoding as positive zero: 0000...00.

FISTP *destination*

FISTP (integer and pop) operates like FIST and also pops the stack following the transfer. The destination may be any of the binary integer data types.

FBLD *source*

FBLD (packed decimal (BCD) load) converts the content of the source operand from packed decimal to temporary real and loads (pushes) the result onto the stack. The sign of the source is preserved, including the case where the value is negative zero. FBLD is an exact operation; the source is loaded with no rounding error.

The packed decimal digits of the source are assumed to be in the range 0–9H. The instruction does not check for invalid digits (A–FH) and the result of attempting to load an invalid encoding is undefined.

FBSTP *destination*

FBSTP (packed decimal (BCD) store and pop) converts the content of the stack top to a packed decimal integer, stores the result at the destination in memory, and pops the stack. FBSTP produces a rounded integer from a nonintegral value by adding 0.5 to the value and then chopping. Users who are concerned about rounding may precede FBSTP with FRNDINT.

Arithmetic Instructions

The 80287's arithmetic instruction set (table 2-2) provides a wealth of variations on the basic add, subtract, multiply, and divide operations, and a number of other useful functions. These range from a simple absolute value to a square root instruction that executes faster than ordinary division; 80287 programmers no longer need to spend valuable time eliminating square roots from algorithms because they run too slowly. Other arithmetic instructions perform exact modulo division, round real numbers to integers, and scale values by powers of two.

The 80287's basic arithmetic instructions (addition, subtraction, multiplication, and division) are designed to encourage the development of very efficient algorithms. In particular, they allow the programmer to minimize memory references and to make optimum use of the NPX register stack.

Table 2-3 summarizes the available operation/operand forms that are provided for basic arithmetic. In addition to the four normal operations, two "reversed" instructions make subtraction and division "symmetrical" like addition and multiplication. The variety of instruction and operand forms give the programmer unusual flexibility:

- Operands may be located in registers or memory.

- Results may be deposited in a choice of registers.

- Operands may be a variety of NPX data types: temporary real, long real, short real, short integer or word integer, with automatic conversion to temporary real performed by the 80287.

Table 2-2. Arithmetic Instructions

Addition	
FADD	Add real
FADDP	Add real and pop
FIADD	Integer add

Subtraction	
FSUB	Subtract real
FSUBP	Subtract real and pop
FISUB	Integer subtract
FSUBR	Subtract real reversed
FSUBRP	Subtract real reversed and pop
FISUBR	Integer subtract reversed

Multiplication	
FMUL	Multiply real
FMULP	Multiply real and pop
FIMUL	Integer multiply

Division	
FDIV	Divide real
FDIVP	Divide real and pop
FIDIV	Integer divide
FDIVR	Divide real reversed
FDIVRP	Divide real reversed and pop
FIDIVR	Integer divide reversed

Other Operations	
FSQRT	Square root
FSCALE	Scale
FPREM	Partial remainder
FRNDINT	Round to integer
FXTRACT	Extract exponent and significand
FABS	Absolute value
FCHS	Change sign

Five basic instruction forms may be used across all six operations, as shown in table 2-3. The classical stack form may be used to make the 80287 operate like a classical stack machine. No operands are coded in this form, only the instruction mnemonic. The NPX picks the source operand from the stack top and the destination from the next stack element. It then pops the stack, performs the operation, and returns the result to the new stack top, effectively replacing the operands by the result.

The register form is a generalization of the classical stack form; the programmer specifies the stack top as one operand and any register on the stack as the other operand. Coding the stack top as the destination provides a convenient way to access a constant, held elsewhere in the stack, from the stack top. The converse coding (ST is the source operand) allows, for example, adding the top into a register used as an accumulator.

Table 2-3. Basic Arithmetic Instructions and Operands

Instruction Form	Mnemonic Form	Operand Forms destination, source	ASM286 Example	
Classical stack	F*op*	{ ST(1),ST }	FADD	
Register	F*op*	ST(i),ST or ST,ST(i)	FSUB	ST,ST(3)
Register pop	F*op*P	ST(i),ST	FMULP	ST(2),ST
Real memory	F*op*	{ ST, } short-real/long-real	FDIV	AZIMUTH
Integer memory	FI*op*	{ ST, } word-integer/short-integer	FIDIV	N_PULSES

NOTES:

Braces ({ }) surround *implicit* operands; these are not coded, and are shown here for information only.

op = ADD   destination ← destination + source
     SUB   destination ← destination − source
     SUBR destination ← source − destination
     MUL   destination ← destination • source
     DIV   destination ← destination ÷ source
     DIVR destination ← source ÷ destination

Often the operand in the stack top is needed for one operation but then is of no further use in the computation. The register pop form can be used to pick up the stack top as the source operand, and then discard it by popping the stack. Coding operands of ST(1),ST with a register pop mnemonic is equivalent to a classical stack operation: the top is popped and the result is left at the new top.

The two memory forms increase the flexibility of the 80287's arithmetic instructions. They permit a real number or a binary integer in memory to be used directly as a source operand. This is a very useful facility in situations where operands are not used frequently enough to justify holding them in registers. Note that any memory addressing mode may be used to define these operands, so they may be elements in arrays, structures, or other data organizations, as well as simple scalars.

The six basic operations are discussed further in the next paragraphs, and descriptions of the remaining seven arithmetic operations follow.

ADDITION
FADD   *//source/destination,source*
FADDP   *//destination/source*
FIADD   *source*

The addition instructions (add real, add real and pop, integer add) add the source and destination operands and return the sum to the destination. The operand at the stack top may be doubled by coding:

```
FADD ST,ST(0)
```

NORMAL SUBTRACTION
FSUB   *//source/destination,source*
FSUBP   *//destination/source*
FISUB   *source*

The normal subtraction instructions (subtract real, subtract real and pop, integer subtract) subtract the source operand from the destination and return the difference to the destination.

REVERSED SUBTRACTION
FSUBR //source/destination,source
FSUBRP //destination/source
FISUBR source

The reversed subtraction instructions (subtract real reversed, subtract real reversed and pop, integer subtract reversed) subtract the destination from the source and return the difference to the destination.

MULTIPLICATION
FMUL //source/destination,source
FMULP destination,source
FIMUL source

The multiplication instructions (multiply real, multiply real and pop, integer multiply) multiply the source and destination operands and return the product to the destination. Coding FMUL ST,ST(0) squares the content of the stack top.

NORMAL DIVISION
FDIV //source/destination,source
FDIVP destination,source
FIDIV source

The normal division instructions (divide real, divide real and pop, integer divide) divide the destination by the source and return the quotient to the destination.

REVERSED DIVISION
FDIVR //source/destination,source
FDIVRP destination,source
FIDIVR source

The reversed division instructions (divide real reversed, divide real reversed and pop, integer divide reversed) divide the source operand by the destination and return the quotient to the destination.

FSQRT

FSQRT (square root) replaces the content of the top stack element with its square root. (Note: The square root of -0 is defined to be -0.)

FSCALE

FSCALE (scale) interprets the value contained in ST(1) as an integer and adds this value to the exponent of the number in ST. This is equivalent to

$$ST \leftarrow ST \cdot 2^{ST(1)}$$

Thus, FSCALE provides rapid multiplication or division by integral powers of 2. It is particularly useful for scaling the elements of a vector.

Note that FSCALE assumes the scale factor in ST(1) is an integral value in the range $-2^{15} \leq X < 2^{15}$. If the value is not integral, but is in-range and is greater in magnitude than 1, FSCALE uses the nearest integer smaller in magnitude; i.e., it chops the value toward 0. If the value is out of range, or $0 < |X| < 1$, the instruction will produce an undefined result and will not signal an exception. The recommended practice is to load the scale factor from a word integer to ensure correct operation.

FPREM

FPREM (partial remainder) performs modulo division of the top stack element by the next stack element, i.e., ST(1) is the modulus. FPREM produces an *exact* result; the precision exception does not occur. The sign of the remainder is the same as the sign of the original dividend.

FPREM operates by performing successive scaled subtractions; obtaining the exact remainder when the operands differ greatly in magnitude can consume large amounts of execution time. Because the 80287 can only be preempted between instructions, the remainder function could seriously increase interrupt latency in these cases. Accordingly, the instruction is designed to be executed iteratively in a software-controlled loop.

FPREM can reduce a magnitude difference of up to 2^{64} in one execution. If FPREM produces a remainder that is less than the modulus, the function is complete and bit C2 of the status word condition code is cleared. If the function is incomplete, C2 is set to 1; the result in ST is then called the partial remainder. Software can inspect C2 by storing the status word following execution of FPREM and re-execute the instruction (using the partial remainder in ST as the dividend), until C2 is cleared. Alternatively, a program can determine when the function is complete by comparing ST to ST(1). If ST>ST(1), then FPREM must be executed again; if ST=ST(1), then the remainder is 0; if ST<ST(1), then the remainder is ST. A higher priority interrupting routine that needs the 80287 can force a context switch between the instructions in the remainder loop.

An important use for FPREM is to reduce arguments (operands) of periodic transcendental functions to the range permitted by these instructions. For example, the FPTAN (tangent) instruction requires its argument to be less than $\pi/4$. Using $\pi/4$ as a modulus, FPREM will reduce an argument so that it is in range of FPTAN. Because FPREM produces an exact result, the argument reduction does *not* introduce roundoff error into the calculation, even if several iterations are required to bring the argument into range. (The rounding of π does not create the effect of a rounded argument, but of a rounded period.)

FPREM also provides the least-significant three bits of the quotient generated by FPREM (in C_3, C_1, C_0). This is also important for transcendental argument reduction, because it locates the original angle in the correct one of eight $\pi/4$ segments of the unit circle (see table 2-4). If the quotient is less than 4, then C0 will be the value of C3 before FPREM was executed. If the quotient is less than 2, then C3 will be the value of C1 before FPREM was executed.

FRNDINT

FRNDINT (round to integer) rounds the top stack element to an integer. For example, assume that ST contains the 80287 real number encoding of the decimal value 155.625. FRNDINT will change the value to 155 if the RC field of the control word is set to down or chop, or to 156 if it is set to up or nearest.

Table 2-4. Condition Code Interpretation after FPREM

Condition Code				Interpretation after FPREM
C3	C2	C1	C0	
X	1	X	X	Incomplete Reduction; further iteration is required for complete reduction.
				Complete Reduction; C1, C3, and C0 contain the three least-significant bits of quotient:
0	0	0	0	(Quotient) MOD 8 = 0
0	0	0	1	(Quotient) MOD 8 = 4
0	0	1	0	(Quotient) MOD 8 = 1
0	0	1	1	(Quotient) MOD 8 = 5
1	0	0	0	(Quotient) MOD 8 = 2
1	0	0	1	(Quotient) MOD 8 = 6
1	0	1	0	(Quotient) MOD 8 = 3
1	0	1	1	(Quotient) MOD 8 = 7

FXTRACT

FXTRACT (extract exponent and significand) "decomposes" the number in the stack top into two numbers that represent the actual value of the operand's exponent and significand fields. The "exponent" replaces the original operand on the stack and the "significand" is pushed onto the stack. Following execution of FXTRACT, ST (the new stack top) contains the value of the original significand expressed as a real number: its sign is the same as the operand's, its exponent is 0 true (16,383 or 3FFFH biased), and its significant is identical to the original operand's. ST(1) contains the value of the original operand's true (unbiased) exponent expressed as a real number. If the original operand is zero, FXTRACT produces zeros in ST and ST(1) and *both* are signed as the original operand.

To clarify the operation of FXTRACT, assume ST contains a number of whose true exponent is $+4$ (i.e., its exponent field contains 4003H). After executing FXTRACT, ST(1) will contain the real number $+4.0$; its sign will be positive, its exponent field will contain 4001H ($+2$ true) and its significand field will contain $1_\triangle 00...00B$. In other words, the value in ST(1) will be $1.0 \times 2^2 = 4$. If ST contains an operand whose true exponent is -7 (i.e., its exponent field contains 3FF8H), then FXTRACT will return an "exponent" of -7.0; after the instruction executes, ST(1)'s sign and exponent fields will contain C001H (negative sign, true exponent of 2), and its significand will be $1_\triangle 1100...00B$. In other words, the value in ST(1) will be $-1.11 \times 2^2 = -7.0$. In both cases, following FXTRACT, ST's sign and significand fields will be the same as the original operand's, and its exponent field will contain 3FFFH (0 true).

FXTRACT is useful in conjunction with FBSTP for converting numbers in 80287 temporary real format to decimal representations (e.g., for printing or displaying). It can also be useful for debugging, because it allows the exponent and significant parts of a real number to be examined separately.

FABS

FABS (absolute value) changes the top stack element to its absolute value by making its sign positive.

FCHS

FCHS (change sign) complements (reverses) the sign of the top stack element.

Comparison Instructions

Each of these instructions (table 2-5) analyzes the top stack element, often in relationship to another operand, and reports the result in the status word condition code. The basic operations are compare, test (compare with zero), and examine (report tag, sign, and normalization). Special forms of the compare operation are provided to optimize algorithms by allowing direct comparisons with binary integers and real numbers in memory, as well as popping the stack after a comparison.

The FSTSW (store status word) instruction may be used following a comparison to transfer the condition code to memory for inspection.

Note that instructions other than those in the comparison group may update the condition code. To ensure that the status word is not altered inadvertently, store it immediately following a comparison operation.

FCOM //source

FCOM (compare real) compares the stack top to the source operand. The source operand may be a register on the stack, or a short or long real memory operand. If an operand is not coded, ST is compared to ST(1). Positive and negative forms of zero compare identically as if they were unsigned. Following the instruction, the condition codes reflect the order of the operands as shown in table 2-6.

Table 2-5. Comparison Instructions

FCOM	Compare real
FCOMP	Compare real and pop
FCOMPP	Compare real and pop twice
FICOM	Integer compare
FICOMP	Integer compare and pop
FTST	Test
FXAM	Examine

Table 2-6. Condition Code Interpretation after FCOM

Condition Code				Interpretation after FCOM
C3	C2	C1	C0	
0	0	X	0	ST > source
0	0	X	1	ST < source
1	0	X	0	ST = source
1	1	X	1	ST is not comparable

NaNs and ∞ (projective) cannot be compared and return $C3 = C0 = 1$ as shown in the table.

FCOMP //*source*

FCOMP (compare real and pop) operates like FCOM, and in addition pops the stack.

FCOMPP

FCOMPP (compare real and pop twice) operates like FCOM and additionally pops the stack twice, discarding both operands. The comparison is of the stack top to ST(1); no operands may be explicitly coded.

FICOM *source*

FICOM (integer compare) converts the source operand, which may reference a word or short binary integer variable, to temporary real and compares the stack top to it.

FICOMP *source*

FICOMP (integer compare and pop) operates identically to FICOM and additionally discards the value in ST by popping the stack.

FTST

FTST (test) tests the top stack element by comparing it to zero. The result is posted to the condition codes as shown in table 2-7.

FXAM

FXAM (examine) reports the content of the top stack element as positive/negative and NaN/unnormal/denormal/normal/zero, or empty. Table 2-8 lists and interprets all the condition code values that FXAM generates. Although four different encodings may be returned for an empty register, bits C3 and C0 of the condition code are both 1 in all encodings. Bits C2 and C1 should be ignored when examining for empty.

Table 2-7. Condition Code Interpretation after FTST

Condition Code				Interpretation after FTST
C3	C2	C1	C0	
0	0	X	0	ST > 0
0	0	X	1	ST < 0
1	0	X	0	ST = 0
1	1	X	1	ST is not comparable; (i.e., it is a NaN or projective infinity)

Table 2-8. FXAM Condition Code Settings

Condition Code				Interpretation
C3	C2	C1	C0	
0	0	0	0	+ Unnormal
0	0	0	1	+ NaN
0	0	1	0	− Unnormal
0	0	1	1	− NaN
0	1	0	0	+ Normal
0	1	0	1	+ ∞
0	1	1	0	− Normal
0	1	1	1	− ∞
1	0	0	0	+ 0
1	0	0	1	Empty
1	0	1	0	− 0
1	0	1	1	Empty
1	1	0	0	+ Denormal
1	1	0	1	Empty
1	1	1	0	− Denormal
1	1	1	1	Empty

Transcendental Instructions

The instructions in this group (table 2-9) perform the time-consuming *core calculations* for all common trigonometric, inverse trigonometric, hyperbolic, inverse hyperbolic, logarithmic, and exponential functions. Prologue and epilogue software may be used to reduce arguments to the range accepted by the instructions and to adjust the result to correspond to the original arguments if necessary. The transcendentals operate on the top one or two stack elements, and they return their results to the stack, also.

NOTE

The transcendental instructions assume that their operands are *valid* and *in-range*. The instruction descriptions in this section provide the allowed operand range of each instruction.

All operands to a transcendental must be normalized; denormals, unnormals, infinities, and NaNs are considered invalid. (Zero operands are accepted by some functions and are considered out-of-range by others). If a transcendental operand is invalid or out-of-range, the instruction will produce an undefined result without signalling an exception. It is the programmer's responsibility to ensure that operands are valid and in-range before executing a transcendental. For periodic functions, FPREM may be used to bring a valid operand into range.

FPTAN
$0 \leq ST(0) \leq \pi/4$

FPTAN (partial tangent) computes the function $Y/X = TAN(\Theta)$. Θ is taken from the top stack element; it must lie in the range $0 \leq \Theta \leq \pi/4$. The result of the operation is a ratio; Y replaces Θ in the stack and X is pushed, becoming the new stack top.

Table 2-9. Transcendental Instructions

FPTAN	Partial tangent
FPATAN	Partial arctangent
F2XM1	$2^x - 1$
FYL2X	$Y \cdot \log_2 X$
FYL2XP1	$Y \cdot \log_2(X + 1)$

The ratio result of FPTAN and the ratio argument of FPATAN are designed to optimize the calculation of the other trigonometric functions, including SIN, COS, ARCSIN, and ARCCOS. These can be derived from TAN and ARCTAN via standard trigonometric identities.

FPATAN
$0 \leq \text{ST(1)} < \text{ST(0)} < \infty$

FPATAN (partial arctangent) computes the function $\Theta = \text{ARCTAN}(Y/X)$. X is taken from the top stack element and Y from ST(1). Y and X must observe the inequality $0 \leq Y < X < \infty$. The instruction pops the stack and returns Θ to the (new) stack top, overwriting the Y operand.

F2XM1
$0 \leq \text{ST(0)} \leq 0.5$

F2XM1 (2 to the X minus 1) calculates the function $Y = 2^x - 1$. X is taken from the stack top and must be in the range $0 \leq X \leq 0.5$. The result Y replaces X at the stack top.

This instruction is designed to produce a very accurate result even when X is close to 0. To obtain $Y = 2^x$, add 1 to the result delivered by F2XM1.

The following formulas show how values other than 2 may be raised to a power of X:

$10^x = 2^{x \cdot \text{LOG}_2 10}$
$e^x = 2^{x \cdot \text{LOG}_2 e}$
$y^x = 2^{x \cdot \text{LOG}_2 Y}$

As shown in the next section, the 80287 has built-in instructions for loading the constants $\text{LOG}_2 10$ and $\text{LOG}_2 e$, and the FYL2X instruction may be used to calculate $X \cdot \text{LOG}_2 Y$.

FYL2X
$0 < \text{ST(0)} < \infty \quad -\infty < \text{ST(1)} < \infty$

FYL2X (Y log base 2 of X) calculates the function $Z = Y \cdot \text{LOG}_2 X$. X is taken from the stack top and Y from ST(1). The operands must be in the ranges $0 < X < \infty$ and $-\infty < Y < +\infty$. The instruction pops the stack and returns Z at the (new) stack top, replacing the Y operand.

This function optimizes the calculations of log to any base other than two, because a multiplication is always required:

$\text{LOG}_n 2 \cdot \text{LOG}_2 X$

FYL2XP1

$$0 \leq |ST(0)| < (1-(\sqrt{2}/2))$$
$$-\infty < ST(1) < \infty$$

FYL2XP1 (Y log base 2 of (X + 1)) calculates the function $Z = Y \cdot LOG_2 (X+1)$. X is taken from the stack top and must be in the range $0 \leq |X| < (1-(\sqrt{2}/2))$. Y is taken from ST(1) and must be in the range $-\infty < Y < \infty$. FYL2XP1 pops the stack and returns Z at the (new) stack top, replacing Y.

The instruction provides improved accuracy over FYL2X when computing the log of a number very close to 1, for example $1 + \epsilon$ where $\epsilon << 1$. Providing ϵ rather than $1 + \epsilon$ as the input to the function allows more significant digits to be retained.

Constant Instructions

Each of these instructions (table 2-10) loads (pushes) a commonly-used constant onto the stack. The values have full temporary real precision (64 bits) and are accurate to approximately 19 decimal digits. Because a temporary real constant occupies 10 memory bytes, the constant instructions, which are only two bytes long, save storage and improve execution speed, in addition to simplifying programming.

FLDZ

FLDZ (load zero) loads (pushes) $+0.0$ onto the stack.

FLD1

FLD1 (load one) loads (pushes) $+1.0$ onto the stack.

FLDPI

FLDPI (load π) loads (pushes) π onto the stack.

FLDL2T

FLDL2T (load log base 2 of 10) loads (pushes) the value $LOG_2 10$ onto the stack.

FLDL2E

FLDL2E (load log base 2 of e) loads (pushes) the value $LOG_2 e$ onto the stack.

Table 2-10. Constant Instructions

FLDZ	Load + 0.0
FLD1	Load + 1.0
FLDPI	Load π
FLDL2T	Load $\log_2 10$
FLDL2E	Load $\log_2 e$
FLDLG2	Load $\log_{10} 2$
FLDLN2	Load $\log_e 2$

FLDLG2

FLDLG2 (load log base 10 of 2) loads (pushes) the value $LOG_{10}2$ onto the stack.

FLDLN2

FLDLN2 (load log base e of 2) loads (pushes) the value LOG_e2 onto the stack.

Processor Control Instructions

The processor control instructions shown in table 2-11 are not typically used in calculations; they provide control over the 80287 NPX for system-level activities. These activities include initialization, exception handling, and task switching.

As shown in table 2-11, many of the NPX processor control instructions have two forms of assembler mnemonic:

• A *wait* form, where the mnemonic is prefixed only with an F, such as FSTSW. This form checks for unmasked numeric errors.

• A *no-wait* form, where the mnemonic is prefixed with an FN, such as FNSTSW. This form ignores unmasked numeric errors.

When the control instruction is coded using the *no-wait* form of the mnemonic, the ASM286 assembler does not precede the ESC instruction with a *wait* instruction, and the CPU does not test the $\overline{ERROR}$ status line from the NPX before executing the processor control instruction.

Only the *processor control* class of instructions have this alternate no-wait form. All numeric instructions are automatically synchronized by the 80286, with the CPU testing the $\overline{BUSY}$ status line and only executing the numeric instruction when this line is inactive. Because of this automatic synchronization by the 80286, *numeric* instructions for the 80287 need not be preceded by a CPU wait instruction in order to execute correctly.

Table 2-11. Processor Control Instructions

FINIT/FNINIT	Initialize processor
FSETPM	Set Protected Mode
FLDCW	Load control word
FSTCW/FNSTCW	Store control word
FSTSW/FNSTSW	Store status word
FSTSW AX/FNSTSW AX	Store status word to AX
FCLEX/FNCLEX	Clear exceptions
FSTENV/FNSTENV	Store Environment
FLDENV	Load environment
FSAVE/FNSAVE	Save state
FRSTOR	Restore state
FINCSTP	Increment stack pointer
FDECSTP	Decrement stack pointer
FFREE	Free register
FNOP	No operation
FWAIT	CPU Wait

It should also be noted that the 8087 instructions FENI and FDISI perform no function in the 80287. If these opcodes are detected in an 80286/80287 instruction stream, the 80287 will perform no specific operation and no internal states will be affected. For programmers interested in porting numeric software from 8087 environments to the 80286, however, it should be noted that program sections containing these exception-handling instructions are not likely to be completely portable to the 80287. Appendix B contains a more complete description of the differences between the 80287 and the 8087 NPX.

FINIT/FNINIT

FINIT/FNINIT (initialize processor) sets the 80287 NPX into a known state, unaffected by any previous activity. The no-wait form of this instruction will cause the 80287 to abort any previous numeric operations currently executing in the NEU. This instruction performs the functional equivalent of a hardware RESET, with one exception; FINIT/FNINIT does not affect the current 80287 operating mode (either Real-Address mode or Protected mode). FINIT checks for unmasked numeric exceptions, FNINIT does not.

Note that if FNINIT is executed while a previous 80287 memory-referencing instruction is running, 80287 bus cycles in progress will be aborted. This instruction may be necessary to clear the 80287 if a Processor Extension Segment Overrun Exception (Interrupt 9) is detected by the CPU.

FSETPM

FSETPM (set Protected mode) sets the operating mode of the 80287 to Protected Virtual-Address mode. When the 80287 is first initialized following hardware RESET, it operates in Real-Address mode, just as does the 80286 CPU. Once the 80287 NPX has been set into Protected mode, only a hardware RESET can return the NPX to operation in Real-Address mode.

When the 80287 operates in Protected mode, the NPX exception pointers are represented differently than they are in Real-Address mode (see the FSAVE and FSTENV instructions that follow). This distinction is evident primarily to writers of numeric exception handlers, however. For general application programmers, the operating mode of the 80287 need not be a concern.

FLDCW *source*

FLDCW (load control word) replaces the current processor control word with the word defined by the source operand. This instruction is typically used to establish or change the 80287's mode of operation. Note that if an exception bit in the status word is set, loading a new control word that unmasks that exception and clears the interrupt enable mask will generate an immediate interrupt request before the next instruction is executed. When changing modes, the recommended procedure is to first clear any exceptions and then load the new control word.

FSTCW/FNSTCW *destination*

FSTCW/FNSTCW (store control word) writes the current processor control word to the memory location defined by the destination. FSTCW checks for unmasked numeric exceptions, FNSTCW does not.

FSTSW/FNSTSW *destination*

FSTSW/FNSTCW (store status word) writes the current value of the 80287 status word to the destination operand in memory. The instruction is used to

- Implement conditional branching following a comparison or FPREM instruction (FSTSW)
- Poll the 80287 to determine if it is busy (FNSTSW)
- Invoke exception handlers in environments that do not use interrupts (FSTSW).

FSTSW checks for unmasked numeric exceptions, FNSTSW does not.

FSTSW AX/FNSTSW AX

FSTSW AX/FNSTSW AX (store status word to AX) is a special 80287 instruction that writes the current value of the 80287 status word directly into the 80286 AX register. This instruction optimizes conditional branching in numeric programs, where the 80286 CPU must test the condition of various NPX status bits. The waited form checks for unmasked numeric exceptions, the non-waited for does not.

When this instruction is executed, the 80286 AX register is updated with the NPX status word before the CPU executes any further instructions. In this way, the 80286 can immediately test the NPX status word without any WAIT or other synchronization instructions required.

FCLEX/FNCLEX

FCLEX/FNCLEX (clear exceptions) clears all exception flags, the error status flag and the busy flag in the status word. As a consequence, the 80287's $\overline{\text{ERROR}}$ line goes inactive. FCLEX checks for unmasked numeric exceptions, FNCLEX does not.

FSAVE/FNSAVE *destination*

FSAVE/FNSAVE (save state) writes the full 80287 state—environment plus register stack—to the memory location defined by the destination operand. Figure 2-1 shows the layout of the 94-byte save area; typically the instruction will be coded to save this image on the CPU stack. FNSAVE delays its execution until all NPX activity completes normally. Thus, the save image reflects the state of the NPX following the completion of any running instruction. After writing the state image to memory, FSAVE/FNSAVE initializes the 80287 as if FINIT/FNINIT had been executed.

FSAVE/FNSAVE is useful whenever a program wants to save the current state of the NPX and initialize it for a new routine. Three examples are

- An operating system needs to perform a context switch (suspend the task that had been running and give control to a new task).
- An exception handler needs to use the 80287.
- An application task wants to pass a "clean" 80287 to a subroutine.

FSAVE checks for unmasked numeric errors before executing, FNSAVE does not. An FWAIT should be executed before CPU interrupts are enabled or any subsequent 80287 instruction is executed. Other CPU instructions may be executed between the FNSAVE/FSAVE and the FWAIT.

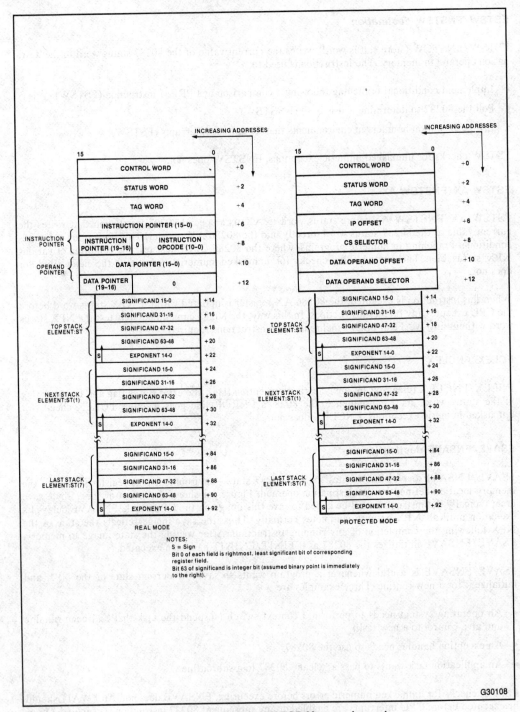

Figure 2-1. FSAVE/FRSTOR Memory Layout

FRSTOR *source*

FRSTOR (restore state) reloads the 80287 from the 94-byte memory area defined by the source operand. This information should have been written by a previous FSAVE/FNSAVE instruction and not altered by any other instruction. An FWAIT is not required after FRSTOR. FRSTOR will automatically wait and check for interrupts until all data transfers are completed before continuing to the next instruction.

Note that the 80287 "reacts" to its new state at the conclusion of the FRSTOR; it will, for example, generate an exception request if the exception and mask bits in the memory image so indicate when the next WAIT or error-checking-ESC instruction is executed.

FSTENV/FNSTENV *destination*

FSTENV/FNSTENV (store environment) writes the 80287's basic status—control, status, and tag words, and exception pointers—to the memory location defined by the destination operand. Typically, the environment is saved on the CPU stack. FSTENV/FNSTENV is often used by exception handlers because it provides access to the exception pointers that identify the offending instruction and operand. After saving the environment, FSTENV/FNSTENV sets all exception masks in the processor. FSTENV checks for pending errors before executing, FNSTENV does not.

Figure 2-2 shows the format of the environment data in memory. FNSTENV does not store the environment until all NPX activity has completed. Thus, the data saved by the instruction reflects the 80287 after any previously decoded instruction has been executed. After writing the environment image to memory, FNSTENV/FSTENV initializes the 80287 state as if FNINIT/FINIT had been executed.

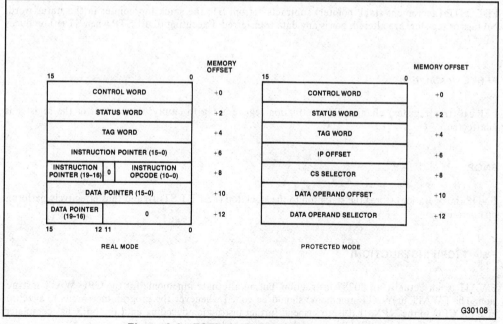

Figure 2-2. FSTENV/FLDENV Memory Layout

FSTENV/FNSTENV must be allowed to complete before any other 80287 instruction is decoded. When FSTENV is coded, an explicit FWAIT, or assembler-generated WAIT, should precede any subsequent 80287 instruction.

FLDENV *source*

FLDENV (load environment) reloads the environment from the memory area defined by the source operand. This data should have been written by a previous FSTENV/FNSTENV instruction. CPU instructions (that do not reference the environment image) may immediately follow FLDENV. An FWAIT is not required after FLDENV. FLDENV will automatically wait for all data transfers to complete before executing the next instruction.

Note that loading an environment image that contains an unmasked exception will cause a numeric exception when the next WAIT or error-checking-ESC instruction is executed.

FINCSTP

FINCSTP (increment stack pointer) adds 1 to the stack top pointer (ST) in the status word. It does not alter tags or register contents, nor does it transfer data. It is not equivalent to popping the stack, because it does not set the tag of the previous stack top to empty. Incrementing the stack pointer when ST=7 produces ST=0.

FDECSTP

FDECSTP (decrement stack pointer) subtracts 1 from ST, the stack top pointer in the status word. No tags or registers are altered, nor is any data transferred. Executing FDECSTP when ST=0 produces ST=7.

FFREE *destination*

FFREE (free register) changes the destination register's tag to empty; the content of the register is unaffected.

FNOP

FNOP (no operation) stores the stack top to the stack top (FST ST,ST(0)) and thus effectively performs no operation.

FWAIT (CPU INSTRUCTION)

FWAIT is not actually an 80287 instruction, but an alternate mnemonic for the CPU WAIT instruction. The FWAIT or WAIT mnemonic should be coded whenever the programmer wants to synchronize the CPU to the NPX, that is, to suspend further instruction decoding until the NPX has completed the current instruction. FWAIT will check for unmasked numeric exceptions.

NOTE

A CPU instruction should not attempt to access a memory operand until the 80287 instruction has completed. For example, the following coding shows how FWAIT can be used to force the CPU instruction to wait for the 80287:

```
FIST        VALUE
FWAIT       ; Wait for FIST to complete
MOV         AX,VALUE
```

More information on when to code an FWAIT instruction is given in a following section of this chapter, "Concurrent Processing with the 80287."

Instruction Set Reference Information

Table 2-14 later in this chapter lists the operating characteristics of all the 80287 instructions. There is one table entry for each instruction mnemonic; the entries are in alphabetical order for quick lookup. Each entry provides the general operand forms accepted by the instruction as well as a list of all exceptions that may be detected during the operation.

One entry exists for each combination of operand types that can be coded with the mnemonic. Table 2-12 explains the operand identifiers allowed in table 2-14. Following this entry are columns that provide execution time in clocks, the number of bus transfers run during the operation, the length of the instruction in bytes, and an ASM286 coding sample.

INSTRUCTION EXECUTION TIME

The execution of an 80287 instruction involves three principal activities, each of which may contribute to the overall execution time of the instruction:

- 80286 CPU overhead involved in handling the ESC instruction opcode and setting up the 80287 NPX

Table 2-12. Key to Operand Types

Identifier	Explanation
ST	Stack top; the register currently at the top of the stack.
ST(i)	A register in the stack i ($0 \leq i \leq 7$) stack elements from the top. ST(1) is the next-on-stack register, ST(2) is below ST(1), etc.
Short-real	A short real (32 bits) number in memory.
Long-real	A long real (64 bits) number in memory.
Temp-real	A temporary real (80 bits) number in memory.
Packed-decimal	A packed decimal integer (18 digits, 10 bytes) in memory.
Word-integer	A word binary integer (16 bits) in memory.
Short-integer	A short binary integer (32 bits) in memory.
Long-integer	A long binary integer (64 bits) in memory.
nn-bytes	A memory area *nn* bytes long.

- Instruction execution by the 80287 NPX

- Operand transfers between the 80287 NPX and memory or a CPU register

The timing of these various activities is affected by the individual clock frequencies of the 80286 CPU and the 80287 NPX. In addition, slow memories requiring the insertion of wait states in bus cycles, and bus contention due to other processors in the system, may lengthen operand transfer times.

In calculating an overall execution time for an individual numeric instruction, analysts must take each of these activities into account. In most cases, it can be assumed that the numeric instructions have already been prefetched by the 80286 and are awaiting execution.

- The CPU overhead in handling the ESC instruction opcode takes only a single CPU bus cycle before the 80287 begins its execution of the numeric instruction. The timing of this bus cycle is determined by the CPU clock. Additional CPU activity is required to set up the 80287's instruction and data pointer registers, but this activity occurs *after* the 80287 has begun executing its instruction, and so this parallel activity does not affect total execution time.

- The duration of individual numeric instructions executing on the 80287 varies for each instruction. Table 2-14 quotes a typical execution clock count and a range for each 80287 instruction. Dividing the figures in the table by 10 (for a 10-MHz 80287 NPX clock) produces an execution time in microseconds. The typical case is an estimate for operand values that normally characterize most applications. The range encompasses best- and worst-case operand values that may be found in extreme circumstances.

- The operand transfer time required to transfer operands between the 80287 and memory or a CPU register depends on the number of words to be transferred, the frequency of the CPU clock controlling bus timing, the number of wait states added to accommodate slower memories, and whether operands are based at even or odd memory addresses. Some (small) additional number of bus cycles may also be lost due to the asynchronous nature of the PEREQ/PEACK handshaking between the 80286 and 80287, and this interaction varies with relative frequencies of the CPU and NPX clocks.

The execution clock counts for the NPX execution of instructions shown in table 2-14 assume that no exceptions are detected during execution. Invalid operation, denormalized operand (unmasked), and zero divide exceptions usually decrease execution time from the typical figure, but execution still falls within the indicated range. The precision exception has no effect on execution time. Unmasked overflow and underflow, and masked denormalized exceptions impose additional execution penalties as shown in table 2-13. Absolute worst-case execution times are therefore the high range figure plus the largest penalty that may be encountered.

BUS TRANSFERS

NPX instructions that reference memory require bus cycles to transfer operands between the NPX and memory. The actual number of transfers depends on the length of the operand and the alignment of

Table 2-13. Execution Penalties

Exception	Additional Clocks
Overflow (unmasked)	14
Underflow (unmasked)	16
Denormalized (masked)	33

the operand in memory. In table 2-14, the first figure gives execution clocks for even-addressed operands, while the second gives the clock count for odd-addressed operands.

For operands aligned at *word boundaries*, that is, based at *even memory addresses*, each word to be transferred requires one bus cycle between the 80286 data channel and memory, and one bus cycle to the NPX. For operands based at *odd memory addresses*, each word transfer requires two bus cycles to transfer individual bytes between the 80286 data channel and memory, and one bus cycle to the NPX.

NOTE

For best performance, operands for the 80287 should be aligned along word boundaries; that is, based at even memory addresses. Operands based at odd memory addresses are transferred to memory essentially byte-at-a-time and may take half again as long to transfer as word-aligned operands.

Additional transfer time is required if slow memories are being used, requiring the insertion of wait states into the CPU bus cycle. In multiprocessor environments, the bus may not be available immediately; this overhead can also increase effective transfer time.

INSTRUCTION LENGTH

80287 instructions that do not reference memory are two bytes long. Memory reference instructions vary between two and four bytes. The third and fourth bytes are for the 8- or 16-bit displacement values used in conjunction with the standard 80286 memory-addressing modes.

Note that the lengths quoted in table 2-14 for the processor control instructions (FNINIT, FNSTCW, FNSTSW, FNSTSW AX, FNCLEX, FNSTENV, and FNSAVE) do not include the one-byte CPU wait instruction inserted by the ASM286 assembler if the control instruction is coded using the wait form of the mnemonic (e.g. FINIT, FSTCW, FSTSW, FSTSW AX, FCLEX, FSTENV, and FSAVE). wait and no-wait forms of the processor control instructions have been described in the preceding section titled "Processor Control Instructions."

Table 2-14. Instruction Set Reference Data

FABS

FABS (no operands)
Absolute value

Exceptions: I

Operands	Execution Clocks		Operand Word Transfers	Code Bytes	Coding Example
	Typical	Range			
(no operands)	14	10-17	0	2	FABS

FADD

FADD //source/destination,source
Add real

Exceptions: I, D, O, U, P

Operands	Execution Clocks		Operand Word Transfers	Code Bytes	Coding Example
	Typical	Range			
//ST,ST(i)/ST(i),ST	85	70-100	0	2	FADD ST,ST(4)
short-real	105	90-120	2	2-4	FADD AIR_TEMP [SI]
long-real	110	95-125	4	2-4	FADD [BX].MEAN

FADDP

FADDP destination, source
Add real and pop

Exceptions: I, D, O, U, P

Operands	Execution Clocks		Operand Word Transfers	Code Bytes	Coding Example
	Typical	Range			
ST(i),ST	90	75-105	0	2	FADDP ST(2),ST

FBLD

FBLD source
Packed decimal (BCD) load

Exceptions: I

Operands	Execution Clocks		Operand Word Transfers	Code Bytes	Coding Example
	Typical	Range			
packed-decimal	300	290-310	5	2-4	FBLD YTD_SALES

FBSTP

FBSTP destination
Packed decimal (BCD) store and pop

Exceptions: I

Operands	Execution Clocks		Operand Word Transfers	Code Bytes	Coding Example
	Typical	Range			
packed-decimal	530	520-540	5	2-4	FBSTP [BX].FORECAST

Table 2-14. Instruction Set Reference Data (Cont'd.)

FCHS

FCHS (no operands)
Change sign Exceptions: I

Operands	Execution Clocks		Operand Word Transfers	Code Bytes	Coding Example
	Typical	Range			
(no operands)	15	10-17	0	2	FCHS

FCLEX/FNCLEX

FCLEX/FNCLEX(no operands)
Clear exceptions Exceptions: None

Operands	Execution Clocks		Operand Word Transfers	Code Bytes	Coding Example
	Typical	Range			
(no operands)	5	2-8	0	2	FNCLEX

FCOM

FCOM //source
Compare real Exceptions: I, D

Operands	Execution Clocks		Operand Word Transfers	Code Bytes	Coding Example
	Typical	Range			
//ST(i)	45	40-50	0	2	FCOM ST(1)
short-real	65	60-70	2	2-4	FCOM [BP].UPPER_LIMIT
long-real	70	65-75	4	2-4	FCOM WAVELENGTH

FCOMP

FCOMP //source
Compare real and pop Exceptions: I, D

Operands	Execution Clocks		Operand Word Transfers	Code Bytes	Coding Example
	Typical	Range			
//ST(i)	47	42-52	0	2	FCOMP ST(2)
short-real	68	63-73	2	2-4	FCOMP [BP + 2].N_READINGS
long-real	72	67-77	4	2-4	FCOMP DENSITY

FCOMPP

FCOMPP (no operands)
Compare real and pop twice Exceptions: I, D

Operands	Execution Clocks		Operand Word Transfers	Code Bytes	Coding Example
	Typical	Range			
(no operands)	50	45-55	0	2	FCOMPP

Table 2-14. Instruction Set Reference Data (Cont'd.)

FDECSTP	FDECSTP (no operands) Decrement stack pointer				Exceptions: None

Operands	Execution Clocks		Operand Word Transfers	Code Bytes	Coding Example
	Typical	Range			
(no operands)	9	6-12	0	2	FDECSTP

FDIV	FDIV //source/destination,source Divide real				Exceptions: I, D, Z, O, U, P

Operands	Execution Clocks		Operand Word Transfers	Code Bytes	Coding Example
	Typical	Range			
//ST(i),ST	198	193-203	0	2	FDIV
short-real	220	215-225	2	2-4	FDIV DISTANCE
long-real	225	220-230	4	2-4	FDIV ARC [DI]

FDIVP	FDIVP destination, source Divide real and pop				Exceptions: I, D, Z, O, U, P

Operands	Execution Clocks		Operand Word Transfers	Code Bytes	Coding Example
	Typical	Range			
ST(i),ST	202	197-207	0	2	FDIVP ST(4),ST

FDIVR	FDIVR //source/destination, source Divide real reversed				Exceptions: I, D, Z, O, U, P

Operands	Execution Clocks		Operand Word Transfers	Code Bytes	Coding Example
	Typical	Range			
//ST,ST(i)/ST(i),ST	199	194-204	0	2	FDIVR ST(2),ST
short-real	221	216-226	2	2-4	FDIVR [BX].PULSE_RATE
long-real	226	221-231	4	2-4	FDIVR RECORDER.FREQUENCY

FDIVRP	FDIVRP destination, source Divide real reversed and pop				Exceptions: I, D, Z, O, U, P

Operands	Execution Clocks		Operand Word Transfers	Code Bytes	Coding Example
	Typical	Range			
ST(i),ST	203	198-208	0	2	FDIVRP ST(1),ST

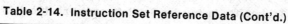

Table 2-14. Instruction Set Reference Data (Cont'd.)

FFREE

FFREE destination
Free register   Exceptions: None

Operands	Execution Clocks		Operand Word Transfers	Code Bytes	Coding Example
	Typical	Range			
ST(i)	11	9-16	0	2	FFREE ST(1)

FIADD

FIADD source
Integer add   Exceptions: I, D, O, P

Operands	Execution Clocks		Operand Word Transfers	Code Bytes	Coding Example
	Typical	Range			
word-integer	120	102-137	1	2-4	FIADD DISTANCE_TRAVELLED
short-integer	125	108-143	2	2-4	FIADD PULSE_COUNT [SI]

FICOM

FICOM source
Integer compare   Exceptions: I, D

Operands	Execution Clocks		Operand Word Transfers	Code Bytes	Coding Example
	Typical	Range			
word-integer	80	72-86	1	2-4	FICOM TOOL.N_PASSES
short-integer	85	78-91	2	2-4	FICOM [BP+4].PARM_COUNT

FICOMP

FICOMP source
Integer compare and pop   Exceptions: I, D

Operands	Execution Clocks		Operand Word Transfers	Code Bytes	Coding Example
	Typical	Range			
word-integer	82	74-88	1	2-4	FICOMP [BP].LIMIT [SI]
short-integer	87	80-93	2	2-4	FICOMP N_SAMPLES

FIDIV

FIDIV source
Integer divide   Exceptions: I, D, Z, O, U, P

Operands	Execution Clocks		Operand Word Transfers	Code Bytes	Coding Example
	Typical	Range			
word-integer	230	224-238	1	2-4	FIDIV SURVEY.OBSERVATIONS
short-integer	236	230-243	2	2-4	FIDIV RELATIVE_ANGLE [DI]

Table 2-14. Instruction Set Reference Data (Cont'd.)

FIDIVR

FIDIVR source
Integer divide reversed

Exceptions: I, D, Z, O, U, P

Operands	Execution Clocks		Operand Word Transfers	Code Bytes	Coding Example
	Typical	Range			
word-integer	230	225-239	1	2-4	FIDIVR [BP].X_COORD
short-integer	237	231-245	2	2-4	FIDIVR FREQUENCY

FILD

FILD source
Integer load

Exceptions: I

Operands	Execution Clocks		Operand Word Transfers	Code Bytes	Coding Example
	Typical	Range			
word-integer	50	46-54	1	2-4	FILD [BX].SEQUENCE
short-integer	56	52-60	2	2-4	FILD STANDOFF [DI]
long-integer	64	60-68	4	2-4	FILD RESPONSE.COUNT

FIMUL

FIMUL source
Integer multiply

Exceptions: I, D, O, P

Operands	Execution Clocks		Operand Word Transfers	Code Bytes	Coding Example
	Typical	Range			
word-integer	130	124-138	1	2-4	FIMUL BEARING
short-integer	136	130-144	2	2-4	FIMUL POSITION.Z_AXIS

FINCSTP

FINCSTP (no operands)
Increment stack pointer

Exceptions: None

Operands	Execution Clocks		Operand Word Transfers	Code Bytes	Coding Example
	Typical	Range			
(no operands)	9	6-12	0	2	FINCSTP

FINIT/FNINIT

FINIT/FNINIT (no operands)
Initialize processor

Exceptions: None

Operands	Execution Clocks		Operand Word Transfers	Code Bytes	Coding Example
	Typical	Range			
(no operands)	5	2-8	0	2	FINIT

Table 2-14. Instruction Set Reference Data (Cont'd.)

FIST

FIST destination
Integer store

Exceptions: I, P

Operands	Execution Clocks		Operand Word Transfers	Code Bytes	Coding Example
	Typical	Range			
word-integer	86	80-90	1	2-4	FIST OBS.COUNT[SI]
short-integer	88	82-92	2	2-4	FIST [BP;].FACTORED_PULSES

FISTP

FISTP destination
Integer store and pop

Exceptions: I, P

Operands	Execution Clocks		Operand Word Transfers	Code Bytes	Coding Example
	Typical	Range			
word-integer	88	82-92	1	2-4	FISTP [BX].ALPHA_COUNT [SI]
short-integer	90	84-94	2	2-4	FISTP CORRECTED_TIME
long-integer	100	94-105	4	2-4	FISTP PANEL.N_READINGS

FISUB

FISUB source
Integer subtract

Exceptions: I, D, O, P

Operands	Execution Clocks		Operand Word Transfers	Code Bytes	Coding Example
	Typical	Range			
word-integer	120	102-137	1	2-4	FISUB BASE_FREQUENCY
short-integer	125	108-143	2	2-4	FISUB TRAIN_SIZE [DI]

FISUBR

FISUBR source
Integer subtract reversed

Exceptions: I, D, O, P

Operands	Execution Clocks		Operand Word Transfers	Code Bytes	Coding Example
	Typical	Range			
word-integer	120	103-139	1	2-4	FISUBR FLOOR [BX] [SI]
short-integer	125	109-144	2	2-4	FISUBR BALANCE

Table 2-14. Instruction Set Reference Data (Cont'd.)

FLD

FLD source
Load real

Exceptions: I, D

Operands	Execution Clocks		Operand Word Transfers	Code Bytes	Coding Example
	Typical	Range			
ST(i)	20	17-22	0	2	FLD ST(0)
short-real	43	38-56	2	2-4	FLD READING [SI].PRESSURE
long-real	46	40-60	4	2-4	FLD [BP].TEMPERATURE
temp-real	57	53-65	5	2-4	FLD SAVEREADING

FLDCW

FLDCW source
Load control word

Exceptions: None

Operands	Execution Clocks		Operand Word Transfers	Code Bytes	Coding Example
	Typical	Range			
2-bytes	10	7-14	1	2-4	FLDCW CONTROL_WORD

FLDENV

FLDENV source
Load environment

Exceptions: None

Operands	Execution Clocks		Operand Word Transfers	Code Bytes	Coding Example
	Typical	Range			
14-bytes	40	35-45	7	2-4	FLDENV [BP + 6]

FLDLG2

FLDLG2 (no operands)
Load $\log_{10}2$

Exceptions: I

Operands	Execution Clocks		Operand Word Transfers	Code Bytes	Coding Example
	Typical	Range			
(no operands)	21	18-24	0	2	FLDLG2

FLDLN2

FLDLN2 (no operands)
Load $\log_{e}2$

Exceptions: I

Operands	Execution Clocks		Operand Word Transfers	Code Bytes	Coding Example
	Typical	Range			
(no operands)	20	17-23	0	2	FLDLN2

Table 2-14. Instruction Set Reference Data (Cont'd.)

FLDL2E

FLDL2E (no operands)
Load $\log_2 e$ Exceptions: I

Operands	Execution Clocks		Operand Word Transfers	Code Bytes	Coding Example
	Typical	Range			
(no operands)	18	15-21	0	2	FLDL2E

FLDL2T

FLDL2T (no operands)
Load $\log_2 10$ Exceptions: I

Operands	Execution Clocks		Operand Word Transfers	Code Bytes	Coding Example
	Typical	Range			
(no operands)	19	16-22	0	2	FLDL2T

FLDPI

FLDPI (no operands)
Load π Exceptions: I

Operands	Execution Clocks		Operand Word Transfers	Code Bytes	Coding Example
	Typical	Range			
(no operands)	19	16-22	0	2	FLDPI

FLDZ

FLDZ (no operands)
Load $+0.0$ Exceptions: I

Operands	Execution Clocks		Operand Word Transfers	Code Bytes	Coding Example
	Typical	Range			
(no operands)	14	11-17	0	2	FLDZ

FLD1

FLD1 (no operands)
Load $+1.0$ Exceptions: I

Operands	Execution Clocks		Operand Word Transfers	Code Bytes	Coding Example
	Typical	Range			
(no operands)	18	15-21	0	2	FLD1

Table 2-14. Instruction Set Reference Data (Cont'd.)

FMUL FMUL //source/destination,source
Multiply real
Exceptions: I, D, O, U, P

Operands	Execution Clocks		Operand Word Transfers	Code Bytes	Coding Example
	Typical	Range			
//ST(i),ST/ST,ST(i)[1]	97	90-105	0	2	FMUL ST,ST(3)
//ST(i),ST/ST,ST(i)	138	130-145	0	2	FMUL ST,ST(3)
short-real	118	110-125	2	2-4	FMUL SPEED_FACTOR
long-real[1]	120	112-126	4	2-4	FMUL [BP].HEIGHT
long-real	161	154-168	4	2-4	FMUL [BP].HEIGHT

FMULP FMULP destination, source
Multiply real and pop
Exceptions: I, D, O, U, P

Operands	Execution Clocks		Operand Word Transfers	Code Bytes	Coding Example
	Typical	Range			
ST(i),ST[1]	100	94-108	0	2	FMULP ST(1),ST
ST(i),ST	142	134-148	0	2	FMULP ST(1),ST

FNOP FNOP (no operands)
No operation
Exceptions: None

Operands	Execution Clocks		Operand Word Transfers	Code Bytes	Coding Example
	Typical	Range			
(no operands)	13	10-16	0	2	FNOP

FPATAN FPATAN (no operands)
Partial arctangent
Exceptions: U, P (operands not checked)

Operands	Execution Clocks		Operand Word Transfers	Code Bytes	Coding Example
	Typical	Range			
(no operands)	650	250-800	0	2	FPATAN

FPREM FPREM (no operands)
Partial remainder
Exceptions: I, D, U

Operands	Execution Clocks		Operand Word Transfers	Code Bytes	Coding Example
	Typical	Range			
(no operands)	125	15-190	0	2	FPREM

Table 2-14. Instruction Set Reference Data (Cont'd.)

FPTAN

FPTAN (no operands)
Partial tangent

Exceptions: I, P (operands not checked)

Operands	Execution Clocks		Operand Word Transfers	Code Bytes	Coding Example
	Typical	Range			
(no operands)	450	30-540	0	2	FPTAN

FRNDINT

FRNDINT (no operands)
Round to integer

Exceptions: I, P

Operands	Execution Clocks		Operand Word Transfers	Code Bytes	Coding Example
	Typical	Range			
(no operands)	45	16-50	0	2	FRNDINT

FRSTOR

FRSTOR source
Restore saved state

Exceptions: None

Operands	Execution Clocks		Operand Word Transfers	Code Bytes	Coding Example
	Typical	Range			
94-bytes		2	47	2-4	FRSTOR [BP]

FSAVE/FNSAVE

FSAVE/FNSAVE destination
Save state

Exceptions: None

Operands	Execution Clocks		Operand Word Transfers	Code Bytes	Coding Example
	Typical	Range			
94-bytes		3	47	2-4	FSAVE [BP]

FSCALE

FSCALE (no operands)
Scale

Exceptions: I, O, U

Operands	Execution Clocks		Operand Word Transfers	Code Bytes	Coding Example
	Typical	Range			
(no operands)	35	32-38	0	2	FSCALE

Table 2-14. Instruction Set Reference Data (Cont'd.)

FSETPM   FSETPM (no operands)   Exceptions: None
Set protected mode

Operands	Execution Clocks		Operand Word Transfers	Code Bytes	Coding Example
	Typical	Range			
(no operands)		2-8	0	2	FSETPM

FSQRT   FSQRT (no operands)   Exceptions: I, D, P
Square root

Operands	Execution Clocks		Operand Word Transfers	Code Bytes	Coding Example
	Typical	Range			
(no operands)	183	180-186	0	2	FSQRT

FST   FST destination   Exceptions: I, O, U, P
Store real

Operands	Execution Clocks		Operand Word Transfers	Code Bytes	Coding Example
	Typical	Range			
ST(i)	18	15-22	0	2	FST ST(3)
short-real	87	84-90	2	2-4	FST CORRELATION [DI]
long-real	100	96-104	4	2-4	FST MEAN_READING

FSTCW/
FNSTCW   FSTCW destination   Exceptions: None
Store control word

Operands	Execution Clocks		Operand Word Transfers	Code Bytes	Coding Example
	Typical	Range			
2-bytes	15	12-18	1	2-4	FSTCW SAVE_CONTROL

FSTENV/
FNSTENV   FSTENV destination   Exceptions: None
Store environment

Operands	Execution Clocks		Operand Word Transfers	Code Bytes	Coding Example
	Typical	Range			
14-bytes	45	40-50	7	2-4	FSTENV [BP]

Table 2-14. Instruction Set Reference Data (Cont'd.)

FSTP

FSTP destination
Store real and pop

Exceptions: I, O, U, P

Operands	Execution Clocks		Operand Word Transfers	Code Bytes	Coding Example
	Typical	Range			
ST(i)	20	17-24	0	2	FSTP ST(2)
short-real	89	86-92	2	2-4	FSTP [BX].ADJUSTED_RPM
long-real	102	98-106	4	2-4	FSTP TOTAL_DOSAGE
temp-real	55	52-58	5	2-4	FSTP REG_SAVE [SI]

FSTSW/ FNSTSW

FSTSW destination
Store status word

Exceptions: None

Operands	Execution Clocks		Operand Word Transfers	Code Bytes	Coding Example
	Typical	Range			
2-bytes	15	12-18	1	2-4	FSTSW SAVE_STATUS

FSTSW AX/ FNSTSWAX

FSTSW AX
Store status word to AX

Exceptions: None

Operands	Execution Clocks		Operand Word Transfers	Code Bytes	Coding Example
	Typical	Range			
AX		10-16	1	2	FSTSW AX

FSUB

FSUB //source/destination,source
Subtract real

Exceptions: I, D, O, U, P

Operands	Execution Clocks		Operand Word Transfers	Code Bytes	Coding Example
	Typical	Range			
//ST,ST(i)/ST(i),ST	85	70-100	0	2	FSUB ST,ST(2)
short-real	105	90-120	2	2-4	FSUB BASE_VALUE
long-real	110	95-125	4	2-4	FSUB COORDINATE.X

FSUBP

FSUBP destination, source
Subtract real and pop

Exceptions: I, D, O, U, P

Operands	Execution Clocks		Operand Word Transfers	Code Bytes	Coding Example
	Typical	Range			
ST(i),ST	90	75-105	0	2	FSUBP ST(2),ST

Table 2-14. Instruction Set Reference Data (Cont'd.)

FSUBR

FSUBR //source/destination, source
Subtract real reversed

Exceptions: I, D, O, U, P

Operands	Execution Clocks		Operand Word Transfers	Code Bytes	Coding Example
	Typical	Range			
//ST,ST(i)/ST(i),ST	87	70-100	0	2	FSUBR ST,ST(1)
short-real	105	90-120	2	2-4	FSUBR VECTOR[SI]
long-real	110	95-125	4	2-4	FSUBR [BX].INDEX

FSUBRP

FSUBRP destination, source
Subtract real reversed and pop

Exceptions: I, D, O, U, P

Operands	Execution Clocks		Operand Word Transfers	Code Bytes	Coding Example
	Typical	Range			
ST(i),ST	90	75-105	0	2	FSUBRP ST(1),ST

FTST

FTST (no operands)
Test stack top against +0.0

Exceptions: I, D

Operands	Execution Clocks		Operand Word Transfers	Code Bytes	Coding Example
	Typical	Range			
(no operands)	42	38-48	0	2	FTST

FWAIT

FWAIT (no operands)
(CPU) Wait while 80287 is busy

Exceptions: None (CPU instruction)

Operands	Execution Clocks		Operand Word Transfers	Code Bytes	Coding Example
	Typical	Range			
(no operands)	$3+5n$*	$3+5n^4$	0	1	FWAIT

FXAM

FXAM (no operands)
Examine stack top

Exceptions: None

Operands	Execution Clocks		Operand Word Transfers	Code Bytes	Coding Example
	Typical	Range			
(no operands)	17	12-23	0	2	FXAM

Table 2-14. Instruction Set Reference Data (Cont'd.)

FXCH	FXCH //destination Exchange registers				Exceptions: I

Operands	Execution Clocks		Operand Word Transfers	Code Bytes	Coding Example
	Typical	Range			
//ST(i)	12	10-15	0	2	FXCH ST(2)

FXTRACT	FXTRACT (no operands) Extract exponent and significant				Exceptions: I

Operands	Execution Clocks		Operand Word Transfers	Code Bytes	Coding Example
	Typical	Range			
(no operands)	50	27-55	0	2	FXTRACT

FYL2X	FYL2X (no operands) $Y \cdot \log_2 X$				Exceptions: P (operands not checked)

Operands	Execution Clocks		Operand Word Transfers	Code Bytes	Coding Example
	Typical	Range			
(no operands)	950	900-1100	0	2	FYL2X

FYL2XP1	FYL2XP1 (no operands) $Y \cdot \log_2(X + 1)$				Exceptions: P (operands not checked)

Operands	Execution Clocks		Operand Word Transfers	Code Bytes	Coding Example
	Typical	Range			
(no operands)	850	700-1000	0	2	FYL2XP1

F2XM1	F2XM1 (no operands) $2^x - 1$				Exceptions: U, P (operands not checked)

Operands	Execution Clocks		Operand Word Transfers	Code Bytes	Coding Example
	Typical	Range			
(no operands)	500	310-630	0	2	F2XM1

[1]Occurs when one or both operands is "short"—it has 40 trailing zeros in its fraction (e.g., it was loaded from a short-real memory operand.

[2]The 80287 execution clock count for this instruction is not meaningful in determining overall instruction execution time. For typical frequency ratios of the 80286 and 80287 clocks, 80287 execution occurs in parallel with the operand transfers, with the operand transfers determining the overall execution time of the instruction. For 80286:80287 clock frequency ratios of 4:8, 1:1, and 8:5, the overall execution clock count for this instruction is estimated at 490, 302, and 227 80287 clocks, respectively.

[3]The 80287 execution clock count for this instruction is not meaningful in determining overall instruction execution time. For typical frequency rations of the 80286 and 80287 clocks, 80287 execution occurs in parallel with the operand transfers, with the operand transfers determining the overall execution time of the instruction. For 80286:80287 clock frequency ratios of 4:8, 1:1, and 8:5, the overall execution clock count for this instruction is estimated at 376, 233, and 174 80287 clocks, respectively.

[4]n = number of times CPU examines $\overline{\text{BUSY}}$ line before 80287 completes execution of previous instruction.

PROGRAMMING FACILITIES

As described previously, the 80287 NPX is programmed simply as an extension of the 80286 CPU. This section describes how programmers in ASM286 and in a variety of higher-level languages can work with the 80287.

The level of detail in this section is intended to give programmers a basic understanding of the software tools that can be used with the 80287, but this information does not document the full capabilities of these facilities. For a complete list of documentation on all the languages available for 80286 systems, readers should consult Intel's *Literature Guide*.

High-Level Languages

For programmers using high-level languages, the programming and operation of the NPX is handled automatically by the compiler. A variety of Intel high-level languages are available that automatically make use of the 80287 NPX when appropriate. These languages include

> PL/M-286
> FORTRAN-286
> PASCAL-286
> C-286

Each of these high-level languages has special numeric libraries allowing programs to take advantage of the capabilities of the 80287 NPX. No special programming conventions are necessary to make use of the 80287 NPX when programming numeric applications in any of these languages.

Programmers in PL/M-286 and ASM286 can also make use of many of these library routines by using routines contained in the 80287 Support Library, described in the *80287 Support Library Reference Manual*, Order Number 122129. These library routines provide many of the functions provided by higher-level languages, including exception handlers, ASCII-to-floating-point conversions, and a more complete set of transcendental functions than that provided by the 80287 instruction set.

PL/M-286

Programmers in PL/M-286 can access a very useful subset of the 80287's numeric capabilities. The PL/M-286 REAL data type corresponds to the NPX's short real (32-bit) format. This data type provides a range of about $8.43*10^{-37} \leq ABS(X) \leq 3.38*10^{38}$, with about seven significant decimal digits. This representation is adequate for the data manipulated by many microcomputer applications.

The utility of the REAL data type is extended by the PL/M-286 compiler's practice of holding intermediate results in the 80287's temporary real format. This means that the full range and precision of the processor are utilized for intermediate results. Underflow, overflow, and rounding errors are most likely to occur during intermediate computations rather than during calculation of an expression's final result. Holding intermediate results in temporary real format greatly reduces the likelihood of overflow and underflow and eliminates roundoff as a serious source of error until the final assignment of the result is performed.

The compiler generates 80287 code to evaluate expressions that contain REAL data types, whether variables or constants or both. This means that addition, subtraction, multiplication, division, comparison, and assignment of REALs will be performed by the NPX. INTEGER expressions, on the other hand, are evaluated on the CPU.

Five built-in procedures (table 2-15) give the PL/M-286 programmer access to 80287 functions manipulated by the processor control instructions. Prior to any arithmetic operations, a typical PL/M-286 program will set up the NPX after power up using the INIT$REAL$MATH$UNIT procedure and then issue SET$REAL$MODE to configure the NPX. SET$REAL$MODE loads the 80287 control word, and its 16-bit parameter has the format shown in figure 1-5. The recommended value of this parameter is 033EH (projective closure, round to nearest, 64-bit precision, all exceptions masked except invalid operation). Other settings may be used at the programmer's discretion.

If any exceptions are unmasked, an exception handler must be provided in the form of an interrupt procedure that is designated to be invoked by CPU interrupt pointer (vector) number 16. The exception handler can use the GET$REAL$ERROR procedure to obtain the low-order byte of the 80287 status word and to then clear the exception flags. The byte returned by GET$REAL$ERROR contains the exception flags; these can be examined to determine the source of the exception.

The SAVE$REAL$STATUS and RESTORE$REAL$STATUS procedures are provided for multi-tasking environments where a running task that uses the 80287 may be preempted by another task that also uses the 80287. It is the responsibility of the preempting task to issue SAVE$REAL$STATUS before it executes any statements that affect the 80287; these include the INIT$REAL$MATH$UNIT

Table 2-15. PL/M-286 Built-In Procedures

Procedure	80287 Instruction	Description
INIT$REAL$MATH$UNIT[1]	FINIT	Initialize processor.
SET$REAL$MODE	FLDCW	Set exception masks, rounding precision, and infinity controls.
GET$REAL$ERROR[2]	FNSTSW & FNCLEX	Store, then clear, exception flags.
SAVE$REAL$STATUS	FNSAVE	Save processor state.
RESTORE$REAL$STATUS	FRSTOR	Restore processor state.

[1]Also initializes interrupt pointers for emulation.
[2]Returns low-order byte of status word.

and SET$REAL$MODE procedures as well as arithmetic expressions. SAVE$REAL$STATUS saves the 80287 state (registers, status, and control words, etc.) on the CPU's stack. RESTORE$REAL$STATUS reloads the state information; the preempting task must invoke this procedure before terminating in order to restore the 80287 to its state at the time the running task was preempted. This enables the preempted task to resume execution from the point of its preemption.

ASM286

The ASM286 assembly language provides programmmers with complete access to all of the facilities of the 80286 and 80287 processors.

The programmer's view of the 80286/80287 hardware is a single machine with these resources:

- 160 instructions
- 12 data types
- 8 general registers
- 4 segment registers
- 8 floating-point registers, organized as a stack

DEFINING DATA

The ASM286 directives shown in table 2-16 allocate storage for 80287 variables and constants. As with other storage allocation directives, the assembler associates a type with any variable defined with these directives. The type value is equal to the length of the storage unit in bytes (10 for DT, 8 for DQ, etc.). The assembler checks the type of any variable coded in an instruction to be certain that it is compatible with the instruction. For example, the coding FIADD ALPHA will be flagged as an error if ALPHA's type is not 2 or 4, because integer addition is only available for word and short integer data types. The operand's type also tells the assembler which machine instruction to produce; although to the programmer there is only an FIADD instruction, a different machine instruction is required for each operand type.

On occasion it is desirable to use an instruction with an operand that has no declared type. For example, if register BX points to a short integer variable, a programmer may want to code FIADD [BX]. This can be done by informing the assembler of the operand's type in the instruction, coding FIADD DWORD PTR [BX]. The corresponding overrides for the other storage allocations are WORD PTR, QWORD PTR, and TBYTE PTR.

Table 2-16. 80287 Storage Allocation Directives

Directive	Interpretation	Data Types
DW	Define Word	Word integer
DD	Define Doubleword	Short integer, short real
DQ	Define Quadword	Long integer, long real
DT	Define Tenbyte	Packed decimal, temporary real

The assembler does not, however, check the types of operands used in processor control instructions. Coding FRSTOR [BP] implies that the programmer has set up register BP to point to the stack location where the processor's 94-byte state record has been previously saved.

The initial values for 80287 constants may be coded in several different ways. Binary integer constants may be specified as bit strings, decimal integers, octal integers, or hexadecimal strings. Packed decimal values are normally written as decimal integers, although the assembler will accept and convert other representations of integers. Real values may be written as ordinary decimal real numbers (decimal point required), as decimal numbers in scientific notation, or as hexadecimal strings. Using hexadecimal strings is primarily intended for defining special values such as infinities, NaNs, and nonnormalized numbers. Most programmers will find that ordinary decimal and scientific decimal provide the simplest way to initialize 80287 constants. Figure 2-3 compares several ways of setting the various 80287 data types to the same initial value.

Note that preceding 80287 variables and constants with the ASM286 EVEN directive ensures that the operands will be word-aligned in memory. This will produce the best system performance. All 80287 data types occupy integral numbers of words so that no storage is "wasted" if blocks of variables are defined together and preceded by a single EVEN declarative.

RECORDS AND STRUCTURES

The ASM286 RECORD and STRUC (structure) declaratives can be very useful in NPX programming. The record facility can be used to define the bit fields of the control, status, and tag words. Figure 2-4 shows one definition of the status word and how it might be used in a routine that polls the 80287 until it has completed an instruction.

Because STRUCtures allow different but related data types to be grouped together, they often provide a natural way to represent "real world" data organizations. The fact that the structure template may be "moved" about in memory adds to its flexibility. Figure 2-5 shows a simple structure that might be used to represent data consisting of a series of test score samples. A structure could also be used to define the organization of the information stored and loaded by the FSTENV and FLDENV instructions.

```
; THE FOLLOWING ALL ALLOCATE THE CONSTANT: -126
; NOTE TWO'S COMPLETE STORAGE OF NEGATIVE BINARY INTEGERS.
;
; EVEN                              ; FORCE WORD ALIGNMENT
WORD_INTEGER      DW  1111111111000010B ; BIT STRING
SHORT_INTEGER     DD  0FFFFFF82H     ; HEX STRING MUST START
                                     ; WITH DIGIT
LONG_INTEGER      DQ  -126           ; ORDINARY DECIMAL
SHORT_REAL        DD  -126.0         ; NOTE PRESENCE OF '.'
LONG_REAL         DD  -1.26E2        ; "SCIENTIFIC"
PACKED_DECIMAL DT   -126             ; ORDINARY DECIMAL INTEGER
; IN THE FOLLOWING, SIGN AND EXPONENT IS 'C005'
;     SIGNIFICAND IS '7E00...00', 'R' INFORMS ASSEMBLER THAT
;     THE STRING REPRESENTS A REAL DATA TYPE.
;
TEMP_REAL         DT  0C0057E00000000000000R  ; HEX STRING
```

Figure 2-3. Sample 80287 Constants

```
; RESERVE SPACE FOR STATUS WORD
STATUS_WORD
; LAY OUT STATUS WORD FIELDS
STATUS RECORD
&       BUSY:               1,
&       COND_CODE3:         1,
&       STACK_TOP:          3,
&       COND_CODE2:         1,
&       COND_CODE1:         1,
&       COND_CODE0:         1,
&       INT_REQ:            1,
&       RESERVED:           1,
&       P_FLAG:             1,
&       U_FLAG:             1,
&       O_FLAG:             1,
&       Z_FLAG:             1,
&       D_FLAG:             1,
&       I_FLAG:             1
; POLL STATUS WORD UNTIL 80287 IS NOT BUSY
POLL:   FNSTSW    STATUS_WORD
        TEST      STATUS_WORD, MASK_BUSY
        JNZ       POLL
```

Figure 2-4. Status Word RECORD Definition

```
SAMPLE      STRUC

    N_OBS           DD      ?   ; SHORT INTEGER
    MEAN            DQ      ?   ; LONG REAL
    MODE            DW      ?   ; WORD INTEGER
    STD_DEV         DQ      ?   ; LONG REAL
    ; ARRAY OF OBSERVATIONS -- WORD INTEGER
    TEST_SCORES     DW      1000 DUP (?)
SAMPLE ENDS
```

Figure 2-5. Structure Definition

ADDRESSING MODES

80287 memory data can be accessed with any of the CPU's five memory addressing modes. This means that 80287 data types can be incorporated in data aggregates ranging from simple to complex according to the needs of the application. The addressing modes, and the ASM286 notation used to specify them in instructions, make the accessing of structures, arrays, arrays of structures, and other organizations direct and straightforward. Table 2-17 gives several examples of 80287 instructions coded with operands that illustrate different addressing modes.

Table 2-17. Addressing Mode Examples

Coding		Interpretation
FIADD	ALPHA	ALPHA is a simple scalar (mode is direct).
FDIVR	ALPHA.BETA	BETA is a field in a structure that is "overlaid" on ALPHA (mode is direct).
FMUL	QWORD PTR [BX]	BX contains the address of a long real variable (mode is register indirect).
FSUB	ALPHA [SI]	ALPHA is an array and SI contains the offset of an array element from the start of the array (mode is indexed).
FILD	[BP].BETA	BP contains the address of a structure on the CPU stack and BETA is a field in the structure (mode is based).
FBLD	TBYTE PTR [BX] [DI]	BX contains the address of a packed decimal array and DI contains the offset of an array element (mode is based indexed).

Comparative Programming Example

Figures 2-6 and 2-7 show the PL/M-286 and ASM286 code for a simple 80287 program, called ARRSUM. The program references an array (X$ARRAY), which contains 0–100 short real values; the integer variable NOFX indicates the number of array elements the program is to consider. ARRSUM steps through X$ARRAY accumulating three sums:

- SUM$X, the sum of the array values

- SUM$INDEXES, the sum of each array value times its index, where the index of the first element is 1, the second is 2, etc.

- SUM$SQUARES, the sum of each array element squared

(A true program, of course, would go beyond these steps to store and use the results of these calculations.) The control word is set with the recommended values: projective closure, round to nearest, 64-bit precision, interrupts enabled, and all exceptions masked invalid operation. It is assumed that an exception handler has been written to field the invalid operation, if it occurs, and that it is invoked by interrupt pointer 16. Either version of the program will run on an actual or an emulated 80287 without altering the code shown.

The PL/M-286 version of ARRSUM (figure 2-6) is very straightforward and illustrates how easily the 80287 can be used in this language. After declaring variables the program calls built-in procedures to initialize the processor (or its emulator) and to load to the control word. The program clears the sum variables and then steps through X$ARRAY with a DO-loop. The loop control takes into account PL/M-286's practice of considering the index of the first element of an array to be 0. In the computation of SUM$INDEXES, the built-in procedure FLOAT converts I+1 from integer to real because the language does not support "mixed mode" arithmetic. One of the strengths of the NPX, of course, is that it *does* support arithmetic on mixed data types (because all values are converted internally to the 80-bit temporary real format).

```
PL/M-286 COMPILER    ARRAYSUM


SERIES-III PL/M-286 V1.0 COMPILATION OF MODULE ARRAYSUM
OBJECT MODULE PLACED IN :F6:D.OBJ
COMPILER INVOKED BY:  PLM286 86 :F6:D.SRC XREF



         /******************************************************
         *                                                     *
         *     A R R A Y S U M   M O D                         *
         *                                                     *
         ******************************************************/

  1      array$sum: do;

  2  1   declare (sum$x,sum$indexes,sum$squares) real;
  3  1   declare x$array(100) real;
  4  1   declare (n$of$x,i) integer;
  5  1   declare control$287 literally '033eh';

         /* Assume x$array and n$of$x are initialized */

         /* Prepare the 80287 of its emulator */
  6  1   call init$real$math$unit;
  7  1   call set$real$mode(control$287);

         /* Clear sums */
  8  1   sum$x, sum$indexes, sum$squares = 0.0;

         /* Loop through array, accumulating sums */
  9  1   do i = 0 to n$of$x-1;
 10  2     sum$x = sum$x + x$array(i);
 11  2     sum$indexes = sum$indexes +
                 (x$array(i) * float(i+1));
 12  2     sum$squares = sum$squares + (x$array(i)*x$array(i));
 13  2   end;

         /* etc. */

 14  1   end array$sum;


PL/M-286 COMPILER    ARRAYSUM
                     CROSS-REFERENCE LISTING


 DEFN  ADDR   SIZE  NAME, ATTRIBUTES, AND REFERENCES
 ----  -----  ----  --------------------------------


  1  0006H  117  ARRAYSUM . . . . . . .    PROCEDURE STACK=0002H
  5               CONTROL287 . . . . . .   LITERALLY '033eh'      7
                  FLOAT. . . . . . . . .   BUILTIN       11
  4  019EH    2  I. . . . . . . . . . .    INTEGER          9*   9  10  11  12  13
                  INITREALMATHUNIT . . .   BUILTIN        6
  4  019CH    2  NOFX . . . . . . . . .    INTEGER          9
                  SETREALMODE. . . . . .   BUILTIN        7
  2  0004H    4  SUMINDEXES . . . . . .    REAL        8*   11  11*
  2  0008H    4  SUMSQUARES . . . . . .    REAL        8*   12  12*
  2  0000H    4  SUMX . . . . . . . . .    REAL        8*   10  10*
  3  000CH  400  XARRAY . . . . . . . .    REAL ARRAY(100)      10  11  12


MODULE INFORMATION:

    CODE AREA SIZE     = 0077H    119D
    CONSTANT AREA SIZE = 0004H      4D
    VARIABLE AREA SIZE = 01A0H    416D
    MAXIMUM STACK SIZE = 0002H      2D
    33 LINES READ
    0 PROGRAM WARNINGS
    0 PROGRAM ERRORS

DICTIONARY SUMMARY:

    96KB MEMORY AVAILABLE
    3KB MEMORY USED  (3%)
    0KB DISK SPACE USED

END OF PL/M-286 COMPILATION
```

Figure 2-6. Sample PL/M-286 Program

The ASM286 version (figure 2-7) defines the external procedure INIT287, which makes the different initialization requirements of the processor and its emulator transparent to the source code. After defining the data and setting up the segment registers and stack pointer, the program calls INIT287 and loads the control word. The computation begins with the next three instructions, which clear three registers by loading (pushing) zeros onto the stack. As shown in figure 2-8, these registers remain at the bottom of the stack throughout the computation while temporary values are pushed on and popped off the stack above them.

The program uses the CPU LOOP instruction to control its iteration through X_ARRAY; register CX, which LOOP automatically decrements, is loaded with N_OF_X, the number of array elements to be summed. Register SI is used to select (index) the array elements. The program steps through X_ARRAY from back to front, so SI is initialized to point at the element just beyond the first element to be processed. The ASM286 TYPE operator is used to determine the number of bytes in each array element. This permits changing X_ARRAY to a long real array by simply changing its definition (DD to DQ) and reassembling.

Figure 2-8 shows the effect of the instructions in the program loop on the NPX register stack. The figure assumes that the program is in its first iteration, that N_OF_X is 20, and that X_ARRAY(19) (the 20th element) contains the value 2.5. When the loop terminates, the three sums are left as the top stack elements so that the program ends by simply popping them into memory variables.

80287 Emulation

The programming of applications to execute on both 80286 and 80287 is made much easier by the existence of an 80287 emulator for 80286 systems. The Intel E80287 emulator offers a complete software counterpart to the 80287 hardware; NPX instructions can be simply emulated in software rather than being executed in hardware. With software emulation, the distinction between 80286 and 80287 systems is reduced to a simple performance differential (see Table 1-2 for a performance comparison between an actual 80287 and an emulator 80287). Identical numeric programs will simply execute more slowly on 80286 systems (using software emulation of NPX instructions) than on executing NPX instructions directly.

When incorporated into the systems software, the emulation of NPX instructions on the 80286 systems is completely transparent to the programmer. Applications software needs no special libraries, linking, or other activity to allow it to run on an 80286 with 80287 emulation.

To the applications programmer, the development of programs for 80286 systems is the same whether the 80287 NPX hardware is available or not. The full 80287 instruction set is available for use, with NPX instructions being either emulated or executed directly. Applications programmers need not be concerned with the hardware configuration of the computer systems on which their applications will eventually run.

For systems programmers, details relating to 80287 emulators are described in a later section of this supplement. An E80287 software emulator for 80286 systems is contained in the iMDX 364 8086 Software Toolbox, available from Intel and described in the *8086 Software Toolbox Manual*.

CONCURRENT PROCESSING WITH THE 80287

Because the 80286 CPU and the 80287 NPX have separate execution units, it is possible for the NPX to execute numeric instructions in parallel with instructions executed by the CPU. This simultaneous execution of different instructions is called concurrency.

```
iAPX286 MACRO ASSEMBLER    EXAMPLE_ASM286_PROGRAM


SERIES-III iAPX286 MACRO ASSEMBLER X108 ASSEMBLY OF MODULE EXAMPLE_ASM286_PROGRAM
OBJECT MODULE PLACED IN :F6:287EXP.OBJ
ASSEMBLER INVOKED BY:   ASM286.86 :F6:287EXP.SRC XREF


LOC  OBJ                    LINE    SOURCE

                           1                name    example_ASM286_program
                           2        ; Define initialization routine
                           3                extrn   init287:far
                           4
                           5        ; Allocate space for data
----                       6        data    segment rw public
0000 3E03                  7        control_287     dw      033eh
0002 ????                  8        n_of_x          dw      ?
0004 (100                  9        x_array         dd      100 dup (?)
     ????????
     )
0194 ????????              10       sum_squares     dd      ?
0198 ????????              11       sum_indexes     dd      ?
019C ????????              12       sum_x           dd      ?
----                       13       data    ends
                           14
                           15       ; Allocate CPU stack space
----                       16       stack   stackseg 400
                           17
                           18       ; Begin code
----                       19       code    segment er public
                           20               assume ds: data, ss: stack, es: nothing
0000                       21       start:
0000 B8----     R          22               mov     ax,data
0003 8ED8                  23               mov     ds,ax
0005 B8----     R          24               mov     ax,stack
0008 8ED0                  25               mov     ss,ax
000A BCFEFF     R          26               mov     sp,stackstart stack
                           27
                           28       ; Assume x_array and n_of_x are initialized
                           29       ;   this pprogram zeroes n_of_x
                           30
                           31       ; Prepare the 80287 or its emulator.
000D 9A0000----  E         32               call    init287
0012 D92E0000    R         33               fldcw   control_287
                           34
                           35       ; Clear three registers to hold running sums
0016 D9EE                  36               fldz
0018 D9EE                  37               fldz
001A D9EE                  38               fldz
                           39
                           40       ; Setup CX as loop counter and
                           41       ; SI as index to x_array
001C 8B0E0200    R         42               mov     cx,n_of_x
0020 F7E9                  43               imul    cx
0022 8BF0                  44               mov     si,ax
                           45
                           46       ; SI now contains index of last element + 1
                           47       ; Loop thru x_array, accumulating sums
0024                       48       sum_next:
0024 83EE04                49               sub     si,type x_array ;backup one element
0027 D9840400    R         50               fld     x_array[si]     ;push it on the stack
002B DCC3                  51               fadd    st(3),st        ;add into sum of x
002D D9C0                  52               fld     st              ;duplicate x on top
002F DCC8                  53               fmul    st,st           ;square it
0031 DEC2                  54               faddp   st(2),st        ;add into sum of (index+x)
                           55                                       ; and discard
0033 FF0E0200    R         56               dec     n_of_x          ;reduce index for next iteration
0037 E2EB                  57               loop    sum_next        ;continue
                           58
                           59       ; Pop running sums into memory
0039                       60       pop_results:
0039 D91E9401    R         61               fstp    sum_squares
003D D91E9801    R         62               fstp    sum_indexes
0041 D91E9C01    R         63               fstp    sum_x
0045 9B                    64               fwait
                           65
                           66       ;
                           67       ; Etc.
                           68       ;
----                       69       code    ends
                           70               end     start
```

Figure 2-7. Sample ASM286 Program

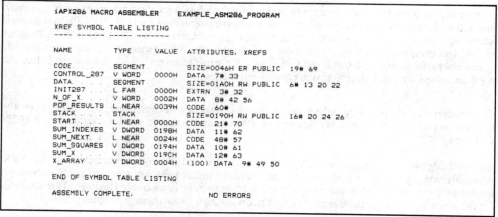

```
iAPX286 MACRO ASSEMBLER     EXAMPLE_ASM286_PROGRAM

XREF SYMBOL TABLE LISTING
---- ------ ----- -------

NAME          TYPE     VALUE   ATTRIBUTES, XREFS

CODE . . .    SEGMENT          SIZE=0046H ER PUBLIC   19# 69
CONTROL_287   V WORD   0000H   DATA  7# 33
DATA. . .     SEGMENT          SIZE=01A0H RW PUBLIC   6# 13 20 22
INIT287       L FAR    0000H   EXTRN  3# 32
N_OF_X . .    V WORD   0002H   DATA  8# 42 56
POP_RESULTS   L NEAR   0039H   CODE  60#
STACK . . .   STACK            SIZE=0190H RW PUBLIC   16# 20 24 26
START . . .   L NEAR   0000H   CODE  21# 70
SUM_INDEXES   V DWORD  0198H   DATA  11# 62
SUM_NEXT.     L NEAR   0024H   CODE  48# 57
SUM_SQUARES   V DWORD  0194H   DATA  10# 61
SUM_X . .     V DWORD  019CH   DATA  12# 63
X_ARRAY . .   V DWORD  0004H   (100) DATA  9# 49 50

END OF SYMBOL TABLE LISTING

ASSEMBLY COMPLETE,               NO ERRORS
```

Figure 2-7. Sample ASM286 Program (Cont'd.)

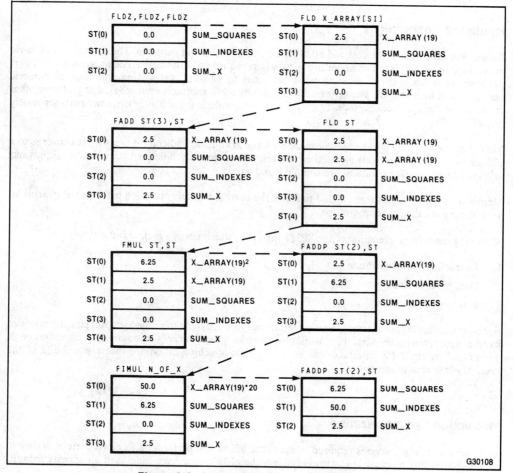

Figure 2-8. Instructions and Register Stack

No special programming techniques are required to gain the advantages of concurrent execution; numeric instructions for the NPX are simply placed in line with the instructions for the CPU. CPU and numeric instructions are initiated in the same order as they are encountered by the CPU in its instruction stream. However, because numeric operations performed by the NPX generally require more time than operations performed by the CPU, the CPU can often execute several of its instructions before the NPX completes a numeric instruction previously initiated.

This concurrency offers obvious advantages in terms of execution performance, but concurrency also imposes several rules that must be observed in order to assure proper synchronization of the 80286 CPU and 80287 NPX.

All Intel high-level languages automatically provide for and manage concurrency in the NPX. Assembly-language programmers, however, must understand and manage some areas of concurrency in exchange for the flexibility and performance of programming in assembly language. This section is for the assembly-language programmer or well-informed high-level-language programmer.

Managing Concurrency

Concurrent execution of the host and 80287 is easy to establish and maintain. The activities of numeric programs can be split into two major areas: program control and arithmetic. The program control part performs activities such as deciding what functions to perform, calculating addresses of numeric operands, and loop control. The arithmetic part simply adds, subtracts, multiplies, and performs other operations on the numeric operands. The NPX and host are designed to handle these two parts separately and efficiently.

Managing concurrency is necessary because both the arithmetic and control areas must converge to a well-defined state before starting another numeric operation. A well-defined state means all previous arithmetic and control operations are complete and valid.

Normally, the host waits for the 80287 to finish the current numeric operation before starting another. This waiting is called synchronization.

Managing concurrent execution of the 80287 involves three types of synchronization:

1. Instruction synchronization
2. Data synchronization
3. Error synchronization

For programmers in higher-level languages, all three types of synchronization are automatically provided by the appropriate compiler. For assembly-language programmers, instruction synchronization is guaranteed by the NPX interface, but data and error synchronization are the responsibility of the assembly-language programmer.

Instruction Synchronization

Instruction synchronization is required because the 80287 can perform only one numeric operation at a time. Before any numeric operation is started, the 80287 must have completed all activity from its previous instruction.

Instruction synchronization is guaranteed for most ESC instructions because the 80286 automatically checks the BUSY status line from the 80287 before commencing execution of most ESC instructions. No explicit WAIT instructions are necessary to ensure proper instruction synchronization.

Data Synchronization

Data synchronization addresses the issue of both the CPU and the NPX referencing the same memory values within a given block of code. Synchronization ensures that these two processors access the memory operands in the proper sequence, just as they would be accessed by a single processor with no concurrency. Data synchronization is not a concern when the CPU and NPX are using different memory operands during the course of one numeric instruction.

The two cases where data synchronization might be a concern are

1. The 80286 CPU reads or alters a memory operand first, then invokes the 80287 to load or alter the same operand.

2. The 80287 is invoked to load or alter a memory operand, after which the 80286 CPU reads or alters the same location.

Due to the instruction synchronization of the NPX interface, data synchronization is automatically provided for the first case—the 80286 will always complete its operation before invoking the 80287.

For the second case, data synchronization is not always automatic. In general, there is no guarantee that the 80287 will have finished its processing and accessed the memory operand before the 80286 accesses the same location.

Figure 2-9 shows examples of the two possible cases of the CPU and NPX sharing a memory value. In the examples of the first case, the CPU will finish with the operand before the 80287 can reference it. The NPX interface guarantees this. In the examples of the second case, the CPU must wait for the 80287 to finish with the memory operand before proceeding to reuse it. The FWAIT instructions shown in these examples are required in order to ensure this data synchronization.

There are several NPX control instructions where automatic data synchronization is provided; however, the FSTSW/FNSTSW, FSTCW/FNSTCW, FLDCW, FRSTOR, and FLDENV instructions are all guaranteed to finish their execution before the CPU can read or alter the referenced memory locations.

The 80287 provides data synchronization for these instructions by making a request on the Processor Extension Data Channel before the CPU executes its next instruction. Since the NPX data transfers occur before the CPU regains control of the local bus, the CPU cannot change a memory value before the NPX has had a chance to reference it. In the case of the FSTSW AX instruction, the 80286 AX register is explicitly updated before the CPU continues execution of the next instruction.

For the numeric instructions not listed above, the assembly-language programmer must remain aware of synchronization and recognize cases requiring explicit data synchronization. Data synchronization can be provided either by programming an explicit FWAIT instruction, or by initiating a subsequent numeric instruction before accessing the operands or results of a previous instruction. After the subsequent numeric instruction has started execution, all memory references in earlier numeric instructions are complete. Reaching the next host instruction after the synchronizing numeric instruction indicates that previous numeric operands in memory are available.

```
     Case 1:                         Case 2:
            MOV    I, 1                     FILD    I
            FILD   I                        FWAIT
                                            MOV     I., 5


            MOV    AX, I                    FISTP   I
            FISTP  I                        FWAIT
                                            MOV     AX, I
```

Figure 2-9. Synchronizing References to Shared Data

The data-synchronization function of any FWAIT or numeric instruction must be well-documented, as shown in figure 2-10. Otherwise, a change to the program at a later time may remove the synchronizing numeric instruction and cause program failure.

High-level languages automatically establish data synchronization and manage it, but there may be applications where a high-level language may not be appropriate.

For assembly-language programmers, *automatic* data synchronization can be obtained using the assembler, although concurrency of execution is lost as a result. To perform automatic data synchronization, the assembler can be changed to always place a WAIT instruction after the ESCAPE instruction. Figure 2-11 shows an example of how to change the ASM286 Code Macro for the FIST instruction to automatically place a WAIT instruction after the ESCAPE instruction. This Code Macro is included in the ASM286 source module. The price paid for this automatic data synchronization is the lack of any possible concurrency between the CPU and NPX.

Error Synchronization

Almost any numeric instruction can, under the wrong circumstances, produce a numeric error. Concurrent execution of the CPU and NPX requires synchronization for these errors just as it does for data references and numeric instructions. In fact, the synchronization required for data and instructions automatically provides error synchronization.

However, incorrect data or instruction synchronization may not be discovered until a numeric error occurs. A further complication is that a programmer may not expect his numeric program to cause numeric errors, but in some systems, they may regularly happen. To better understand these points, let's look at what can happen when the NPX detects an error.

The NPX can perform one of two things when a numeric exception occurs:

- The NPX can provide a default fix-up for selected numeric errors. Programs can mask individual error types to indicate that the NPX should generate a safe, reasonable result whenever that error occurs. The default error fix-up activity is treated by the NPX as part of the instruction causing the error; no external indication of the error is given. When errors are detected, a flag is set in the numeric status register, but no information regarding where or when is available. If the NPX performs its default action for all errors, then error synchronization is never exercised. This is no reason to ignore error synchronization, however.

```
FISTP   I
FMUL        ; I is updated before FMUL is executed
MOV     AX,I  ; I is now safe to use
```

Figure 2-10. Documenting Data Synchronization

```
;
; This is an ASM286 code macro to redefine the FIST
; instruction to prevent any concurrency
; while the instruction runs. A wait
; instruction is placed immediately after the
; escape to ensure the store is done
; before the program may continue.
;
CodeMacro FIST memop: Mw
RfixM 111B, memop
ModRM 010B, memop
RWfix
EndM
```

Figure 2-11. Nonconcurrent FIST Instruction Code Macro

- As an alternative to the NPX default fix-up of numeric errors, the 80286 CPU can be notified whenever an exception occurs. The CPU can then implement any sort of recovery procedures desired, for any numeric error detectable by the NPX. When a numeric error is unmasked and the error occurs, the NPX stops further execution of the numeric instruction and signals this event to the CPU. On the next occurrence of an ESC or WAIT instruction, the CPU traps to a software exception handler. Some ESC instructions do not check for errors. These are the nonwaited forms FNINIT, FNSTENV, FNSAVE, FNSTSW, FNSTCW, and FNCLEX.

When the NPX signals an unmasked exception condition, it is requesting help. The fact that the error was unmasked indicates that further numeric program execution under the arithmetic and programming rules of the NPX is unreasonable.

If concurrent execution is allowed, the state of the CPU when it recognizes the exception is undefined. The CPU may have changed many of its internal registers and be executing a totally different program by the time the exception occurs. To handle this situation, the NPX has special registers updated at the start of each numeric instruction to describe the state of the numeric program when the failed instruction was attempted.

Error synchronization ensures that the NPX is in a well-defined state after an unmasked numeric error occurs. Without a well-defined state, it would be impossible for exception recovery routines to figure out why the numeric error occurred, or to recover successfully from the error.

INCORRECT ERROR SYNCHRONIZATION

An example of how some instructions written without error synchronization will work initially, but fail when moved into a new environment is shown in figure 2-12.

In figure 2-12, three instructions are shown to load an integer, calculate its square root, then increment the integer. The NPX interface and synchronous execution of the NPX emulator will allow this program to execute correctly when no errors occur on the FILD instruction.

This situation changes if the 80287 numeric register stack is extended to memory. To extend the NPX stack to memory, the invalid error is unmasked. A push to a full register or pop from an empty register will cause an invalid error. The recovery routine for the error must recognize this situation, fix up the stack, then perform the original operation.

The recovery routine will not work correctly in the first example shown in the figure. The problem is that the value of COUNT is incremented before the NPX can signal the exception to the CPU. Because COUNT is incremented before the exception handler is invoked, the recovery routine will load an incorrect value of COUNT, causing the program to fail or behave unreliably

PROPER ERROR SYNCHRONIZATION

Error Synchronization relies on the WAIT instructions required by instruction and data synchronization and the BUSY and ERROR signals of the 80287. When an unmasked error occurs in the 80287, it asserts the ERROR signal, signalling to the CPU that a numeric error has occurred. The next time the CPU encounters an error-checking ESC or WAIT instruction, the CPU acknowledges the ERROR signal by trapping automatically to Interrupt #16, the Processor Extension Error vector. If the following ESC or WAIT instruction is properly placed, the CPU will not yet have disturbed any information vital to recovery from the error.

```
                    INCORRECT ERROR SYNCHRONIZATION
FILD    COUNT   ; NPX instruction
INC     COUNT   ; CPU instruction alters operand
FSQRT   COUNT   ; subsequent NPX instruction -- error from
                ;     previous NPX instruction detected here

                     PROPER ERROR SYNCHRONIZATION
FILD    COUNT   ; NPX instruction
FSQRT           ; subsequent NPX instruction -- error from
                ;     previous NPX instruction detected here
INC     COUNT   ; CPU instruction alters operand
```

Figure 2-12. Error Synchronization Examples

System-Level Numeric Programming

3

CHAPTER 3
SYSTEM-LEVEL NUMERIC PROGRAMMING

System programming for 80287 systems requires a more detailed understanding of the 80287 NPX than does application programming. Such things as emulation, initialization, exception handling, and data and error synchronization are all the responsibility of the systems programmer. These topics are covered in detail in the sections that follow.

80287 ARCHITECTURE

On a software level, the 80287 NPX appears as an extension of the 80286 CPU. On the hardware level, however, the mechanisms by which the 80286 and 80287 interact are a bit more complex. This section describes how the 80287 NPX and 80286 CPU interact and points out features of this interaction that are of interest to systems programmers.

Processor Extension Data Channel

All transfers of operands between the 80287 and system memory are performed by the 80286's internal Processor Extension Data Channel. This independent, DMA-like data channel permits all operand transfers of the 80287 to come under the supervision of the 80286 memory-management and protection mechanisms. The operation of this data channel is completely transparent to software.

Because the 80286 actually performs all transfers between the 80287 and memory, no additional bus drivers, controllers, or other components are necessary to interface the 80287 NPX to the local bus. Any memory accessible to the 80286 CPU is accessible by the 80287. The Processor Extension Data Channel is described in more detail in Chapter Six of the *80286 Hardware Reference Manual*.

Real-Address Mode and Protected Virtual-Address Mode

Like the 80286 CPU, the 80287 NPX can operate in both Real-Address mode and in Protected mode. Following a hardware RESET, the 80287 is initially activated in Real-Address mode. A single, privileged instruction (FSETPM) is necessary to set the 80287 into Protected mode.

As an extension to the 80286 CPU, the 80287 can access any memory location accessible by the task currently executing on the 80286. When operating in Protected mode, all memory references by the 80287 are automatically verified by the 80286's memory management and protection mechanisms as for any other memory references by the currently-executing task. Protection violations associated with NPX instructions automatically cause the 80286 to trap to an appropriate exception handler.

To the programmer, these two 80287 operating modes differ only in the manner in which the NPX instruction and data pointers are represented in memory following an FSAVE or FSTENV instruction. When the 80287 operates in Protected mode, its NPX instruction and data pointers are each represented in memory as a 16-bit segment selector and a 16-bit offset. When the 80287 operates in Real-Address mode, these same instruction and data pointers are represented simply as the 20-bit physical addresses of the operands in question (see figure 1-7 in Chapter One).

Dedicated and Reserved I/O Locations

The 80287 NPX does not require that any memory addresses be set aside for special purposes. The 80287 does make use of I/O port addresses in the range 00F8H through 00FFH, although these I/O operations are completely transparent to the 80286 software. 80286 programs must not reference these reserved I/O addresses directly.

To prevent any accidental misuse or other tampering with numeric instructions in the 80287, the 80286's I/O Privilege Level (IOPL) should be used in multiuser reprogrammable environments to restrict application program access to the I/O address space and so guarantee the integrity of 80287 computations. Chapter Eight of the *80286 Operating System Writer's Guide* contains more details regarding the use of the I/O Privilege Level.

PROCESSOR INITIALIZATION AND CONTROL

One of the principal responsibilities of systems software is the initialization, monitoring, and control of the hardware and software resources of the system, including the 80287 NPX. In this section, issues related to system initialization and control are described, including recognition of the NPX, emulation of the 80287 NPX in software if the hardware is not available, and the handling of exceptions that may occur during the execution of the 80287.

System Initialization

During initialization of an 80286 system, systems software must

- Recognize the presence or absence of the NPX
- Set flags in the 80286 MSW to reflect the state of the numeric environment

If an 80287 NPX is present in the system, the NPX must be

- Initialized
- Switched into Protected mode (if desired)

All of these activities can be quickly and easily performed as part of the overall system initialization.

Recognizing the 80287 NPX

Figure 3-1 shows an example of a recognition routine that determines whether an NPX is present, and distinguishes between the 80387 and the 8087/80287. This routine can be executed on any 80386, 80286, or 8086 hardware configuration that has an NPX socket.

The example guards against the possibility of accidentally reading an expected value from a floating data bus when no NPX is present. Data read from a floating bus is undefined. By expecting to read a specific bit pattern from the NPX, the routine protects itself from the indeterminate state of the bus. The example also avoids depending on any values in reserved bits, thereby maintaining compatibility with future numerics coprocessors.

```
8086/87/88/186 MACRO ASSEMBLER    Test for presence of a Numerics Chip, Revision 1.0                    PAGE    1


DOS 3.20 (033-N) 8086/87/88/186 MACRO ASSEMBLER V2.0 ASSEMBLY OF MODULE TEST_NPX
OBJECT MODULE PLACED IN FINDNPX.OBJ


LOC  OBJ              LINE    SOURCE

                         1 +1  $title('Test for presence of a Numerics Chip, Revision 1.0')
                         2
                         3             name    Test_NPX
                         4
....                     5     stack   segment stack 'stack'
0000 (100                6             dw      100 dup (?)
     ????
     )
00C8 ????                7     sst     dw                  ?
....                     8     stack   ends
                         9
....                    10     data    segment public 'data'
0000 0000               11     temp    dw      0h
....                    12     data    ends
                        13
                        14     dgroup  group   data, stack
                        15     cgroup  group   code
                        16
....                    17     code    segment public 'code'
                        18             assume  cs:cgroup, ds:dgroup
                        19
0000                    20     start:
                        21     ;
                        22     ;       Look for an 8087, 80287, or 80387 NPX.
                        23     ;       Note that we cannot execute WAIT on 8086/88 if no 8087 is present.
                        24     ;
0000                    25     test_npx:
0000 90DBE3             26             fninit                      ; Must use non-wait form
0003 BE0000       R     27             mov     si,offset dgroup:temp
0006 C7045A5A           28             mov     word ptr [si],5A5AH ; Initialize temp to non-zero value
000A 90DD3C             29             fnstsw  [si]                ; Must use non-wait form of fstsw
                        30                                         ; It is not necessary to use a WAIT instruction
                        31                                         ; after fnstsw or fnstcw.  Do not use one here.
000D 803C00             32             cmp     byte ptr [si],0     ; See if correct status with zeroes was read
0010 752A               33             jne     no_npx              ; Jump if not a valid status word, meaning no NPX
                        34     ;
                        35     ;       Now see if ones can be correctly written from the control word.
                        36     ;
0012 90D93C             37             fnstcw  [si]                ; Look at the control word; do not use WAIT form
                        38                                         ; Do not use a WAIT instruction here!
0015 8B04               39             mov     ax,[si]             ; See if ones can be written by NPX
0017 253F10             40             and     ax,103fh            ; See if selected parts of control word look OK
001A 3D3F00             41             cmp     ax,3fh              ; Check that ones and zeroes were correctly read
001D 751D               42             jne     no_npx              ; Jump if no NPX is installed
                        43     ;
                        44     ;       Some numerics chip is installed. NPX instructions and WAIT are now safe.
                        45     ;       See if the NPX is an 8087, 80287, or 80387.
                        46     ;       This code is necessary if a denormal exception handler is used or the
                        47     ;       new 80387 instructions will be used.
                        48     ;
001F 9BD9E8             49             fld1                        ; Must use default control word from FNINIT
0022 9BD9EE             50             fldz                        ; Form infinity
0025 9BDEF9             51             fdiv                        ; 8087/287 says +inf = -inf
0028 9BD9C0             52             fld     st                  ; Form negative infinity
002B 9BD9E0             53             fchs                        ; 80387 says +inf <> -inf
002E 9BDED9             54             fcompp                      ; See if they are the same and remove them
0031 9BDD3C             55             fstsw   [si]                ; Look at status from FCOMPP
0034 8B04               56             mov     ax,[si]
0036 9E                 57             sahf                        ; See if the infinities matched
0037 7406               58             je      found_87_287        ; Jump if 8087/287 is present
                        59     ;
```

Figure 3-1. Software Routine to Recognize the 80287

```
8086/87/88/186 MACRO ASSEMBLER   Test for presence of a Numerics Chip, Revision 1.0                    PAGE   2

LOC  OBJ              LINE      SOURCE
                      60      ;        An 80387 is present.  If denormal exceptions are used for an 8087/287,
                      61      ;        they must be masked.  The 80387 will automatically normalize denormal
                      62      ;        operands faster than an exception handler can.
                      63      ;
0039 EB0790           64               jmp      found_387
003C                  65      no_npx:
                      66      ;        set up for no NPX
                      67      ;        ...
                      68      ;
003C EB0490           69               jmp exit
003F                  70      found_87_287:
                      71      ;        set up for 87/287
                      72      ;        ...
                      73      ;
003F EB0190           74               jmp exit
0042                  75      found_387:
                      76      ;        set up for 387
                      77      ;        ...
                      78      ;
0042                  79      exit:
....                  80      code     ends
                      81               end      start,ds:dgroup,ss:dgroup:sst

ASSEMBLY COMPLETE, NO ERRORS FOUND
```

Figure 3-1. Software Routine to Recognize the 80287 (Cont'd.)

Configuring the Numerics Environment

Once the 80286 CPU has determined the presence or absence of the 80287 NPX, the 80286 must set either the MP or the EM bit in its own machine status word accordingly. The initialization routine can either

- Set the MP bit in the 80286 MSW to allow numeric instructions to be executed directly by the 80287 NPX component
- Set the EM bit in the 80286 MSW to permit software emulation of the 80287 numeric instructions

The Math Present (MP) flag of the 80286 machine status word indicates to the CPU whether an 80287 NPX is physically available in the system. The MP flag controls the function of the WAIT instruction. When executing a WAIT instruction, the 80286 tests only the Task Switched (TS) bit if MP is set; if it finds TS set under these conditions, the CPU traps to exception #7.

The Emulation Mode (EM) bit of the 80286 machine status word indicates to the CPU whether NPX functions are to be emulated. If the CPU finds EM set when it executes an ESC instruction, program control is automatically trapped to exception #7, giving the exception handler the opportunity to emulate the functions of an 80287. The 80286 EM flag can be changed only by using the LMSW (load machine status word) instruction (legal only at privilege level 0) and examined with the aid of the SMSW (store machine status word) instruction (legal at any privilege level).

The EM bit also controls the function of the WAIT instruction. If the CPU finds EM set while executing a WAIT, the CPU does not check the ERROR pin for an error indication.

For correct 80286 operation, the EM bit must never be set concurrently with MP. The EM and MP bits of the 80286 are described in more detail in the *80286 Operating System Writer's Guide*. More information on software emulation for the 80287 NPX is described in the "80287 Emulation" section later in this chapter.

In any case, if ESC instructions are to be executed, either the MP or EM bit must be set, but not both.

Initializing the 80287

Initializing the 80287 NPX simply means placing the NPX in a known state unaffected by any activity performed earlier. The example software routine to recognize the 80287 (table 3-1) performed this initialization using a single FNINIT instruction. This instruction causes the NPX to be initialized in the same way as that caused by the hardware RESET signal to the 80287. All the error masks are set, all registers are tagged empty, the ST is set to zero, and default rounding, precision, and infinity controls are set. Table 3-1 shows the state of the 80287 NPX following initialization.

Following a hardware RESET signal, such as after initial power-up, the 80287 is initialized in Real-Address mode. Once the 80287 has been switched to Protected mode (using the FSETPM instruction), only another hardware RESET can switch the 80287 back to Real-Address mode. The FNINIT instruction does not switch the operating state of the 80287.

80287 Emulation

If it is determined that no 80287 NPX is available in the system, systems software may decide to emulate ESC instructions in software. This emulation is easily supported by the 80286 hardware, because the 80286 can be configured to trap to a software emulation routine whenever it encounters an ESC instruction in its instruction stream.

Table 3-1. NPX Processor State Following Initialization

Field	Value	Interpretation
Control Word		
Infinity Control	0	Projective
Rounding Control	00	Round to nearest
Precision Control	11	64 bits
Interrupt-Enable Mask	1	Interrupts disabled
Exception Masks	111111	All exceptions masked
Status Word		
Busy	0	Not busy
Condition Code	????	(Indeterminate)
Stack Top	000	Empty stack
Interrupt Request	0	No interrupt
Exception Flags	000000	No exceptions
Tag Word		
Tags	11	Empty
Registers	N.C.	Not changed
Exception Pointers		
Instruction Code	N.C.	Not changed
Instruction Address	N.C.	Not changed
Operand Address	N.C.	Not changed

As described previously, whenever the 80286 CPU encounters an ESC instruction, and its MP and EM status bits are set appropriately (MP=0, EM=1), the 80286 will automatically trap to interrupt #7, the Processor Extension Not Available exception. The return link stored on the stack points to the first byte of the ESC instruction, including the prefix byte(s), if any. The exception handler can use this return link to examine the ESC instruction and proceed to emulate the numeric instruction in software.

The emulator must step the return pointer so that, upon return from the exception handler, execution can resume at the first instruction following the ESC instruction.

To an application program, execution on an 80286 system with 80287 emulation is almost indistinguishable from execution on an 80287 system, except for the difference in execution speeds.

There are several important considerations when using emulation on an 80286 system:

- When operating in Protected-Address mode, numeric applications using the emulator must be executed in execute-readable code segments. Numeric software cannot be emulated if it is executed in execute-only code segments. This is because the emulator must be able to examine the particular numeric instruction that caused the Emulation trap.

- Only privileged tasks can place the 80286 in emulation mode. The instructions necessary to place the 80286 in Emulation mode are privileged instructions, and are not typically accessible to an application.

An emulator package (E80287) that runs on 80286 systems is available from Intel in the *8086 Software Toolbox*, Order Number 122203. This emulation package operates in both Real and Protected mode, providing a complete functional equivalent for the 80287 emulated in software.

When using the E80287 emulator, writers of numeric exception handlers should be aware of one slight difference between the emulated 80287 and the 80287 hardware:

- On the 80287 hardware, exception handlers are invoked by the 80286 at the first WAIT or ESC instruction following the instruction causing the exception. The return link, stored on the 80286 stack, points to this second WAIT or ESC instruction where execution will resume following a return from the exception handler.

- Using the E80287 emulator, numeric exception handlers are invoked from within the emulator itself. The return link stored on the stack when the exception handler is invoked will therefore point back to the E80287 emulator, rather than to the program code actually being executed (emulated). An IRET return from the exception handler returns to the emulator, which then returns immediately to the emulated program. This added layer of indirection should not cause confusion, however, because the instruction causing the exception can always be identified from the 80287's instruction and data pointers.

Handling Numeric Processing Exceptions

Once the 80287 has been initialized and normal execution of applications has been commenced, the 80287 NPX may occasionally require attention in order to recover from numeric processing errors. This section provides details for writing software exception handlers for numeric exceptions. Numeric processing exceptions have already been introduced in previous sections of this manual.

As discussed previously, the 80287 NPX can take one of two actions when it recognizes a numeric exception:

- If the exception is masked, the NPX will automatically perform its own masked exception response, correcting the exception condition according to fixed rules, and then continuing with its instruction execution.
- If the exception is unmasked, the NPX signals the exception to the 80286 CPU using the $\overline{\text{ERROR}}$ status line between the two processors. Each time the 80286 encounters an ESC or WAIT instruction in its instruction stream, the CPU checks the condition of this $\overline{\text{ERROR}}$ status line. If $\overline{\text{ERROR}}$ is active, the CPU automatically traps to Interrupt vector #16, the Processor Extension Error trap.

Interrupt vector #16 typically points to a software exception handler, which may or may not be a part of systems software. This exception handler takes the form of an 80286 interrupt procedure.

When handling numeric errors, the CPU has two responsibilities:

- The CPU must not disturb the numeric context when an error is detected.
- The CPU must clear the error and attempt recovery from the error.

Although the manner in which programmers may treat these responsibilities varies from one implementation to the next, most exception handlers will include these basic steps:

- Store the NPX environment (control, status, and tag words, operand and instruction pointers) as it existed at the time of the exception.
- Clear the exception bits in the status word.
- Enable interrupts on the CPU.
- Identify the exception by examining the status and control words in the save environment.
- Take some system-dependent action to rectify the exception.
- Return to the interrupted program and resume normal execution.

It should be noted that the NPX exception pointers contained in the stored NPX environment will take different forms, depending on whether the NPX is operating in Real-Address mode or in Protected mode. The earlier discussion of Real versus Protected mode details how this information is presented in each of the two operating modes.

Simultaneous Exception Response

In cases where multiple exceptions arise simultaneously, the 80287 signals one exception according to the precedence sequence shown in table 3-2. This means, for example, that zero divided by zero will result in an invalid operation, and not a zero divide exception.

Exception Recovery Examples

Recovery routines for NPX exceptions can take a variety of forms. They can change the arithmetic and programming rules of the NPX. These changes may redefine the default fix-up for an error, change the appearance of the NPX to the programmer, or change how arithmetic is defined on the NPX.

A change to an error response might be to automatically normalize all denormals loaded from memory. A change in appearance might be extending the register stack into memory to provide an "infinite"

Table 3-2. Precedence of NPX Exceptions

Signaled First:	Denormalized operand (if unmasked)
	Invalid operation
	Zero divide
	Denormalized (if masked)
	Over/Underflow
Signaled Last:	Precision

number of numeric registers. The arithmetic of the NPX can be changed to automatically extend the precision and range of variables when exceeded. All these functions can be implemented on the NPX via numeric errors and associated recovery routines in a manner transparent to the application programmer.

Some other possible system-dependent actions, mentioned previously, may include:

- Incrementing an exception counter for later display or printing
- Printing or displaying diagnostic information (e.g., the 80287 environment and registers)
- Aborting further execution
- Storing a diagnostic value (a NaN) in the result and continuing with the computation

Notice that an exception may or may not constitute an error, depending on the implementation. Once the exception handler corrects the error condition causing the exception, the floating-point instruction that caused the exception can be restarted, if appropriate. This cannot be accomplished using the IRET instruction, however, because the trap occurs at the ESC or WAIT instruction following the offending ESC instruction. The exception handler must obtain from the NPX the address of the offending instruction in the task that initiated it, make a copy of it, execute the copy in the context of the offending task, and then return via IRET to the current CPU instruction stream.

In order to correct the condition causing the numeric exception, exception handlers must recognize the precise state of the NPX at the time the exception handler was invoked, and be able to reconstruct the state of the NPX when the exception initially occurred. To reconstruct the state of the NPX, programmers must understand when, during the execution of an NPX instruction, exceptions are actually recognized.

Invalid operation, zero divide, and denormalized exceptions are detected before an operation begins, whereas overflow, underflow, and precision exceptions are not raised until a true result has been computed. When a *before* exception is detected, the NPX register stack and memory have not yet been updated, and appear as if the offending instructions has not been executed.

When an *after* exception is detected, the register stack and memory appear as if the instruction has run to completion; i.e., they may be updated. (However, in a store or store-and-pop operation, unmasked over/underflow is handled like a before exception; memory is not updated and the stack is not popped.) The programming examples contained in Chapter Four include an outline of several exception handlers to process numeric exceptions for the 80287.

Numeric Programming Examples 4

CHAPTER 4
NUMERIC PROGRAMMING EXAMPLES

The following sections contain examples of numeric programs for the 80287 NPX written in ASM286. These examples are intended to illustrate some of the techniques for programming the 80287 computing system for numeric applications.

CONDITIONAL BRANCHING EXAMPLES

As discussed in Chapter Two, several numeric instructions post their results to the condition code bits of the 80287 status word. Although there are many ways to implement conditional branching following a comparison, the basic approach is as follows:

- Execute the comparison.
- Store the status word. (80287 allows storing status directly into AX register.)
- Inspect the condition code bits.
- Jump on the result.

Figure 4-1 is a code fragment that illustrates how two memory-resident long real numbers might be compared (similar code could be used with the FTST instruction). The numbers are called A and B, and the comparison is A to B.

The comparison itself requires loading A onto the top of the 80287 register stack and then comparing it to B, while popping the stack with the same instruction. The status word is then written into the 80286 AX register.

A and B have four possible orderings, and bits C3, C2, and C0 of the condition code indicate which ordering holds. These bits are positioned in the upper byte of the NPX status word so as to correspond to the CPU's zero, parity, and carry flags (ZF, PF, and CF), when the byte is written into the flags. The code fragment sets ZF, PF, and CF of the CPU status word to the values of C3, C2, and C0 of the NPX status word, and then uses the CPU conditional jump instructions to test the flags. The resulting code is extremely compact, requiring only seven instructions.

The FXAM instruction updates all four condition code bits. Figure 4-2 shows how a jump table can be used to determine the characteristics of the value examined. The jump table (FXAM_TBL) is initialized to contain the 16-bit displacement of 16 labels, one for each possible condition code setting. Note that four of the table entries contain the same value, because four condition code settings correspond to "empty."

The program fragment performs the FXAM and stores the status word. It then manipulates the condition code bits to finally produce a number in register BX that equals the condition code times 2. This involves zeroing the unused bits in the byte that contains the code, shifting C3 to the right so that it is adjacent to C2, and then shifting the code to multiply it by 2. The resulting value is used as an index that selects one of the displacements from FXAM_TBL (the multiplication of the condition code is required because of the 2-byte length of each value in FXAM_TBL). The unconditional JMP instruction effectively vectors through the jump table to the labelled routine that contains code (not shown in the example) to process each possible result of the FXAM instruction.

```
                 .
                 .
                 .
A       DQ       ?
B       DQ       ?
                 .
                 .
                 .
        FLD      A               ; LOAD A ONTO TOP OF 287 STACK
        FCOMP    B               ; COMPARE A:B, POP A
        FSTSW    AX              ; STORE RESULT TO CPU AX REGISTER
        ;
        ; CPU AX REGISTER CONTAINS CONDITION CODES (RESULTS OF
        ; COMPARE)
        ;    LOAD CONDITION CODES INTO CPU FLAGS
        SAHF
        ;
        ; USE CONDITIONAL JUMPS TO DETERMINE ORDERING OF A TO
        ; B
        ;
        JP       A_B_UNORDERED   ; TEST C2 (PF)
        JB       A_LESS          ; TEST C0 (CF)
        JE       A_EQUAL         ; TEST C3 (ZF)
A_GREATER:                       ; C0 (CF) = 0, C3 (ZF) = 0
                 .
                 .
A_EQUAL:                         ; C0 (CF) = 0, C3 (ZF) = 1
                 .
                 .
A_LESS:                          ; C0 (CF) = 1, C3 (ZF) = 0
                 .
                 .
A_B_UNORDERED:                   ; C2 (PF) = 1
```

Figure 4-1. Conditional Branching for Compares

```
        ; JUMP TABLE FOR EXAMINE ROUTINE
        ;
FXAM_TBL   DW POS_UNNORM, POS_NAN, NEG_UNNORM, NEG_NAN,
   &          POS_NORM, POS_INFINITY, NEG_NORM,
   &          NEG_INFINITY, POS_ZERO, EMPTY, NEG_ZERO,
   &          EMPTY, POS_DENORM, EMPTY, NEG_DENORM, EMPTY
                 .
                 .
                 .
        ; EXAMINE ST AND STORE RESULT (CONDITION CODES)
        FXAM
        FSTSW   AX
```

Figure 4-2. Conditional Branching for FXAM

```
        ;
        ;   CALCULATE OFFSET INTO JUMP TABLE
        MOV     BH,0      ; CLEAR UPPER HALF OF BX,
        MOV     BL,AH     ; LOAD CONDITION CODE INTO BL
        AND     BL,00000111B    ; CLEAR ALL BITS EXCEPT C2-C0
        AND     AH,01000000B    ; CLEAR ALL BITS EXCEPT C3
        SHR     AH,2      ; SHIFT C3 TWO PLACES RIGHT
        SAL     BX,1      ; SHIFT C2-C0 1 PLACE LEFT (MULTIPLY
                          ; BY 2)
        OR      BL,AH     ; DROP C3 BACK IN ADJACENT TO C2
                          ; (000XXXX0)
        ;
        ;   JUMP TO THE ROUTINE 'ADDRESSED' BY CONDITION CODE
        JMP     FXAM_TBL[BX]
        ;
        ;   HERE ARE THE JUMP TARGETS, ONE TO HANDLE
        ;      EACH POSSIBLE RESULT OF FXAM
POS_UNNORM:
            .
POS_NAN:
            .
NEG_UNNORM:
            .
NEG_NAN:
            .
POS_NORM:
            .
POS_INFINITY:
            .
NEG_NORM:
            .
NEG_INFINITY:
            .
POS_ZERO:
            .
EMPTY:
            .
NEG_ZERO:
            .
POS_DENORM:
            .
NEG_DENORM:
```

Figure 4-2. Conditional Branching for FXAM (Cont'd.)

EXCEPTION HANDLING EXAMPLES

There are many approaches to writing exception handlers. One useful technique is to consider the exception handler procedure as consisting of "prologue," "body," and "epilogue" sections of code. (For compatibility with the 80287 emulators, this procedure should be invoked by interrupt pointer (vector) number 16.)

At the beginning of the prologue, CPU interrupts have been disabled. The prologue performs all functions that must be protected from possible interruption by higher-priority sources. Typically, this will involve saving CPU registers and transferring diagnostic information from the 80287 to memory. When the critical processing has been completed, the prologue may enable CPU interrupts to allow higher-priority interrupt handlers to preempt the exception handler.

The exception handler body examines the diagnostic information and makes a response that is necessarily application-dependent. This response may range from halting execution, to displaying a message, to attempting to repair the problem and proceed with normal execution.

The epilogue essentially reverses the actions of the prologue, restoring the CPU and the NPX so that normal execution can be resumed. The epilogue must *not* load an unmasked exception flag into the 80287 or another exception will be requested immediately.

Figure 4-3 through 4-5 show the ASM286 coding of three skeleton exception handlers. They show how prologues and epilogues can be written for various situations, but provide comments indicating only where the application-dependent exception handling body should be placed.

Figure 4-3 and 4-4 are very similar; their only substantial difference is their choice of instructions to save and restore the 80287. The tradeoff here is between the increased diagnostic information provided by FNSAVE and the faster execution of FNSTENV. For applications that are sensitive to interrupt latency or that do not need to examine register contents, FNSTENV reduces the duration of the "critical region," during which the CPU will not recognize another interrupt request (unless it is a nonmaskable interrupt).

After the exception handler body, the epilogues prepare the CPU and the NPX to resume execution from the point of interruption (i.e., the instruction following the one that generated the unmasked exception). Notice that the exception flags in the memory image that is loaded into the 80287 are cleared to zero prior to reloading (in fact, in these examples, the entire status word image is cleared).

The examples in figures 4-3 and 4-4 assume that the exception handler itself will not cause an unmasked exception. Where this is a possibility, the general approach shown in figure 4-5 can be employed. The basic technique is to save the full 80287 state and then to load a new control word in the prologue. Note that considerable care should be taken when designing an exception handler of this type to prevent the handler from being reentered endlessly.

```
SAVE_ALL            PROC
;
; SAVE CPU REGISTERS, ALLOCATE STACK SPACE
; FOR 80287 STATE IMAGE
      PUSH      BP
      MOV       BP,SP
      SUB       SP,94
; SAVE FULL 80287 STATE, WAIT FOR COMPLETION,
; ENABLE CPU INTERRUPTS
      FNSAVE    [BP-94]
      FWAIT
      STI
;
; APPLICATION-DEPENDENT EXCEPTION HANDLING
; CODE GOES HERE
```

Figure 4-3. Full-State Exception Handler

```
;
; CLEAR EXCEPTION FLAGS IN STATUS WORD
; RESTORE MODIFIED STATE
; IMAGE
    MOV         BYTE PTR [BP-92], 0H
    FRSTOR      [BP-94]
; DE-ALLOCATE STACK SPACE, RESTORE CPU REGISTERS
    MOV         SP,BP
        .
        .
    POP         BP
;
; RETURN TO INTERRUPTED CALCULATION
    IRET
SAVE_ALL            ENDP
```

Figure 4-3. Full-State Exception Handler (Cont'd.)

```
SAVE_ENVIRONMENT PROC
;
; SAVE CPU REGISTERS, ALLOCATE STACK SPACE
; FOR 80287 ENVIRONMENT
    PUSH        BP
        .
    MOV         BP,SP
    SUB         SP,14
; SAVE ENVIRONMENT, WAIT FOR COMPLETION,
; ENABLE CPU INTERRUPTS
    FNSTENV     [BP-14]
    FWAIT
    STI
;
; APPLICATION EXCEPTION-HANDLING CODE GOES HERE
;
; CLEAR EXCEPTION FLAGS IN STATUS WORD
; RESTORE MODIFIED
; ENVIRONMENT IMAGE
    MOV         BYTE PTR [BP-12], 0H
    FLDENV      [BP-14]
; DE-ALLOCATE STACK SPACE, RESTORE CPU REGISTERS
    MOV         SP,BP
    POP         BP
;
; RETURN TO INTERRUPTED CALCULATION
    IRET
SAVE_ENVIRONMENT ENDP
```

Figure 4-4. Reduced-Latency Exception Handler

```
              .
              .
              .
       LOCAL_CONTROL   DW   ?   ; ASSUME INITIALIZED
              .
              .
              .
REENTRANT               PROC
;
; SAVE CPU REGISTERS, ALLOCATE STACK SPACE FOR
; 80287 STATE IMAGE
     PUSH     BP
              .
              .
              .
     MOV      BP,SP
     SUB      SP,94
; SAVE STATE, LOAD NEW CONTROL WORD,
; FOR COMPLETION, ENABLE CPU INTERRUPTS
     FNSAVE   [BP-94]
     FLDCW    LOCAL_CONTROL
     STI
              .
              .
              .
; APPLICATION EXCEPTION HANDLING CODE GOES HERE.
; AN UNMASKED EXCEPTION GENERATED HERE WILL
; CAUSE THE EXCEPTION HANDLER TO BE REENTERED.
; IF LOCAL STORAGE IS NEEDED, IT MUST BE
; ALLOCATED ON THE CPU STACK.
              .
              .
              .
; CLEAR EXCEPTION FLAGS IN STATUS WORD
; RESTORE MODIFIED STATE IMAGE
     MOV      BYTE PTR [BP-92], 0H
     FRSTOR   [BP-94]
; DE-ALLOCATE STACK SPACE, RESTORE CPU REGISTERS
     MOV      SP,BP
              .
              .
              .
     POP      BP
; RETURN TO POINT OF INTERRUPTION
     IRET
REENTRANT               ENDP
```

Figure 4-5. Reentrant Exception Handler

FLOATING-POINT TO ASCII CONVERSION EXAMPLES

Numeric programs must typically format their results at some point for presentation and inspection by the program user. In many cases, numeric results are formatted as ASCII strings for printing or display. This example shows how floating-point values can be converted to decimal ASCII character strings. The function shown in figure 4-6 can be invoked from PL/M-286, Pascal-286, FORTRAN-286, or ASM286 routines.

Shortness, speed, and accuracy were chosen rather than providing the maximum number of significant digits possible. An attempt is made to keep integers in their own domain to avoid unnecessary conversion errors.

Using the extended precision real number format, this routine achieves a worst case accuracy of three units in the 16th decimal position for a noninteger value or integers greater than 10^{18}. This is double precision accuracy. With values having decimal exponents less than 100 in magnitude, the accuracy is one unit in the 17th decimal position.

Higher precision can be achieved with greater care in programming, larger program size, and lower performance.

```
iAPX286 MACRO ASSEMBLER    80287 Floating-Point to 18-Digit ASCII Conversion          10:12:38  09/25/83  PAGE   1

SERIES-III iAPX286 MACRO ASSEMBLER X108 ASSEMBLY OF MODULE FLOATING_TO_ASCII
OBJECT MODULE PLACED IN :F3:FPASC.OBJ
ASSEMBLER INVOKED BY:  ASM286.86 :F3:FPASC.AP2


LOC  OBJ                 LINE    SOURCE

                            1 +1  $title("80287 Floating-Point to 18-Digit ASCII Conversion")
                            2
                            3                name    floating_to_ascii
                            4
                            5                public  floating_to_ascii
                            6                extrn   get_power_10:near, tos_status:near
                            7     ;
                            8     ;        This subroutine will convert the floating point number in tne
                            9     ;        top of the 80287 stack to an ASCII string and separate power of 10
                           10     ;        scaling value (in binary).  The maximum width of the ASCII string
                           11     ;        formed is controlled by a parameter which must be > 1.  Unnormal values,
                           12     ;        denormal values, and psuedo zeroes will be correctly converted.
                           13     ;        A returned value will indicate how many binary bits of
                           14     ;        precision were lost in an unnormal or denormal value.  The magnitude
                           15     ;        (in terms of binary power) of a psuedo zero will also be indicated.
                           16     ;        Integers less than 10**18 in magnitude are accurately converted if the
                           17     ;        destination ASCII string field is wide enough to hold all the
                           18     ;        digits.  Otherwise the value is converted to scientific notation.
                           19     ;
                           20     ;        The status of the conversion is identified by the return value,
                           21     ;        it can be:
                           22     ;
                           23     ;            0         conversion complete, string_size is defined
                           24     ;            1         invalid arguments
                           25     ;            2         exact integer conversion, string_size is defined
                           26     ;            3         indefinite
                           27     ;            4       + NAN (Not A Number)
                           28     ;            5       - NAN
                           29     ;            6       + Infinity
                           30     ;            7       - Infinity
                           31     ;            8         psuedo zero found, string_size is defined
                           32     ;
                           33     ;        The PLM/286 calling convention is:
                           34     ;
                           35     ; floating_to_ascii:
                           36     ;        procedure (number, denormal_ptr, string_ptr, size_ptr, field_size,
                           37     ;            power_ptr) word external;
                           38     ;        declare (denormal_ptr, string_ptr, power_ptr, size_ptr) pointer,
                           39     ;        declare field_size word, string_size based size_ptr word;
                           40     ;        declare number real;
                           41     ;        declare denormal integer based denormal_ptr;
                           42     ;        declare power integer based power_ptr;
                           43     ;        end floating_to_ascii;
                           44     ;
                           45     ;        The floating point value is expected to be on the top of the NPX
                           46     ;        stack.  This subroutine expects 3 free entries on the NPX stack and
                           47     ;        will pop the passed value off when done.  The generated ASCII string
                           48     ;        will have a leading character either '-' or '+' indicating the sign
                           49     ;        of the value.  The ASCII decimal digits will immediately follow.
                           50     ;        The numeric value of the ASCII string is (ASCII STRING.)*10**POWER.
```

Figure 4-6. Floating-Point to ASCII Conversion Routine

```
iAPX286 MACRO ASSEMBLER     80287 Floating-Point to 18-Digit ASCII Conversion          10:12:38  09/25/83  PAGE   2

LOC  OBJ                LINE    SOURCE

                         51     ;        If the given number was zero, the ASCII string will contain a sign
                         52     ;        and a single zero chacter.  The value string_size indicates the total
                         53     ;        length of the ASCII string including the sign character.  String(O) will
                         54     ;        always hold the sign.  It is possible for string_size to be less than
                         55     ;        field_size.  This occurs for zeroes or integer values.  A psuedo zero
                         56     ;        will return a special return code.  The denormal count will indicate
                         57     ;        the power of two originally associated with the value.  The power of
                         58     ;        ten and ASCII string will be as if the value was an ordinary zero.
                         59     ;
                         60     ;        This subroutine is accurate up to a maximum of 18 decimal digits for
                         61     ;        integers.  Integer values will have a decimal power of zero associated
                         62     ;        with them.  For non integers, the result will be accurate to within 2
                         63     ;        decimal digits of the 16th decimal place (double precision).  The
                         64     ;        exponentiation instruction is also used for scaling the value into the
                         65     ;        range acceptable for the BCD data type.  The rounding mode in effect
                         66     ;        on entry to the subroutine is used for the conversion.
                         67     ;
                         68     ;        The following registers are not transparent:
                         69     ;
                         70     ;            ax bx cx dx si di flags
                         71     ;
                         72  +1 $eject
                         73     ;
                         74     ;            Define the stack layout.
                         75     ;
0000[]                   76     bp_save         equ     word ptr [bp]
0002[]                   77     es_save         equ     bp_save + size bp_save
0004[]                   78     return_ptr      equ     es_save + size es_save
0006[]                   79     power_ptr       equ     return_ptr + size return_ptr
0008[]                   80     field_size      equ     power_ptr + size power_ptr
000A[]                   81     size_ptr        equ     field_size + size field_size
000C[]                   82     string_ptr      equ     size_ptr + size size_ptr
000E[]                   83     denormal_ptr    equ     string_ptr + size string_ptr
                         84
                         85     parms_size      equ     power_ptr + size field_size + size size_ptr +
000A                     86        &                    size string_ptr + size denormal_ptr
                         87     ;
                         88     ;            Define constants used
                         89     ;
0012                     90     BCD_DIGITS      equ     18                  ; Number of digits in bcd_value
0002                     91     WORD_SIZE       equ     2
000A                     92     BCD_SIZE        equ     10
0001                     93     MINUS           equ     1                   ; Define return values
0004                     94     NAN             equ     4                   ; The exact values chosen here are
0006                     95     INFINITY        equ     6                   ; important.  They must correspond to
0003                     96     INDEFINITE      equ     3                   ; the possible return values and be in
0008                     97     PSUEDO_ZERO     equ     8                   ; the same numeric order as tested by
-0002                    98     INVALID         equ     -2                  ; the program.
-0004                    99     ZERO            equ     -4
-0006                   100     DENORMAL        equ     -6
-0008                   101     UNNORMAL        equ     -8
0000                    102     NORMAL          equ     0
0002                    103     EXACT           equ     2
                        104     ;
                        105     ;            Define layout of temporary storage area.
                        106     ;
-0002[]                 107     status          equ     word ptr [bp-WORD_SIZE]
-0004[]                 108     power_two       equ     status - WORD_SIZE
-0006[]                 109     power_ten       equ     power_two - WORD_SIZE
-0010[]                 110     bcd_value       equ     tbyte ptr power_ten - BCD_SIZE
-0010[]                 111     bcd_byte        equ     byte ptr bcd_value
-0010[]                 112     fraction        equ     bcd_value
                        113
                        114     local_size      equ     size status + size power_two + size power_ten
0010                    115        &                    + size bcd_value
                        116
----                    117     stack           stackseg (local_size+6) ; Allocate stack space for locals
                        118  +1 $eject
----                    119     code            segment er public
                        120                     extrn   power_table:qword
                        121     ;
                        122     ;            Constants used by this function.
                        123     ;
                        124                     even                        ; Optimize for 16 bits
0000 0A00               125     const10         dw      10                  ; Adjustment value for too big BCD
                        126     ;
                        127     ;            Convert the C3,C2,C1,C0 encoding from tos_status into meaningful bit
                        128     ;            flags and values.
                        129     ;
0002 F8                 130     status_table    db      UNNORMAL, NAN, UNNORMAL + MINUS, NAN + MINUS,
0003 04
0004 F9
0005 05
0006 00                 131        &                    NORMAL, INFINITY, NORMAL + MINUS, INFINITY + MINUS,
0007 06
0008 01
0009 07
000A FC                 132        &                    ZERO, INVALID, ZERO + MINUS, INVALID,
000B FE
000C FD
000D FE
000E FA                 133        &                    DENORMAL, INVALID, DENORMAL + MINUS, INVALID
000F FA
0010 FB
0011 FE
```

Figure 4-6. Floating-Point to ASCII Conversion Routine (Cont'd.)

```
iAPX286 MACRO ASSEMBLER      80287 Floating-Point to 18-Digit ASCII Conversion         10:12:38 09/25/83  PAGE   3


 LOC  OBJ                    LINE   SOURCE

                            134
 0012                       135    floating_to_ascii proc
                            136
 0012 E80000          E     137            call    tos_status                    ; Look at status of ST(0)
 0015 8BD8                  138            mov     bx,ax                         ; Get descriptor from table
 0017 2E8A870200      R     139            mov     al,status_table[bx]
 001C 3CFE                  140            cmp     al,INVALID                    ; Look for empty ST(0)
 001E 752B                  141            jne     not_empty
                            142    ;
                            143    ;      ST(0) is empty!  Return the status value.
                            144    ;
 0020 C20A00                145            ret     parms_size
                            146    ;
                            147    ;      Remove infinity from stack and exit.
                            148    ;
 0023                       149    found_infinity:
                            150
 0023 DDD8                  151            fstp    st(0)                         ; OK to leave fstp running
 0025 EB02                  152            jmp     short exit_proc
                            153    ;
                            154    ;      String space is too small! Return invalid code.
                            155    ;
 0027                       156    small_string:
                            157
 0027 B0FE                  158            mov     al,INVALID
                            159
 0029                       160    exit_proc:
                            161
 0029 C9                    162            leave                                 ; Restore stack
 002A 07                    163            pop     es
 002B C20A00                164            ret     parms_size
                            165    ;
                            166    ;      ST(0) is NAN or indefinite.  Store the value in memory and look
                            167    ;      at the fraction field to separate indefinite from an ordinary NAN.
                            168    ;
 002E                       169    NAN_or_indefinite:
                            170
 002E DB7EF0                171            fstp    fraction                      ; Remove value from stack for examination
 0031 A801                  172            test    al,MINUS                      ; Look at sign bit
 0033 9B                    173            fwait                                 ; Insure store is done
 0034 74F3                  174            jz      exit_proc                     ; Can't be indefinite if positive
                            175
 0036 BB00C0                176            mov     bx,0C000H                     ; Match against upper 16 bits of fraction
 0039 2B5EF6                177            sub     bx,word ptr fraction+6        ; Compare bits 63-48
 003C 0B5EF4                178            or      bx,word ptr fraction+4        ; Bits 32-47 must be zero
 003F 0B5EF2                179            or      bx,word ptr fraction+2        ; Bits 31-16 must be zero
 0042 0B5EF0                180            or      bx,word ptr fraction          ; Bits 15-0 must be zero
 0045 75E2                  181            jnz     exit_proc
                            182
 0047 B003                  183            mov     al,INDEFINITE                 ; Set return value for indefinite value
 0049 EBDE                  184            jmp     exit_proc
                            185    ;
                            186    ;      Allocate stack space for local variables and establish parameter
                            187    ;      addressibility.
                            188    ;
 004B                       189    not_empty:
                            190
 004B 06                    191            push    es                            ; Save working register
 004C C8100000              192            enter   local_size,0                  ; Format stack
                            193
 0050 8B4E08                194            mov     cx,field_size                 ; Check for enough string space
 0053 83F902                195            cmp     cx,2
 0056 7CCF                  196            jl      small_string
                            197
 0058 49                    198            dec     cx                            ; Adjust for sign character
 0059 83F912                199            cmp     cx,BCD_DIGITS                 ; See if string is too large for BCD
 005C 7603                  200            jbe     size_ok
                            201
 005E B91200                202            mov     cx,BCD_DIGITS                 ; Else set maximum string size
                            203
 0061                       204    size_ok:
                            205
 0061 3C06                  206            cmp     al,INFINITY                   ; Look for infinity
 0063 7DBE                  207            jge     found_infinity                ; Return status value for + or - inf.
                            208
 0065 3C04                  209            cmp     al,NAN                        ; Look for NAN or INDEFINITE
 0067 7DC5                  210            jge     NAN_or_indefinite
                            211
                            212    ;      Set default return values and check that the number is normalized.
                            213    ;
 0069 D9E1                  214            fabs                                  ; Use positive value only
                            215                                                  ; sign bit in al has true sign of value
 006B 8BD0                  216            mov     dx,ax                         ; Save return value for later
 006D 33C0                  217            xor     ax,ax                         ; Form 0 constant
 006F 8B7E0E                218            mov     di,denormal_ptr               ; Zero denormal count
 0072 8905                  219            mov     word ptr [di],ax
 0074 8B5E06                220            mov     bx,power_ptr                  ; Zero power of ten value
 0077 8907                  221            mov     word ptr [bx],ax
 0079 80FAFC                222            cmp     dl,ZERO                       ; Test for zero
 007C 732B                  223            jae     real_zero                     ; Skip power code if value is zero
                            224
 007E 80FAFA                225            cmp     dl,DENORMAL                   ; Look for a denormal value
 0081 732C                  226            jae     found_denormal                ; Handle it specially
                            227
```

Figure 4-6. Floating-Point to ASCII Conversion Routine (Cont'd.)

```
iAPX286 MACRO ASSEMBLER      80287 Floating-Point to 18-Digit ASCII Conversion               10:12:38  09/25/83  PAGE   4


LOC  OBJ               LINE     SOURCE

0083 D9F4               228          fxtract                             ; Separate exponent from significand
0085 80FAF8             229          cmp      d1,UNNORMAL                 ; Test for unnormal value
0088 7240               230          jb       normal_value
                        231
008A 80EAF8             232          sub      d1,UNNORMAL-NORMAL          ; Return normal status with correct sign
                        233      ;
                        234      ;      Normalize the fraction, adjust the power of two in ST(1) and set
                        235      ;      the denormal count value.
                        236      ;
                        237      ;      Assert: 0 <= ST(0) < 1.0
                        238      ;
008D D9E8               239          fld1                                ; Load constant to normalize fraction
                        240
008F                    241      normalize_fraction:
                        242
008F DCC1               243          fadd     st(1),st                   ; Set integer bit in fraction
0091 DEE9               244          fsub                                ; Form normalized fraction in ST(0)
0093 D9F4               245          fxtract                             ; Power of two field will be negative
                        246                                              ;   of denormal count
0095 D9C9               247          fxch                                ; Put denormal count in ST(0)
0097 DF15               248          fist     word ptr [di]              ; Put negative of denormal count in memory
0099 DEC2               249          faddp    st(2),st                   ; Form correct power of two in st(1)
                        250                                              ; OK to use word ptr [di] now
009B F71D               251          neg      word ptr [di]              ; Form positive denormal count
009D 752B               252          jnz      not_psuedo_zero
                        253      ;
                        254      ;      A psuedo zero will appear as an unnormal number.  When attempting
                        255      ;      to normalize it, the resultant fraction field will be zero.  Performing
                        256      ;      an fxtract on zero will yield a zero exponent value.
                        257      ;
009F D9C9               258          fxch                                ; Put power of two value in st(0)
00A1 DF1D               259          fistp    word ptr [di]              ; Set denormal count to power of two value
                        260                                              ; Word ptr [di] is not used by convert
                        261                                              ;   integer, OK to leave running
00A3 80EAFB             262          sub      d1,NORMAL-PSUEDO_ZERO      ; Set return value saving the sign bit
00A6 E9A400             263          jmp      convert_integer            ; Put zero value into memory
                        264      ;
                        265      ;      The number is a real zero, set the return value and setup for
                        266      ;      conversion to BCD.
                        267      ;
00A9                    268      real_zero:
                        269
00A9 80EAFC             270          sub      d1,ZERO-NORMAL             ; Convert status to normal value
00AC E99E00             271          jmp      convert_integer            ; Treat the zero as an integer
                        272      ;
                        273      ;      The number is a denormal.  FXTRACT will not work correctly in this
                        274      ;      case.  To correctly separate the exponent and fraction, add a fixed
                        275      ;      constant to the exponent to guarantee the result is not a denormal.
                        276      ;
00AF                    277      found_denormal:
                        278
00AF D9E8               279          fld1                                ; Prepare to bump exponent
00B1 D9C9               280          fxch                                ; Force denormal to smallest representable
00B3 D9F8               281          fprem                               ;   extended real format exponent
                        282                                              ; This will work correctly now
00B5 D9F4               283          fxtract
                        284      ;
                        285      ;      The power of the original denormal value has been safely isolated.
                        286      ;      Check if the fraction value is an unnormal.
                        287      ;
00B7 D9E5               288          fxam                                ; See if the fraction is an unnormal
00B9 9BDFE0             289          fstsw    ax                         ; Save 80287 status in CPU AX reg for later
00BC D9C9               290          fxch                                ; Put exponent in ST(0)
00BE D9CA               291          fxch     st(2)                      ; Put 1.9 into ST(0), exponent in ST(2)
00C0 80EAFA             292          sub      d1,DENORMAL-NORMAL         ; Return normal status with correct sign
00C3 A90044             293          test     ax,4400H                   ; See if C3=C2=0 impling unnormal or NAN
00C6 74C7               294          jz       normalize_fraction         ; Jump if fraction is an unnormal
                        295
00C8 DDD8               296          fstp     st(0)                      ; Remove unnecessary 1.0 from st(0)
                        297      ;
                        298      ;      Calculate the decimal magnitude associated with this number to
                        299      ;      within one order.  This error will always be inevitable due to
                        300      ;      rounding and lost precision.  As a result, we will deliberately fail
                        301      ;      to consider the LOG10 of the fraction value in calculating the order.
                        302      ;      Since the fraction will always be 1 <= F < 2, its LOG10 will not change
                        303      ;      the basic accuracy of the function.  To get the decimal order of magnitude,
                        304      ;      simply multiply the power of two by LOG10(2) and truncate the result to
                        305      ;      an integer.
                        306      ;
00CA                    307      normal_value:
00CA                    308      not_psuedo_zero:
                        309
00CA DB7EF0             310          fstp     fraction                   ; Save the fraction field for later use
00CD DF56FC             311          fist     power_two                  ; Save power of two
00D0 D9EC               312          fldlg2                              ; Get LOG10(2)
                        313                                              ; Power_two is now safe to use
00D2 DEC9               314          fmul                                ; Form LOG10(of exponent of number)
00D4 DF5EFA             315          fistp    power_ten                  ; Any rounding mode will work here
                        316      ;
                        317      ;      Check if the magnitude of the number rules out treating it as
                        318      ;      an integer.
                        319      ;
                        320      ;      CX has the maximum number of decimal digits allowed.
                        321      ;
```

Figure 4-6. Floating-Point to ASCII Conversion Routine (Cont'd.)

```
LOC  OBJ              LINE   SOURCE

00D7 9B               322            fwait                            ; Wait for power_ten to be valid
00D8 8B46FA           323            mov     ax,power_ten             ; Get power of ten of value
00DB 2BC1             324            sub     ax,cx                    ; Form scaling factor necessary in ax
00DD 7722             325            ja      adjust_result            ; Jump if number will not fit
                      326     ;
                      327     ;      The number is between 1 and 10**(field_size).
                      328     ;      Test if it is an integer.
                      329     ;
00DF DF46FC           330            fild    power_two                ; Restore original number
00E2 8BF2             331            mov     si,dx                    ; Save return value
00E4 80EAFE           332            sub     dl,NORMAL-EXACT          ; Convert to exact return value
00E7 DB6EF0           333            fld     fraction
00EA D9FD             334            fscale                           ; Form full value, this is safe here
00EC DDD1             335            fst     st(1)                    ; Copy value for compare
00EE D9FC             336            frndint                          ; Test if its an integer
00F0 D8D9             337            fcomp                            ; Compare values
00F2 9BDD7EFE         338            fstsw   status                   ; Save status
00F6 F746FE0040       339            test    status,4000H             ; C3=1 implies it was an integer
00FB 7550             340            jnz     convert_integer
                      341
00FD DDD8             342            fstp    st(0)                    ; Remove non integer value
00FF 8BD6             343            mov     dx,si                    ; Restore original return value
                      344     ;
                      345     ;      Scale the number to within the range allowed by the BCD format.
                      346     ;      The scaling operation should produce a number within one decimal order
                      347     ;      of magnitude of the largest decimal number representable within the
                      348     ;      given string width.
                      349     ;
                      350     ;      The scaling power of ten value is in ax.
                      351     ;
0101                  352     adjust_result:
                      353
0101 8907             354            mov     word ptr [bx],ax         ; Set initial power of ten return value
0103 F7D8             355            neg     ax                       ; Subtract one for each order of
                      356                                             ; magnitude the value is scaled by
0105 E80000        E  357            call    get_power_10             ; Scaling factor is returned as exponent
                      358                                             ; and fraction
0108 DB6EF0           359            fld     fraction                 ; Get fraction
010B DEC9             360            fmul                             ; Combine fractions
010D 8BF1             361            mov     si,cx                    ; Form power of ten of the maximum
010F D1E6             362            shl     si,1                     ; BCD value to fit in the string
0111 D1E6             363            shl     si,1                     ; Index in si
0113 D1E6             364            shl     si,1
0115 DF46FC           365            fild    power_two                ; Combine powers of two
0118 DEC2             366            faddp   st(2),st
011A D9FD             367            fscale                           ; Form full value, exponent was safe
011C DDD9             368            fstp    st(1)                    ; Remove exponent
                      369     ;
                      370     ;      Test the adjusted value against a table of exact powers of ten.
                      371     ;      The combined errors of the magnitude estimate and power function can
                      372     ;      result in a value one order of magnitude too small or too large to fit
                      373     ;      correctly in the BCD field.  To handle this problem, pretest the
                      374     ;      adjusted value, if it is too small or large, then adjust it by ten and
                      375     ;      adjust the power of ten value.
                      376     ;
011E                  377     test_power:
                      378
011E 2EDC940800    E  379            fcom    power_table[si]+type power_table; Compare against exact power
                      380                                             ; entry.  Use the next entry since cx
                      381                                             ; has been decremented by one
0123 9BDFE0           382            fstsw   ax                       ; No wait is necessary
0126 A90041           383            test    ax,4100H                 ; If C3 = C0 = 0 then too big
0129 750C             384            jnz     test_for_small
                      385
012B 2EDE360000    R  386            fidiv   const10                  ; Else adjust value
0130 80E2FD           387            and     dl,not EXACT             ; Remove exact flag
0133 FF07             388            inc     word ptr [bx]            ; Adjust power of ten value
0135 EB14             389            jmp     short in_range           ; Convert the value to a BCD integer
                      390
0137                  391     test_for_small:
                      392
0137 2EDC940000    E  393            fcom    power_table[si]          ; Test relative size
013C 9BDFE0           394            fstsw   ax                       ; No wait is necessary
013F A90001           395            test    ax,100H                  ; If CO = 0 then st(0) >= lower bound
0142 7407             396            jz      in_range                 ; Convert the value to a BCD integer
                      397
0144 2EDE0E0000    R  398            fimul   const10                  ; Adjust value into range
0149 FF0F             399            dec     word ptr [bx]            ; Adjust power of ten value
                      400
014B                  401     in_range:
                      402
014B D9FC             403            frndint                          ; Form integer value
                      404     ;
                      405     ;      Assert: 0 <= TOS <= 999,999,999,999,999,999
                      406     ;      The TOS number will be exactly representable in 18 digit BCD format.
                      407     ;
014D                  408     convert_integer:
                      409
014D DF76F0           410            fbstp   bcd_value                ; Store as BCD format number
                      411     ;
                      412     ;      While the store BCD runs, setup registers for the conversion to
                      413     ;      ASCII.
                      414     ;
0150 BE0800           415            mov     si,BCD_SIZE-2            ; Initial BCD index value
```

Figure 4-6. Floating-Point to ASCII Conversion Routine (Cont'd.)

```
iAPX286 MACRO ASSEMBLER    80287 Floating-Point to 18-Digit ASCII Conversion        10:12:38  09/25/83  PAGE   6


LOC  OBJ          LINE      SOURCE

0153 B9040F        416          mov     cx,0F04h             ; Set shift count and mask
0156 BB0100        417          mov     bx,1                 ; Set initial size of ASCII field for sign
0159 8B7E0C        418          mov     di,string_ptr        ; Get address of start of ASCII string
015C 8CD8          419          mov     ax,ds                ; Copy ds to es
015E 8EC0          420          mov     es,ax
0160 FC            421          cld                          ; Set autoincrement mode
0161 B02B          422          mov     al,'+'               ; Clear sign field
0163 F6C201        423          test    dl,MINUS             ; Look for negative value
0166 7402          424          jz      positive_result
                   425
0168 B02D          426          mov     al,'-'
                   427
016A               428      positive_result:
                   429
016A AA            430          stosb                        ; Bump string pointer past sign
016B 80E2FE        431          and     dl,not MINUS         ; Turn off sign bit
016E 9B            432          fwait                        ; Wait for fbstp to finish
                   433      ;
                   434      ;           Register usage:
                   435      ;                                ah:   BCD byte value in use
                   436      ;                                al:   ASCII character value
                   437      ;                                dx:   Return value
                   438      ;                                ch:   BCD mask = 0fh
                   439      ;                                cl:   BCD shift count = 4
                   440      ;                                bx:   ASCII string field width
                   441      ;                                si:   BCD field index
                   442      ;                                di:   ASCII string field pointer
                   443      ;                                ds,es: ASCII string segment base
                   444      ;
                   445      ;           Remove leading zeroes from the number.
                   446      ;
016F               447      skip_leading_zeroes:
                   448
016F 8A62F0        449          mov     ah,bcd_byte[si]      ; Get BCD byte
0172 8AC4          450          mov     al,ah                ; Copy value
0174 D2E8          451          shr     al,cl                ; Get high order digit
0176 22C5          452          and     al,ch                ; Set zero flag
0178 7516          453          jnz     enter_odd            ; Exit loop if leading non zero found
                   454
017A 8AC4          455          mov     al,ah                ; Get BCD byte again
017C 22C5          456          and     al,ch                ; Get low order digit
017E 7518          457          jnz     enter_even           ; Exit loop if non zero digit found
                   458
0180 4E            459          dec     si                   ; Decrement BCD index
0181 79EC          460          jns     skip_leading_zeroes
                   461      ;
                   462      ;           The significand was all zeroes.
                   463      ;
0183 B030          464          mov     al,'0'               ; Set initial zero
0185 AA            465          stosb
0186 43            466          inc     bx                   ; Bump string length
0187 EB16          467          jmp     short exit_with_value
                   468      ;
                   469      ;           Now expand the BCD string into digit per byte values 0-9.
                   470      ;
0189               471      digit_loop:
                   472
0189 8A62F0        473          mov     ah,bcd_byte[si]      ; Get BCD byte
018C 8AC4          474          mov     al,ah
018E D2E8          475          shr     al,cl                ; Get high order digit
                   476
0190               477      enter_odd:
                   478
0190 0430          479          add     al,'0'               ; Convert to ASCII
0192 AA            480          stosb                        ; Put digit into ASCII string area
0193 8AC4          481          mov     al,ah                ; Get low order digit
0195 22C5          482          and     al,ch
0197 43            483          inc     bx                   ; Bump field size counter
                   484
0198               485      enter_even:
                   486
0198 0430          487          add     al,'0'               ; Convert to ASCII
019A AA            488          stosb                        ; Put digit into ASCII area
019B 43            489          inc     bx                   ; Bump field size counter
019C 4E            490          dec     si                   ; Go to next BCD byte
019D 79EA          491          jns     digit_loop
                   492      ;
                   493      ;           Conversion complete.  Set the string size and remainder.
                   494      ;
019F               495      exit_with_value:
                   496
019F 8B7E0A        497          mov     di,size_ptr
01A2 891D          498          mov     word ptr [di],bx
01A4 8BC2          499          mov     ax,dx                ; Set return value
01A6 E980FE        500          jmp     exit_proc
                   501
                   502      floating_to_ascii            endp
----               503      code                         ends
                   504                                   end

ASSEMBLY COMPLETE.    NO WARNINGS.    NO ERRORS
```

Figure 4-6. Floating-Point to ASCII Conversion Routine (Cont'd.)

```
iAPX286 MACRO ASSEMBLER   Calculate the value of 10**ax                    12:11:08  09/25/83  PAGE   1


SERIES-III iAPX286 MACRO ASSEMBLER X108 ASSEMBLY OF MODULE GET_POWER_10
OBJECT MODULE PLACED IN :F3:POW10.OBJ
ASSEMBLER INVOKED BY:   ASM286.86 :F3:POW10.AP2


LOC  OBJ                    LINE        SOURCE

                           1 +1    $title("Calculate the value of 10**ax")
                           2    ;
                           3    ;           This subroutine will calculate the value of 10**ax.
                           4    ;       For values of 0 <= ax < 19, the result will be exact.
                           5    ;       All 80286 registers are transparent and the value is returned on
                           6    ;       the TOS as two numbers, exponent in ST(1) and fraction in ST(0).
                           7    ;       The exponent value can be larger than the largest exponent of an
                           8    ;       extended real format number.  Three stack entries are used.
                           9    ;
                          10            name    get_power_10
                          11
                          12            public  get_power_10, power_table
                          13
----                      14    stack   stackseg 8
                          15
----                      16    code    segment er public
                          17    ;
                          18    ;       Use exact values from 1.0 to 1e18.
                          19    ;
                          20            even                                    ; Optimize 16 bit access
0000 000000000000F0        21    power_table     dq      1.0, 1e1, 1e2, 1e3
     3F
0008 00000000000024
     40
0010 00000000000059
     40
0018 0000000000408F
     40
0020 00000000088C3         22            dq      1e4, 1e5, 1e6, 1e7
     40
0028 000000006AF8
     40
0030 000000080842E
     41
0038 00000000D01263
     41
0040 0000000084D797        23            dq      1e8, 1e9, 1e10, 1e11
     41
0048 0000000065CDCD
     41
0050 000000205FA002
     42
0058 00000E8764837
     42
0060 000000A2941A6D        24            dq      1e12, 1e13, 1e14, 1e15
     42
0068 000040E59C30A2
     42
0070 0000901EC4BCD6
     42
0078 00003426F56B0C
     43
0080 0080E03779C341        25            dq      1e16, 1e17, 1e18
     43
0088 00A0D885573476
     43
0090 00C84E676DC1AB
     43

                          26
                          27    get_power_10    proc
                          28
0098 3D1200               29            cmp     ax, 18                  ; Test for 0 <= ax < 19
009B 770F                 30            ja      out_of_range
                          31
009D 53                   32            push    bx                      ; Get working index register
009E 8BD8                 33            mov     bx, ax                  ; Form table index
00A0 C1E303               34            shl     bx, 3
00A3 2EDDB70000     R     35            fld     power_table[bx]         ; Get exact value
00A8 5B                   36            pop     bx                      ; Restore register value
00A9 D9F4                 37            fxtract                         ; Separate power and fraction
00AB C3                   38            ret                             ; OK to leave fxtract running
                          39    ;
                          40    ;       Calculate the value using the exponentiate instruction.
                          41    ;       The following relations are used:
                          42    ;           10**x = 2**(log2(10)*x)
                          43    ;           2**(I+F) = 2**I * 2**F
                          44    ;           if st(1) = I and st(0) = 2**F then fscale produces 2**(I+F)
                          45    ;
00AC                      46    out_of_range:
                          47
00AC D9E9                 48            fld12t                          ; TOS = LOG2(10)
00AE C8040000             49            enter   4, 0                    ; Format stack
00B2 8946FE               50            mov     [bp-2], ax              ; Save power of 10 value
00B5 DE4EFE               51            fimul   word ptr [bp-2]         ; TOS, X = LOG2(10)*P = LOG2(10**P)
00B8 9BD97EFC             52            fstcw   word ptr [bp-4]         ; Get current control word
00BC 8B46FC               53            mov     ax, word ptr [bp-4]     ; Get control word, no wait necessary
00BF 25FFF3               54            and     ax, not 0C00H           ; Mask off current rounding field
00C2 0D0004               55            or      ax, 0400H               ; Set round to negative infinity
00C5 8746FC               56            xchg    ax, word ptr [bp-4]     ; Put new control word in memory
                          57                                            ; old control word is in ax
00C8 D9E8                 58            fld1                            ; Set TOS = -1.0
```

Figure 4-6. Floating-Point to ASCII Conversion Routine (Cont'd.)

```
iAPX286 MACRO ASSEMBLER    Calculate the value of 10**ax                    12:11:08  09/25/83  PAGE    2


LOC  OBJ              LINE      SOURCE

OOCA D9EO             59            fchs                              ; Copy power value in base two
OOCC D9C1            60            fld     st(1)                     ; Set new control word value
OOCE D96EFC          61            fldcw   word ptr [bp-4]
OOD1 D9FC            62            frndint                           ; TOS = I; -inf < I <= X, I is an integer
OOD3 8946FC          63            mov     word ptr [bp-4],ax        ; Restore original rounding control
OOD6 D96EFC          64            fldcw   word ptr [bp-4]
OOD9 D9CA            65            fxch    st(2)                     ; TOS = X, ST(1) = -1.0, ST(2) = I
OODB D8E2            66            fsub    st,st(2)                  ; TOS,F = X-I; 0 <= TOS < 1.0
OODD 8B46FE          67            mov     ax,[bp-2]                 ; Restore power of ten
OOEO D9FD            68            fscale                            ; TOS = F/2; 0 <= TOS < 0.5
OOE2 D9FO            69            f2xm1                             ; TOS = 2**(F/2) - 1.0
OOE4 C9              70            leave                             ; Restore stack
OOE5 DEE1            71            fsubr                             ; Form 2**(F/2)
OOE7 DCC8            72            fmul    st,st(0)                  ; Form 2**F
OOE9 C3              73            ret                               ; OK to leave fmul running
                     74
                     75      get_power_10    endp
                     76
----                 77      code            ends
                     78                      end

ASSEMBLY COMPLETE,   NO WARNINGS,   NO ERRORS



iAPX286 MACRO ASSEMBLER    Determine TOS register contents                   12:12:13  09/25/83  PAGE    1


SERIES-III iAPX286 MACRO ASSEMBLER X108 ASSEMBLY OF MODULE TOS_STATUS
OBJECT MODULE PLACED IN :F3:TOSST.OBJ
ASSEMBLER INVOKED BY:  ASM286.86 :F3:TOSST.AP2


LOC  OBJ              LINE      SOURCE

                     1 +1     $title("Determine TOS register contents")
                     2   ;
                     3   ;         This subroutine will return a value from 0-15 in AX corresponding
                     4   ;     to the contents of 80287 TOS.  All registers are transparent and no
                     5   ;     errors are possible.  The return value corresponds to c3,c2,c1,c0
                     6   ;     of FXAM instruction.
                     7   ;
                     8         name    tos_status
                     9
                    10         public  tos_status
                    11
----                12  stack          stackseg 6         ; Allocate space on the stack
                    13
----                14  code           segment er public
                    15
0000                16  tos_status     proc
                    17
0000 D9E5           18            fxam                     ; Get register contents status
0002 9BDFEO         19            fstsw   ax               ; Get status
0005 8AC4           20            mov     al,ah            ; Put bit 10-8 into bits 2-0
0007 250740         21            and     ax,4007h         ; Mask out bits c3,c2,c1,c0
OOOA COECO3         22            shr     ah,3             ; Put bit c3 into bit 11
OOOD OAC4           23            or      al,ah            ; Put c3 into bit 3
OOOF B400           24            mov     ah,0             ; Clear return value
0011 C3             25            ret
                    26
                    27  tos_status     endp
                    28
----                29  code           ends
                    30                 end

ASSEMBLY COMPLETE,   NO WARNINGS,   NO ERRORS
```

Figure 4-6. Floating-Point to ASCII Conversion Routine (Cont'd.)

Function Partitioning

Three separate modules implement the conversion. Most of the work of the conversion is done in the module FLOATING_TO_ASCII. The other modules are provided separately, because they have a more general use. One of them, GET_POWER_10, is also used by the ASCII to floating-point conversion routine. The other small module, TOS_STATUS, will identify what, if anything, is in the top of the numeric register stack.

Exception Considerations

Care is taken inside the function to avoid generating exceptions. Any possible numeric value will be accepted. The only exceptions possible would occur if insufficient space exists on the numeric register stack.

The value passed in the numeric stack is checked for existence, type (NaN or infinity), and status (unnormal, denormal, zero, sign). The string size is tested for a minimum and maximum value. If the top of the register stack is empty, or the string size is too small, the function will return with an error code.

Overflow and underflow is avoided inside the function for very large or very small numbers.

Special Instructions

The functions demonstrate the operation of several numeric instructions, different data types, and precision control. Shown are instructions for automatic conversion to BCD, calculating the value of 10 raised to an integer value, establishing and maintaining concurrency, data synchronization, and use of directed rounding on the NPX.

Without the extended precision data type and built-in exponential function, the double precision accuracy of this function could not be attained with the size and speed of the shown example.

The function relies on the numeric BCD data type for conversion from binary floating-point to decimal. It is not difficult to unpack the BCD digits into separate ASCII decimal digits. The major work involves scaling the floating-point value to the comparatively limited range of BCD values. To print a 9-digit result requires accurately scaling the given value to an integer between 10^8 and 10^9. For example, the number $+0.123456789$ requires a scaling factor of 10^9 to produce the value $+123456789.0$, which can be stored in 9 BCD digits. The scale factor must be an exact power of 10 to avoid to changing any of the printed digit values.

These routines should exactly convert all values exactly representable in decimal in the field size given. Integer values that fit in the given string size will not be scaled, but directly stored into the BCD form. Noninteger values exactly representable in decimal within the string size limits will also be exactly converted. For example, 0.125 is exactly representable in binary or decimal. To convert this floating-point value to decimal, the scaling factor will be 1000, resulting in 125. When scaling a value, the function must keep track of where the decimal point lies in the final decimal value.

Description of Operation

Converting a floating-point number to decimal ASCII takes three major steps: identifying the magnitude of the number, scaling it for the BCD data type, and converting the BCD data type to a decimal ASCII string.

Identifying the magnitude of the result requires finding the value X such that the number is represented by $I*10^X$, where $1.0 <= I < 10.0$. Scaling the number requires multiplying it by a scaling factor 10^S, so that the result is an integer requiring no more decimal digits than provided for in the ASCII string.

Once scaled, the numeric rounding modes and BCD conversion put the number in a form easy to convert to decimal ASCII by host software.

Implementing each of these three steps requires attention to detail. To begin with, not all floating-point values have a numeric meaning. Values such as infinity, indefinite, or Not a Number (NaN) may be encountered by the conversion routine. The conversion routine should recognize these values and identify them uniquely.

Special cases of numeric values also exist. Denormals, unnormals, and pseudo zero all have a numeric value but should be recognized, because all of them indicate that precision was lost during some earlier calculations.

Once it has been determined that the number has a numeric value, and it is normalized setting appropriate unnormal flags, the value must be scaled to the BCD range.

Scaling the Value

To scale the number, its magnitude must be determined. It is sufficient to calculate the magnitude to an accuracy of 1 unit, or within a factor of 10 of the given value. After scaling the number, a check will be made to see if the result falls in the range expected. If not, the result can be adjusted one decimal order of magnitude up or down. The adjustment test after the scaling is necessary due to inevitable inaccuracies in the scaling value.

Because the magnitude estimate need only be close, a fast technique is used. The magnitude is estimated by multiplying the power of 2, the unbiased floating-point exponent, associated with the number by $\log_{10}2$. Rounding the result to an integer will produce an estimate of sufficient accuracy. Ignoring the fraction value can introduce a maximum error of 0.32 in the result.

Using the magnitude of the value and size of the number string, the scaling factor can be calculated. Calculating the scaling factor is the most inaccurate operation of the conversion process. The relation $10^x = 2^{**}(X^*\log_2 10)$ is used for this function. The exponentiate instruction (F2XM1) will be used.

Due to restrictions on the range of values allowed by the F2XM1 instruction, the power of 2 value will be split into integer and fraction components. The relation $2^{**}(I + F) = 2^{**}I * 2^{**}F$ allows using the FSCALE instruction to recombine the $2^{**}F$ value, calculated through F2XM1, and the $2^{**}I$ part.

INACCURACY IN SCALING

The inaccuracy of these operations arises because of the trailing zeros placed into the fraction value when stripping off the integer valued bits. For each integer valued bit in the power of 2 value separated from the fraction bits, one bit of precision is lost in the fraction field due to the zero fill occurring in the least significant bits.

Up to 14 bits may be lost in the fraction because the largest allowed floating point exponent value is $2^{14}-1$.

AVOIDING UNDERFLOW AND OVERFLOW

The fraction and exponent fields of the number are separated to avoid underflow and overflow in calculating the scaling values. For example, to scale 10^{-4932} to 10^8 requires a scaling factor of 10^{4950}, which cannot be represented by the NPX.

By separating the exponent and fraction, the scaling operation involves adding the exponents separate from multiplying the fractions. The exponent arithmetic will involve small integers, all easily represented by the NPX.

FINAL ADJUSTMENTS

It is possible that the power function (Get_Power_10) could produce a scaling value such that it forms a scaled result larger than the ASCII field could allow. For example, scaling $9.9999999999999999 \times 10^{4900}$ by $1.00000000000000010 \times 10^{-4883}$ would produce $1.00000000000000009 \times 10^{18}$. The scale factor is within the accuracy of the NPX and the result is within the conversion accuracy, but it cannot be represented in BCD format. This is why there is a post-scaling test on the magnitude of the result. The result can be multiplied or divided by 10, depending on whether the result was too small or too large, respectively.

Output Format

For maximum flexibility in output formats, the position of the decimal point is indicated by a binary integer called the power value. If the power value is zero, then the decimal point is assumed to be at the right of the rightmost digit. Power values greater than zero indicate how many trailing zeros are not shown. For each unit below zero, move the decimal point to the left in the string.

The last step of the conversion is storing the result in BCD and indicating where the decimal point lies. The BCD string is then unpacked into ASCII decimal characters. The ASCII sign is set corresponding to the sign of the original value.

TRIGONOMETRIC CALCULATION EXAMPLES

The 80287 instruction set does not provide a complete set of trigonometric functions that can be used directly in calculations. Rather, the basic building blocks for implementing trigonometric functions are provided by the FPTAN and FPREM instructions. The example in figure 4-7 shows how three trigonometric functions (sine, cosine, and tangent) can be implementing using the 80287. All three functions accept a valid angle argument between -2^{62} and $+2^{62}$. These functions may be called from PL/M-286, Pascal-286, FORTRAN-286, or ASM286 routines.

These trigonometric functions use the partial tangent instruction together with trigonometric identities to calculate the result. They are accurate to within 16 units of the low 4 bits of an extended precision value. The functions are coded for speed and small size, with tradeoffs available for greater accuracy.

FPTAN and FPREM

These trigonometric functions use the FPTAN instruction of the NPX. FPTAN requires that the angle argument be between 0 and $\pi/4$ radians, 0 to 45 degrees. The FPREM instruction is used to reduce the argument down to this range. The low three quotient bits set by FPREM identify which octant the original angle was in.

One FPREM instruction iteration can reduce angles of 10^{18} radians or less in magnitude to $\pi/4$! Larger values can be reduced, but the meaning of the result is questionable, because any errors in the least significant bits of that value represent changes of 45 degrees or more in the reduced angle.

Cosine Uses Sine Code

To save code space, the cosine function uses most of the sine function code. The relation $\sin(|A| + \pi/2) = \cos(A)$ is used to convert the cosine argument into a sine argument. Adding $\pi/2$ to the angle is performed by adding 010_2 to the FPREM quotient bits identifying the argument's octant.

It would be very inaccurate to add $\pi/2$ to the cosine argument if it was very much different from $\pi/2$.

Depending on which octant the argument falls in, a different relation will be used in the sine and tangent functions. The program listings show which relations are used.

For the tangent function, the ratio produced by FPTAN will be directly evaluated. The sine function will use either a sine or cosine relation depending on which octant the angle fell into. On exit, these functions will normally leave a divide instruction in progress to maintain concurrency.

If the input angles are of a restricted range, such as from 0 to 45 degrees, then considerable optimization is possible since full angle reduction and octant identification is not necessary.

All three functions begin by looking at the value given to them. Not a Number (NaN), infinity, or empty registers must be specially treated. Unnormals need to be converted to normal values before the FPTAN instruction will work correctly. Denormals will be converted to very small unnormals that do work correctly for the FPTAN instruction. The sign of the angle is saved to control the sign of the result.

Within the functions, close attention was paid to maintain concurrent execution of the 80287 and host. The concurrent execution will effectively hide the execution time of the decision logic used in the program.

```
iAPX286 MACRO ASSEMBLER    80287 Trignometric Functions                          10:13:51  09/25/83  PAGE   1


SERIES-III iAPX286 MACRO ASSEMBLER X108 ASSEMBLY OF MODULE TRIG_FUNCTIONS
OBJECT MODULE PLACED IN  :F3:TRIG.OBJ
ASSEMBLER INVOKED BY:  ASM286.86 :F3:TRIG.AP2


LOC  OBJ                LINE     SOURCE

                           1 +1  $title("80287 Trignometric Functions")
                           2
                           3                name     trig_functions
                           4                public   sine,cosine,tangent
                           5
----                       6      stack      stackseg    6                      ; Reserve local space
                           7
  *                        8      sw_287     record   res1:1,cond3:1,top:3,cond2:1,cond1:1,cond0:1,
                           9      &                    res2:8
                          10
----                      11      code       segment er public
                          12      ;
                          13      ;        Define local constants.
                          14      ;
                          15                even
0000 35C26821A2DA0F       16      pi_quarter dt       3FFEC90FDAA22168C235R      ; PI/4
     C9FE3F
000A 0000C0FF             17      indefinite dd       0FFC00000R                 ; Indefinite special value
                          18 +1  $eject
```

Figure 4-7. Calculating Trigonometric Functions

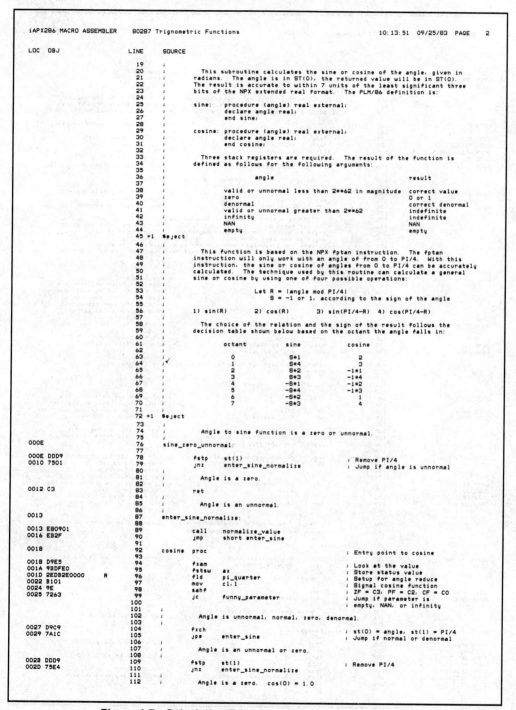

```
LOC  OBJ           LINE    SOURCE

                   19    ;
                   20    ;            This subroutine calculates the sine or cosine of the angle, given in
                   21    ;     radians.  The angle is in ST(0), the returned value will be in ST(0).
                   22    ;     The result is accurate to within 7 units of the least significant three
                   23    ;     bits of the NPX extended real format.  The PLM/86 definition is:
                   24    ;
                   25    ;     sine:  procedure (angle) real external;
                   26    ;            declare angle real;
                   27    ;            end sine;
                   28    ;
                   29    ;     cosine: procedure (angle) real external;
                   30    ;            declare angle real;
                   31    ;            end cosine;
                   32    ;
                   33    ;            Three stack registers are required.  The result of the function is
                   34    ;     defined as follows for the following arguments:
                   35    ;
                   36    ;                  angle                                  result
                   37    ;
                   38    ;            valid or unnormal less than 2**62 in magnitude  correct value
                   39    ;            zero                                           0 or 1
                   40    ;            denormal                                       correct denormal
                   41    ;            valid or unnormal greater than 2**62           indefinite
                   42    ;            infinity                                       indefinite
                   43    ;            NAN                                            NAN
                   44    ;            empty                                          empty
                   45 +1 $eject
                   46    ;
                   47    ;            This function is based on the NPX fptan instruction.  The fptan
                   48    ;     instruction will only work with an angle of from 0 to PI/4.  With this
                   49    ;     instruction, the sine or cosine of angles from 0 to PI/4 can be accurately
                   50    ;     calculated.  The technique used by this routine can calculate a general
                   51    ;     sine or cosine by using one of four possible operations:
                   52    ;
                   53    ;                  Let R = |angle mod PI/4|
                   54    ;                      S = -1 or 1, according to the sign of the angle
                   55    ;
                   56    ;            1) sin(R)     2) cos(R)     3) sin(PI/4-R) 4) cos(PI/4-R)
                   57    ;
                   58    ;            The choice of the relation and the sign of the result follows the
                   59    ;     decision table shown below based on the octant the angle falls in:
                   60    ;
                   61    ;                  octant        sine            cosine
                   62    ;
                   63    ;                  0             S*1             2
                   64    ;                  1             S*4             3
                   65    ;                  2             S*2             -1*1
                   66    ;                  3             S*3             -1*4
                   67    ;                  4             -S*1            -1*2
                   68    ;                  5             -S*4            -1*3
                   69    ;                  6             -S*2            1
                   70    ;                  7             -S*3            4
                   71    ;
                   72 +1 $eject
                   73    ;
                   74    ;            Angle to sine function is a zero or unnormal.
                   75    ;
000E               76    sine_zero_unnormal:
                   77    ;
000E DDD9          78            fstp    st(1)                          ; Remove PI/4
0010 7501          79            jnz     enter_sine_normalize           ; Jump if angle is unnormal
                   80    ;
                   81    ;            Angle is a zero.
                   82    ;
0012 C3            83            ret
                   84    ;
                   85    ;            Angle is an unnormal.
                   86    ;
0013               87    enter_sine_normalize:
                   88
0013 E80901        89            call    normalize_value
0016 EB2F          90            jmp     short enter_sine
                   91
0018               92    cosine  proc                                   ; Entry point to cosine
                   93
0018 D9E5          94            fxam                                   ; Look at the value
001A 9BDFE0        95            fstsw   ax                             ; Store status value
001D 2EDB2E0000  R 96            fld     pi_quarter                     ; Setup for angle reduce
0022 B101          97            mov     cl,1                           ; Signal cosine function
0024 9E            98            sahf                                   ; ZF = C3, PF = C2, CF = C0
0025 7263          99            jc      funny_parameter                ; Jump if parameter is
                   100   ;                                              ; empty, NAN, or infinity
                   101   ;
                   102   ;            Angle is unnormal, normal, zero, denormal.
                   103   ;
0027 D9C9          104           fxch                                   ; st(0) = angle, st(1) = PI/4
0029 7A1C          105           jpe     enter_sine                     ; Jump if normal or denormal
                   106   ;
                   107   ;            Angle is an unnormal or zero.
                   108   ;
002B DDD9          109           fstp    st(1)                          ; Remove PI/4
002D 75E4          110           jnz     enter_sine_normalize
                   111   ;
                   112   ;            Angle is a zero.  cos(0) = 1.0
```

Figure 4-7. Calculating Trigonometric Functions (Cont'd.)

```
LOC  OBJ                LINE    SOURCE

                        113   ;
002F DDD8               114           fstp    st(0)                           ; Remove 0
0031 D9E8               115           fld1                                    ; Return 1
0033 C3                 116           ret
                        117   ;
                        118   ;          All work is done as a sine function.  By adding PI/2 to the angle
                        119   ;          a cosine is converted to a sine.  Of course the angle addition is not
                        120   ;          done to the argument but rather to the program logic control values.
                        121   ;
0034                    122   sine:                                           ; Entry point for sine function
                        123   ;
0034 D9E5               124           fxam                                    ; Look at the parameter
0036 9BDFE0             125           fstsw   ax                              ; Look at fxam status
0039 2EDB2E0000    R    126           fld     pi_quarter                      ; Get PI/4 value
003E 9E                 127           sahf                                    ; CF = C0, PF = C2, ZF = C3
003F 7249               128           jc      funny_parameter                 ; Jump if empty, NAN, or infinity
                        129   ;
                        130   ;          Angle is unnormal, normal, zero, or denormal.
                        131   ;
0041 D9C9               132           fxch                                    ; ST(1) = PI/4, st(0) angle
0043 B100               133           mov     cl,0                            ; Signal sine
0045 7BC7               134           jpo     sine_zero_unnormal              ; Jump if zero or unnormal
                        135   ;
                        136   ;          ST(0) is either a normal or denormal value.  Both will work.
                        137   ;          Use the fprem instruction to accurately reduce the range of the given
                        138   ;          angle to within 0 and PI/4 in magnitude.  If fprem cannot reduce the
                        139   ;          angle in one shot, the angle is too big to be meaningful, > 2**62
                        140   ;          radians.  Any roundoff error in the calculation of the angle given
                        141   ;          could completely change the result of this function.  It is safest to
                        142   ;          call this very rare case an error.
                        143   ;
0047                    144   enter_sine:
0047 D9F8               145           fprem                                   ; Reduce angle
                        146   ;                                               ; Note that fprem will force a
                        147   ;                                               ; denormal to a very small unnormal
                        148   ;                                               ; Fptan of a very small unnormal
                        149   ;                                               ; will be the same very small
                        150   ;                                               ; unnormal, which is correct.
0049 93                 151           xchg    ax,bx                           ; Save old status in BX
004A 9BDFE0             152           fstsw   ax                              ; Check if reduction was complete
                        153   ;                                               ; Quotient in C0,C3,C1
004D 93                 154           xchg    ax,bx                           ; Put new status in bx
004E F6C704             155           test    bh,high(mask cond2)             ; sin(2*N*PI+x) = sin(x)
0051 7544               156           jnz     angle_too_big
                        157   ;
                        158   ;          Set sign flags and test for which eighth of the revolution the
                        159   ;          angle fell into.
                        160   ;
                        161   ;          Assert: -PI/4 < st(0) < PI/4
                        162   ;
0053 D9E1               163           fabs                                    ; Force the argument positive
                        164   ;                                               ; cond1 bit in bx holds the sign
0055 0AC9               165           or      cl,cl                           ; Test for sine or cosine function
0057 740F               166           jz      sine_select                     ; Jump if sine function
                        167   ;
                        168   ;          This is a cosine function.  Ignore the original sign of the angle
                        169   ;          and add a quarter revolution to the octant id from the fprem instruction.
                        170   ;          cos(A) = sin(A+PI/2) and cos(|A|) = cos(A)
                        171   ;
0059 80E4FD             172           and     ah,not high(mask cond1)         ; Turn off sign of argument
005C 80CFB0             173           or      bh,80H                          ; Prepare to add 010 to C0,C3,C1
                        174   ;                                               ; status value in ax
                        175   ;                                               ; Set busy bit so carry out from
005F 80C740             176           add     bh,high(mask cond3)             ; C3 will go into the carry flag
0062 3000               177           mov     al,0                            ; Extract carry flag
0064 D0D0               178           rcl     al,1                            ; Put carry flag in low bit
0066 32F8               179           xor     bh,al                           ; Add carry to C0 not changing
                        180   ;                                               ; C1 flag
                        181   ;
                        182   ;          See if the argument should be reversed, depending on the octant in
                        183   ;          which the argument fell during fprem.
                        184   ;
0068                    185   sine_select:
                        186   ;
0068 F6C702             187           test    bh,high(mask cond1)             ; Reverse angle if C1 = 1
006B 7404               188           jz      no_sine_reverse
                        189   ;
                        190   ;          Angle was in octants 1,3,5,7.
                        191   ;
006D DEE9               192           fsub                                    ; Invert sense of rotation
006F EB0E               193           jmp     short do_sine_fptan             ; 0 < arg <= PI/4
                        194   ;
                        195   ;          Angle was in octants 0,2,4,6.
                        196   ;          Test for a zero argument since fptan will not work if st(0) = 0
                        197   ;
0071                    198   no_sine_reverse:
                        199   ;
0071 D9E4               200           ftst                                    ; Test for zero angle
0073 91                 201           xchg    ax,cx
0074 9BDFE0             202           fstsw   ax                              ; cond3 = 1 if st(0) = 0
0077 91                 203           xchg    ax,cx
0078 DDD9               204           fstp    st(1)                           ; Remove PI/4
007A F6C540             205           test    ch,high(mask cond3)             ; If C3=1, argument is zero
007D 7514               206           jnz     sine_argument_zero
```

Figure 4-7. Calculating Trigonometric Functions (Cont'd.)

```
iAPX286 MACRO ASSEMBLER    80287 Trignometric Functions                         10:13:51  09/25/83  PAGE   4

LOC  OBJ                   LINE    SOURCE

                           207     ;
                           208     ;            Assert:  0 < st(0) <= PI/4
                           209     ;
007F                       210     do_sine_fptan:
                           211
007F D9F2                  212             fptan                                 ; TAN ST(0) = ST(1)/ST(0) = Y/X
                           213
0081                       214     after_sine_fptan:
                           215
0081 F6C742                216             test    bh,high(mask cond3 + mask cond1); Look at octant angle fell into
0084 7B1A                  217             jpo     X_numerator                   ; Calculate cosine for octants
                           218     ;                                              ; 1, 2, 5, 6
                           219     ;
                           220     ;         Calculate the sine of the argument.
                           221     ;         sin(A) = tan(A)/sqrt(1+tan(A)**2)     if tan(A) = Y/X then
                           222     ;         sin(A) = Y/sqrt(X*X + Y*Y)
                           223     ;
0086 D9C1                  224             fld     st(1)                         ; Copy Y value
0088 EB1A                  225             jmp     short finish_sine             ; Put Y value in numerator
                           226     ;
                           227     ;         The top of the stack is either NAN, infinity, or empty.
                           228     ;
008A                       229     funny_parameter:
                           230
008A DDD8                  231             fstp    st(0)                         ; Remove PI/4
008C 7404                  232             jz      return_empty                  ; Return empty if no parm
                           233
008E 7B02                  234             jpo     return_NAN                    ; Jump if st(0) is NAN
                           235
                           236     ;         st(0) is infinity.  Return an indefinite value.
                           237     ;
0090 D9F8                  238             fprem                                 ; ST(1) can be anything
                           239
0092                       240     return_NAN:
0092                       241     return_empty:
                           242
0092 C3                    243             ret                                   ; Ok to leave fprem running
                           244     ;
                           245     ;         Simulate fptan with st(0) = 0
                           246     ;
0093                       247     sine_argument_zero:
                           248
0093 D9E8                  249             fld1                                  ; Simulate tan(0)
0095 EBEA                  250             jmp     after_sine_fptan              ; Return the zero value
                           251     ;
                           252     ;         The angle was too large.  Remove the modulus and dividend from the
                           253     ;         stack and return an indefinite result.
                           254     ;
0097                       255     angle_too_big:
                           256
0097 DED9                  257             fcompp                                ; Pop two values from the stack
0099 2ED9060A00      R     258             fld     indefinite                    ; Return indefinite
009E 9B                    259             fwait                                 ; Wait for load to finish
009F C3                    260             ret
                           261     ;
                           262     ;         Calculate the cosine of the argument.
                           263     ;         cos(A) = 1/sqrt(1+tan(A)**2)     if tan(A) = Y/X then
                           264     ;         cos(A) = X/sqrt(X*X + Y*Y)
                           265     ;
00A0                       266     X_numerator:
                           267
00A0 D9C0                  268             fld     st(0)                         ; Copy X value
00A2 D9CA                  269             fxch    st(2)                         ; Put X in numerator
                           270
00A4                       271     finish_sine:
                           272
00A4 DCC8                  273             fmul    st,st(0)                      ; Form X*X + Y*Y
00A6 D9C9                  274             fxch
00A8 DCC8                  275             fmul    st,st(0)
00AA DEC1                  276             fadd                                  ; st(0) = X*X + Y*Y
00AC D9FA                  277             fsqrt                                 ; st(0) = sqrt(X*X + Y*Y)
                           278
                           279
                           280     ;         Form the sign of the result.  The two conditions are the C1 flag from
                           281     ;         FXAM in bh and the CO flag from fprem in ah.
                           282     ;
00AE 80E701                283             and     bh,high(mask cond0)           ; Look at the fprem CO flag
00B1 80E402                284             and     ah,high(mask cond1)           ; Look at the fxam C1 flag
00B4 0AFC                  285             or      bh,ah                         ; Even number of flags cancel
00B6 7A02                  286             jpe     positive_sine                 ; Two negatives make a positive
                           287
00B8 D9E0                  288             fchs                                  ; Force result negative
                           289
00BA                       290     positive_sine:
                           291
00BA DEF9                  292             fdiv                                  ; Form final result
00BC C3                    293             ret                                   ; Ok to leave fdiv running
                           294
                           295     cosine  endp
                           296  +1 $eject
                           297     ;
                           298     ;         This function will calculate the tangent of an angle.
                           299     ;         The angle, in radians is passed in ST(0), the tangent is returned
                           300     ;         in ST(0).  The tangent is calculated to an accuracy of 4 units in the
```

Figure 4-7. Calculating Trigonometric Functions (Cont'd.)

```
iAPX286 MACRO ASSEMBLER    80287 Trignometric Functions                          10:13:51  09/25/83  PAGE   5

LOC  OBJ                   LINE    SOURCE
                           301     ;        least three significant bits of an extended real format number.   The
                           302     ;        PLM/86 calling format is:
                           303     ;
                           304     ;      tangent: procedure (angle) real external;
                           305     ;               declare angle real;
                           306     ;               end tangent;
                           307     ;
                           308     ;        Two stack registers are used.  The result of the tangent function is
                           309     ;      defined for the following cases:
                           310     ;
                           311     ;                       angle                               result
                           312     ;
                           313     ;      valid or unnormal < 2**62 in magnitude          correct value
                           314     ;      0                                               0
                           315     ;      denormal                                        correct denormal
                           316     ;      valid or unnormal > 2**62 in magnitude          indefinite
                           317     ;      NAN                                             NAN
                           318     ;      infinity                                        indefinite
                           319     ;      empty                                           empty
                           320     ;
                           321     ;        The tangent instruction uses the fptan instruction.  Four possible
                           322     ;      relations are used:
                           323     ;
                           324     ;      Let R = !angle MOD PI/4!
                           325     ;          S = -1 or 1 depending on the sign of the angle
                           326     ;
                           327     ;      1) tan(R)     2) tan(PI/4-R)  3) 1/tan(R)    4) 1/tan(PI/4-R)
                           328     ;
                           329     ;        The following table is used to decide which relation to use depending
                           330     ;      on in which octant the angle fell.
                           331     ;
                           332     ;      octant          relation
                           333     ;
                           334     ;         0              S*1
                           335     ;         1              S*4
                           336     ;         2             -S*3
                           337     ;         3             -S*2
                           338     ;         4              S*1
                           339     ;         5              S*4
                           340     ;         6             -S*3
                           341     ;         7             -S*2
                           342     ;
00BD                       343     tangent proc
                           344
00BD  D9E5                 345             fxam                                    ; Look at the parameter
00BF  9BDFE0               346             fstsw   ax                              ; Get fxam status
00C2  2EDB2E0000    R      347             fld     pi_quarter                      ; Get PI/4
00C7  9E                   348             sahf                                    ; CF = C0, PF = C2, ZF = C3
00C8  72C0                 349             jc      funny_parameter
                           350     ;
                           351     ;        Angle is unnormal, normal, zero, or denormal.
                           352     ;
00CA  D9C9                 353             fxch                                    ; st(0) = angle, st(1) = PI/4
00CC  7A17                 354             jpe     tan_zero_unnormal
                           355     ;
                           356     ;        Angle is either an normal or denormal.
                           357     ;      Reduce the angle to the range -PI/4 < result < PI/4.
                           358     ;      If fprem cannot perform this operation in one try, the magnitude of the
                           359     ;      angle must be > 2**62.  Such an angle is so large that any rounding
                           360     ;      errors could make a very large difference in the reduced angle.
                           361     ;      It is safest to call this very rare case an error.
                           362     ;
00CE                       363     tan_normal:
                           364
00CE  D9F8                 365             fprem                                   ; Quotient in C0,C3,C1
                           366                                                     ; Convert denormals into unnormals
00D0  93                   367             xchg    ax,bx
00D1  9BDFE0               368             fstsw   ax                              ; Quotient identifies octant
                           369                                                     ; original angle fell into
00D4  93                   370             xchg    ax,bx
00D5  F6C704               371             test    bh,high(mask cond2)             ; Test for complete reduction
00D8  75BD                 372             jnz     angle_too_big                   ; Exit if angle was too big
                           373     ;
                           374     ;        See if the angle must be reversed.
                           375     ;
                           376     ;        Assert: -PI/4 < st(0) < PI/4
                           377     ;
00DA  D9E1                 378             fabs                                    ; 0 <= st(0) < PI/4
                           379                                                     ; C3 in bx has the sign flag
00DC  F6C702               380             test    bh,high(mask cond1)             ; must be reversed
00DF  740E                 381             jz      no_tan_reverse
                           382     ;
                           383     ;        Angle fell in octants 1,3,5,7.  Reverse it, subtract it from PI/4.
                           384     ;
00E1  DEE9                 385             fsub                                    ; Reverse angle
00E3  EB18                 386             jmp     short do_tangent
                           387     ;
                           388     ;        Angle is either zero or an unnormal.
                           389     ;
00E5                       390     tan_zero_unnormal:
                           391
00E5  DDD9                 392             fstp    st(1)                           ; Remove PI/4
00E7  7405                 393             jz      tan_angle_zero
                           394     ;
                           395     ;        Angle is an unnormal.
```

```
iAPX286 MACRO ASSEMBLER     80287 Trignometric Functions                        10:13:51  09/25/83  PAGE   6


 LOC  OBJ              LINE    SOURCE

                       396    ;
00E9 E83300            397              call     normalize_value
00EC EBE0              398              jmp      tan_normal
                       399    ;
00EE                   400    tan_angle_zero:
                       401    ;
00EE C3                402              ret
                       403    ;
                       404    ;       Angle fell in octants 0,2,4,6.  Test for st(0) = 0, fptan won't work.
                       405    ;
00EF                   406    no_tan_reverse:
                       407    ;
00EF D9E4              408              ftst                              ; Test for zero angle
00F1 91                409              xchg     ax,cx
00F2 9BDFE0            410              fstsw    ax                       ; C3 = 1 if st(0) = 0
00F5 91                411              xchg     ax,cx
00F6 DDD9              412              fstp     st(1)                    ; Remove PI/4
00F8 F6C540            413              test     ch,high(mask cond3)
00FB 7515              414              jnz      tan_zero
                       415    ;
00FD                   416    do_tangent:
                       417    ;
00FD D9F2              418              fptan                             ; tan ST(0) = ST(1)/ST(0)
                       419    ;
00FF                   420    after_tangent:
                       421    ;
                       422    ;       Decide on the order of the operands and their sign for the divide
                       423    ;       operation while the fptan instruction is working.
                       424    ;
00FF 8AC7              425              mov      al,bh                    ; Get a copy of fprem C3 flag
0101 254002            426              and      ax,mask cond1 + high(mask cond3); Examine fprem C3 flag and
                       427                                               ; FXAM C1 flag
0104 F6C742            428              test     bh,high(mask cond1 + mask cond3); Use reverse divide if in
                       429                                               ; octants 1,2,5,6
0107 7B0D              430              jpo      reverse_divide           ; Note! parity works on low
                       431                                               ; 8 bits only!
                       432    ;
                       433    ;       Angle was in octants 0,3,4,7.
                       434    ;       Test for the sign of the result.  Two negatives cancel.
                       435    ;
0109 0AC4              436              or       al,ah
010B 7A02              437              jpe      positive_divide
                       438    ;
010D D9E0              439              fchs                             ; Force result negative
                       440    ;
010F                   441    positive_divide:
                       442    ;
010F DEF9              443              fdiv                             ; Form result
0111 C3                444              ret                              ; Ok to leave fdiv running
                       445    ;
0112                   446    tan_zero:
                       447    ;
0112 D9E8              448              fld1                             ; Force 1/0 = tan(PI/2)
0114 EBE9              449              jmp      after_tangent
                       450    ;
                       451    ;       Angle was in octants 1,2,5,6.
                       452    ;       Set the correct sign of the result.
                       453    ;
0116                   454    reverse_divide:
                       455    ;
0116 0AC4              456              or       al,ah
0118 7A02              457              jpe      positive_r_divide
                       458    ;
011A D9E0              459              fchs                             ; Force result negative
                       460    ;
011C                   461    positive_r_divide:
                       462    ;
011C DEF1              463              fdivr                            ; Form reciprocal of result
011E C3                464              ret                              ; Ok to leave fdiv running
                       465    ;
                       466    tangent endp
                       467    ;
                       468    ;       This function will normalize the value in st(0).
                       469    ;       Then PI/4 is placed into st(1).
                       470    ;
011F                   471    normalize_value:
                       472    ;
011F D9E1              473              fabs                             ; Force value positive
0121 D9F4              474              fxtract                          ; 0 <= st(0) < 1
0123 D9E8              475              fld1                             ; Get normalize bit
0125 DCC1              476              fadd     st(1),st                 ; Normalize fraction
0127 DEE9              477              fsub                             ; Restore original value
0129 D9FD              478              fscale                           ; Form original normalized value
012B DDD9              479              fstp     st(1)                    ; Remove scale factor
012D 2EDB2E0000     R  480              fld      pi_quarter               ; Get PI/4
0132 D9C9              481              fxch
0134 C3               482              ret
                       483    ;
----                   484    code     ends
                       485              end


ASSEMBLY COMPLETE,   NO WARNINGS,   NO ERRORS
```

Figure 4-7. Calculating Trigonometric Functions (Cont'd.)

Figure 4-7. Calculating Trigonometric Functions (Cont'd)

Appendix
Machine Instruction
Encoding and Decoding

A

APPENDIX A
MACHINE INSTRUCTION ENCODING AND DECODING

Machine instructions for the 80287 come in one of five different forms as shown in table A-1. In all cases, the instructions are at least two bytes long and begin with the bit pattern 11011B, which identifies the ESCAPE class of instructions. Instructions that reference memory operands are encoded much like similar CPU instructions, because all of the CPU memory-addressing modes may be used with ESCAPE instructions.

Note that several of the processor control instructions (see table 2-11 in Chapter Two) may be preceded by an assembler-generated CPU WAIT instruction (encoding: 10011011B) if they are programmed using the WAIT form of their mnemonics. The ASM286 assembler inserts a WAIT instruction only before these specific *processor control* instructions—all of the *numeric* instructions are automatically synchronized by the 80286 CPU and an explicit WAIT instruction, though allowed, is not necessary.

Table A-1. 80287 Instruction Encoding

	Lower-Addressed Byte								Higher-Addressed Byte								0, 1, or 2 bytes
(1)	1	1	0	1	1	OP-A		1	MOD		1	OP-B		R/M			DISPLACEMENT
(2)	1	1	0	1	1	FORMAT		OP-A	MOD		OP-B			R/M			DISPLACEMENT
(3)	1	1	0	1	1	R	P	OP-A	1		1	OP-B			REG		
(4)	1	1	0	1	1	0	0	1	1	1	1		OP				
(5)	1	1	0	1	1	0	1	1	1	1	1		OP				
	7	6	5	4	3	2	1	0	7	6	5	4	3	2	1	0	

NOTES:

(1) Memory transfers, including applicable processor control instructions; 0, 1, or 2 displacement bytes may follow.

(2) Memory arithmetic and comparison instructions; 0, 1, or 2 displacement bytes may follow.

(3) Stack arithmetic and comparison instructions.

(4) Constant, transcendental, some arithmetic instructions.

(5) Processor control instructions that do not reference memory.

OP, OP-A, OP-B: Instruction opcode, possibly split into two fields.

MOD: Same as 80286 CPU mode field.

R/M: Same as 80286 CPU register/memory field.

FORMAT: Defines memory operand
  00 = short real
  01 = short integer
  10 = long real
  11 = word integer

R: 0 = return result to stack top
  1 = return result to other register

P: 0 = do not pop stack
 1 = pop stack after operation

REG: register stack element
 000 = stack top
 001 = next on stack
 010 = third stack element, etc.

Table A-2 lists all 80287 machine instructions in binary sequence. This table may be used to "disassemble" instructions in unformatted memory dumps or instructions monitored from the data bus. Users writing exception handlers may also find this information useful to identify the offending instruction.

Table A-2. Machine Instruction Decoding Guide

1st Byte Hex	1st Byte Binary	2nd Byte	Bytes 3, 4	ASM286 Instruction Format	
D8	1101 1000	MOD00 0R/M	(disp-lo),(disp-hi)	FADD	short-real
D8	1101 1000	MOD00 1R/M	(disp-lo),(disp-hi)	FMUL	short-real
D8	1101 1000	MOD01 0R/M	(disp-lo),(disp-hi)	FCOM	short-real
D8	1101 1000	MOD01 1R/M	(disp-lo),(disp-hi)	FCOMP	short-real
D8	1101 1000	MOD10 0R/M	(disp-lo),(disp-hi)	FSUB	short-real
D8	1101 1000	MOD10 1R/M	(disp-lo),(disp-hi)	FSUBR	short-real
D8	1101 1000	MOD11 0R/M	(disp-lo),(disp-hi)	FDIV	short-real
D8	1101 1000	MOD11 1R/M	(disp-lo),(disp-hi)	FDIVR	short-real
D8	1101 1000	1100 0REG		FADD	ST,ST(i)
D8	1101 1000	1100 1REG		FMUL	ST,ST(i)
D8	1101 1000	1101 0REG		FCOM	ST(i)
D8	1101 1000	1101 1REG		FCOMP	ST(i)
D8	1101 1000	1110 0REG		FSUB	ST,ST(i)
D8	1101 1000	1110 1REG		FSUBR	ST,ST(i)
D8	1101 1000	1111 0REG		FDIV	ST,ST(i)
D8	1101 1000	1111 1REG		FDIVR	ST,ST(i)
D9	1101 1001	MOD00 0R/M	(disp-lo),(disp-hi)	FLD	short-real
D9	1101 1001	MOD00 1R/M		reserved	
D9	1101 1001	MOD01 0R/M	(disp-lo),(disp-hi)	FST	short-real
D9	1101 1001	MOD01 1R/M	(disp-lo),(disp-hi)	FSTP	short-real
D9	1101 1001	MOD10 0R/M	(disp-lo),(disp-hi)	FLDENV	14-bytes
D9	1101 1001	MOD10 1R/M	(disp-lo),(disp-hi)	FLDCW	2-bytes
D9	1101 1001	MOD11 0R/M	(disp-lo),(disp-hi)	FSTENV	14-bytes
D9	1101 1001	MOD11 1R/M	(disp-lo),(disp-hi)	FSTCW	2-bytes
D9	1101 1001	1100 0REG		FLD	ST(i)
D9	1101 1001	1100 1REG		FXCH	ST(i)
D9	1101 1001	1101 0000		FNOP	
D9	1101 1001	1101 0001		reserved	
D9	1101 1001	1101 001-		reserved	
D9	1101 1001	1101 01--		reserved	
D9	1101 1001	1101 1REG		*(1)	
D9	1101 1001	1110 0000		FCHS	
D9	1101 1001	1110 0001		FABS	
D9	1101 1001	1110 001-		reserved	
D9	1101 1001	1110 0100		FTST	
D9	1101 1001	1110 0101		FXAM	
D9	1101 1001	1110 011-		reserved	
D9	1101 1001	1110 1000		FLD1	

Table A-2. Machine Instruction Decoding Guide (Cont'd.)

1st Byte		2nd Byte		Bytes 3, 4	ASM286 Instruction Format	
Hex	Binary					
D9	1101 1001	1110	1001		FLDL2T	
D9	1101 1001	1110	1010		FLDL2E	
D9	1101 1001	1110	1011		FLDPI	
D9	1101 1001	1110	1100		FLDLG2	
D9	1101 1001	1110	1101		FLDLN2	
D9	1101 1001	1110	1110		FLDZ	
D9	1101 1001	1110	1111		reserved	
D9	1101 1001	1111	0000		F2XM1	
D9	1101 1001	1111	0001		FYL2X	
D9	1101 1001	1111	0010		FPTAN	
D9	1101 1001	1111	0011		FPATAN	
D9	1101 1001	1111	0100		FXTRACT	
D9	1101 1001	1111	0101		reserved	
D9	1101 1001	1111	0110		FDECSTP	
D9	1101 1001	1111	0111		FINCSTP	
D9	1101 1001	1111	1000		FPREM	
D9	1101 1001	1111	1001		FYL2XP1	
D9	1101 1001	1111	1010		FSQRT	
D9	1101 1001	1111	1011		reserved	
D9	1101 1001	1111	1100		FRNDINT	
D9	1101 1001	1111	1101		FSCALE	
D9	1101 1001	1111	111-		reserved	
DA	1101 1010	MOD00	0R/M	(disp-lo),(disp-hi)	FIADD	short-integer
DA	1101 1010	MOD00	1R/M	(disp-lo),(disp-hi)	FIMUL	short-integer
DA	1101 1010	MOD01	0R/M	(disp-lo),(disp-hi)	FICOM	short-integer
DA	1101 1010	MOD01	1R/M	(disp-lo),(disp-hi)	FICOMP	short-integer
DA	1101 1010	MOD10	0R/M	(disp-lo),(disp-hi)	FISUB	short-integer
DA	1101 1010	MOD10	1R/M	(disp-lo),(disp-hi)	FISUBR	short-integer
DA	1101 1010	MOD11	0R/M	(disp-lo),(disp-hi)	FIDIV	short-integer
DA	1101 1010	MOD11	1R/M	(disp-lo),(disp-hi)	FIDIVR	short-integer
DA	1101 1010	11--	----		reserved	
DB	1101 1011	MOD00	0R/M	(disp-lo),(disp-hi)	FILD	short-integer
DB	1101 1011	MOD00	1R/M	(disp-lo),(disp-hi)	reserved	
DB	1101 1011	MOD01	0R/M	(disp-lo),(disp-hi)	FIST	short-integer
DB	1101 1011	MOD01	1R/M	(disp-lo),(disp-hi)	FISTP	short-integer
DB	1101 1011	MOD10	0R/M	(disp-lo),(disp-hi)	reserved	
DB	1101 1011	MOD10	1R/M	(disp-lo),(disp-hi)	FLD	temp-real
DB	1101 1011	MOD11	0R/M	(disp-lo),(disp-hi)	reserved	
DB	1101 1011	MOD11	1R/M	(disp-lo),(disp-hi)	FSTP	temp-real
DB	1101 1011	110-	----		reserved	
DB	1101 1011	1110	0000		reserved (8087 FENI)	
DB	1101 1011	1110	0001		reserved (8087 FDISI)	
DB	1101 1011	1110	0010		FCLEX	
DB	1101 1011	1110	0011		FINIT	
DB	1101 1011	1110	0100		FSETPM	
DB	1101 1011	1110	1---		reserved	
DB	1101 1011	1111	----		reserved	
DC	1101 1100	MOD00	0R/M	(disp-lo),(disp-hi)	FADD	long-real
DC	1101 1100	MOD00	1R/M	(disp-lo),(disp-hi)	FMUL	long-real
DC	1101 1100	MOD01	0R/M	(disp-lo),(disp-hi)	FCOM	long-real
DC	1101 1100	MOD01	1R/M	(disp-lo),(disp-hi)	FCOMP	long-real
DC	1101 1100	MOD10	0R/M	(disp-lo),(disp-hi)	FSUB	long-real

Table A-2. Machine Instruction Decoding Guide (Cont'd.)

Hex	Binary	2nd Byte	Bytes 3, 4	ASM286 Instruction Format	
DC	1101 1100	MOD10 1R/M	(disp-lo),(disp-hi)	FSUBR	long-real
DC	1101 1100	MOD11 0R/M	(disp-lo),(disp-hi)	FDIV	long-real
DC	1101 1100	MOD11 1R/M	(disp-lo),(disp-hi)	FDIVR	long-real
DC	1101 1100	1100 0REG		FADD	ST(i),ST
DC	1101 1100	1100 1REG		FMUL	ST(i),ST
DC	1101 1100	1101 0REG		*(2)	
DC	1101 1100	1101 1REG		*(3)	
DC	1101 1100	1110 0REG		FSUB	ST(i),ST
DC	1101 1100	1110 1REG		FSUBR	ST(i),ST
DC	1101 1100	1111 0REG		FDIV	ST(i),ST
DC	1101 1100	1111 1REG		FDIVR	ST(i),ST
DD	1101 1101	MOD00 0R/M	(disp-lo),(disp-hi)	FLD	long-real
DD	1101 1101	MOD00 1R/M		reserved	
DD	1101 1101	MOD01 0R/M	(disp-lo),(disp-hi)	FST	long-real
DD	1101 1101	MOD01 1R/M	(disp-lo),(disp-hi)	FSTP	long-real
DD	1101 1101	MOD10 0R/M	(disp-lo),(disp-hi)	FRSTOR	94-bytes
DD	1101 1101	MOD10 1R/M	(disp-lo),(disp-hi)	reserved	
DD	1101 1101	MOD11 0R/M	(disp-lo),(disp-hi)	FSAVE	94-bytes
DD	1101 1101	MOD11 1R/M	(disp-lo),(disp-hi)	FSTSW	2-bytes
DD	1101 1101	1100 0REG		FFREE	ST(i)
DD	1101 1101	1100 1REG		*(4)	
DD	1101 1101	1101 0REG		FST	ST(i)
DD	1101 1101	1101 1REG		FSTP	ST(i)
DD	1101 1101	111- ----		reserved	
DE	1101 1110	MOD00 0R/M	(disp-lo),(disp-hi)	FIADD	word-integer
DE	1101 1110	MOD00 1R/M	(disp-lo),(disp-hi)	FIMUL	word-integer
DE	1101 1110	MOD01 0R/M	(disp-lo),(disp-hi)	FICOM	word-integer
DE	1101 1110	MOD01 1R/M	(disp-lo),(disp-hi)	FICOMP	word-integer
DE	1101 1110	MOD10 0R/M	(disp-lo),(disp-hi)	FISUB	word-integer
DE	1101 1110	MOD10 1R/M	(disp-lo),(disp-hi)	FISUBR	word-integer
DE	1101 1110	MOD11 0R/M	(disp-lo),(disp-hi)	FIDIV	word-integer
DE	1101 1110	MOD11 1R/M	(disp-lo),(disp-hi)	FIDIVR	word-integer
DE	1101 1110	1100 0REG		FADDP	ST(i),ST
DE	1101 1110	1100 1REG		FMULP	ST(i),ST
DE	1101 1110	1101 0---		*(5)	
DE	1101 1110	1101 1000		reserved	
DE	1101 1110	1101 1001		FCOMPP	
DE	1101 1110	1101 101-		reserved	
DE	1101 1110	1101 11--		reserved	
DE	1101 1110	1110 0REG		FSUBP	ST(i),ST
DE	1101 1110	1110 1REG		FSUBRP	ST(i),ST
DE	1101 1110	1111 0REG		FDIVP	ST(i),ST
DE	1101 1110	1111 1REG		FDIVRP	ST(i),ST
DF	1101 1111	MOD00 0R/M	(disp-lo),(disp-hi)	FILD	word-integer
DF	1101 1111	MOD00 1R/M	(disp-lo),(disp-hi)	reserved	
DF	1101 1111	MOD01 0R/M	(disp-lo),(disp-hi)	FIST	word-integer
DF	1101 1111	MOD01 1R/M	(disp-lo),(disp-hi)	FISTP	word-integer
DF	1101 1111	MOD10 0R/M	(disp-lo),(disp-hi)	FBLD	packed-decimal
DF	1101 1111	MOD10 1R/M	(disp-lo),(disp-hi)	FILD	long-integer
DF	1101 1111	MOD11 0R/M	(disp-lo),(disp-hi)	FBSTP	packed-decimal
DF	1101 1111	MOD11 1R/M	(disp-lo),(disp-hi)	FISTP	long-integer
DF	1101 1111	1100 0REG		*(6)	

Table A-2. Machine Instruction Decoding Guide (Cont'd.)

1st Byte		2nd Byte		Bytes 3, 4	ASM286 Instruction Format
Hex	Binary				
DF	1101 1111	1100	1REG		*(7)
DF	1101 1111	1101	0REG		*(8)
DF	1101 1111	1101	1REG		*(9)
DF	1101 1111	1110	000		FSTSW AX
DF	1101 1111	1111	XXX		reserved

NOTE:

* The marked encodings are *not* generated by the language translators. If, however, the 80287 encounters one of these encodings in the instruction stream, it will execute it as follows:

(1) FSTP   ST(i)

(2) FCOM   ST(i)

(3) FCOMP ST(i)

(4) FXCH   ST(i)

(5) FCOMP ST(i)

(6) FFREE   ST(i) and pop stack

(7) FXCH   ST(i)

(8) FSTP   ST(i)

(9) FSTP   ST(i)

Appendix
Compatibility Between the
80287 NPX and the 8087

B

APPENDIX B
COMPATIBILITY BETWEEN
THE 80287 NPX AND THE 8087

The 80286/80287 operating in Real-Address mode will execute 8087 programs without major modification. However, because of differences in the handling of numeric exceptions by the 80287 NPX and the 8087 NPX, exception-handling routines *may* need to be changed.

This appendix summarizes the differences between the 80287 NPX and the 8087 NPX, and provides details showing how 8087 programs can be ported to the 80287.

1. The 80287 signals exceptions through a dedicated $\overline{\text{ERROR}}$ line to the 80286. The 80287 error signal does not pass through an interrupt controller (the 8087 INT signal does). Therefore, any interrupt-controller-oriented instructions in numeric exception handlers for the 8087 should be deleted.

2. The 8087 instructions FENI/FNENI and FDISI/FNDISI perform no useful function in the 80287. If the 80287 encounters one of these opcodes in its instruction stream, the instruction will effectively be ignored—none of the 80287 internal states will be updated. While 8087 code containing these instructions may be executed on the 80287, it is unlikely that the exception-handling routines containing these instructions will be completely portable to the 80287.

3. Interrupt vector 16 must point to the numeric exception handling routine.

4. The ESC instruction address saved in the 80287 includes any leading prefixes before the ESC opcode. The corresponding address saved in the 8087 does not include leading prefixes.

5. In Protected-Address mode, the format of the 80287's saved instruction and address pointers is different than for the 8087. The instruction opcode is not saved in Protected mode—exception handlers will have to retrieve the opcode from memory if needed.

6. Interrupt 7 will occur in the 80286 when executing ESC instructions with either TS (task switched) or EM (emulation) of the 80286 MSW set (TS=1 or EM=1). If TS is set, then a WAIT instruction will also cause interrupt 7. An exception handler should be included in 80287 code to handle these situations.

7. Interrupt 9 will occur if the second or subsequent words of a floating-point operand fall outside a segment's size. Interrupt 13 will occur if the starting address of a numeric operand falls outside a segment's size. An exception handler should be included in 80287 code to report these programming errors.

8. Except for the processor control instructions, all of the 80287 numeric instructions are automatically synchronized by the 80286 CPU—the 80286 automatically tests the $\overline{\text{BUSY}}$ line from the 80287 to ensure that the 80287 has completed its previous instruction before executing the next ESC instruction. No explicit WAIT instructions are required to assure this synchronization. For the 8087 used with 8086 and 8088 processors, explicit WAITs are required before each numeric instruction to ensure synchronization. Although 8087 programs having explicit WAIT instructions will execute perfectly on the 80287 without reassembly, these WAIT instructions are unnecessary.

9. Since the 80287 does not require WAIT instructions before each numeric instruction, the ASM286 assembler does not automatically generate these WAIT instructions. The ASM86 assembler, however, automatically precedes every ESC instruction with a WAIT instruction. Although numeric routines generated using the ASM86 assembler will generally execute correctly on the 80286/20, reassembly using ASM286 may result in a more compact code image.

The processor control instructions for the 80287 may be coded using either a WAIT or No-WAIT form of mnemonic. The WAIT forms of these instructions cause ASM286 to precede the ESC instruction with a CPU WAIT instruction, in the identical manner as does ASM86.

10. A recommended way to detect the presence of an 80287 in an 80286 system (or an 8087 in an 8086 system) is shown below. It assumes that the sytem hardware causes the data bus to be high if no 80287 is present to drive the data lines during the FSTSW (Store 80287 Status Word) instruction.

```
FND_287: FNINIT              ; initialize numeric processor.
         FSTSTW    STAT      ; store status word into location
                             ; STAT.

         MOV       AX,STAT
         OR        AL,AL     ; Zero Flag reflects result of OR.
         JZ        GOT_287   ; Zero in AL means 80287 is
                             ; present.

;
;     No 80287 Present
;
         SMSW      AX
         OR        AX,0004H  ; set EM bit in Machine Status
                             ; Word.
         LMSW      AX        ; to enable software emulation of
                             ; 287.
         JMP       CONTINUE

;
;     80287 is present in system
;
GOT_287: SMSW      AX
         OR        AX,0002H  ; set MP bit in Machine Status Word
         LMSW      AX        ; to permit normal 80287 operation
;
;     Continue . . .
;
CONTINUE:                    ; and off we go
```

An 80286/80287 design must place a pullup resistor on one of the low eight data bus bits of the 80286 to be sure it is read as a high when no 80287 is present.

Appendix
Implementing the
IEEE P754 Standard

C

APPENDIX C
IMPLEMENTING THE IEEE P754 STANDARD

The 80287 NPX and standard support library software, provides an implementation of the IEEE "A Proposed Standard for Binary Floating-Point Arithmetic," Draft 10.0, Task P754, of December 2, 1982. The *80287 Support Library*, described in *80287 Support Library Reference Manual*, Order Number 122129, is an example of such a support library.

This appendix describes the relationship between the 80287 NPX and the IEEE Standard. Where the Standard has options, Intel's choices in implementing the 80287 are described. Where portions of the Standard are implemented through software, this appendix indicates which modules of the 80287 Support Library implement the Standard. Where special software in addition to the Support Library may be required by your application, this appendix indicates how to write this software.

This appendix contains many terms with precise technical meanings, specified in the 754 Standard. Where these terms are used, they have been capitalized to emphasize the precision of their meanings. The Glossary provides the definitions for all capitalized phrases in this appendix.

OPTIONS IMPLEMENTED IN THE 80287

The 80287 SHORT_REAL and LONG_REAL formats conform precisely to the Standard's Single and Double Floating-Point Numbers, respectively. The 80287 TEMP_REAL format is the same as the Standard's Double Extended format. The Standard allows a choice of Bias in representing the exponent; the 80287 uses the Bias 16383 decimal.

For the Double Extended format, the Standard contains an option for the meaning of the minimum exponent combined with a nonzero significand. The Bias for this special case can be either 16383, as in all the other cases, or 16382, making the smallest exponent equivalent to the second-smallest exponent. The 80287 uses the Bias 16382 for this case. This allows the 80287 to distinguish between Denormal numbers (integer part is zero, fraction is nonzero, Biased exponent is 0) and Unnormal numbers of the same value (same as the denormal except the Biased Exponent is 1).

The Standard allows flexibility in specifying which NaNs are trapping and which are nontrapping. The EH287.LIB module of the 80287 Support Library provides a software implementation of nontrapping NaNs, and defines one distinction between trapping and nontrapping NaNs: If the most significant bit of the fractional part of a NaN is 1, the NaN is nontrapping. If it is 0, the NaN is trapping.

When a masked Invalid Operation error involves two NaN inputs, the Standard allows flexibility in choosing which NaN is output. The 80287 selects the NaN whose absolute value is greatest.

AREAS OF THE STANDARD IMPLEMENTED IN SOFTWARE

There are five areas of the Standard that are not implemented directly in the 80287 hardware; these areas are instead implemented in software as part of the 80287 Support Library.

1. The Standard requires that a Normalizing Mode be provided, in which any nonnormal operands to functions are automatically normalized before the function is performed. The NPX provides a "Denormal operand" exception for this case, allowing the exception handler the opportunity to perform the normalization specified by the Standard. The Denormal operand exception handler provided by EH287.LIB implements the Standard's Normalizing Mode completely for Single- and Double-precision arguments. Normalizing mode for Double Extended operands is implemented in EH287.LIB with one non-Standard feature, discussed in the next section.

2. The Standard specifies that in comparing two operands whose relationship is "unordered," the equality test yield an answer of FALSE, with no errors or exceptions. The 80287 FCOM and FTST instructions themselves issue an Invalid Operation exception in this case. The error handler EH287.LIB filters out this Invalid Operation error using the following convention: Whenever an FCOM or FTST instruction is followed by a MOV AX,AX instruction (8BC0 Hex), and neither argument is a trapping NaN, the error handler will assume that a Standard equality comparison was intended, and return the correct answer with the Invalid Operation exception flag erased. Note that the Invalid Operation exception must be unmasked for this action to occur.

3. The Standard requires that two kinds of NaN's be provided: trapping and nontrapping. Nontrapping NaNs will not cause further Invalid Operation errors when they occur as operands to calculations. The NPX hardware directly supports only trapping NaN's; the EH287.LIB software implements nontrapping NaNs by returning the correct answer with the Invalid Operation exception flag erased. Note that the Invalid Operation exception must be unmasked for this action to occur.

4. The Standard requires that all functions that convert real numbers to integer formats automatically normalize the inputs if necessary. The integer conversion functions contained in CEL287.LIB fully meet the Standard in this respect; the 80287 FIST instruction alone does not perform this normalization.

5. The Standard specifies the remainder function which is provided by mqerRMD in CEL287.LIB. The 80287 FPREM instruction returns answers within a different range.

ADDITIONAL SOFTWARE TO MEET THE STANDARD

There are two cases in which additional software is required in conjunction with the 80287 Support Library in order to meet the standard. The 80287 Support Library does not provide this software in the interest of saving space and because the vast majority of applications will never encounter these cases.

1. When the Invalid Operation exception is masked, Nontrapping NaNs are not implemented fully. Likewise, the Standard's equality test for "unordered" operands is not implemented when the Invalid Operation exception is masked. Programmers can simulate the Standard notion of a masked Invalid Operation exception by unmasking the 80287 Invalid Operation exception, and providing an Invalid Operation exception handler that supports nontrapping NaNs and the equality test, but otherwise acts just as if the Invalid Operation exception were masked. The *80287 Support Library Reference Manual* contains examples for programming this handler in both ASM286 and PL/M-286.

2. In Normalizing Mode, Denormal operands in the TEMP_REAL format are converted to 0 by EH287.LIB, giving sharp Underflow to 0. The Standard specifies that the operation be performed on the real numbers represented by the denormals, giving gradual underflow. To correctly perform such arithmetic while in Normalizing Mode, programmers would have to normalize the operands into a format identical to TEMP_REAL except for two extra exponent bits, then perform the operation on those numbers. Thus, software must be written to handle the 17-bit exponent explicitly.

In designing the EH287.LIB, it was felt that it would be a disadvantage to most users to increase the size of the Normalizing routine by the amount necessary to provide this expanded arithmetic. Because the TEMP_REAL exponent field is so much larger than the LONG_REAL exponent field, it is extremely unlikely that TEMP_REAL underflow will be encountered in most applications.

If meeting the Standard is a more important criterion for your application than the choice between Normalizing and warning modes, then you can select warning mode (Denormal operand exceptions masked), which fully meets the Standard.

If you do wish to implement the Normalization of denormal operands in TEMP_REAL format using extra exponent bits, the list below indicates some useful pointers about handling Denormal operand exceptions:

1. TEMP_REAL numbers are considered Denormal by the NPX whenever the Biased Exponent is 0 (minimum exponent). This is true even if the explicit integer bit of the significand is 1. Such numbers can occur as the result of Underflow.

2. The 80287 FLD instruction can cause a Denormal Operand error if a number is being loaded from memory. It will not cause this exception if the number is being loaded from elsewhere in the 80287 stack.

3. The 80287 FCOM and FTST instructions will cause a Denormal Operand exception for unnormal operands as well as for denormal operands.

4. In cases where both the Denormal Operand and Invalid Operation exceptions occur, you will want to know which is signalled first. When a comparison instruction operates between a nonexistent stack element and a denormal number in 80286 memory, the D and I exceptions are issued simultaneously In all other situations, a Denormal Operand exception takes precedence over a nonstack Invalid operation exception, while a stack Invalid Operation exception takes precedence over a Denormal Operand exception.

Glossary of 80287 and Floating-Point Terminology

GLOSSARY OF 80287
AND FLOATING-POINT TERMINOLOGY

This glossary defines many terms that have precise technical meanings as specified in the IEEE 754 Standard. Where these terms are used, they have been capitalized to emphasize the precision of their meanings. In reading these definitions, you may therefore interpret any capitalized terms or phrases as cross-references.

Affine Mode: a state of the 80287, selected in the 80287 Control Word, in which infinities are treated as having a sign. Thus, the values +INFINITY and −INFINITY are considered different; they can be compared with finite numbers and with each other.

Base: (1) a term used in logarithms and exponentials. In both contexts, it is a number that is being raised to a power. The two equations (y = log base b of x) and (b^y = x) are the same.

Base: (2) a number that defines the representation being used for a string of digits. Base 2 is the binary representation; Base 10 is the decimal representation; Base 16 is the hexadecimal representation. In each case, the Base is the factor of increased significance for each succeeding digit (working up from the bottom).

Bias: the difference between the unsigned Integer that appears in the Exponent field of a Floating-Point Number and the true Exponent that it represents. To obtain the true Exponent, you must subtract the Bias from the given Exponent. For example, the Short Real format has a Bias of 127 whenever the given Exponent is nonzero. If the 8-bit Exponent field contains 10000011, which is 131, the true Exponent is 131 − 127, or +4.

Biased Exponent: the Exponent as it appears in a Floating-Point Number, interpreted as an unsigned, positive number. In the above example, 131 is the Biased Exponent.

Binary Coded Decimal: a method of storing numbers that retains a base 10 representation. Each decimal digit occupies 4 full bits (one hexadecimal digit). The hex values A through F (1010 through 1111) are not used. The 80287 supports a Packed Decimal format that consists of 9 bytes of Binary Coded Decimal (18 decimal digits) and one sign byte.

Binary Point: an entity just like a decimal point, except that it exists in binary numbers. Each binary digit to the right of the Binary Point is multiplied by an increasing negative power of two.

C3—C0: the four "condition code" bits of the 80287 Status Word. These bits are set to certain values by the compare, test, examine, and remainder functions of the 80287.

Characteristic: a term used for some non-Intel computers, meaning the Exponent field of a Floating-Point Number.

Chop: to set the fractional part of a real number to zero, yielding the nearest integer in the direction of zero.

Control Word: a 16-bit 80287 register that the user can set, to determine the modes of computation the 80287 will use, and the error interrupts that will be enabled.

Denormal: a special form of Floating-Point Number, produced when an Underflow occurs. On the 80287, a Denormal is defined as a number with a Biased Exponent that is zero. By providing a Significand with leading zeros, the range of possible negative Exponents can be extended by the number of bits in the Significand. Each leading zero is a bit of lost accuracy, so the extended Exponent range is obtained by reducing significance.

Double Extended: the Standard's term for the 80287 Temporary Real format, with more Exponent and Significand bits than the Double (Long Real) format, and an explicit Integer bit in the Significand.

Double Floating Point Number: the Standard's term for the 80287's 64-bit Long Real format.

Environment: the 14 bytes of 80287 registers affected by the FSTENV and FLDENV instructions. It encompasses the entire state of the 80287, except for the 8 Temporary Real numbers of the 80287 stack. Included are the Control Word, Status Word, Tag Word, and the instruction, opcode, and operand information provided by interrupts.

Exception: any of the six error conditions (I, D, O, U, Z, P) signalled by the 80287.

Exponent: (1) any power that is raised by an exponential function. For example, the operand to the function mqerEXP is an Exponent. The Integer operand to mqerYI2 is an Exponent.

Exponent: (2) the field of a Floating-Point Number that indicates the magnitude of the number. This would fall under the above more general definition (1), except that a Bias sometimes needs to be subtracted to obtain the correct power.

Floating-Point Number: a sequence of data bytes that, when interpreted in a standardized way, represents a Real number. Floating-Point Numbers are more versatile than Integer representations in two ways. First, they include fractions. Second, their Exponent parts allow a much wider range of magnitude than possible with fixed-length Integer representations.

Gradual Underflow: a method of handling the Underflow error condition that minimizes the loss of accuracy in the result. If there is a Denormal number that represents the correct result, that Denormal is returned. Thus, digits are lost only to the extent of denormalization. Most computers return zero when Underflow occurs, losing all significant digits.

Implicit Integer Bit: a part of the Significand in the Short Real and Long Real formats that is not explicitly given. In these formats, the entire given Significand is considered to be to the right of the Binary Point. A single Implicit Integer Bit to the left of the Binary Point is always 1, except in one case. When the Exponent is the minimum (Biased Exponent is 0), the Implicit Integer Bit is 0.

Indefinite: a special value that is returned by functions when the inputs are such that no other sensible answer is possible. For each Floating-Point format there exists one Nontrapping NaN that is designated as the Indefinite value. For binary Integer formats, the negative number furthest from zero is often considered the Indefinite value. For the 80287 Packed Decimal format, the Indefinite value contains all 1's in the sign byte and the uppermost digits byte.

Infinity: a value that has greater magnitude than any Integer or any Real number. The existence of Infinity is subject to heated philosophical debate. However, it is often useful to consider Infinity as another number, subject to special rules of arithmetic. All three Intel Floating-Point formats provide representations for +INFINITY and −INFINITY. They support two ways of dealing with Infinity: Projective (unsigned) and Affine (signed).

Integer: a number (positive, negative, or zero) that is finite and has no fractional part. Integer can also mean the computer representation for such a number: a sequence of data bytes, interpreted in a standard way. It is perfectly reasonable for Integers to be represented in a Floating-Point format; this is what the 80287 does whenever an Integer is pushed onto the 80287 stack.

Invalid Operation: the error condition for the 80287 that covers all cases not covered by other errors. Included are 80287 stack overflow and underflow, NaN inputs, illegal infinite inputs, out-of-range inputs, and illegal unnormal inputs.

Long Integer: an Integer format supported by the 80287 that consists of a 64-bit Two's Complement quantity.

Long Real: a Floating-Point Format supported by the 80287 that consists of a sign, an 11-bit Biased Exponent, an Implicit Integer Bit, and a 52-bit Significand—a total of 64 explicit bits.

Mantissa: a term used for some non-Intel computers, meaning the Significand of a Floating-Point Number.

Masked: a term that applies to each of the six 80287 Exceptions I,D,Z,O,U,P. An exception is Masked if a corresponding bit in the 80287 Control Word is set to 1. If an exception is Masked, the 80287 will not generate an interrupt when the error condition occurs; it will instead provide its own error recovery.

NaN: an abbreviation for Not a Number; a Floating-Point quantity that does not represent any numeric or infinite quantity. NaNs should be returned by functions that encounter serious errors. If created during a sequence of calculations, they are transmitted to the final answer and can contain information about where the error occurred.

Nontrapping NaN: a NaN in which the most significant bit of the fractional part of the Significand is 1. By convention, these NaNs can undergo certain operations without visible error. Nontrapping NaNs are implemented for the 80287 via the software in EH87.LIB.

Normal: the representation of a number in a Floating-Point format in which the Significand has an Integer bit 1 (either explicit or Implicit).

Normalizing Mode: a state in which nonnormal inputs are automatically converted to normal inputs whenever they are used in arithmetic. Normalizing Mode is implemented for the 80287 via the software in EH87.LIB.

NPX: Numeric Processor Extension. This is the 80287.

Overflow: an error condition in which the correct answer is finite, but has magnitude too great to be represented in the destination format.

Packed Decimal: an Integer format supported by the 80287. A Packed Decimal number is a 10-byte quantity, with nine bytes of 18 Binary Coded Decimal digits, and one byte for the sign.

Pop: to remove from a stack the last item that was placed on the stack.

Precision Control: an option, programmed through the 80287 Control Word, that allows all 80287 arithmetic to be performed with reduced precision. Because no speed advantage results from this option, its only use is for strict compatibility with the IEEE Standard, and with other computer systems.

Precision Exception: an 80287 error condition that results when a calculation does not return an exact answer. This exception is usually Masked and ignored; it is used only in extremely critical applications, when the user must know if the results are exact.

Projective Mode: a state of the 80287, selected in the 80287 Control Word, in which infinities are treated as not having a sign. Thus the values +INFINITY and −INFINITY are considered the same. Certain operations, such as comparison to finite numbers, are illegal in Projective Mode but legal in Affine Mode. Thus Projective Mode gives you a greater degree of error control over infinite inputs.

Pseudo Zero: a special value of the Temporary Real format. It is a number with a zero significand and an Exponent that is neither all zeros or all ones. Pseudo zeros can come about as the result of multiplication of two Unnormal numbers; but they are very rare.

Real: any finite value (negative, positive, or zero) that can be represented by a decimal expansion. The fractional part of the decimal expansion can contain an infinite number of digits. Reals can be represented as the points of a line marked off like a ruler. The term Real can also refer to a Floating-Point Number that represents a Real value.

Short Integer: an Integer format supported by the 80287 that consists of a 32-bit Two's Complement quantity. Short Integer is not the shortest 80287 Integer format—the 16-bit Word Integer is.

Short Real: a Floating-Point Format supported by the 80287, which consists of a sign, an 8-bit Biased Exponent, an Implicit Integer Bit, and a 23-bit Significand—a total of 32 explicit bits.

Significand: the part of a Floating-Point Number that consists of the most significant nonzero bits of the number, if the number were written out in an unlimited binary format. The Significand alone is considered to have a Binary Point after the first (possibly Implicit) bit; the Binary Point is then moved according to the value of the Exponent.

Single Extended: a Floating-Point format, required by the Standard, that provides greater precision than Single; it also provides an explicit Integer Significand bit. The 80287's Temporary Real format meets the Single Extended requirement as well as the Double Extended requirement.

Single Floating-Point Number: the Standard's term for the 80287's 32-bit Short Real format.

Standard: "a Proposed Standard for Binary Floating-Point Arithmetic," Draft 10.0 of IEEE Task P754, December 2, 1982.

Status Word: A 16-bit 80287 register that can be manually set, but which is usually controlled by side effects to 80287 instructions. It contains condition codes, the 80287 stack pointer, busy and interrupt bits, and error flags.

Tag Word: a 16-bit 80287 register that is automatically maintained by the 80287. For each space in the 80287 stack, it tells if the space is occupied by a number; if so, it gives information about what kind of number.

Temporary Real: the main Floating-Point Format used by the 80287. It consists of a sign, a 15-bit Biased Exponent, and a Significand with an explicit Integer bit and 63 fractional-part bits.

Transcendental: one of a class of functions for which polynomial formulas are always approximate, never exact for more than isolated values. The 80287 supports trigonometric, exponential, and logarithmic functions; all are Transcendental.

Trapping NaN: a NaN that causes an I error whenever it enters into a calculation or comparison, even a nonordered comparison.

Two's Complement: a method of representing Integers. If the uppermost bit is 0, the number is considered positive, with the value given by the rest of the bits. If the uppermost bit is 1, the number is negative, with the value obtained by subtracting ($2^{bit\ count}$) from all the given bits. For example, the 8-bit number 11111100 is −4, obtained by subtracting 2^8 from 252.

Unbiased Exponent: the true value that tells how far and in which direction to move the Binary Point of the Significand of a Floating-Point Number. For example, if a Short Real Exponent is 131, we subtract the Bias 127 to obtain the Unbiased Exponent +4. Thus, the Real number being represented is the Significand with the Binary Point shifted 4 bits to the right.

Underflow: an error condition in which the correct answer is nonzero, but has a magnitude too small to be represented as a Normal number in the destination Floating-Point format. The Standard specifies that an attempt be made to represent the number as a Denormal.

Unmasked: a term that applies to each of the six 80287 Exceptions: I,D,Z,O,U,P. An exception is Unmasked if a corresponding bit in the 80287 Control Word is set to 0. If an exception is Unmasked, the 80287 will generate an interrupt when the error condition occurs. You can provide an interrupt routine that customizes your error recovery.

Unnormal: a Temporary Real representation in which the explicit Integer bit of the Significand is zero, and the exponent is nonzero. We consider Unnormal numbers distinct from Denormal numbers.

Word Integer: an Integer format supported by both the 80286 and the 80287 that consists of a 16-bit Two's Complement quantity.

Zero divide: an error condition in which the inputs are finite, but the correct answer, even with an unlimited exponent, has infinite magnitude.

INDEX

DOMESTIC SALES OFFICES

ALABAMA

†Intel Corp.
5015 Bradford Dr., #2
Huntsville 35805
Tel: (205) 830-4010

ARIZONA

†Intel Corp.
11225 N. 28th Dr., #D214
Phoenix 85029
Tel: (602) 869-4980

Intel Corp.
1161 N. El Dorado Place
Suite 301
Tucson 85715
Tel: (602) 299-6815

CALIFORNIA

†Intel Corp.
21515 Vanowen Street
Suite 116
Canoga Park 91303
Tel: (818) 704-8500

†Intel Corp.
2250 E. Imperial Highway
Suite 218
El Segundo 90245
Tel: (213) 640-6040

Intel Corp.
1510 Arden Way, Suite 101
Sacramento 95815
Tel: (916) 920-8096

†Intel Corp.
4350 Executive Drive
Suite 105
San Diego 92121
Tel: (619) 452-5880

Intel Corp.*
400 N. Tustin Avenue
Suite 450
Santa Ana 92705
Tel: (714) 835-9642
TWX: 910-595-1114

†Intel Corp.*
San Tomas 4
2700 San Tomas Expressway
Santa Clara, CA 95051
Tel: (408) 986-8086
TWX: 910-338-0255

COLORADO

Intel Corp.
4445 Northpark Drive
Suite 100
Colorado Springs 80907
Tel: (303) 594-6622

†Intel Corp.*
650 S. Cherry St., Suite 915
Denver 80222
Tel: (303) 321-8086
TWX: 910-931-2289

CONNECTICUT

†Intel Corp.
26 Mill Plain Road
Danbury 06811
Tel: (203) 748-3130
TWX: 710-456-1199

FLORIDA

†Intel Corp.
242 N. Westmonte Dr.
Suite 105
Altamonte Springs 32714
Tel: (305) 869-5588

Intel Corp.
6363 N.W. 6th Way, Suite 100
Ft. Lauderdale 33309
Tel: (305) 771-0600
TWX: 510-956-9407

Intel Corp.
11300 4th Street North
Suite 170
St. Petersburg 33702
Tel: (813) 577-2413

GEORGIA

†Intel Corp.
3280 Pointe Parkway
Suite 200
Norcross 30092
Tel: (404) 449-0541

ILLINOIS

Intel Corp.*
300 N. Martingale Road, Suite 400
Schaumburg 60173
Tel: (312) 310-8031

INDIANA

†Intel Corp.
8777 Purdue Road
Suite 125
Indianapolis 46268
Tel: (317) 875-0623

IOWA

Intel Corp.
St. Andrews Building
1930 St. Andrews Drive N.E.
Cedar Rapids 52402
Tel: (319) 393-5510

KANSAS

†Intel Corp.
8400 W. 110th Street
Suite 170
Overland Park 66210
Tel: (913) 345-2727

MARYLAND

Intel Corp.*
7321 Parkway Drive South
Suite C
Hanover 21076
Tel: (301) 796-7500
TWX: 710-862-1944

Intel Corp.
5th Floor
7833 Walker Drive
Greenbelt 20770
Tel: (301) 441-1020

MASSACHUSETTS

†Intel Corp.*
Westford Corp. Center
3 Carlisle Road
Westford 01886
Tel: (617) 692-3222
TWX: 710-343-6333

MICHIGAN

†Intel Corp.
7071 Orchard Lake Road
Suite 100
West Bloomfield 48033
Tel: (313) 851-8096

MINNESOTA

Intel Corp.
3500 W. 80th St., Suite 360
Bloomington 55431
Tel: (612) 835-6722
TWX: 910-576-2867

MISSOURI

Intel Corp.
4203 Earth City Expressway
Suite 131
Earth City 63045
Tel: (314) 291-1990

NEW JERSEY

Intel Corp.*
Parkway 109 Office Center
328 Newman Springs Road
Red Bank 07701
Tel: (201) 747-2233

Intel Corp.
280 Corporate Center
75 Livingston Avenue
First Floor
Roseland 07068
Tel: (201) 740-0111

NEW MEXICO

Intel Corp.
8500 Menual Boulevard N.E.
Suite B 295
Albuquerque 87112
Tel: (505) 292-8086

NEW YORK

Intel Corp.
127 Main Street
Binghamton 13905
Tel: (607) 773-0337

Intel Corp.*
850 Cross Keys Office Park
Fairport 14450
Tel: (716) 425-2750
TWX: 510-253-7391

Intel Corp.*
300 Motor Parkway
Hauppauge 11787
Tel: (516) 231-3300
TWX: 510-227-6236

Intel Corp.
Suite 2B Hollowbrook Park
15 Myers Corners Road
Wappinger Falls 12590
Tel: (914) 297-6161
TWX: 510-248-0060

NORTH CAROLINA

Intel Corp.
5700 Executive Center Drive
Suite 213
Charlotte 28212
Tel: (704) 568-8966

†Intel Corp.
2700 Wycliff Road
Suite 102
Raleigh 27607
Tel: (919) 781-8022

OHIO

Intel Corp.*
3401 Park Center Drive
Suite 220
Dayton 45414
Tel: (513) 890-5350
TWX: 810-450-2528

Intel Corp.*
25700 Science Park Dr., Suite 100
Beachwood 44122
Tel: (216) 464-2736
TWX: 810-427-9298

OKLAHOMA

Intel Corp.
6801 N. Broadway
Suite 115
Oklahoma City 73116
Tel: (405) 848-8086

OREGON

†Intel Corp.
15254 N.W. Greenbrier Parkway, Bldg. B
Beaverton 97006
Tel: (503) 645-8051
TWX: 910-467-8741

PENNSYLVANIA

Intel Corp.
1513 Cedar Cliff Drive
Camp Hill 17011
Tel: (717) 737-5035

Intel Corp.*
455 Pennsylvania Avenue
Fort Washington 19034
Tel: (215) 641-1000
TWX: 510-661-2077

Intel Corp.*
400 Penn Center Blvd., Suite 610
Pittsburgh 15235
Tel: (412) 823-4970

PUERTO RICO

Intel Microprocessor Corp.
South Industrial Park
P.O. Box 910
Las Piedras 00671
Tel: (809) 733-8616

TEXAS

†Intel Corp.
313 E. Anderson Lane
Suite 314
Austin 78752
Tel: (512) 454-3628

†Intel Corp.*
12300 Ford Road
Suite 380
Dallas 75234
Tel: (214) 241-8087
TWX: 910-860-5617

Intel Corp.*
7322 S.W. Freeway
Suite 1490
Houston 77074
Tel: (713) 988-8086
TWX: 910-881-2490

UTAH

Intel Corp.
5201 Green Street
Suite 290
Murray 84123
Tel: (801) 263-8051

VIRGINIA

†Intel Corp.
1603 Santa Rosa Road
Suite 109
Richmond 23288
Tel: (804) 282-5668

WASHINGTON

Intel Corp.
155-108 Avenue N.E.
Suite 386
Bellevue 98004
Tel: (206) 453-8086
TWX: 910-443-3002

Intel Corp.
408 N. Mullan Road
Suite 102
Spokane 99206
Tel: (509) 928-8086

WISCONSIN

†Intel Corp.
330 S. Executive Dr.
Suite 102
Brookfield 53005
Tel: (414) 784-8087
FAX: (414) 796-2115

CANADA

BRITISH COLUMBIA

Intel Semiconductor of Canada, Ltd.
4585 Canada Way, Suite 202
Burnaby V5G 4L6
Tel: (604) 298-0387
FAX: (604) 298-8234

ONTARIO

†Intel Semiconductor of Canada, Ltd.
2650 Queensview Drive
Suite 250
Ottawa K2B 8H6
Tel: (613) 829-9714
TLX: 053-4115

†Intel Semiconductor of Canada, Ltd.
190 Attwell Drive
Suite 500
Rexdale M9W 6H8
Tel: (416) 675-2105
TLX: 06983574
FAX: (416) 675-2438

QUEBEC

†Intel Semiconductor of Canada, Ltd.
620 St. Jean Boulevard
Pointe Claire H9R 3K3
Tel: (514) 694-9130
TWX: 514-694-9134

†Sales and Service Office
*Field Application Location

CG-6/29/87

DOMESTIC DISTRIBUTORS

ALABAMA

Arrow Electronics, Inc.
1015 Henderson Road
Huntsville 35805
Tel: (205) 837-6955

†Hamilton/Avnet Electronics
4940 Research Drive
Huntsville 35805
Tel: (205) 837-7210
TWX: 810-726-2162

Pioneer/Technologies Group Inc.
4825 University Square
Huntsville 35805
Tel: (205) 837-9300
TWX: 810-726-2197

ARIZONA

†Hamilton/Avnet Electronics
505 S. Madison Drive
Tempe 85281
Tel: (602) 231-5100
TWX: 910-950-0077

Kierulff Electronics, Inc.
4134 E. Wood Street
Phoenix 85040
Tel: (602) 437-0750
TWX: 910-951-1550

Wyle Distribution Group
17855 N. Black Canyon Highway
Phoenix 85023
Tel: (602) 866-2888

CALIFORNIA

Arrow Electronics, Inc.
19748 Dearborn Street
Chatsworth 91311
Tel: (818) 701-7500
TWX: 910-493-2086

Arrow Electronics, Inc.
1502 Crocker Avenue
Hayward 94544
Tel: (408) 487-4600

Arrow Electronics, Inc.
9511 Ridgehaven Court
San Diego 92123
Tel: (619) 565-4800
TLX: 888064

†Arrow Electronics, Inc.
521 Weddell Drive
Sunnyvale 94086
Tel: (408) 745-6600
TWX: 910-339-9371

Arrow Electronics, Inc.
2961 Dow Avenue
Tustin 92680
Tel: (714) 838-5422
TWX: 910-595-2860

†Avnet Electronics
350 McCormick Avenue
Costa Mesa 92626
Tel: (714) 754-6051
TWX: 910-595-1928

Hamilton/Avnet Electronics
1175 Bordeaux Drive
Sunnyvale 94086
Tel: (408) 743-3300
TWX: 910-339-9332

†Hamilton/Avnet Electronics
4545 Viewridge Avenue
San Diego 92123
Tel: (619) 571-7500
TWX: 910-595-2638

†Hamilton/Avnet Electronics
20501 Plummer Street
Chatsworth 91311
Tel: (818) 700-6271
TWX: 910-494-2207

†Hamilton/Avnet Electronics
4103 Northgate Boulevard
Sacramento 95834
Tel: (916) 920-3150

†Hamilton/Avnet Electronics
3002 G Street
Ontario 91311
Tel: (714) 989-9411

Hamilton Electro Sales
19515 So. Vermont Avenue
Torrance 90502
Tel: (213) 615-3909
TWX: 910-349-6263

Hamilton Electro Sales
9650 De Soto Avenue
Chatsworth 91311
Tel: (818) 700-6500

CALIFORNIA (Cont'd)

†Hamilton Electro Sales
10950 W. Washington Blvd.
Culver City 90230
Tel: (213) 558-2458
TWX: 910-340-6364

Hamilton Electro Sales
1361 B West 190th Street
Gardena 90248
Tel: (213) 558-2131

†Hamilton Electro Sales
3170 Pullman Street
Costa Mesa 92626
Tel: (714) 641-4150
TWX: 910-595-2638

Kierulff Electronics, Inc.
10824 Hope Street
Cypress 90430
Tel: (714) 220-6300

†Kierulff Electronics, Inc.
1180 Murphy Avenue
San Jose 95131
Tel: (408) 971-2600
TWX: 910-379-6430

†Kierulff Electronics, Inc.
14101 Franklin Avenue
Tustin 92680
Tel: (714) 731-5711
TWX: 910-595-2599

†Kierulff Electronics, Inc.
5650 Jillson Street
Commerce 90040
Tel: (213) 725-0325
TWX: 910-580-3666

Wyle Distribution Group
26560 Agoura Street
Calabasas 91302
Tel: (818) 880-9000
TWX: 818-372-0232

†Wyle Distribution Group
124 Maryland Street
El Segundo 90245
Tel: (213) 322-8100
TWX: 910-348-7140 or 7111

†Wyle Distribution Group
17872 Cowan Avenue
Irvine 92714
Tel: (714) 863-9953
TWX: 910-595-1572

Wyle Distribution Group
11151 Sun Center Drive
Rancho Cordova 95670
Tel: (916) 638-5282

†Wyle Distribution Group
9525 Chesapeake Drive
San Diego 92123
Tel: (619) 565-9171
TWX: 910-335-1590

†Wyle Distribution Group
3000 Bowers Avenue
Santa Clara 95051
Tel: (408) 727-2500
TWX: 910-338-0296

Wyle Military
18910 Teller Avenue
Irvine 92750
Tel: (714) 851-9958
TWX: 310-371-9127

Wyle Systems
7382 Lampson Avenue
Garden Grove 92641
Tel: (714) 891-1717
TWX: 910-595-2642

COLORADO

Arrow Electronics, Inc.
1390 S. Potomac Street
Suite 136
Aurora 80012
Tel: (303) 696-1111

†Hamilton/Avnet Electronics
8765 E. Orchard Road
Suite 708
Englewood 80111
Tel: (303) 740-1017
TWX: 910-935-0787

†Wyle Distribution Group
451 E. 124th Avenue
Thornton 80241
Tel: (303) 457-9953
TWX: 910-936-0770

CONNECTICUT

†Arrow Electronics, Inc.
12 Beaumont Road
Wallingford 06492
Tel: (203) 265-7741
TWX: 710-476-0162

Hamilton/Avnet Electronics
Commerce Industrial Park
Commerce Drive
Danbury 06810
Tel: (203) 797-2800
TWX: 710-456-9974

†Pioneer Northeast Electronics
112 Main Street
Norwalk 06851
Tel: (203) 853-1515
TWX: 710-468-3373

FLORIDA

†Arrow Electronics, Inc.
350 Fairway Drive
Deerfield Beach 33441
Tel: (305) 429-8200
TWX: 510-955-9456

Arrow Electronics, Inc.
1001 N.W. 62nd St., Ste. 108
Ft. Lauderdale 33309
Tel: (305) 776-7790
TWX: 510-955-9456

†Arrow Electronics, Inc.
50 Woodlake Drive W., Bldg. B
Palm Bay 32905
Tel: (305) 725-1480
TWX: 510-959-6337

†Hamilton/Avnet Electronics
6801 N.W. 15th Way
Ft. Lauderdale 33309
Tel: (305) 971-2900
TWX: 510-956-3097

Hamilton/Avnet Electronics
3197 Tech Drive North
St. Petersburg 33702
Tel: (813) 576-3930
TWX: 810-863-0374

Hamilton/Avnet Electronics
6947 University Boulevard
Winterpark 32792
Tel: (305) 628-3888
TWX: 810-853-0322

†Pioneer Electronics
337 N. Lake Blvd., Ste. 1000
Alta Monte Springs 32701
Tel: (305) 834-9090
TWX: 810-853-0284

Pioneer Electronics
674 S. Military Trail
Deerfield Beach 33442
Tel: (305) 428-8877
TWX: 510-955-9653

GEORGIA

†Arrow Electronics, Inc.
3155 Northwoods Parkway
Suite A
Norcross 30071
Tel: (404) 449-8252
TWX: 810-766-0439

Hamilton/Avnet Electronics
5825 D. Peachtree Corners
Norcross 30092
Tel: (404) 447-7500
TWX: 810-766-0432

Pioneer Electronics
3100 F. Northwoods Place
Norcross 30071
Tel: (404) 448-1711
TWX: 810-766-4515

ILLINOIS

†Arrow Electronics, Inc.
2000 E. Alonquin Street
Schaumberg 60195
Tel: (312) 397-3440
TWX: 910-291-3544

†Hamilton/Avnet Electronics
1130 Thorndale Avenue
Bensenville 60106
Tel: (312) 860-7780
TWX: 910-227-0060

Kierulff Electronics, Inc.
1140 W. Thorndale
Itasca 60143
Tel: (312) 250-0500

ILLINOIS (Cont'd)

MTI Systems Sales
1100 West Thorndale
Itasca 60143
Tel: (312) 773-2300

†Pioneer Electronics
1551 Carmen Drive
Elk Grove Village 60007
Tel: (312) 437-9680
TWX: 910-222-1834

INDIANA

†Arrow Electronics, Inc.
2495 Directors Row, Suite H
Indianapolis 46241
Tel: (317) 243-9353
TWX: 810-341-3119

Hamilton/Avnet Electronics
485 Gradle Drive
Carmel 46032
Tel: (317) 844-9333
TWX: 810-260-3966

†Pioneer Electronics
6408 Castleplace Drive
Indianapolis 46250
Tel: (317) 849-7300
TWX: 810-260-1794

KANSAS

†Hamilton/Avnet Electronics
9219 Quivera Road
Overland Park 66215
Tel: (913) 888-8900
TWX: 910-743-0005

Pioneer Electronics
10551 Lackman Rd.
Lenexa 66215
Tel: (913) 492-0500

KENTUCKY

Hamilton/Avnet Electronics
1051 D. Newton Park
Lexington 40511
Tel: (606) 259-1475

MARYLAND

Arrow Electronics, Inc.
8300 Guilford Road #H
Rivers Center
Columbia 21046
Tel: (301) 995-0003
TWX: 710-236-9005

†Hamilton/Avnet Electronics
6822 Oak Hall Lane
Columbia 21045
Tel: (301) 995-3500
TWX: 710-862-1861

†Mesa Technology Corp.
9720 Patuxentwood Dr.
Columbia 21046
Tel: (301) 720-5020
TWX: 710-828-9702

†Pioneer Electronics
9100 Gaither Road
Gaithersburg 20877
Tel: (301) 921-0660
TWX: 710-828-0545

MASSACHUSETTS

†Arrow Electronics, Inc.
1 Arrow Drive
Woburn 01801
Tel: (617) 933-8130
TWX: 710-393-6770

†Hamilton/Avnet Electronics
10D Centennial Drive
Peabody 01960
Tel: (617) 532-3701
TWX: 710-393-0382

Kierulff Electronics, Inc.
13 Fortune Dr.
Billerica 01821
Tel: (617) 667-8331

MTI Systems Sales
13 Fortune Drive
Billerica 01821

Pioneer Northeast Electronics
44 Hartwell Avenue
Lexington 02173
Tel: (617) 861-9200
TWX: 710-326-6617

MICHIGAN

Arrow Electronics, Inc.
755 Phoenix Drive
Ann Arbor 48104
Tel: (313) 971-8220
TWX: 810-223-6020

†Hamilton/Avnet Electronics
32487 Schoolcraft Road
Livonia 48150
Tel: (313) 522-4700
TWX: 810-242-8775

Hamilton/Avnet Electronics
2215 29th Street S.E.
Space A5
Grand Rapids 49508
Tel: (616) 243-8805
TWX: 810-273-6921

Pioneer Electronics
4505 Broadmoor Ave. S.E.
Grand Rapids 49508
Tel: (616) 555-1800

†Pioneer Electronics
13485 Stamford
Livonia 48150
Tel: (313) 525-1800
TWX: 810-242-3271

MINNESOTA

†Arrow Electronics, Inc.
5230 W. 73rd Street
Edina 55435
Tel: (612) 830-1800
TWX: 910-576-3125

Hamilton/Avnet Electronics
12400 White Water Drive
Minnetonka 55343
Tel: (612) 932-0600
TWX: (910) 576-2720

†Pioneer Electronics
10203 Bren Road East
Minnetonka 55343
Tel: (612) 935-5444
TWX: 910-576-2738

MISSOURI

†Arrow Electronics, Inc.
2380 Schuetz
St. Louis 63141
Tel: (314) 567-6888
TWX: 910-764-0882

†Hamilton/Avnet Electronics
13743 Shoreline Court
Earth City 63045
Tel: (314) 344-1200
TWX: 910-762-0684

Kierulff Electronics, Inc.
11804 Borman Dr.
St. Luis 63146
Tel: (314) 997-4956

NEW HAMPSHIRE

†Arrow Electronics, Inc.
3 Perimeter Road
Manchester 03103
Tel: (603) 668-6968
TWX: 710-220-1684

Hamilton/Avnet Electronics
444 E. Industrial Drive
Manchester 03104
Tel: (603) 624-9400

NEW JERSEY

†Arrow Electronics, Inc.
6000 Lincoln East
Marlton 08053
Tel: (609) 596-8000
TWX: 710-897-0829

†Arrow Electronics, Inc.
2 Industrial Road
Fairfield 07006
Tel: (201) 575-5300
TWX: 710-998-2206

†Hamilton/Avnet Electronics
1 Keystone Avenue
Bldg. 36
Cherry Hill 08003
Tel: (609) 424-0110
TWX: 710-940-0262

DOMESTIC DISTRIBUTORS

NEW JERSEY (Cont'd)

†Hamilton/Avnet Electronics
10 Industrial
Fairfield 07006
Tel: (201) 575-3390
TWX: 701-734-4388

†Pioneer Northeast Electronics
45 Route 46
Pinebrook 07058
Tel: (201) 575-3510
TWX: 710-734-4382

†MTI Systems Sales
383 Route 46 W
Fairfield 07006
Tel: (201) 227-5552

NEW MEXICO

Alliance Electronics Inc.
11030 Cochiti S.E.
Albuquerque 87123
Tel: (505) 292-3360
TWX: 910-989-1151

Hamilton/Avnet Electronics
2524 Baylor Drive S.E.
Albuquerque 87106
Tel: (505) 765-1500
TWX: 910-989-0614

NEW YORK

Arrow Electronics, Inc.
25 Hub Drive
Melville 11747
Tel: (516) 694-6800
TWX: 510-224-6126

†Arrow Electronics, Inc.
3375 Brighton-Henrietta Townline Rd.
Rochester 14623
Tel: (716) 427-0300
TWX: 510-253-4766

Arrow Electronics, Inc.
7705 Maltage Drive
Liverpool 13088
Tel: (315) 652-1000
TWX: 710-545-0230

Arrow Electronics, Inc.
20 Oser Avenue
Hauppauge 11788
Tel: (516) 231-1000
TWX: 510-227-6623

Hamilton/Avnet Electronics
333 Metro Park
Rochester 14623
Tel: (716) 475-9130
TWX: 510-253-5470

†Hamilton/Avnet Electronics
103 Twin Oaks Drive
Syracuse 13206
Tel: (315) 437-2641
TWX: 710-541-1560

†Hamilton/Avnet Electronics
933 Motor Parkway
Hauppauge 11788
Tel: (516) 231-9800
TWX: 510-224-6166

†MTI Systems Sales
38 Harbor Park Drive
P.O. Box 271
Port Washington 11050
Tel: (516) 621-6200
TWX: 510-223-0846

†Pioneer Northeast Electronics
1806 Vestal Parkway East
Vestal 13850
Tel: (607) 748-8211
TWX: 510-252-0893

†Pioneer Northeast Electronics
60 Crossway Park West
Woodbury, Long Island 11797
Tel: (516) 921-8700
TWX: 510-221-2184

NEW YORK (Cont'd)

†Pioneer Northeast Electronics
840 Fairport Park
Fairport 14450
Tel: (716) 381-7070
TWX: 510-253-7001

NORTH CAROLINA

†Arrow Electronics, Inc.
5240 Greendairy Road
Raleigh 27604
Tel: (919) 876-3132
TWX: 510-928-1856

†Hamilton/Avnet Electronics
3510 Spring Forest Drive
Raleigh 27604
Tel: (919) 878-0819
TWX: 510-928-1836

Pioneer Electronics
9801 A-Southern Pine Blvd.
Charlotte 28210
Tel: (704) 527-8188
TWX: 810-621-0366

OHIO

Arrow Electronics, Inc.
7620 McEwen Road
Centerville 45459
Tel: (513) 435-5563
TWX: 810-459-1611

†Arrow Electronics, Inc.
6238 Cochran Road
Solon 44139
Tel (216) 248-3990
TWX: 810-427-9409

Hamilton/Avnet Electronics
777 Brookedge Blvd.
Westerville 43081
Tel: (614) 882-7004

†Hamilton/Avnet Electronics
954 Senate Drive
Dayton 45459
Tel: (513) 433-0610
TWX: 810-450-2531

†Hamilton/Avnet Electronics
4588 Emery Industrial Parkway
Warrensville Heights 44128
Tel: (216) 831-3500
TWX: 810-427-9452

†Pioneer Electronics
4433 Interpoint Blvd.
Dayton 45424
Tel: (513) 236-9900
TWX: 810-459-1622

†Pioneer Electronics
4800 E. 131st Street
Cleveland 44105
Tel: (216) 587-3600
TWX: 810-422-2211

OKLAHOMA

Arrow Electronics, Inc.
4719 S. Memorial Drive
Tulsa 74145
Tel: (918) 665-7700

OREGON

†Almac Electronics Corpora-
tion
1885 N.W. 169th Place
Beaverton 97006
Tel: (503) 629-8090
TWX: 910-467-8743

†Hamilton/Avnet Electronics
6024 S.W. Jean Road
Bldg. C, Suite 10
Lake Oswego 97034
Tel: (503) 635-7848
TWX: 910-455-8179

OREGON (Cont'd)

Wyle Distribution Group
5250 N.E. Elam Young Parkway
Suite 600
Hillsboro 97124
Tel: (503) 640-6000
TWX: 910-460-2203

PENNSYLVANIA

Arrow Electronics, Inc.
650 Seco Road
Monroeville 15146
Tel: (412) 856-7000

Hamilton/Avnet Electronics
2800 Liberty Ave., Bldg. E
Pittsburg 15238
Tel: (412) 281-4150

Pioneer Electronics
259 Kappa Drive
Pittsburgh 15238
Tel: (412) 782-2300
TWX: 710-795-3122

†Pioneer Electronics
261 Gibralter Road
Horsham 19044
Tel: (215) 674-4000
TWX: 510-665-6778

TEXAS

†Arrow Electronics, Inc.
3220 Commander Drive
Carrollton 75006
Tel: (214) 380-6464
TWX: 910-860-5377

†Arrow Electronics, Inc.
10899 Kinghurst
Suite 100
Houston 77099
Tel: (713) 530-4700
TWX: 910-880-4439

†Arrow Electronics, Inc.
10125 Metropolitan
Austin 78758
Tel: (512) 835-4180
TWX: 910-874-1348

†Hamilton/Avnet Electronics
2401 Rutland
Austin 78758
Tel: (512) 837-8911
TWX: 910-874-1319

†Hamilton/Avnet Electronics
2111 W. Walnut Hill Lane
Irving 75062
Tel: (214) 659-4100
TWX: 910-860-5929

†Hamilton/Avnet Electronics
4850 Wright Road #190
Stafford 77477
Tel: (713) 780-1771
TWX: 910-881-5523

Kierulff Electronics, Inc.
9610 Skillman
Dallas 75243
Tel: (214) 343-2400

†Pioneer Electronics
1826 D. Kramer Lane
Austin 78758
Tel: (512) 835-4000
TWX: 910-874-1323

†Pioneer Electronics
13710 Omega Road
Dallas 75234
Tel: (214) 386-7300
TWX: 910-850-5563

†Pioneer Electronics
5853 Point West Drive
Houston 77036
Tel: (713) 988-5555
TWX: 910-881-1606

UTAH

†Hamilton/Avnet Electronics
1585 West 2100 South
Salt Lake City 84119
Tel: (801) 972-2800
TWX: 910-925-4018

Kierulff Electronics, Inc.
1946 W. Parkway Blvd.
Salt Lake City 84119
Tel: (801) 973-6913

Wyle Distribution Group
1325 West 2200 South
Suite E
Salt Lake City 84119
Tel: (801) 974-9953

WASHINGTON

†Almac Electronics Corp.
14360 S.E. Eastgate Way
Bellevue 98007
Tel: (206) 643-9992
TWX: 910-444-2067

Arrow Electronics, Inc.
14320 N.E. 21st Street
Bellevue 98007
Tel: (206) 643-4800
TWX: 910-444-2017

Hamilton/Avnet Electronics
14212 N.E. 21st Street
Bellevue 98005
Tel: (206) 453-5874
TWX: 910-443-2469

Wyle Distribution Group
1750 132nd Ave., N.E.
Bellvue 98005
Tel: (206) 453-8300

WISCONSIN

†Arrow Electronics, Inc.
430 W. Rausson Avenue
Oakcreek 53154
Tel: (414) 764-6600
TWX: 910-262-1193

Hamilton/Avnet Electronics
2975 Moorland Road
New Berlin 53151
Tel: (414) 784-4510
TWX: 910-262-1182

Kierulff Electronics, Inc.
2238-E W. Bluemound Rd.
Waukeshaw 53186
Tel: (414) 784-8160

CANADA

ALBERTA

Hamilton/Avnet Electronics
2816 21st Street N.E.
Calgary T2E 6Z2
Tel: (403) 250-9380
TWX: 03-827-642

Hamilton/Avnet Electronics
6845 Rexwood Road Unit 6
Mississauga, Ontario L4V1R2
Tel: (416) 677-0484

Zentronics
6815 8th Street, N.E., Ste. 100
Calgary T2E 7H7
Tel: (403) 295-8838

BRITISH COLUMBIA

Hamilton/Avnet Electronics
105-2550 Boundary Road
Burnaby V5M 3Z3
Tel: (604) 437-6667

BRITISH COLUMBIA (Cont'd)

Zentronics
108-11400 Bridgeport Road
Richmond V6X 1T2
Tel: (604) 273-5575
TWX: 04-5077-89

MANITOBA

Zentronics
60-1313 Border Street
Winnipeg R3H 0X4
Tel: (204) 694-1957
FAX: (204) 633-9255

ONTARIO

Arrow Electronics Inc.
24 Martin Ross Avenue
Downsview M3J 2K9
Tel: (416) 661-0220
TLX: 06-218213

Arrow Electronics Inc.
148 Colonnade Road
Nepean K2E 7J5
Tel: (613) 226-6903

†Hamilton/Avnet Electronics
6845 Rexwood Road
Units G & H
Mississauga L4V 1R2
Tel: (416) 677-7432
TWX: 610-492-8867

†Hamilton/Avnet Electronics
210 Colonnade Road South
Nepean K2E 7L5
Tel: (613) 226-1700
TWX: 05-349-71

†Zentronics
8 Tilbury Court
Brampton L6T 3T4
Tel: (416) 451-9600
TWX: 06-976-78

Zentronics
564/10 Weber Street North
Waterloo N2L 5C6
Tel: (519) 884-5700

†Zentronics
155 Colonnade Road
Unit 17
Nepean K2E 7K1
Tel: (613) 225-8840
TWX: 06-976-78

SASKATCHEWAN

Zentronics
173-1222 Alberta Avenue
Saskatoon S7K 1R4
Tel: (306) 955-2202, 2207
FAX: (306) 244-3731

QUEBEC

†Arrow Electronics Inc.
4050 Jean Talon Quest
Montreal H4P 1W1
Tel: (514) 735-5511
TLX: 05-25596

Arrow Electronics Inc.
909 Charest Blvd.
Quebec 61N 269
Tel: (418) 687-4231
TLX: 05-13388

Hamilton/Avnet Electronics
2795 Rue Halpern
St. Laurent H4S 1P8
Tel: (514) 335-1000
TWX: 610-421-3731

Zentronics
505 Locke Street
St. Laurent H4T 1X7
Tel: (514) 735-5361
TWX: 05-827-535

EUROPEAN SALES OFFICES

BELGIUM

Intel Corporation S.A.
Rue de Cottages 65
B-1180 Brussels
Tel: (02) 347-0566

DENMARK

Intel Denmark A/S*
Glentevej 61 - 3rd Floor
DK-2400 Copenhagen
Tel: (01) 19-80-33
TLX: 19567

FINLAND

Intel Finland OY
Rousilantie 2
00390 Helsinki
Tel: (8) 0544-644
TLX: 123332

FRANCE

Intel Paris
1 Rue Edison, BP 303
78054 Saint-Quentin-en-Yvelines Cedex
Tel: (33) 1-30-57-7000
TLX: 69901677

Intel Corporation, S.A.R.L.
Immeuble BBC
4 Quai des Etroits
69005 Lyon
Tel: (7) 842-4089
TLX: 305153

WEST GERMANY

Intel Semiconductor GmbH*
Seidlstrasse 27
D-8000 Muenchen 2
Tel: (89) 53891
TLX: 05-23177 INTL D

Intel Semiconductor GmbH
Verkaufsbuero Wiesbaden
Abraham-Lincoln Str. 16-18
6200 Wiesbaden
Tel: (6121) 76050
TLX: 04186183 INTW D

Intel Semiconductor GmbH
Verkaufsbuero Hannover
Hohenzollernstrasse 5
3000 Hannover 1
Tel: (511) 34-40-81
TLX: 923625 INTH D

Intel Semiconductor GmbH
Verkaufsbuero Stuttgart
Bruckstrasse 61
7012 Fellbach
Tel: (711) 58-00-82
TLX: 7254826 INTS D

ISRAEL

Intel Semiconductor Ltd*
Attidim Industrial Park
Neve Sharet
Dvora Hanevia
Bldg. No. 13, 4th Floor
P.O. Box 43202
Tel Aviv 61430
Tel: (3) 491-099, 491-098
TLX: 371215

ITALY

Intel Corporation S.P.A.*
Milanofiori, Palazzo E/4
20090 Assago (Milano)
Tel: (02) 824-4071
TLX: 341286 INTMIL

NETHERLANDS

Intel Semiconductor (Nederland) B.V.*
Alexanderpoort Building
Marten Meesweg 93
3068 Rotterdam
Tel: (10) 21-23-77
TLX: 22283

NORWAY

Intel Norway A/S
P.O. Box 92
Hvamveien 4
N-2013, Skjetten
Tel: 06-842420
TLX: 78018

SPAIN

Intel Iberia
Calle Zurbaran 28-IZQDA
28010 Madrid
Tel: (1) 410-4004
TLX: 46880

SWEDEN

Intel Sweden A.B.*
Dalvagen 24
S-171 36 Solna
Tel: (8) 734-0100
TLX: 12261

SWITZERLAND

Intel Semiconductor A.G.*
Talackerstrasse 17
8152 Glattbrugg
CH-8065 Zurich
Tel: (01) 829-2977
TLX: 57989 ICH CH

UNITED KINGDOM

Intel Corporation (U.K.) Ltd.*
Pipers Way
Swindon, Wiltshire SN3 1RJ
Tel: (0793) 696000
TLX: 444447 INT SWN

EUROPEAN DISTRIBUTORS/REPRESENTATIVES

AUSTRIA

Bacher Elektronics Ges.m.b.H.
Rotenmuehlgasse 26
A-1120 Wien
Tel: (222) 835-6460
TLX: 131532

BELGIUM

Inelco Belgium S.A.
Ave. des Croix de Guerre, 94
Bruxelles 1120
Tel: (02) 216-01-60
TLX: 64475

BENELUX

Koning en Hartman Electrotechniek B.V.
Postbus 125
2600 AC Delft
Tel: (15) 609-906
TLX: 38250

DENMARK

ITT MultiKomponent
Naverland 29
DK-2600 Glostrup
Tel: (02) 456-66-45
TLX: 33355 ITTCG DK

FINLAND

Oy Fintronic AB
Melkonkatu 24A
SF-00211 Helsinki 21
Tel: (0) 692-60-22
TLX: 124224 FTRON SF

FRANCE

Generim
Zone d'Activite de Courtaboeuf
Avenue de la Baltique
91943 Les Ulis Cedex
Tel: (1) 69-07-78-78
TLX: 691700

Jermyn
73-79 Rue des Solets
Silic 585
94663 Rungis Cedex
Tel: (1) 45-80-04-00
TLX: 290967

Metrologie
Tour d'Asnieres
4, Avenue Laurent Cely
92606 Asnieres
Tel: (1) 47-90-62-40
TLX: 611448

FRANCE (Cont'd)

Tekelec Airtronic
Cite des Bruyeres
Rue Carle Vernet BP 2
92310 Sevres
Tel: (1) 45-34-75-35
TLX: 204552

WEST GERMANY

Electronic 2000 Vertriebs AG
Stahlgruberring 12
8000 Muenchen 82
Tel: (089) 42-00-10
TLX: 522561 ELEC D

Jermyn GmbH
Schulstrasse 84
6277 Bad Camberg
Tel: (064) 34-231
TLX: 415257-0 JERM D

Metrologie GmbH
Meglingerstr. 49
8000 Muenchen 71
Tel: (089) 570-940
TLX: 5213189

Metrologie GmbH
Rheinstr. 94-96
6100 Darmstadt
Tel: (06151) 33661
TLX: 176151820

Proelectron Vertriebs AG
Max-Planck-Strasse 1-3
6072 Dreieich
Tel: (06103) 3040
TLX: 417972

ITT-MultiKomponent
Bahnhofstrasse 44
7141 Moeglingen
Tel: (07141) 4879
TLX: 7264399 MUKO D

ISRAEL

Eastronics Ltd.
11 Rosanis Street
P.O. Box 39300
Tel Aviv 61392
Tel: (3) 47-51-51
TLX: 342610 DATIX IL or
33838 RONIX IL

ITALY

Eledra Componenti S.P.A.
Via Giacomo Watt, 37
20143 Milano
Tel: (02) 82821
TLX: 332332

ITALY (Cont'd)

Intesi
Milanofiori E5
20090 Assago
Tel: (02) 824701
TLX: 311351

Lasi Elettronica S.P.A.
Viale Fulvio Testi, 126
20092 Cinisello Balsamo
Tel: (02) 244-0012, 244-0212
TLX: 352040

NORWAY

Nordisk Electronik A/S
Postboks 130
N-1364 Hvalstad
Tel: (2) 846-210
TLX: 77546 NENAS N

PORTUGAL

Ditram
Avenida Marques de Tomar, 46A
Lisboa P-1000
Tel: (1) 545-313
TWX: (0404) 14182

SPAIN

A.T.D. Electronica S.A.
Pl. Ciudad de Viena 6
28040 Madrid
Tel: (1) 234-40-00
TWX: 42477

ITT SESA
21-3 Miguel Angel
Madrid 28010
Tel: (1) 419-54-00
TWX: 27461

SWEDEN

Nordisk Elektronik AB
Box 1409
S-171 27 Solna
Tel: (8) 734-97-70
TLX: 10547

SWITZERLAND

Industrade AG
Hertistrasse 31
CH-8304 Wallisellen
Tel: (01) 830-5040
TLX: 56788

UNITED KINGDOM

Accent Electronic Components Ltd.
Jubilee House, Jubilee Way
Letchworth, Herts SG6 1QH
England
Tel: (0462) 686666
TLX: 626923

Bytech Ltd.
Unit 2 Western Centre
Western Industrial Estate
Bracknell, Berkshire RG12 1RW
England
Tel: (0344) 482211
TLX: 848215

Comway Microsystems Ltd.
John Scott House, Market St.
Bracknell, Berkshire RJ12 1QP
England
Tel: (0344) 55333
TLX: 847201

IBR Microcomputers Ltd.
Unit 2 Western Centre
Western Industrial Estate
Bracknell, Berkshire RG12 1RW
England
Tel: (0344) 486-555
TLX: 849381

Jermyn Industries
Vestry Estate, Otford Road
Sevenoaks, Kent TN14 5EU
England
Tel: (0732) 450144
TLX: 95142

Rapid Silicon
Rapid House, Denmark St.
High Wycombe, Bucks HP11 2ER
England
Tel: (0494) 442266
TLX: 837931

Rapid Systems
Rapid House, Denmark St.
High Wycombe, Bucks HP11 2ER
England
Tel: (0494) 450244
TLX: 837931

Micro Marketing
Glenageary Office Park
Glenageary, Co. Dublin
Ireland
Tel: (0001) 856288
TLX: 31584

YUGOSLAVIA

H.R. Microelectronics Corp.
2005 De La Cruz Blvd., Ste. 223
Santa Clara, CA 95050 U.S.A.
Tel: (408) 988-0286
TLX: 387452